WISDOM AND CULT

SOCIETY OF BIBLICAL LITERATURE
DISSERTATION SERIES

edited by
Howard C. Kee
and
Douglas A. Knight

Number 30

WISDOM AND CULT

A Critical Analysis of the Views of Cult
in the Wisdom Literatures of Israel
and the Ancient Near East

by
Leo G. Perdue

SCHOLARS PRESS
Missoula, Montana

WISDOM AND CULT
A Critical Analysis of the Views of Cult
in the Wisdom Literatures of Israel
and the Ancient Near East

by
Leo G. Perdue

Published by
SCHOLARS PRESS
for
The Society of Biblical Literature

Distributed by

SCHOLARS PRESS

University of Montana
Missoula, Montana 59812

WISDOM AND CULT

A Critical Analysis of the Views of Cult
in the Wisdom Literatures of Israel
and the Ancient Near East

by
Leo G. Perdue
Phillips University
Enid, Oklahoma

Ph.D., 1976
Vanderbilt University

Advisors:
James L. Crenshaw
Walter Harrelson

Library of Congress Cataloging in Publication Data
Perdue, Leo G
    Wisdom and cult.

    (Dissertation series ; no. 30)
    Originally presented as the author's thesis,
Vanderbilt University, 1976.
    Bibliography: p.
    1. Wisdom literature—Criticism, interpretation,
etc. 2. Cultus, Jewish. 3. Egyptian literature—
Relation to the Old Testament. 4. Assyro-Babylonian
literature-Relation to the Old Testament. I. Ti-
tle. II. Series: Society of Biblical Literature.
Dissertation series ; no. 30.
BS1455.P4   1977   223'.06   76-47453
ISBN 0-89130-094-5

Printed in the United States of America

1 2 3 4 5

Printing Department
University of Montana
Missoula, Montana 59812

TABLE OF CONTENTS

Page

TABLE OF ABBREVIATIONS   ix

ACKNOWLEDGMENTS   xiii

CHAPTER I
INTRODUCTION   1

A. The Posing of the Problem   1
B. The Question of Wisdom and Cult in Recent
   Scholarship   2
C. Towards a Definition of Cult   9
D. The Task before Us   11

CHAPTER II
THE VIEWS OF CULT IN EGYPTIAN WISDOM LITERATURE   19

A. The World View of Egyptian Wisdom Literature . . .   19
   Ma'at and Wisdom   19
   Ma'at and Cosmology   20
   Ma'at and the Gods   21
   Ma'at and the State: the Pharaoh   22
   Ma'at and the State: the Men of the King   24
   Ma'at and Mankind   27

B. Views of Cult in Egyptian Wisdom Literature   28
   The Old Kingdom   29
      The Instruction for Ka-gem-ni   29
      The Instruction of Prince Hor-dedef   29
      The Instruction of Ptah-hotep   30
   The First Intermediate Period   31
      Introduction   31
      The Dialogue of a Man Tired of Life with his Ba . 31
      A Harper's Song   37
      The Admonitions of Ipu-wer   38
      The Instruction for King Meri ka Re   42
   The Middle Kingdom   46
      Introduction   46
      The Instruction of King Amen-em-het   47
      The Instruction of a Man for his Son   47
      The Instruction of Sehetep-ib-Re   49
   The New Kingdom   50
      Introduction   50
      In Praise of Learned Scribes   50
      The Instruction of Ani   52
      The Instruction of Amen-em-Opet   54
   The Late Dynastic Period and Hellenistic Rule . . .   59
      Introduction   59
      The Instruction of 'Onchsheshonqy   59
      The Instruction of the Papyrus Insinger   61

Conclusions   62

CHAPTER III
THE VIEWS OF CULT IN MESOPOTAMIAN WISDOM LITERATURE . . 85

A. The World View of Mesopotamian Wisdom Literature . 85
   Wisdom and the Cosmos 85
   Wisdom and the Gods 88
   Wisdom and the King 90
   Wisdom and Mankind 91
   Wisdom and the Sages 93

B. The Views of Cult in Mesopotamian Wisdom
   Literature 95
   Sumerian Wisdom Literature 95
     The Sumerian "Man and his God" 95
     Sumerian Proverbs 97
   Akkadian Wisdom Literature 99
     Advice to a Prince 99
     The Counsels of Wisdom 100
     Counsels of a Pessimist 101
     The Shamash Hymn 103
     The Babylon Theodicy 105
     I Will Praise the Lord of Wisdom 108
     Dialogue of Pessimism 115

Conclusions 118

CHAPTER IV
THE VIEWS OF CULT IN ISRAELITE WISDOM LITERATURE 135

A. The World View of Israelite Wisdom Literature . . . 135
   Wisdom and the Cosmos 135
   Wisdom and God 137
   Wisdom and Society 138
   Wisdom and Mankind 139
   Wisdom and the Sages 140

B. The Views of Cult in Israelite Wisdom Literature . 142
   Proverbs 1-9 142
     Introduction 142
     Proverbs 3:9-10 144
     The Strange Woman 146
   Proverbs 10-31 155
     Sacrifice and Prayer 155
     The Vow 162
     The Sacred Lots 164
     Cultic Language in Proverbs 165
   Job (The Narrative) 166
     Introduction 166
     Cultic Devotion 167
   Job (The Dialogues) 170
     Introduction 170
     The Lament-Thanksgiving Cycle 171
     Apostasy: The Unforgivable Sin 177
   Koheleth 178
     Introduction 178
     Koheleth's Views of Cult 180

Sirach 188
    Introduction 188
    The Identification of Wisdom with Cult 189
    Cultic Orders in "The Praise of the Fathers" . . 190
    Cultic Rituals: Sacrificial Offerings, Ritual
        Washings, and Fasting 196
    Cultic Rituals: Prayer and the Lament-
        Thanksgiving Cycle 199
    Didactic Hymns 204
    The Vow 208
    Urim and Thummim 209
    Holy Times 209
    The Temple 210
    The Attack against Illicit Cultic Practices . . . 210
    Conclusion 211
The Wisdom of Solomon 211
    Introduction 211
    The Attack Against Foreign Religions 213
    Egyptian Religion: The Animal Cults 213
    Mystery Religions: The Cult of Dionysus 216
    Philosophical Religion: The Worship of Nature . . 218
    The Religion of Idolatry 219
    Prayer 222
    The Passover 223
    Aaron, the High-Priest 224
    Conclusion 225

Conclusions 225

CHAPTER V
DIDACTIC POEMS AND THE WISDOM PSALMS 261

A. Introduction 261
    Wisdom Psalms in Modern Scholarship 261
    Methodology 265
    Life Situation 266

B. Proverb Poems 269
    Psalm 1 269
    Psalm 34 273
    Psalm 37 279
    Psalm 73 286
    Psalm 112 291
    Psalm 19B 294
    Psalm 127 297

C. 'Ashrê Poems 299
    Psalm 32 299
    Psalm 119 303

D. Riddle Poems 313
    Psalm 49 313
    Psalm 19A 319

E. Conclusion 323

CHAPTER VI
CONCLUSIONS   345

  A. Introduction   345

  B. The Approaches of the Wise to Cultic Religion . . .   346
     Cult as a Compartment of Order   346
     Elements of Cult in Ancient Near Eastern Wisdom
       Literature   347
     Affirmations of Cultic Dogmas   351
     Motivations for Cultic Participation   354
     The Decorum of the Wise within the Realm of the
       Cult   355

  C. The Wise as Critics of the Cult   356

  D. The Question of Sapiential Avoidance of Cultic
     Provincialism   359

  E. The Wise as Creators of Cultic Literature   360

  F. The Question of Sapiential Usage of Cultic
     Language   360

  G. Sapiential Forms and References to Cult   361

  H. Conclusion   362

BIBLIOGRAPHY   365

TABLE OF ABBREVIATIONS

AB	Anchor Bible
AcAnt	*Acta Antiqua*
AJSL	*American Journal of Semitic Literatures and Languages*
AnBib	Analecta Biblica
ANET	*Ancient Near Eastern Texts*
ASAÉ	*Annales du service des antiquités de l'Égypte*
ATD	Das Alte Testament Deutsch
BBB	Bonner biblische Beiträge
BH³	Biblia Hebraica; third edition
BHT	Beiträge zur historischen Theologie
Bib	*Biblica*
BIFAO	*Bulletin de l'institut français d'archéologie orientale*
BO	*Bibliotheca Orientalis*
BWANT	Beiträge zur Wissenschaft vom Alten und Neuen Testament
BWL	Babylonian Wisdom Literature
BZAW	Beiheft zur Zeitschrift für die alttestamentliche Wissenschaft
CAH	Cambridge Ancient History
CBQ	*Catholic Biblical Quarterly*
CJTh	*Canadian Journal of Theology*
DAWBIO	Deutsche Akademie der Wissenschaften zu Berlin Institut für Orientforschung
ET	*Expository Times*
ETL	*Ephemerides theologicae lovanienses*
EvT	*Evangelische Theologie*
FRLANT	Forschungen zur Religion und Literatur des Alten und Neuen Testaments
HAT	Handbuch zum Alten Testament
Herder-B	Herders Bibelkommentar
HKAT	Handkommentar zum Alten Testament
HO	Handbuch der Orientalistik
HTR	*Harvard Theological Review*
HUCA	*Hebrew Union College Annual*
IB	*The Interpreter's Bible*

ICC	International Critical Commentary
IDB	*The Interpreter's Dictionary of the Bible*
IEJ	*Israel Exploration Journal*
Int	*Interpretation*
JAOS	*Journal of the American Oriental Society*
JBL	*Journal of Biblical Literature*
JCS	*Journal of Cuneiform Studies*
JEA	*Journal of Egyptian Archaeology*
JEOL	*Jaarbericht...ex oriente lux*
JNES	*Journal of Near Eastern Studies*
JQR	*Jewish Quarterly Review*
JR	*Journal of Religion*
JSS	*Journal of Semitic Studies*
KAT	Kommentar zum AT
KuD	*Kerygma und Dogma*
MDAIK	Mitteilungen des deutschen archäologischen Instituts
MDOG	Mitteilungen der deutschen Orient-Gesellschaft
MIO	Mitteilungen des Instituts für Orientforschung
MthSt	Münchener theologische Studien
MVAG	Mitteilungen der vorderasiatisch-ägyptischen Gesellschaft
NTT	*Nieuw theologisch Tijdschrift*
OLZ	*Orientalische Literaturzeitung*
Or	*Orientalia*
OrAnt	*Oriens antiqvvs*
OTL	Old Testament Library
OTS	*Oudtestamentische Studiën*
PEQ	*Palestine Exploration Quarterly*
RB	*Revue biblique*
RQ	*Revue de Qumrân*
RHPR	*Revue d'histoire et de philosophie religieuses*
RHR	*Revue de l'histoire des religions*
RSR	*Recherches de science religieuse*
RTP	*Revue de théologie et de philosophie*
SAHG	Sumerische und akkadische Hymnen und Gebete
SAT	Die Schriften des AT
SBT	Studies in Biblical Theology

SJT	*Scottish Journal of Theology*
SPOA	Les sagesse du Proche-Orient ancien
StANT	*Studien zum Alten und Neuen Testament*
ST	*Studia Theologica*
TLZ	*Theologische Literaturzeitung*
ThRu	*Theologische Rundschau*
ThSt	*Theologische Studiën*
ThZ	*Theologische Zeitschrift*
VT	*Vetus Testamentum*
VTSup	Vetus Testamentum, Supplements
WMANT	Wissenschaftliche Monographien zum Alten und Neuen Testament
WO	*Die Welt des Orients*
WUNT	Wissenschaftliche Untersuchungen zum Neuen Testament
ZA	*Zeitschrift für Assyriologie*
ZÄS	*Zeitschrift für ägyptische Sprache und Altertumskunde*
ZAW	*Zeitschrift für die alttestamentliche Wissenschaft*
ZNW	*Zeitschrift für die neutestamentliche Wissenschaft*
ZRGG	*Zeitschrift für Religions- und Geistesgeschichte*
ZTK	*Zeitschrift für Theologie und Kirche*

ACKNOWLEDGMENTS

This investigation of the assessments of cult by the sages of the ancient Near East was originally a dissertation presented to the Graduate Faculty of Vanderbilt University in partial fulfillment of the requirements for the Ph.D. degree, and, as such, represents the culmination of a long and arduous journey, the completion of which would have been impossible without the encouragement and assistance of many people. I wish to express my warmest appreciation to my wife, Sharon, whose companionship, understanding, and hard work over the years contributed so much to the completion of this project. Special thanks also go to Professors James L. Crenshaw and Walter Harrelson whose guidance and assistance were of considerable importance during the various stages of this dissertation.

I also wish to express my gratitude to both the United States-Israel Educational Foundation for a Fulbright scholarship and the American Schools of Oriental Research for appointing me the Nelson Glueck Fellow during 1973-74. These awards made possible much of the research that went into this study.

In addition, I wish to thank both the anonymous readers of this dissertation for their recommending of this manuscript for publication and Prof. Douglas A. Knight, Old Testament editor, for his acceptance of this study into the SBL Dissertation Series.

Finally, one man stands out above all others for special thanks and recognition, the late J. Philip Hyatt, Distinguished Professor of Old Testament, Vanderbilt University, under whose direction this investigation was initiated. Professor Hyatt's outstanding professional skills as scholar and teacher, personal integrity, religious concern, and human warmth made him an exemplary model for his many students. I count myself most fortunate to have studied under his very wise and kind tutelage, and it is to his memory that I wish to dedicate this book.

Leo G. Perdue
February, 1977

CHAPTER I

INTRODUCTION

A. *The Posing of the Problem*

A perusal of Old Testament scholarship during the past
century points to an impressive concern to define and compare
the nature and development of the three major traditions of
Israelite literature: prophecy, cult, and wisdom. Among the
most suggestive inquiries into the realm of these Old Testament
traditions have been those studies which have sought to define
the relationships between the various institutions and traditions of prophet, priest, and sage by centering primarily upon
the critical assessments expressed by one institution and its
traditions toward another. Such a critical approach has provided the modern scholar a better understanding not only of how
an institution has been viewed in terms of its character and
value by contemporaries outside its own sphere, but also has
provided incisive insight concerning those who have given vent
to an assessment of a contemporary group. Of course, critical
efforts by scholars to analyze the viewpoints of an institution
and its traditions which evaluate a contemporary group are
fraught with major difficulties. These include the realization
that each institution has its own unique diversity which issues
forth from conflicting attitudes from competing members, fac-
tions, and ideologues, and the fact that institutions, their
traditions, and individual members often share certain ideas
and elements of language which are inherited from a common
cultural milieu.[1] A case in point is the central dogma of
retribution which is shared by prophet, priest, and sage,
though, of course, the general concept of *Tun-Ergehen-
Zusammenhang* was given its own specific set of nuances by each
tradition. Furthermore, it has become increasingly evident
that a tremendous amount of diversity exists among modern
scholars as pertains to which pieces of literature belong to
which institution and its traditions.[2] Even so, by assuming
this approach, important, interpretative analyses of these
institutions and their respective literatures and ideologies

have resulted. In earlier years, the primary sphere of concern was the relationship between prophecy and cult,[3] with primary emphasis being given to the prophetic view of the Israelite cultus,[4] while more recently growing interest has been elicited in the area of prophecy and wisdom.[5]

In view of the recent proliferation of scholarly literature concerning wisdom literature, it is surprising that no systematic examination has been undertaken to explore the relationship of wisdom and cult. Such a study would be most significant at a time when continuing efforts are being made to delineate the office, function, thought world, and literature of the sages. Therefore, we shall conduct a critical examination of the evaluation of cult by the sages of the ancient Near East to determine what place is given to cult.

B. *The Question of Wisdom and Cult in Recent Scholarship*

In surveying the major interpretations of the sages of ancient Israel and their literary productions, many scholars have believed that an examination of the relationship of wisdom and cult is nigh impossible, not because of the difficulties to which we have referred, but rather, it seems, because most Old Testament savants have accepted the argument that cult was of little or no concern whatsoever to the sage. To demonstrate this point, let us purvey a brief summary of viewpoints of the major scholarly literature with respect to our topic.

The most extensive analysis of wisdom and cult that could be deemed as comprehensive in scope was undertaken in the classic monograph published in 1933 by Johannes Fichtner.[6] In a brief ten pages, Fichtner summarized the ancient Near Eastern sapiential comments pertaining to cult. His examination of Egyptian wisdom literature led him to conclude that older Egyptian wisdom made no efforts whatsoever to speak to cult, and, in fact, that only four sages in the entire sapiential literature expressed any views of cult whatsoever: Meri-ka-Re, Ani, Amen-em-Opet, and the Papyrus Insinger, thus leading him to conclude that cult was of little interest to Egyptian wise men. Even in these texts the few references to cult are interpreted to be of little significance, since the sages tended

to relegate cultic religion to the periphery of their interest
and to emphasize the ethical import of cult. A case in point
is Amen-em-Opet who, in his chapter concerning the contrast between the "silent man" and the "heated man," is said by Fichtner
to attack the value of cult as *opus operatum* and to teach that
the "silent" man finds life even if he does not participate in
cult, whereas the "heated man" is destroyed even if he zealous-
ly participates as a priest or a layman in cult. Even the
Papyrus Insinger, which is filled with admonitions concerning
the cult, is said by Fichtner to result not from an interest by
the sapiential writer to fulfill the legal dictates of the
cult, but rather from his ethical concerns, especially in regard to caring for the poor who are fed by means of sacrifices.
And the sage teaches that cultic participation will not be accepted unless the observant cultist is ethically aware of his
social responsibilities in providing for the sustenance of the
poor.

Fichtner then proceeds into the area of Mesopotamian wisdom literature, and admits that the wise were positive in their
orientation to the Babylonian cults, though he argues that the
wise were part and parcel of the priesthood, and thus their
many references which often convey a positive evaluation of
cultic religion may be easily explained.[7]

Finally, Fichtner enters into the realm of the Israelite
wise. With regard to Proverbs, Fichtner argues that the older
parts of Proverbs demonstrate almost no concern at all for the
cult, and, when the cult is mentioned, it is done so with a
negative critique. The only positive evaluation of cultic
religion by the older wise rests in the practice of prayer. In
his brief examination of Job, he concludes: "der Kult spielt
also für das Hiobbuch keine Rolle." Koheleth is given a rather
brief analysis by Fichtner whose main comment is that the Israelite sage placed morality and ethical behavior high above
the practices and rituals of cultic religion. Sirach's numerous references to cult are evaluated by Fichtner as being of
only secondary importance to individual ethics, and even the
references to cult demonstrate a primary concern for the ethical
behavior of the wise and righteous cultic participant.

Fichtner concludes his survey with brief references to the Wisdom of Solomon, Tobit, Ezra, Aristeas, IV Maccabees, and Pirke Aboth, and concludes that there is evidence for a growing interest in cult. Thus one may see an historical development from old wisdom, which protested against the overstressing of the value of cultic religion and affirmed the superiority of ethical behavior over cultic ritual, to late wisdom, most especially Pirke Aboth, in which the value of cultic religion was "dangerously" accentuated.[8]

The problems inherent in Fichtner's investigation, in addition to the obvious one of brevity, include an omission of many important texts, an omission not entirely due to an oversight by the scholar, but often to the fact that much of the literature we now have was neither available nor critically investigated. He does not examine such important Egyptian sapiential pieces as "The Admonitions of Ipu-wer," "The Instruction of 'Onchsheshonqy," "The Dialogue between a Man Tired of Life with his Soul," "A Harper's Song," "In Praise of Learned Scribes," "The Instruction of a Man for his Son," and "The Instruction of Sehetep-ib-Re." As concerns Mesopotamia, there was no investigation of Sumerian Proverbs, the Sumerian "A Man and His God," "The Advice to a Prince," "Counsels of a Pessimist," and the "Shamash Hymn." In addition, his tendency to regard the older sages as secularistic humanists, his lack of appreciation for the concerns of the priests for ethical behavior, and his conclusion that the wise evidence only passing concern for cult while exalting ethical behavior are subject to serious criticisms which we shall unfold in the following chapters.

An earlier study by Paul Humbert which takes a more judicious view of wisdom and cult is hampered only by a failure to explore in depth several incisive observations.[9] Humbert is still not a convert to the idea that the wise of Egypt and Israel were overly concerned with cult, as his comment concerning proverbial literature demonstrates:

> Les devoirs envers la divinité ne jouent qu'un rôle
> de second plan dans les écrits gnomiques égyptiens
> et israélites, cela même leur est déjà commun.

Yet he argues that there was not necessarily a divorce between
wisdom and cult in Egypt, but rather, on the contrary, the
Egyptian sages recommended faithful practice of cultic duties.
The same is true of Israel, for while there are not many references to cult in Israelite wisdom literature, especially in
Proverbs, still the sages were not hostile toward cult. In
fact he argues:

> Mais cette discrétion sur les devoirs proprement
> cultuels n'implique aucunement leur rejet, car maint
> passage en présuppose au contraire l'exercice.

Thus he suggests that wisdom could proceed along the periphery
of cult without ignoring it. Humbert concludes that the wise,
like the prophets, were more concerned with ethical religion
than external rites, though neither group completely rejected
their importance. The major weakness of Humbert's treatment
of cult is his affirmation of the secondary place of cult in
Egyptian and Israelite literature which obviously influenced
his own abbreviated analysis of the topic.

Another well known French treatment of the sages of the
ancient Near East is the massive volume of Duesberg and Fransen
who rarely mention the topic of wisdom and cult and when doing
so usually comment on the lack of interest shown by the sages
of Israel in cultic religion or on the critical evaluation by
the sages when they assess the cultic institution. To these
scholars Proverbs presents a rather detached apathy with respect to cultic religion, choosing rather to place primary emphasis on individual morality:

> Sa religion est certainement celle d'Israël, mais
> allégée ou amputée de son zéle pour la *tôrah*, pour
> l'alliance, pour le culte, et assez indifférente,
> en entour, à l'horreur de l'idolatrie.[10]

In explaining such an observation, a suggestion is made which
would be carried forward by McKane: the older wise were governmental and royal functionaries who set forth a secular *poli-
ique*, devoid of the doctrinaire idiosyncracies of religious
traditions and institutions.[11] While almost ignoring the matter of cult in Job, they comment that Koheleth was quite comparable to the prophets and psalms in his opposition to a

ritual detached from morality. The comments made concerning
Sirach are deprecatory of the Jerusalem sage whose interests in
cult are taken as evidence of his being a rigid legalist, and
possibly even a priest. But Sirach is rescued from legalism
and priestly religion by Duesberg and Fransen who stress that
Sirach is more concerned with the moral character of the worshipper than the religious value of cultic rites.

Our topic also receives little attention in Scott's treatment of the sages and their literature, for he almost completely passes over the subject except for a brief comment that is
typical of scholars who have approached wisdom while still
maintaining their devotion to the "highest expression of Israelite religion," the prophets.[12] Scott mentions in passing
Prov. 21:3 and 16:6, following a comment in which he asserts
that the wise almost ignored cultic religion and its ceremonies. He believes that 21:3 may be taken as a "prophetic summary" of the prophetic view of cult, while he affirms that 16:6
was possibly influenced by the prophets, thus making the sages
of Israel the spiritual and ethical inferiors to their prophetic contemporaries.

Whybray has briefly dealt with the views of the wise concerning cult in his efforts to regard the Succession Narrative
as wisdom literature.[13] Whybray regarded what he believed to
be a paucity of remarks made by the wise concerning cult to be
directly linked to their very unique view of God's working
through the channels of individual men and natural events
rather than by a direct intervention in the course of salvation
history, thus leading them to diminish the importance of the
cult and its institutions as a means of communication between
God and man and as the conduit of divine blessing. However, he
rejects the argument that the cult lay outside the sphere of
concerns of the wise, since this could be a valid argument only
if there existed no references to cult whatsoever. But this
was not true, for the wise did speak of the value of cult as
"one aspect of the 'way of life' which led to happiness and
prosperity." However, the assumed paucity of references to
cult in Israelite as well as in Egyptian wisdom literature led
Whybray to conclude that this demonstrated the rather small

position cult held among the interests of the wise.[14] Once
more Whybray, like his predecessors, chooses to argue that
ethical conduct is the primary domain of the wise, though
prayer is an important, but not really a "cultic," pursuit.

Hans Heinrich Schmid in his study of the wisdom traditions
in Israel and the ancient Near East has offered a very brief
mentioning of wisdom and cult in Egypt, and, while we find a
number of his arguments to be questionable, he has made several
suggestive comments which unfortunately suffer from the failure
on his part to develop their possible ramifications.[15] Schmid
addresses himself primarily to the appearance of references to
cult in literature of the First Intermediate Period and the
early Middle Kingdom, and especially selects for scrutiny a
number of texts from Meri-ka-Re in which one finds side by side
a *do-ut-des* faith and, paradoxically, critical comments concerning cult. Schmid proceeds to argue that the failure of the
sages of the Old Kingdom to refer to cult was primarily due to
the unquestioned acceptance of the importance of cult as self-
evident. There were no problems with regard to cult, and thus
there was no critical reflection by the wise. Secondly, the
wise were involved in non-mythical and non-cultic understandings of time and reality and, therefore, blazed a path in their
own particular way.

However, according to Schmid, with the chaos of the First
Intermediate Period, the wise were forced to enter into an
evaluation of their orientation towards cult. The powers of
individuality of this period demanded an *Auseinandersetzung*
with the previously accepted cultic practices. What had been
formerly self-evident became the subject of rigid scrutiny.
Thus sapiential views of cult, along with those of God and
King, had to be reassessed in a new comprehensive analysis of
the totality of reality as perceived by the sages. In this
reassessment one does not find the wise espousing cultic participation without some duly noted reservations. Schmid contends that whether or not a cultic activity is to be pursued
depends entirely upon the ability to perceive in that activity
an order-inducing and sustaining process. If an activity of
cult corresponded to the dictates of order and helped in

maintaining that order, then it should be done; but if not, the practice should be rejected. Yet, throughout the sapiential reflections the wise had views radically different from cult, especially as concern myth and time,[16] thus causing them never to embrace totally cultic religion. Unfortunately Schmid ignores the question of cult in Mesopotamia and Israel and in the majority of the Egyptian texts. His ideas are intriguing, but he fails to develop them adequately.

Finally, the late dean of Old Testament scholars, Gerhard von Rad, devoted a short excursus to wisdom and cult which he refused to make a major subject of his investigation of wisdom due to his conclusion that the wise never regarded cultic matters to be of any primary interest.[17] After briefly referring to a small number of proverbs pertaining to cult in Proverbs and the passage in Sir. 34:19f., he states: "But in all this, the concern is not with the cultic, but with human presuppositions which are indispensable for cultic participation." Thus von Rad aligns himself with earlier scholars who had argued that the ethical predisposition of the individual worshipper was the only real concern of the wise.

Von Rad also speaks to the problem of the usage of what may be described as "cultic terminology," and suggests two possible methods of approaching this issue. First, it might be concluded that the wise used such language in a "spiritualized" way, thus demonstrating that, intellectually speaking, the wise had "outgrown" the faith and practices of cultic religion. The second suggestion, more preferable to von Rad, is the argument that the wise, not being priests, had no opportunity to use the terms in their cultic context, for they spoke in the "humanized, generalized" language of everyday existence. Finally, von Rad admits that there is still a wisdom and cult problem which has not been addressed, which seems to be in the area of a comparison between the various ways that the wise and the priests sought to approach "order" and in the area of the relation between wisdom and cultic genres, especially the hymn and the individual thanksgiving.[18]

In summation, the question of wisdom and cult has rarely been raised, and when raised it was usually answered with the

passing remark that cult rested only on the periphery of
sapiential concern, for the wise were more concerned with ethical behavior. If this assessment were true, it would indeed be
rather important in itself, and would lead us to ask why the
wise would ignore or, at the very best, severly criticize and
then delegate to obscurity the cultic realm. But is this assessment completely accurate? Thus it will be our major task
to examine closely the major wisdom texts of the ancient Near
East to determine if the wise were inclined to treat with
aloofness or even disdained the practices and beliefs of their
cultic contemporaries, or if such aloofness and disdain are
assessments which are not completely in line with a number of
ancient Near Eastern wisdom sources.

C. *Towards a Definition of Cult*

Of course, one of the major problems in proceeding with
our investigation, and also one that has plagued earlier scholars in their comments about cult and wisdom, is that of defining the meaning and the limits of the term cult.[19] Such a
definition is no easy task as a perusal of major cultic studies
of the past decade demonstrates, but we shall proceed with the
following. Cult is the ordered response of a society and its
individuals to their belief that a deity has appeared within
its midst.[20] The concern of cult is to maintain a continuing
relationship with that deity in the hopes of securing divine
blessings for the community by means of obeying the commands
of the deity, providing for the deity's needs, propitiating his
anger, and maintaining the integrity of his sanctity which must
be guarded from the contact with or incursions from the profane.
Thus cult is seen as the channel for the blessings of the deity,
the means for avoiding the destructive power resulting from the
profanation of divine holiness, and the method of revelatory
communications between deity and society. In fact, the cultic
institution itself is believed to have been originated and continues to be legitimated by this deity.

In the developed societies which we shall examine, this
response[21] came to consist, first of all, of holy places

(especially high places and temples), believed to be intimately
linked with the divine, life-giving sphere, where perhaps a
theophany occurred or where a deity dwells. Because of its
association with the world of gods, this space, along with the
cultic paraphernalia (censers, altars, idols, etc.) devoted to
divine service, was believed to be permeated by sacredness and
had to be protected from unlawful incursions of the profane
world of men. Thus, we find the need for sacred personnel who
in a state of holiness may approach the realm of the divine in
order to perform cultic service and may avoid the destructive
forces of the holy, unleashed against the profanation of sacred
space and objects. Throughout these societies, then, we find
orders of priests and priestesses dedicated to divine service.

In general, the rituals performed in cultic services by
these sacred persons were carefully and exactly performed,
dramatic, and symbolic re-enactments of the divine actions
believed responsible for the creation and maintenance of those
vital forces so essential for the existence of the community.
By carefully following the divine prescriptions for cultic
rituals, these creative and salvific forces were renewed and
unleashed for the benefit of the community.[22] In addition,
these rituals were performed at specific times, and took on
added significance during those sacred seasons of the year in
which the divine powers of life were considered to be at their
high point and thus could be garnered for the blessing of society or, conversely, were at their low ebb and thus needed
revitalizing by cultic rituals. The recreating of the cosmos
and the community thus occurred on a seasonal basis.

Finally, cultic officials produced a wealth of cultic
traditions concerning dogmatics and ritual in cultic forms,
including communications from the deity, prescriptions for
various rituals, liturgical prayers, laments, hymns, cultic
legends which speak of the founding of a cult or a cultic site,
festal legends, liturgies of service, priestly instructions
directed towards the communicants, and cultic myths which especially center upon creation.

In our investigation of the views of the wise expressed
towards cult, we shall not limit ourselves merely to sacrifice

or even to cultic ritual, a self-imposed limitation by earlier scholars which, we believe, led to the denigration of the importance of the realm of cult to the ancient wise. Rather we shall be concerned to look for references to cultic places, times, personnel, rituals, beliefs, and language. We shall especially attempt to assess how the wise viewed these various components of the cult, and, in so doing, compare them with the ideas of the cultists themselves. With regard to cultic language, we shall look primarily at prayers and various kinds of psalms with the purpose of discovering if the wise used, and perhaps even created, cultic genres in their writings. Further, we shall attempt to assess whether certain psalms may have been intended to be used in cultic liturgies.

D. *The Task Before Us*

Wisdom has been defined as the wise man's quest for self-understanding, an understanding in terms of the relationships of the wise with things, persons, deity, and, we would add, the societal and religious institutions of the society in which a sage lived and functioned.[23] Such a quest was founded upon the belief of the wise person that there existed an all embracing "order" to the compartments of reality, whether he called this *Ma'at*, *Ṣedaqâh*, or the system of *mes*, an order often bearing the connotations of truth, orderliness, and even justice.[24] Thus the wise man's task was to discover his place, function, and time within the structure of this order which permeated the spheres of the cosmos, society, man, and the realm and nature of the holy. By successfully integrating himself within these spheres of reality, or "order", the wise man thereby becomes aware of the meaning of existence for himself and may achieve self-understanding, knowing who he is and what he is about. And by gaining harmony with the spheres of order, he achieves harmony within himself.

But the quest was motivated by the attempt of the wise to master life, for wisdom was very much a search for security in what very often turned out to be a relatively insecure existence. Thus the wise man, through his endowment with wisdom by the gods, had within his grasp the means to come to terms with the demands of living in accord with reality, knowing how to act or what to do in every conceivable situation and every possible time. By his wisdom he had the means to achieve the blessings and rewards of life: honor, respect, longevity, family, prosperity, and peace within himself. These were believed to result, because the wise attributed a beneficent quality to the spheres of order. While it is true that the wise never naively ignored the destructive, and even seemingly hostile, character of reality, they did deny that this could overwhelm the wise man who had found how to live in harmony with the components of reality. Only the fools, the ones untrained in the ways of wisdom, were destroyed by the destructive forces in reality. This belief became legislated in the dogma that almost led to the demise of the wisdom tradition in the ancient Near East.

If the wise were comprehensive in their attempts to assess the compartments of reality and to discover the proper relationships between these compartments and themselves, which is an oft heard claim, it would be amazing indeed to find the wise ignoring the realm of cult, especially when the wise themselves admitted certain limitations in their quest for understanding, and, in difficult times, when their faith in the principle of retribution was sore afflicted, the only recourse appeared to be a turning to divine mercy and aid. So we should not be terribly surprised as we proceed with our own quest if the comments of past scholars and the relative obscurity of cult in modern analyses of wisdom literature perhaps were hastily made conclusions and oversights which did not result from a close scrutiny of the appropriate texts.

We shall begin with the literature of the Egyptian wise, move into the realm of Mesopotamian wisdom literature, and conclude with Israelite wisdom to determine what place cult may have had in the assessments of the sages of the ancient Near East with respect to the spheres of the order of reality. But we shall also be concerned with wisdom psalms, that is, didactic poems which are closely similar to the cultic psalms, especially since von Rad believes that this is one of the primary means by which the problem of wisdom and cult may be broached. And, as we stated earlier, our study should demonstrate not only how the priestly tradition was viewed by the wise contemporaries who were perhaps not professionally associated with that tradition, but at the same time should provide us with important insights into the thought world of the ancient sages themselves.

CHAPTER I

[1]See the comments of James L. Crenshaw, "Review of *Isaiah and Wisdom*, J. William Whedbee," *Int* 36 (1972) pp. 74-77.

[2]If trends continue, we may see in the not too distant future large portions of Old Testament literature being assigned to the creation or the influence of the wise, who only a short time ago were the unwanted, illegitimate children of Old Testament research. For example, Weinfeld has concluded that the once time-honored cultic life situation of Deuteronomy was actually a sapiential one, for the real authors of Deuteronomy were not priests, but the wise scribes(*Deuteronomy and the Deuteronomic School* [Oxford: At the Clarendon Press, 1972]). For a treatment of supposed wisdom texts or wisdom influenced texts, supported by the rigorous application of a precise methodology for identifying wisdom literature and wisdom influence, see James L. Crenshaw, "Method in Determining Wisdom Influence upon 'Historical' Literature," *JBL* 88 (1969) pp. 129-42.

[3]See, e.g., Alfred Haldar, *Associations of Cult Prophets among the Ancient Semites* (Uppsala: Almqvist and Wiksellsboktryckeri, 1945); and Aubrey Johnson, *The Cultic Prophet in Ancient Israel* (Cardiff: University of Wales Press, 1962).

[4]See W. Beyerlin, *Die Kulttraditionen Israels in der Verkündigung des Prophetes Micha*, FRLANT (Göttingen: Vandenhoeck und Ruprecht, 1959); R. E. Clements, *Prophecy and Covenant*, SBT 43 (Naperville, Ill.: Alec Allenson, Inc., 1965); R. Hentschke, *Die Stellung der vorexilischen Schriftpropheten zum Kultus*, BZAW 75 (Berlin: Alfred Töpelmann, 1957); H. W. Hertzberg, "Die prophetische Kritik am Kult," *TLZ* 75 (1950) pp. 219-26; J. P. Hyatt, *The Prophetic Criticism of Israelite Worship*, Goldenson Lectures (Cincinnati: H.U.C. Press, 1963); *Prophetic Religion* (Nashville: Abingdon Press, 1947); O. Plöger, "Priester und Prophet," *ZAW* 63 (1951) pp. 157-92; R. Rendtorff, "Priesterliche Kulttheologie und prophetische Kultpolemik," *TLZ* 81 (1956) pp. 339-42; H. H. Rowley, "Ritual and the Hebrew Prophets," *JSS* 1 (1956) pp. 338-60.

[5]James L. Crenshaw, "The Influence of the Wise upon Amos," *ZAW* 79 (1967) pp. 42-52; Johannes Fichtner, "Jesaja unter den Weisen," *Gottes Weisheit* (Stuttgart: Calwer) pp. 18-26; J. Lindblom, "Wisdom in the Old Testament Prophets," VTSup 3 (1955) pp. 192-204; William McKane, *Prophets and Wise Men*, SBT 44 (Naperville, Ill.: Alec R. Allenson, 1965); Samuel Terrien, "Amos and Wisdom," *Israel's Prophetic Heritage* (New York: Harper, 1962) pp. 108-15; J. W. Whedbee, *Isaiah and Wisdom* (Nashville: Abingdon Press, 1971); and H. W. Wolff, *Amos' geistige Heimat*, WMANT 18 (Neukirchen-Vluyn: Neukirchener Verlag, 1964).

[6]*Die altorientalische Weisheit in ihrer israelitisch-jüdischen Ausprägung*, BZAW 62 (Giessen: Alfred Töpelmann) pp. 36-46.

[7]Fichtner bases his argument on the observation made by Meissner that the same Akkadian ideogram is used for both priest and scribe (*Babylonien und Assyrien*, p. 326). However, this does not lead Landsberger to accept the idea that the wise were priests: "One must castigate as false romanticism the conception of the so-called *Priesterweisheit*, still to be found in secondary handbooks. The scribes, although the greater number of them were deeply religious, were completely a lay group." ("Scribal Concepts of Education," *City Invincible*, A Symposium on Urbanization and Cultural Development in the Ancient Near East [Chicago: The University of Chicago Press, 1958] p. 98). Furthermore, Oppenheim has argued that it was the sphere of the court, not that of the temple, which gave shape to the Mesopotamian artistic, literary, and scholarly traditions, and provided the circles through which the traditions were nourished and transmitted ("The Intellectual in Mesopotamian Society," *Daedalus* 104 [1975] pp. 40f.).

[8]He concludes this section by stating: "Neben die ethische Forderung, die die ältere isr.-jüd. Wsht fast völlig und auch die jüngere noch stark beherrscht, tritt in der jüngsten Entwicklung immer deutlicher die kultische, die in den Pirke Aboth sogar die überragende Bedeutung des ethischen Gebotes zu gefährden droht" (p. 46).

[9]*Recherchés sur les sources égyptiennes de la litterature sapientiale d'Israël* (Neuchâtel: Paul Attinger, 1929).

[10]H. Duesberg et I. Fransen, *Les scribes inspirés* (Maredsous: Éditions de Maredsous, 1966) p. 332. Their observations concerning wisdom and cult are scattered throughout their book.

[11]*Prophets and Wise Men*.

[12]R. B. Y. Scott, *The Way of Wisdom* (New York: The Macmillan Co., 1971) pp. 123-24. Rankin's comment that the wise actually influenced the prophets in this case is just as possible, though, as we shall see, we lean to the position that both groups had their own reasons for criticizing cult (*Israel's Wisdom Literature* [Edinburgh: T. and T. Clark, 1954] p. 71).

[13]R. N. Whybray, *The Succession Narrative*, SBT 14 (Naperville, Ill.: Alec R. Allenson, Inc., 1968) pp. 66f.

[14]Whybray makes some rather odd choices when he points to the "paucity" of cultic references in Egyptian Wisdom literature, for he uses as his examples Meri-ka-Re and Ani. We shall deal with these two sapiential pieces later in Chapter II. However, of the 13 instructions given by Ani, three concern one's wife, two deal with the observances of social etiquette, four pertain to the following: home and garden, mother, the "foreign woman," and control of the tongue, while four concern the cult. Thus almost one-third of his instruction concerns the cult. In terms of Meri-ka-Re, out of 130 preserved lines of instruction which deal with a myriad of subjects, approximately 20 refer to the cult, or 15 percent. One might as well

say the paucity of references to the control of the tongue in these two texts demonstrates the lack of interest of the sages in correct speaking.

[15]H.-H. Schmid, *Wesen und Geschichte der Weisheit*, BZAW 101 (Berlin: Alfred Töpelmann, 1966), pp. 50-53.

[16]We find ourselves puzzled by the strong contrasts Schmid makes between wisdom and myth, for it is our opinion that the intellectual progenitors of the sages were the cosmological myths.

[17]*Wisdom in Israel* (Nashville: Abingdon Press, 1972), pp. 186-89.

[18]Von Rad's point is important, for, as we shall see, there are abundant wisdom texts which contain didactic poems which are most similar to the cultic genres of the psalms, leading us to ask whether or not they were actually composed by the wise, and, if so, whether or not they were intended for cultic use.

[19]For a very useful and succinct examination of the major critical approaches to cult since the period of German Romanticism, see H.-J. Kraus, *Worship in Israel* (Richmond: John Knox Press, 1966), pp. 1-25.

[20]Walter Harrelson, *From Fertility Cult to Worship* (Garden City, New York: Doubleday, 1970), pp. 1 and 36.

[21]For a detailed examination of the institution of the cult, see Roland de Vaux, *Ancient Israel* 2 (New York: McGraw-Hill, 1965).

[22]Specific rituals were designed for expressing devotion (e.g., hymns), appeasing divine anger (laments, fasts, sacrifices, libations), sacralization and desacralization (ablutions, sacrifices), divine communications (priestly oracles), establishing communal unity with the deity (communion meals), and providing for divine needs (sacrifices, libations, gifts).

[23]Crenshaw, "Method in Determining Wisdom Influence on 'Historical' Literature," pp. 130-32.

[24]See H. H. Schmid, *Gerechtigkeit als Weltordnung*, BHT 40 (Tübingen: J. C. M. Mohr [Paul Siebeck], 1968).

CHAPTER II

THE VIEWS OF CULT IN EGYPTIAN WISDOM LITERATURE

A. *The World View of Egyptian Wisdom Literature*

Ma'at and Wisdom

In one of the oldest extant pieces of Egyptian Wisdom
Literature, "The Instruction of Ptah-hotep," the vizier of
Pharaoh Izezi of the Fifth Dynasty, one immediately confronts
the cornerstone upon which was erected the structure of wisdom
thinking in ancient Egypt, an edifice which was to outlast all
but the greatest of the pyramids:

> IF THOU ART A LEADER commanding the affairs of the
> multitude, seek out for thyself every beneficial deed
> until it may be that thy own affairs are without
> wrong. Justice[1] is great, and its appropriateness is
> lasting; it has not been disturbed since the time of
> him who made it,[2] (whereas) there is punishment for
> him who passes over its laws. It is the (right) path
> before him who knows nothing. Wrongdoing has never
> brought its undertaking into port. (It may be that)
> it is fraud that gains riches, (but) the strength of
> justice is that it lasts, and a man may say: "It is
> the property of my father."[3]

As may be deduced from this and numerous other sapiential
texts,[4] *Ma'at* ("truth," "justice") is the constitutive order of
creation established by the primeval creator deity to direct
the harmonious regularity of the cosmos for all eternity. Yet,
the passage elicits the further deduction that *Ma'at* is also
the constitutive order of society, a point well taken, since it
has been recognized for a long time that in Egyptian as well as
other ancient Near Eastern thought, the two spheres of cosmos
and society are inextricably bound. Furthermore, *Ma'at* is the
constitutive order of the individual wise man who, instructed
by wisdom, is able to live according to her dictates.[5]

In presupposing the static existence of world order in its
cosmic, social, and anthropological spheres, sapiential propo-
nents endeavored to observe, evaluate, and formulate the regulations of *Ma'at* into the written form of wisdom instructions
which would, therefore, provide essential guidelines for

19

enabling the adherent of wisdom to integrate himself in harmonious fashion within the ubiquitous compartments of orderly existence, and thus come to achieve self-understanding. The wise man is able by wisdom to understand and to know his place and function within the order of the universe and society, and he is able to experience the beneficence attributed to the spheres of order provided for the one who existed in tune with that order.[6] At the same time, the wisdom[7] devotee has the means by which he could avoid the disastrous pitfalls which result in being out of step with order, pitfalls which entrapped and destroyed the non-initiated. As Schmid has concisely observed: "Weisheitliches Denken, Fragen und Lehren zielt auf die Eingliederung des menschlichen Verhaltens in die allen umfassende Weltordnung."[8]

Ma'at and Cosmology

According to Egyptian mythology, the *Urgott* (Re, Amon-Re, Ptah)[9] stood upon the primeval hill[10] which rose forth from the watery abyss,[11] and created the lower gods and subsequently the universe. In this act of creation, the creator deity established *Ma'at* (considered in mythological thought to be both the daughter and mother of Re)[12] as the divinely instituted order which permeated the cosmos. One sapiential text which reminisces about this primeval activity is "The Instruction for King Meri-ka-Re":

> Well directed are men, the cattle of the god. He made heaven and earth according to their desire, and he repelled the water-monster. He made the breath of life (for) their nostrils. They who have issued from his body are his images. He arises in heaven according to their desire. He made for them plants, animals, fowl, and the fish to feed them. He slew his enemies and injured (even) his (own) children because they thought of making rebellion. HE MAKES THE LIGHT OF DAY according to their desire, and he *sails by* in order to see them, and when they weep he hears. He made for them rulers (even) in the egg, a supporter to support the back of the disabled. He made for them magic as weapons to ward off what might happen or dreams by night as well as day. He has slain the treacherous of heart among them, as a man beats his son for his brother's sake. For the god knows every name.[13]

This text amply illustrates the view of creation in wisdom literature and especially the beneficent nature of the spheres of world order. This optimistic view of creation and the order which permeated it made possible the beginnings of the sapiential literary production in Egypt, a literature that seeks to create, extend, and perpetuate order by means of the correct guidance of its adherents within the Kingdom of *Ma'at*.

Ma'at and the Gods

According to the sapiential understanding of the divine, the *Urgott* is not only the creator who established *Ma'at* as the constitutive order of the universe, but also is the one responsible for the maintenance and preservation of this order he initiated,[14] a task he accomplishes by means of the principle of retribution. According to this idea, a particular act or thought sets into motion a force which eventually will lead to a particular result. Therefore, a wise/righteous act leads to a beneficial result, whereas a foolish/wicked action leads to the punishment and possibly the destruction of the perpetrator, and, at times, even the social unit or units with which the offender is associated. Yet retribution is not a self-generative, self-perpetuating force, but rather is regulated and overseen by the *Urgott* who blesses society and the individual for the maintenance and perpetuation of *Ma'at*, but punishes and even destroys the society or the individual which transgresses social and cosmological order.[15] Brunner has perceptibly remarked: "Jedes Abirren von dem Weg der Ordnung betrafft Gott, und zwar in der Regel ohne ausdrücklich Willensakt, vielmehr muss der (Bewusst oder unbewusst) sich vergehende Mensch zwangsläufig anstossen."[16] Yet, one should not conclude from this observation that the deity is totally bound to a system of *Vergeltung*, because he possesses divine freedom which allows him to act independently of any regulatory system,[17] a freedom leading to the observation of one sage: "One thing are the words which men say, another is that which the god does."[18] Even during the Old Kingdom the Egyptian sage recognized that order was not immutable due to the deity's volition, and that the deity very well could be remote and quite inscrutable.

Such an observation assumed tremendous proportions during periods of extreme societal and personal crisis when orientation to world order was impossible due to the loss of any tangible, easily perceived order. As we shall see, the response of despair was most noticeable after the dissolution of the Old Kingdom during the First Intermediate Period.[19]

One of the most intriguing aspects of wisdom theology is the customary generic reference to the deity as "god" or "the god" (*ntr*), thus avoiding in general any overt participation in the extremely complex polytheism so characteristic of Egyptian religion. While a variety of reasons have been suggested to explain this phenomenon, the most plausible is that these generic references reflect the central concern of the wise with the *Urgott* who has created and continues to maintain world order, and who is revealed not in one specific cultus, but rather in all cults as well as in the order for which he is responsible.[20]

Finally, the remoteness of the *Urgott* never seemed to negate the belief in that deity's personal concern for the individual, a point well expressed in the above citation from Meri-ka-Re: "the god knows every name" and "is aware of him who acts for him."[21]

Ma'at and the State: the Pharoah

With the establishment of world order in creation, the social expression of that order became the Egyptian body politic which was regarded as the microcosm of the created cosmos. In Egypt kingship was the state, and the purpose delegated to the king by the creator deity was to maintain the order established by the *Urgott*, the divine author of the political, social, and religious institutions.[22] This he was to do in the realms of justice, war, and cult, and the result of creating and maintaining order was the integration of the Egyptian state within the beneficent spheres of the cosmos which led, of course, to the well-being of Egyptian society.[23]

Since there were no promulgated law-codes, the divine pharaoh himself was considered the incarnation of divine justice, a justice he was to administer by means of his possession

of the divine gifts of *Hu*, *Sia*, and *Ma'at*. The ideal wise king
was to be concerned with justice, as may be seen in the instruction given to King Meri-ka-Re:

> Do Justice whilst thou endurest upon the earth.
> Quiet the weeper; do not oppress the widow; sup-
> plant no man in the property of his father; and im-
> pair no officials at their *posts*. Be on thy guard
> against punishing wrongfully. Do not slaughter: it
> is not of advantage to thee.[24]

Failure to adhere to the standards of *Ma'at* was considered the
worst possible breach of divine responsibility, and was thought
to be the chief cause of the dissolution of the stately embodiment of order, a point made strikingly vivid by the attack
levelled against a pharaoh by Ipu-wer during the First Intermediate Period:

> Authority, Perception, and Justice[25] are with thee,
> (but) it is confusion which thou wouldst set through-
> out the land, together with the noise of contention.
> Behold, one thrusts against another. Men conform to
> that which thou hast commanded....[26]

As commander of the army and protector of the boundaries
of Upper and Lower Egypt, the pharaoh was responsible for military conquest, considered to be the extension of the Kingdom of
Ma'at, and the defense of Egyptian territory from the onslaughts
of foreign invaders. King Amen-em-het boasts of his military
prowess in his announcement:

> Never has there been the like of my reputation as the
> doer of valiant deeds. I trod as far as Elephantine;
> I attained to the marshes of the Delta. I stood upon
> the margins of the land and saw its enclosure. I
> reached the limits *of the armed territory*, by my (own)
> strong arm and in my (own) form of being.
> . . . .
> I overcame lions; I caught crocodiles. I subjugated
> them of Wawat; I carried off the Madjoi; I made the
> Asiatics do the dog-walk.[27]

In a candid, extremely atypical, confession of failure, Meri-
ka-Re's "divine" father admitted that because of his inade-
quacy in defending the Thinite regions, he suffered the pains
of retributive punishment for allowing the order of the kingdom
to be disrupted:

> Behold, a misfortune happened in my time. The Thinite
> regions were hacked up. It really happened through
> what I had done, and I knew of it (only) after (it)
> was done. Behold, my recompense (came) out of what I
> had done.[28]

Being the principal guarantor and proponent of *Ma'at*, the
king also was a central focus of wisdom instruction. Of all
the adherents to the guidelines of *Ma'at*, he must be the one
who follows unswervingly sagacious instructions in both his
training and his reign, and, in turn, must transmit them to his
successor. Extant royal instructions include Hor-dedef, Meri-
ka-Re, and Amen-em-het.[29] Throughout these sapiential writings
one finds the same concern for order expressed in instructions
and observations that one finds in writings intended for the
training of scribal and bureaucratic officials, though, of
course, certain ones are applicable only to the unique position
of the king. Yet, he is given greater powers than ordinary
mortals, for he incorporates the divine qualities of *Hu* (authoritative utterance), *Sia* (intellectual perception), and *Ma'a*
(justice/truth), qualities which were to empower him to follow
the rules of *Ma'at* and subsequently maintain societal order.

As stated earlier, the just king who maintained societal
order produced for his people well-being and prosperity, most
commonly expressed in the productivity of the natural world.[30]
And, of course, failure by the king led to the disruption of
order and consequently to the chaos of civil war and the upset-
ting of the natural cycle. Nefer-rohu lamented the horrid
conditions of the kingdom of his time which was suffering from
a misguided king:

> THE RIVERS of Egypt are empty, (so that) the water is
> crossed on foot. Men seek water for the ships to
> sail on it. Its course is (become) a sandbank. The
> sandbank *is against* the flood; the place of water *is
> against* the (flood)-(both) the place of water *and* the
> sandbank.[31]

Ma'at and the State: the Men of the King

The creation and transmission of wisdom literature in ancient Egypt occurred within the circles of the scribal officials who theoretically were conceived to be the functional
extension of the pharaonic institution in which they found the

raison d'être. In "The Installation of the Vizier," the statement is made: "As for him who shall do justice before all men,
he is the vizier" (ll. 18-19).[32] The wise vizier was chiefly
responsible for the maintenance of judicial justice, a responsibility delegated to him by the king. Additional areas of authority and duties filtered down throughout the ranks of the
scribal hierarchy in the administration of the royal state.
Through this vast scribal bureaucracy were channeled the powers
and responsibilities of the royal institution. Through devoted
service to the king came not only the continuation of the divine order of the state, but also personal achievement and success. Ptah-hotep points to his own experiences of achievement
as the validation of the merits of obedience to sagacious instruction:

> An obedient son is a follower of Horus.[33] What I have
> done on earth is not inconsiderable. I attained one
> hundred and ten years of life which the king gave me,
> with favor foremost among the ancestors, through doing
> right for the king up to the point of veneration.[34]

Perhaps the height of scribal adulation and loyalty expressed for the king as the incarnation of stately order is
expressed in "The Instruction of a Man for his Son" which has
an obvious propagandistic *tendance*:

> Do not turn away from the god,[35] (but) adore him,
> love him as (loyal) supporters. He will bless as
> his power shall grant; whom he neglects is one who
> has no prospects; worth more is he than millions of
> men, to him whom he has favored.[36]

Such undying devotion to the king in the Old Kingdom may have
been partially the result of the cultic dogma that eternal life
was possible only for the pharaoh and that small entourage of
courtiers and nobles upon whose devoted service the pharaoh
grew to depend during his earthly existence.[37]

The high esteem in which the scribal profession was held
is most noticeable in two wisdom documents: "In Praise of
Learned Scribes"[38] and "The Instructions of Khety."[39] In exalting the scribal profession above all others, Khety presents
sardonic glimpses into other less enticing professions. He
tells his prospective scribe who is about to embark on his
journey to the school for officials in the capital:

> BEHOLD, I HAVE SET THEE ON THE WAY of god.   The
> Renenut of a scribe is on his shoulder on the day
> of his birth.   He reaches the halls of the magistrates,
> when he *has become a man*.   Behold there is no scribe
> who lacks food for the property of the House of the
> King--life, prosperity, health!   Meskhenet is (the
> source of) the scribe's welfare, he being set before
> the magistrates.   His father and his mother praise
> god, he being set upon the way of the living.[40]

Adulation bordering on worship was given to certain truly distinguished teachers in the wisdom schools, as is evidenced by the Papyrus Chester Beatty IV:

> As for those learned scribes from the time of those
> who lived after the gods, they could foretell what
> was to come, their names have become everlasting,
> (even though) they are gone, they completed their
> lives, and all their relatives are forgotten.   THEY
> DID NOT MAKE FOR THEMSELVES pyramids of metal, with
> the tombstone thereof of iron.   They were not able
> to have heirs in children...pronouncing their names,
> but they made heirs for themselves in the writings
> and in the (books of) wisdom which they composed....
> Their mortuary service is (*gone*); their tombstones
> are covered with dirt; and their graves are forgotten,
> (but) their names are (still) pronounced because of
> their books which they made, since they were good and
> the memory of him who made them (lasts) to the limits
> of eternity.[41]

The primary form of Egyptian wisdom literature was the "Instruction" (*sb3yt*) which consisted of "admonitions" and "sayings".   The literary structure consists of the following parts:

1. Title--"The beginning of the Instruction which X has composed for his son Y."
2. Prose Introduction--the setting forth of the details of why the instruction is given.
3. Contents--the linking together of admonitions and sayings in contiguous sections.[42]

Such instructions were created with the express purpose of training officials and scribes to observe the dictates of *Ma'at*, to function within their particular scribal and official capacities, and to achieve success, fortune, and well-being.[43] Amen-em-Opet instructs his 'son':

> If thou spendest thy time while this is in thy heart,
> Thou wilt find it a success;
> Thou wilt find my words a treasury of life,
> And thy body will prosper upon earth.[44]

Not only did the wise conceive of themselves as "men of the king," but, in addition, they considered their roles to be the means by which the *Urgott* continued to maintain order in the Egyptian state. In fact, these sages considered their activities as actually creating *Ma'at*. Such an understanding becomes increasingly apparent in the wisdom instructions produced in the Middle and New Kingdoms, and can be seen, for example, in the constant references of Amen-em-Opet to the will of "god" (or "the god") as the basis for any activity. In speaking of the sage's function as a judge in a law court, the sage is to be just and free from corruption, for his just decisions are the carrying out of the designs of god (XXI, 1ff.). And the same is true of the sage who is to keep honest records (XXI, 13f.).

Ma'at and Mankind

Not only were the wise concerned with cosmological and societal spheres of order, but equally were concerned with the creating of *Ma'at* within the hearts of their students which would result in their being able to orient themselves within the beneficent orders of reality and to avoid the disaster caused by the aberration of that order. The seat of learning and the receptacle for the embodiment of sapiential instruction was thought to be the heart. Thus Amen-em-Opet begins his instruction with the admonition:

> Give thy ears, hear what is said,
> Give thy heart to understand them.
> To put them in thy heart is worth while,
> (But) it is damaging to him who neglects them.
> Let them rest in the casket of thy belly,
> That they may be a *key* in thy heart.
> At a time when there is a whirlwind of words,
> They shall be a mooring-stake *for* thy tongue.
> If thou spendest time while this is in thy heart,
> Thou wilt find my words a treasury of life,
> And thy body will prosper upon earth.[45]

On the contrary, a fool is one whose heart does not receive instruction. While divine determination of one's ability or inability to receive instruction at times is denied, certain students' inability to follow wisdom's path led to the occasional conclusion that the deity must have created them to be forever ignorant: "He whom the god loves is a hearkener, (but) he whom god hates cannot hear."[46]

It is especially true in Egypt that the instructions are to be seen as incorporating a *Standesethik* which set forth the important criteria prerequisite to a successful career in the service to the king.[47] Each admonition and observation, whether concerned with social ethics or dining etiquette, contributed to the same purpose--the providing of guidance for young students in the dictates of *Ma'at*. Thus in the dichotomy drawn between the "Heated Man" and the "Silent Man," the "Silent Man" is the ideal wise professional who, because of his training, is considered to have complete mastery over his passions, especially his tongue, and is able to practice the moderation of self-control. By way of contrast, the "Heated Man" is the untrained, illiterate, unskilled, foolish intemperate who, being dominated by his passions which are allowed to run to full course, has no regard for order and consequently is brought to self-destruction.[48]

The active principle which operates within the spheres of *Ma'at* in order to assure reward for the wise-righteous and punishment for the foolish-wicked is *Tat-Ergehen-Zusammenhang*, or retribution, the idea that there is a causative connection between one's behavior and the results of that behavior. However, it should be stressed that the Egyptian wise recognized the limitations of the human ability to perceive and follow the guidelines of *Ma'at*, and, as a result, incongruities which arose were usually not blamed on the deity's capricious disruption of order, but rather were attributed to the lack of complete understanding and the inability to adapt perfectly one's behavior to the dictates of order. Furthermore, the deity was recognized to possess freedom of will, and, therefore, was never completely bound to the principle of retribution.

B. *Views of Cult in Egyptian Wisdom Literature*

Having surveyed the basic tenets of the world-view of the Egyptian wise with its central orientation to *Ma'at*, we must

now consider whether or not cult had any role within that
world-view. Was cult of little or no concern to the sages, or
did it receive a penetrating assessment and subsequently an important place in sapiential concerns? Certainly Fichtner's
opinion is overstated: "Wie die ältere isr.-jüd. so nimmt auch
die ägyptische Wshtslit. vielfach keine Notiz vom Kult." Yet,
Fichtner does admit that exceptions to this lack of concern for
cult in older wisdom may be found in later texts: Meri-ka-Re,
Ani, Amem-em-Opet, and the Papyrus Insinger.[49] As mentioned in
Chapter I, many scholars have argued that the realm of wisdom
is the secular, profane sphere of everyday existence, and,
therefore, cult and cultic duties are of very little concern to
the wise. Such a generalization would be important if correct,
but as we shall hope to prove from the following investigation,
cult did receive significant attention from many sages in their
attempts to assess the compartments of world order.

The Old Kingdom (2686-2160 B.C.)[50]

   The Instruction for Ka-gem-ni.[51] In probably the oldest
extant instruction, "The Instruction for Ka-gem-ni," we have an
instruction dating from perhaps the third or fourth dynasty,
but, unfortunately the text is corrupt.[52] From the historical
introduction, an anonymous vizier apparently has become old in
his service to Pharaoh Huni, and, therefore, begins to set
forth rules of life for his children, especially Ka-gem-ni who
is designated to be his successor as vizier under the next
pharaoh, Snefru. None of the fragmentary admonitions contains
any reference to cult, though it would be a hasty conclusion to
draw from this omission the conclusion that the wise were unconcerned with cult, since the text is fragmentary and the entire piece extremely brief.

   The Instruction of Prince Hor-dedef. Another instruction
from the Old Kingdom is that of Prince Hor-dedef, certainly one
of the most revered Egyptian sages of antiquity, who was a son
of Khufu, though apparently not the crown prince.[53] His instruction, also truncated and fragmentary, has preserved material which concerns the making of proper mortuary preparations

which will insure one of participation in the future life.[54]
These preparations include the importance of taking a wife and
producing a son, with the obvious concern being that one may in
this way make sure that the proper mortuary rituals will be
carried through. The other preparations involve the building
and embellishing of one's tomb, for the sage states that those
who have made these preparations will continue to exist in the
life after death.[55] This material gives us an initial insight
into the attitude of the wise with respect to mortuary religion, and demonstrates that the wise shared the cultic ideology
of the priests especially in the concern for continuation into
the future life by means of mortuary religion.[56]

   The Instruction of Ptah-hotep.[57] One of the most famous
instructions of the Old Kingdom is that of Ptah-hotep, the
vizier of Pharaoh Izezi of the fifth dynasty (2494-2345),
written during the height of Egyptian culture and optimistic
well-being. According to this sage, well-being and success
come to the wise man who is faithfully devoted in his service
to the divine king. Firm is this wise man's faith in the doctrine of *Ma'at* which provides the basis for orderly existence
and professional success. As Spiegel states concerning the
central concern of Ptah-hotep: "Harmonische Einfügung in diese
allumfassend gottegewollte Ordnung ist die vornehmste Pflicht
des Menschen."[58]

   While we may search in vain for explicit admonitions or
observations referring to cult, it becomes obvious that Ptah-
hotep, like Hor-dedef, also avows the cultic dogma of a future
life obtainable by the scribe faithful in his service to the
divine pharaoh, and, related to this, by one who has a tomb
prepared. The latter point may be seen in the 19th maxim,
ll. 298f.:

>   Dagegen dauert der Mann, dessen Lebensprinzip die
>   Gerechtigkeit ist, und der den ihm vorgezeichneten
>   Weg geht. Er macht ein Vermögen dabei, aber der
>   Gierige bleibe ohne Grab![59]

This interesting passage demonstrates that it is one's righteousness, defined in terms of one's adherence to the dictates
of *Ma'at*, that assures one of a participation in the future

life, whereas the "passionate man," who neither stands in conformity to *Ma'at* nor faithfully serves the king, is not granted the gift of a grave, and, therefore, is denied participation in the continuance of a life following death.[60] Furthermore, a number of statements demonstrate that the sage who is devoted to the divine pharaoh also, as a result of that service, will be granted a place in the entourage of the king in his future life: "Mayest thou reach me, with thy body sound, and with the king satisfied with all that has taken place."[61]

The royal cult centered around the kings is not expressly discussed in Ptah-hotep, though the vizier certainly shared the ideology of the divine pharaoh, since he refers to the king as 'god' (ll. 38f., 199, 339). Furthermore he instructs his 'son' to be a "follower of Horus," reflecting the Osiris-Horus ritual in Egypt (l. 593).[62]

In conclusion, it seems apparent the wise of the Old Kingdom shared the dogma of participation in the future life by means of mortuary religion, conformity to *Ma'at*, and service to the divine king.

The First Intermediate Period (2160-2040 B.C.)

Introduction.[63] The optimism and placidity which characterized the sapiential literature of the Old Kingdom is changed to despair, pessimism, and at times outrage and a demand for the return of *Ma'at*, a change brought about by the dissolution of the Kingdom of *Ma'at* in terms of civil wars, invasions, and natural disasters. These catastrophes led the savants of ancient Egypt to question the very foundations of their ideological structure. In general, one can see two very different responses to the crisis in the sapiential ranks: the response of biting criticism, cynicism with respect to traditional dogmas (especially mortuary religion and the cult of the divine pharaoh), and even black despair; and the 'political response,' intended to bring about by political action and sapiential propaganda a re-establishing of order and a return to the traditional beliefs of old wisdom.

The Dialogue of a Man Tired of Life with his Ba.[64] By far the most devastating critique of the belief so prominent in

sapiential literature in the Old Kingdom concerning an orderly
transition to the future life by means of the mortuary cult[65]
is the *Streitgespräch* between a wise man and his Ba, a debate
which provides us not only with one of the most vivid depictions of agonizing despair in Egyptian Wisdom literature,[66]
but also destroys the firm belief in the effectiveness of mortuary religion in being able to guarantee one's continuation
into the future realm.[67]

As Alfred Hermann and Raymond Weill have correctly perceived, the primary concern of the dialogue is neither the
issue of suicide[68] nor hedonism, but rather at the heart of the
dialogue is the presentation of two contrasting views of death
and the future life.[69] Part of the orthodox view of death and
the future life developing during the Old Kingdom is represented by the man. The orthodox dogma involved three, never completely integrated, facets. The most important of these was
the one which received expression in the development of the
mortuary cult which included magical incantations (Pyramid
Texts), a well constructed tomb, mummification, proper provisions for sustenance in the afterlife, mortuary priests, and
heirs who would faithfully see that the deceased received his
proper burial and continued to receive the sustaining rituals
and provisions. During the period of the Old Kingdom, a future
life was possible only for a very few--the divine pharaoh, his
royal family and entourage, and a few needed servants. A second concept of the future life developed around the Ba, "the
personification of the vital forces, physical as well as
psychic, of the deceased, his alter ego, one of the modes of
existence in which he continues to live after death."[70] Along
with the mummy in the tomb, the Ba was seen as another mode of
existence after death, though it seems to have had considerably
more freedom, being able to leave the tomb at various times,
only to return to the mummified body. Such a mode of existence,
however, was not believed to be present until death. A third
idea of life after death involved the belief that at death man
continued to exist as an *Akh*, a 'transfigured spirit,' which
became part of the cosmic order, though it had no human contact.[71]

The disruption of the tranquility of the Old Kingdom brought about by the chaos experienced during the First Intermediate Period led to the creation of new and at times radically opposite views concerning death and the future life. One new view (represented by the Ba) considered the mortuary cult and its expensive, elaborate trappings quite inadequate, and, therefore, superfluous; an empirically developed view resulting from the obvious observation that many tombs were destroyed and neglected during those times.[72] A second view, seen in the "Song of the Harper," remains completely agnostic with respect to any certainty of a future life. Finally, a new anthropological perspective began to make some headway during this period as can be derived from the coffin texts of the Heracleopolitan period in which the Ba was perceived to be a part of a man before death.[73] Such a view raised the vital question as to what would happen to a man if his Ba, considered to be the incorporation of his vital forces and efficacious qualities as well as essential for future existence, should separate from him before death.[74]

The first two facets of the orthodox dogma concerning death and the future life are to be seen in the position of the man, though he is troubled by the new concept concerning the Ba that was beginning to appear in certain cultic circles. The man is presented as a sage who has lost any semblance of meaningful existence due to both the lack of a perceivable world order and his own personal loss of wealth, prestige, honor, and health, values common in the wisdom literature of the Old Kingdom.[75] Such a catastrophic situation led him to begin to consider making preparations for an orderly transition to the future life. And though the serenity of death and the bliss of a longed for future life beckon to him, he has recognized that he is ill-prepared for an orderly transition, since he has neither a tomb nor an heir, needed to insure that he would receive the proper burial. In addition, due to his misfortune, he begins to contemplate the distressing possibility that he is being abandoned by his Ba, and, if true, his hope for an escape from a tormented present through death to a future life would be crushed.[76] By way of contrast, the Ba is presented as the sapiential cynic who despises the man because of his misfortune and is ready to abandon him. In addition, he represents the newly developing idea that mortuary religion is an ineffectual facade for rotting bodies, though it remains inconclusive as to whether or not he equally denies a future existence by means of the Ba. With this background in mind, let us consider the dialogue.

The opening section of the dialogue is missing, and, unfortunately, complicates our understanding of it. It may be suggested, however, that the setting appears to be that of a sacrificial scene in which the wise man, his spirit crushed by his current dilemma, has started to initiate the ritual preparations for his imminent demise by offering up a mortuary sacrifice and by appealing to the divine tribunal which will soon face him in judgement.[77] Though the Ba's opening speech is missing, it appears from the first speech of the wise man that the Ba has threatened to abandon him because of his current misfortune, and in cruel derision has suggested that the man offer himself as a burnt offering to Re, a rather blasphemous idea completely repugnant to the man, for he believes the preservation of the body is essential for his future life, but an idea rather pleasant for the Ba who would subsequently be free of the destitute man once and for all.[78] The man longs for death as an escape, but not premature death, certainly not suicide, since he has not made the proper mortuary preparations. The retort of the Ba to this speech is curt and mockingly cynical. He lampoons the impoverished and dishonored wise man for foolishly concerning himself with an impossible dream of a tomb, as though he were rich and able to afford such expensive preparations.

The wise man, stung by such a biting criticism, implores his Ba not to abandon him before his death, for this would destroy all hopes for a future existence. He tries to tempt the Ba into remaining with him by indicating that if the Ba will have patience, he will eventually be able to complete the necessary arrangements and will provide the Ba with a pleasing tomb for the future life that they can share together. However, if the Ba is successful in his urging[79] him on to self-immolation, then neither of them may hope for any future life. The Ba responds by pointing to the eventual ineffectiveness of mortuary religion. Even the powerful and rich, the pharaohs, who had the large pyramids built as their tombs are in the final analysis no better off than those who lie dead on the dyke and decompose in the water and the natural elements without the benefit of a proper burial, for their tombs have been destroyed and their mortuary services have been discontinued. As a consequence, he admonishes the man to heed a sapiential admonition that he cease to worry about mortuary concerns and "pursue the happy day and forget care"! This life affirming admonition is illustrated by the Ba with two parables. The first involves a fisherman who loses a young daughter in a crocodile infested lake. And he is presented as weeping not for her, but rather for her unborn children who have not seen the joys of living, the only true value accorded to man.[80] The second parable depicts a foolish peasant whose afternoon appetite remains unsatiated after his wife's counsel that for the poor there is food only for supper. Instead of accepting her advice, he foolishly loses his temper and goes away to sulk, thus loosing any chance for an inner tranquility.[81] These parables, coupled with the admonition, stress that the destitute wise man should accept his current situation, put away foolish concerns about ineffective mortuary preparations, and, like a true wise man, come to an inner peace which will allow him to enjoy his present life.

The man, ignoring the advice of his Ba, clings to his mortuary faith and offers up a lament, beautifully constructed in four strophes strung together by four recurring refrains in which he bemoans his own despicable situation and the lack of order in the world. In the first strophe, he condemns the faithless soul whose abandonment will mean that his name, that is his honor and memory, will become a repugnant odor. In the second strophe, he turns to ponder the loss of world order which is evident in the total disruption of current existence and to bemoan his own loss of position which has left him alone and deserted in a world whose unrighteous people have no desire to listen to the counsel of a destitute wise man. In the third

strophe, he longs for the serenity of death which beckons to
him as an entrancing odor of myrrh and lotus blossoms, and,
finally in the fourth strophe, he looks to the blissful future
life in which he will exist as a god in a realm where security,
order, and cultic observance are present.[82]

The conclusion is perplexing,[83] but it appears that the Ba
continues to admonish the man to put aside thoughts of death
and live, though he agrees to remain with the man whether he
lives or dies, a concession that, at least to the man's thinking, will allow him a means of existence in the future life.[84]
His fear that the Ba would abandon him before death is put to
rest.

What is most significant for our investigation, of course,
is the complete repudiation by the Ba, and perhaps this is the
position of the wise man who wrote the Dialogue, of the efficacy and, therefore, the necessity of mortuary religion. As
the position of the Ba has effectively demonstrated, even if
the ritual were necessary for a future life, the few wealthy
who could afford the trappings of the elaborately expensive
funerary cult could find small solace in the fact that during
this period tombs were neglected and even despoiled. Thus it
appears that during periods of tranquility such as the Old
Kingdom, the wise gave expression to their acceptance of the
importance of mortuary religion (Hor-dedef, Ptah-hotep). However, with the onslaught of disruptive social, historical, and
economic forces so strong during the First Intermediate Period,
the wise despaired of the effectiveness of mortuary religion,
some even reaching the conclusion that it should be totally
abandoned as worthless. If there is a future life, and the Ba
certainly never clearly commits himself to this belief, it results from the nature of man. It is through the Ba that all
men may share in the future life, and not only the wealthy few
who were ranked high enough in social and economic categories
to be able to afford the mortuary cult. The Ba's position,
however, places primary emphasis upon the achievement of inner
tranquility and joy in this life and a refusal to allow undue
duress caused by thoughts of death to disturb one's quest for
inner peace and joy.

A Harper's Song. Embedded among Egyptian literature is a genre of songs commonly referred to as "Harper Songs," so named because they often accompany tomb reliefs which depict a harper entertaining guests who are participating in a feast.[85] Egyptologists tend to regard the songs in two conflicting ways: either as songs which have their life situation within mortuary religion, and are, therefore, pious in spirit and positive in regards to death, for they joyously assure the deceased that his mortuary preparations are completed and, consequently, his future life is guaranteed; or as secular songs having their life situation in secular banquets, and, therefore, are skeptical in spirit and thoroughly pessimistic with respect to death and the future life.[86]

Though there exists a number of these songs, the one that has received the most attention is the one found in the Papyrus Harris 500 manuscript which dates from the 19th dynasty, during the reign of Ramses II, and which is assumed to have come originally from the tomb of one of the Intef Kings, though whether it is to be dated before or after the twelfth dynasty (1991-1786 B.C.) is not certain.[87] The importance for our investigation rests on the conclusion that the song may be included within the skeptical wisdom tradition which appears at the end of the Old Kingdom,[88] though a certain king of the house of Intef had a regular funerary introduction added when the song was apparently placed within his tomb.[89]

In contrast to most of the Harper Songs, this song is addressed to the living and not to a deceased king, and betrays a total skepticism toward any affirmations made about a future life in the first strophe, and in the second turns to a positive admonition that the living should "make holiday, and weary not therein!," an admonition followed by two sayings: "Behold, it is not given to a man to take his property with him" and "Behold, there is not one who departs (dies) who comes back again!" Most significant for our investigation into the attitudes of the wise with respect to cult is the reference to two legendary savants of Egypt's past, Imhotep and Hor-dedef, and what may be assumed to be a satirical repudiation of the positive admonitions to their followers to take seriously mortuary religion:

> I have heard the words of Ii-em-hotep and Hor-dedef,
> With whose discourses men speak so much.
> What are their places (now)?
> Their walls are broken apart, and their places are
> not--As though they have never been!

In a vein similar to the grim observations of the "Ba" in the
"Dialogue of a Man Tired of Life," the Harper has perceived
that the hope for a future life based on one's preservation in
a tomb and a continuation of mortuary rituals has been decimated by the chaotic conditions of the First Intermediate
Period. Instead of speculating on the state of the dead, the
iconoclastic harper remarks concerning death:

> There is none who comes back from (over) there,
> That he may tell their state,
> That he may tell their needs,
> That he may still our hearts,
> Until, we (too) may travel to the place where they have
> gone.

Like the Hebrew sage Koheleth, he avoids speculating on the
subject of death and any possible future life, and advises his
audience to "follow thy desire, as long as thou shalt live,...
until there comes for thee that day of mourning."[90]

This text adds to the contention that the historical and
personal crises which resulted from this traumatic age led to
a bitter sarcasm with respect to the mortuary cult.

The Admonitions of Ipu-wer.[91] During the chaotic upheav-
als of the First Intermediate Period, another sage[92] responded
to the disruption of political, social, and religious order by
levelling the most bitter denunciation against a pharaoh in
Egyptian wisdom literature.[93] Regreting his earlier silence in
the court before conditions had deteriorated so precipitously,[94]
this sage describes in a strikingly vivid depiction the breakdown of Egyptian society until disorder and corruption had
literally become the 'order of the day,' a reality so painfully
depressing that suicide seemed for many a better alternative to
living.[95]

In a progressively more vitriolic and damning indictment
of the failures of the 'divine' pharaoh to respond aggressive-
ly to the current state of disruption, Ipu-wer draws up a 'Bill

of Particulars' to set before the august feet of pharaoh upon which he bases his judgment of damnation.[96] In the initial part of the piece, introduced by the recurring emphatic "WHY REALLY," the sage lists the various kinds of disruptive forces which have thrown the kingdom into chaos: robbery, cessation of labor, infertility of land and people, the topsy-turvy nature of the social structure in which nobles are impoverished and the poor become rich, external attacks from "barbarians," the discontinuation of the mortuary services, and sabre-rattling among the vassals. The next major section, introduced by the recurring word "BEHOLD," shifts the emphasis to disasters which concern more the personal interests of the king: rebellion against the authority and prestige of the pharaoh whose awesome mystique and great authority are being spurned to such a degree that even despoilation of the royal tombs is taking place. And the sage stresses that fires of revolution could ignite at any moment. Then he points to the king's cultic duties in a section initiated by the repeated "Remember," indicating that in times past whenever such concerns were scrupulously pursued order was maintained, suggesting that such a renewed cultic interest by the king is essential for order to return. Then he attacks Re, the sun god, in a livid accusation for failing both to perceive the wickedness of men even in the "first generation" after creation and to act to eradicate it, thus laying the blame for the wickedness of man before the divine throne of the creator. Then turning to the reigning pharaoh, the one supposedly commissioned by the creator to establish and maintain order in the Kingdom of *Ma'at*, he damns the king for his failures and for his promotion of discord and destruction of order. Finally, he concludes with a section, introduced by the recurring "It is still, however, good," which combines nostalgic glances at the harmony of the past with a wistful hope for the return of the beneficent orders in the future.[97]

It is obvious that this Egyptian sage is a stalwart advocate of the beneficent powers of the cult, and is most distressed because the spheres of mortuary religion, the Egyptian temple cults, and the pharaonic duty as overseer and chief

priest are transgressed, neglected, and even treated with contempt. The response of the fool which seems representative of
the *Vox Populi* is that of growing pessimism with respect to the
concern for or even the power of retribution; especially is
this true of the creator Re, who, ironically, since he is the
'sun god,' has become a *Deus absconditus*! "Indeed, the hot-
tempered man says: If I knew where God is, then would I serve
him."[98]   Such cultic cynicism has apparently penetrated the
royal court.

The discontinuation of mortuary services and the profanation by blatant robbery of the sacred rombs of the glorious
dead is lamented by Ipu-wer:

> WHY REALLY, many dead are buried in the river. The
> stream is a tomb, and the embalming-place has really
> become the stream.[99]

Even the expensive cedars and other opulent materials of the
mortuary religion are unobtainable, because of the impoverished
state of the kingdom, thus making impossible the building of
pyramids and mummification. Brigands have become so crass and
disdainful of royal power that they have robbed and desecrated
the royal tombs:

> BEHOLD now, something has been done which never hap-
> pened for a long time: the king has been taken away
> by poor men.
> BEHOLD, he who was buried as a falcon (now lies) on
> a (mere) bier. What the pyramid hid has become
> empty.[100]

Not only has mortuary religion been impossible to maintain
and the realm of the powerful dead been profaned, but even the
cults of Egypt have lost their mystique and secretive holiness:

> WHY REALLY, the writings of the august enclosure are
> read. The place of secrets which was (so formerly)
> is (now) laid bare.
> WHY REALLY, magic is exposed. *Go-spells* and *enfold-
> spells* are made ineffectual because they are repeated
> by (ordinary) people.[101]

In a nostalgic look at the past with an implicit imperative that the present Pharaoh reassert his role in the sacred
cult, Ipu-wer reminds the royal head of his cultic duties which
are necessary for the beneficent powers of cult to be released
once again:

Remember...how fumigation is made with incense, how
water is offered from a jar in the early morning.
Remember fattened *ro*-geese, *terep*-geese, and *sat*-
geese, how the divine offerings are made to the gods.
Remember how natron is chewed and how white bread is
prepared by a man on the day of moistening the head.
Remember how flagstaffs are set up and a stela[102] is
carved, while a priest purifies the temples and the
house of god is whitewashed like milk; how the frag-
rance of the horizon is made sweet, and how offering-
bread is established.
Remember how (ritual) regulations are adhered to, how
(religious) dates are distributed, how one who has
been inducted into priestly service may be removed
for *personal* weakness--that is, it was carried out
wrongfully...[103]

Then in an apparent accusation levelled against Re,[104] the
creator and the one responsible for maintaining world order, he
blames the sun god for creating men with wicked character and
for failing to perceive that such wickedness would lead to the
present period of the breakdown of order. Re should have acted
as divine retributor and removed the wickedness. Otto remarks
in a perceptive article:

Dem Schöpfer, der eigentlich ein 'guter Hirte' sein
sollte, wird vorgeworden, er habe die Menschen in
ihrem Charakter unzulänglich erschaffen und damit
selbst die Weltordnung zerstört; die Götter werden
als mitschuldig in dem Sinne bezeichnet, als sie auf
Geheiss des Schöpfers in immer neuen Schöpfungsakten
die Welt bis auf die trostlose Gegenwart fortgeführt
haben.[105]

Ipu-wer then moves from his brazen attack upon the failures of the deity to his divine son sitting on the throne of
Egypt whose failure to create and maintain order in society is
painfully obvious.[106] In an impassioned accusation filled with
heavy-handed irony, Ipu-wer declares:

...Authority, Perception, and Justice are with thee,
(but) it is confusion which thou wouldst set throughout the land, together with noise of contention.
Behold, one thrusts against another. Men conform
to that which thou hast commanded. If three men go
along a road, they are found to be two men: it is the
greater number that kills the lesser. Does then the
herdsman love death? So then thou wilt command that
a reply be made: "It is *because* one man *loves* and
another hates. *That is, their forms* are few every-
where." *This really means that thou hast acted* to

> bring such (a situation) into being, and thou hast
> spoken lies....All these years are civil strife.
> A man may be slain on his (own) roof, while he is
> on the watch in his boundary house. Is he brave and
> saves himself?--that means that he will live....Would
> that thou mightest taste of some of the oppressions
> thereof![107]

Finally, Ipu-wer looks to the future when orderly existence will allow cultic concerns to be once more the norm of
Egyptian society:

> But it is still good when the hands of men construct
> pyramids, when canals are dug, and when groves of
> trees are made for the gods (XIII, 10).

Such a longing for the restoration of order and therewith
a restoration of the sacral orders of cult vividly describe the
positive orientation of this Egyptian sage toward the beneficent powers of cult and mortuary religion. Their abusive neglect by the ideal chief priest, the reigning Pharaoh, has contributed to the withering decay of the political, religious,
and social fabric of the Kingdom of *Ma'at*. To this sage both
cultic rituals and sapiential instructions are necessary for
the creation and the maintaining of order incorporated ideally
within the Egyptian kingdom.

The Instruction for King Meri-ka-Re.[108] Another sapiential piece written during the troubled First Intermediate
Period is the "Instruction for King Meri-ka-Re." This instruction originated in the Heracleopolitan court of King Meri-ka-
Re, an Egyptian ruler of the tenth dynasty (2160-2040 B.C.)
which was in competition with the kings of the eleventh dynasty
of Thebes.[109] As the title indicates, the formal structure of
the writing is that of the instruction genre, though a new
twist is added by court propagandists who present the Instruction as that of the dead father of Meri-ka-Re who is instructing his son from the realm of the after-life in matters pertaining to the wise and righteous guidance of the kingdom of
Ma'at.[110] In this piece of court propaganda, Meri-ka-Re sets
forth a delineation of his political, social, and religious
policies which should be in direct contrast to the mistaken,
and sometimes catastrophic, policies of his predecessor.[111] He

gives an authoritative basis to his policies by having them placed on the lips of his dead father, thus making his policies appear to come from his dead father who has joined the world of the divine. Thus in this instruction, the sages of the court seek to reaffirm the importance of the old orders.

The content of the instruction involves sapiential admonitions with numerous motivation, causal, and result clauses concerning the correct sapiential policies to follow in the administration of the Egyptian Kingdom, which, as has been stressed, is regarded by the Egyptian wise as the incorporation of world order. Thus all of the wise admonitions emanate from the central locus of the king's responsibility for the establishment and maintenance of *Ma'at*, a responsibility that is most urgently needed in the current period of distress, and which was not forcefully and adequately carried forth by the dead king as may be seen in a number of extremely frank and quite unique admissions of failure by a supposedly divine pharaoh:

> Behold, a misfortune happened in my time. The Thinite regions were hacked up. It really happened through what I had done, and I knew of it (only) after (it) was done. Behold, my recompense (came) out of what I had done.[112]

By contrast the young king Meri-ka-Re is advised:

> DO JUSTICE WHILST THOU ENDUREST UPON EARTH. Quiet the weeper; do not oppress the widow; supplant no man in the property of his father; and impair no officials at their posts.[113]

The motivation for establishing and maintaining *Ma'at* is clearly stated in a reference to Meri-ka-Re's eventually being able to join the world of the gods, having successfully passed through the place of judgment: "Thou shalt reach me, without having an accuser."[114] Revolving around this central concern to establish and maintain *Ma'at* are the social, political, and, most important for our study, religious admonitions.[115] In the area of political concerns, the 'dead' king instructs his successor to remove troublemakers from the kingdom, establish safe boundaries, foster young political supporters, and maintain a strong and aggressive military policy. Just social policies are to be implemented, including the refraining from oppressing the weak, maintaining a just legal system, rewarding the just, and punishing the wicked.

This concern for establishing and maintaining *Ma'at* and following the proper rules of attitude and conduct which result from the cogent analyses of the spheres of world order also enters into the cultic realm, and, as we shall see, this instruction provides us with one of the most important Egyptian sapiential texts for assessing the views of the Egyptian wise toward cult. The father instructs his son who theoretically is the one responsible for maintaining the cults of Egypt, especially the state cult, not to neglect cultic concerns, but rather to participate whole-heartedly in the performance of his cultic role:

> Make monuments...for the god. That is what makes to
> live the name of him who does it. A man should do
> what is of advantage to his soul: the monthly service
> of the priest, putting on the white sandals, visiting
> the temple, revealing the mysteries, having access to
> the shrine, and eating bread in the temple. MAKE THE
> OFFERING-TABLE FLOURISH, INCREASE THE LOAVES, and add
> to the daily offerings. It is an advantage to him who
> does it. Make thy monuments to endure according as
> thou art able. A single day gives for eternity, and
> an hour effects accomplishment for the future. The
> god is aware of him who works for him.[116]

In this admonition extended by a number of motivation clauses, the king's ideal role as the chief priest and overseer of the Egyptian cult is stressed. Religious obligations such as the building of temples and shrines for 'the god' and participation in the cult are to be dutifully carried out. Several motivations are listed as to why these cultic duties should not be shirked. The perpetuation of the memory of the pharaoh probably by means of his name being carved in the building inscriptions of temples under his direction is one, but the most important is the same as the general one given at the end of the instruction: by fulfilling his cultic duties the king will come successfully into the realm of the future life, since 'the god' who is responsible for creating and overseeing world order is aware of the pharaoh who does his cultic duties and, therefore, will reward him accordingly, not only in this life, but in the one to come.[117]

The orderly transition from this life to the future life
by means of mortuary religion is also an accepted dogma in this
instruction, as may be seen in the admonition that Meri-ka-Re
should not destroy the necropolis as his predecessor apparently
did by re-using the stones of earlier tombs in the construction
of his own tomb:

> Granite comes to thee without hindrance. Do not
> injure the monument of another; thou shouldst quarry
> stone in Troia. Do not build thy tomb out of ruins,
> what had been made (going) into what is to be made.[118]

The implication is that the mortuary cult centered around the
tombs of the former pharaohs and nobles should not be disturbed
by destroying their resting places, for such an evil atrocity
is punished: "Egypt fights even in the necropolis, by hacking
up graves, by...I did the same, and the same happened as is
done to one who transgressed *the way* of the god." Thus 'the
god' punishes the king who disrupts this orderly transition to
the future life and the continuance of a future existence in a
tomb.[119]

The most significant admonition concerning mortuary religion is the admonition: "Enrich thy house of the West; embellish
thy place of the necropolis."[120] But even more important is the
means by which Meri-ka-Re is to embellish his tomb. He is to
do so by being "an upright man" and "one who executes the justice upon which (men's) hearts rely."[121] Thus by establishing
and maintaining justice, the king's participation in the future
life is assured. The admonition is followed by the comparative
proverb: "More acceptable is the character of one upright of
heart than the ox of the evildoer," a stunningly ethical observation that condemns the perfunctory religiosity of the wicked
who may participate in a grandiose scale in the proper ritual
observances of cult, but who, by reason of their wickedness,
negate the value of these observances. The god prefers one who
is upright even though he may appear empty-handed before him in
the temple.[122]

The instruction incorporates within its text a hymn to the
creator god which is quite comparable to Egyptian cultic hymns
to the creator deities. In glowing praise and joyous

thanksgiving, the god's creation, the concern for his creation, and his maintenance of justice which pervades the creation are magnificently described. Such an example of a cultic genre within a sapiential text illustrates a point that will be most important when we consider Hebrew Wisdom Psalms, for, as may be seen here as well as in the lament of the *Lebensmüde*, the wise utilized and composed poetic psalms.

From this very important instruction, we have excellent testimony to the views of the pious sages toward cult in Egypt. To the composers of this instruction, cult is certainly one of the spheres of world order overseen by the *Urgott* who created the world and established *Ma'at*. Consequently, the pharaoh is not to neglect his cultic responsibilities as the overseer and chief priest of Egyptian cults. If he does so, he will be punished according to the principle of retribution, a fate apparently suffered by Meri-ka-Re's predecessor. Mortuary religion is again a primary means for the orderly transition of the pharaoh to the future world, but in this text there is injected a close connection between mortuary ritual and the justice of the king, both of which insure his glorious participation in the future life. Thus cultic devotion and the maintenance of justice are closely interwoven duties of the king.

The Middle Kingdom (2040-1558 B.C.)

Introduction. The chaos of the First Intermediate Period was finally put to an end by the vigorous rulers of the twelfth dynasty at Thebes, and gradually we see these kings reasserting a strong, authoritarian rule which slowly strangled the individualism and demands for individual justice which had blossomed during the earlier period. A reassertion of the divine nature of the kings became accepted dogma, and once more scribal texts point not only to this but also to the importance of service to and worship of kings upon whom one's transition to the future life by means of mortuary religion depended.[123] But the rebuilding of the forces which had held together the Kingdom of *Ma'at* during the Old Kingdom was not easily accomplished, and the first king of the twelfth dynasty, as we shall see, is presented as quite frankly admitting his assassination.

The Instruction of King Amen-em-het.[124] Once more we find words placed on the lips of a dead Pharaoh, Amen-em-het I. Written by a court scribe under the patronage of Sen-Usert I (1971-1928 B.C.) upon the occasion of his ascent to the throne, this text purports to be an instruction coming from his dead predecessor on the throne.[125] The text probably had as its primary purpose the legitimation of the right of succession of the new pharaoh, and thus is rightly considered a piece of royal propaganda.[126]

The most noteworthy feature of the piece is reflected in the candid admission of the failures of the now defunct king who, to his obvious chagrin, was caught off guard and subsequently assassinated by his own treacherous subordinates. Yet efforts are made to present the dead king in glowing terms, for he vaunts his seemingly unparalleled achievements in the areas of military conquests, building projects, administration of justice, and national prosperity. His major failure lay in his lack of perception in choosing loyal courtiers and supporters, and thus this is his major emphasis to his new successor: he should be wise and perceptive in the appointing of loyal supporters to strategic posts.

What is important for us is a re-emphasis of the dogma of the divine pharaoh seen in the titulary and in the conclusion. Also the statement made to Sen-Usert that in his succession to the throne he "has appeared as a god" coupled with the good possibility that the text was read during the coronation festival of the new king make it probable that the sapiential text accepts the virtues of loyal service to and worship of the divine king. The attack against the kings made in the First Intermediate Period by the critical wise is now being countered by the loyalist sages of the Middle Kingdom.

In addition, he makes reference to his pyramid, indicating again a positive affirmation of the value of the mortuary cult (iii, 1f.).

The Instruction of a Man for his Son.[127] One of the most obvious pieces of sapiential propaganda, originating in the early part of the twelfth dynasty (1991-1786 B.C.),[128] is "The

Instruction of a Man for his Son" which attempts to inculcate
within the lesser officials, scribes, and bureaucrats of the
kingdom a zealous loyalty to the pharaoh, thereby solidifying
the structure of the kingdom around the cohesive center of the
Egyptian throne.[129] Once again we are able to see the response
of the loyalist wise to the earlier attacks against the authority and divinity of the Pharaoh, by means of pacifying potential sources of discontent, disorder, and even anarchy. This
attempt to generate the spirit of an enthusiastic devotee within the breasts of the minor officials was to be effectuated by
the emphasis upon an achievable and prosperous elevation in the
royal ranks, an elevation open to the scribal opportunists
whose loyalty and devotion would bring them more directly into
contact with the divine blessing radiating forth from the royal
god.[130]

> Great (shall be) thy portion for thee,
>   (If) thou spendest thy lifetime within the counsels
>   of thy god.
> Adore the King of Upper Egypt, revere the King of
> Lower Egypt (ll. 18-19).

Following the title and typical summons to gather and listen to his wisdom, this anonymous wise man articulates in the
form of admonitions the various qualities which should be developed within the character of the young official: repute,
diligence, silence, trustworthiness, reliability, and atten-
tiveness. Then in the central section of the teaching, he
turns to his primary concern, the indoctrination of his youth-
ful audience in the loyalist creed of the aspiring young 'man
of the king.'

> Do not turn away from the god,[131]
>   But adore him, love him as (loyal) supporters.
> He will bless as his power shall grant;
>   Whom he neglects is one who has no prospects,
>   Worth more is he than millions of men, to him
>   whom he favoured (ll. 8-9).

Such a sapiential document is a clear expression of the dogma
of royal divinity which should make the pharaoh the center of
piety and devotion to the scribes serving within the royal
domain.[132]

The Instruction of Sehetep-ib-Re.[133] Another sapiential
instruction bearing the noticeable marks of court propaganda is
the hymnic "Instruction[134] of Sehetep-ib-Re," a high official,
perhaps even the vizier, of Pharaoh Amen-em-het III (Ni-maat-Re)
(1842-1797 B.C.) of the Twelfth Dynasty, which is written for
the primary purpose of engendering within the hearts of the
students[135] a cultist attitude of fervent devotion toward the
divine Pharaoh.[136] The entire counsel is imbued with a venera-
tive reverence concerning the divinity of the royal personage,
a reverence which is incorporated in the admonition to serve
the Pharaoh with adoration, for such counsel is

> ....a counsel of eternity
> And a manner of living aright
> And for passing a lifetime in peace.[137]

Following the admonition to "worship King Ni-maat-Re," in
hymnic fashion the divine qualities of the monarch are listed
which should inspire awe and the concomitant loyalty that the
sage wished to infuse within the audience. Thus the ruler is

> Perception which is in (men's) hearts,
> ....
> He is Re, by whose beams one sees,
> ....
> He is the Khnum of all bodies,
> ....
> He is the Bastet who protects the Two Lands,
> ....
> He is Sekhmet against him who transgresses his command.

In this catalogue,[138] the wise man has presented the major emphases of Egyptian royal ideology which centers upon the king
as the incorporation of the spheres of world order and by whom
order, peace, prosperity, and the tranquility of eternity are
created and maintained. Therefore, he admonishes the officials
and nobles of the kingdom to serve with unswerving loyalty the
divine king and by this service perform as the functional ex-
tensions of the royal blessing and creative power. By so doing,
they will share in the rewards for such service by receiving
the blissful abundance of the present and the future life.

The obvious contrast between those who faithfully execute
their duties of service and those who contribute to disorder by
engendering a festering spirit of hostility or even rebellion
is seen in the following:

He is Bastet who protects the two lands
He who worships him will be one whom his arm shelters.
He is Sekhmet against him who transgresses his command;
He whom he hates will bear woes.

He concludes with a passionate summons to service and
loyalty, and with a reference to the attendant benefits:

Fight on behalf of his name,
And be scrupulous in the oath to him
(That) ye may be free from a taint of *disloyalty*.
He whom the king has loved will be a revered one,
(But) there is no tomb for a rebel against his majesty,
And his corpse is cast into the water.
If ye do this, your persons shall be unblemished--
Ye will find it (so) forever.

Thus the loyal servant will participate in the blissful after-
life with the pharaoh, a reward gained through obedient service.
However, the preparations of mortuary religion will be denied
to the disloyal fool who in death will find himself without
tomb and subsequently without eternal life.

The New Kingdom (1558-1085 B.C.)

Introduction.[139] Following the debacle of the Second
Intermediate Period, the Egyptians, especially during the Thut-
mosid dynasty, established a tremendous empire in Africa and
Asia, and once more we find literary creations of the wise: "In
Praise of Learned Scribes," "The Instruction of Ani," and "The
Instruction of Amen-em-Opet."

In Praise of Learned Scribes.[140] One of the most provoca-
tive sapiential texts which bespeaks the sage's concern to continue into the future life is Papyrus Chester Beatty IV, which
takes the form of a panegyric to the illustrious savants of the
distant past whose august fame and renowned writings provided
schoolboys of ancient Egypt with human models after which to
pattern their careers and with instructions concerning the
moulding of such careers.

Written with the express purpose of creating a self-
motivating spirit of diligent dedication to the scribal professions within the Egyptian empire, this sage bases his admonitions to diligent study and labor on the idea that the achievement of undisputed fame and prestige as a sage is the only

certain means for realizing eternal existence. But such an emphasis may involve not only the commonly held idea of an existence predicated upon indisputable renown which comes to the scholar who promulgates famous writings, but also the intimation that the schoolboys throughout the ages who study the writings of their august predecessors will remember their names in mortuary prayers and thereby ensure their continued existence in the realm of the living dead.

First of all, the sage contrasts the coveted position of the famous wise who continue to exist eternally by means of their writings and that of the person who stakes his eternal existence upon the trappings of mortuary religion. The celebrated wise may have had their tombs and mortuary services, but now, centuries later, "their mortuary service is (gone); their tombstones are covered with dirt; and their graves are forgotten." However, they possess something infinitely better. Their papyrus roll is their lector priest, their students are their children, their writing boards are their "beloved sons," their reed-pens are their children,[141] their stone ostraca are their wives,[142] and, most important, their writings which provide them with continued existence are their tombs. Thus, "their names are (still) pronounced because of their books which they made, since they were good and the memory of him who made them (lasts) to the limits of eternity."

Then the sage turns directly to his students and admonishes them to work in order to achieve such lasting fame, and, consequently, continuance into the future life, for famous writings handed down through the ages not only serve the same function as tombs and the reliefs and mortuary texts placed upon the walls, but are actually superior in providing existence into the future life for the savant, because the famous writings easily outlast the crumbling tombs, the mummies which turn to dust, and the extinction of one's survivors:

> More effective is a book than a decorated tombstone
> or an established *tomb-wall*. Such things make
> buildings and pyramids for the sake of pronouncing
> their names.[143] Without doubt a name in the mouth
> of men is of benefit in the necropolis. A MAN IS
> PERISHED, his corpse is dust, all his relatives are

> come to the ground--(But) it is writing that makes
> him remembered in the mouth of a reciter. More
> effective is a book than the house of the builder
> or tombs in the West. It is better than a (well-)
> founded castle or a stela in a temple.

Therefore a famous sage can be assured of future existence, because his students will remember his name and will recite the
necessary mortuary texts which magically insure his future life.
The wise, being cogent observers of reality, readily recognized
the shortcomings of mortuary religion, for the crumbled tombs,
destroyed mortuary stelae, and long forgotten names of the deceased were constant reminders that future existence predicated
upon mortuary religion was illusory. But in contrast, the
writings of the famous scribe provided him permanency in the
future realm: "Though they are gone and their names are forgotten, it is writing that makes them remembered."

Once more a sage reflects over the sacred rituals and dogmas of mortuary religion and disputes much of their cogency and
effectiveness, preferring to achieve immortality through the
means of acquiring an august reputation, and hoping that his
name will continue on the lips of scribes throughout the centuries, and in that way find the future life that mortuary religion had so obviously failed to provide.

The Instruction of Ani.[144] During the 18th dynasty (1558-
1303 B.C.), another sage, this time a lower echelon temple
scribe, produced a wisdom writing meant to instruct his son, a
scribal novitiate, in the general areas of social, civic, and
religious duties and responsibilities which would be his in the
scribal profession.[145] As will become obvious, this is another
sage who is most concerned to bring the realm of cult under
sagacious scrutiny.

In iii 3-9, Ani instructs his young son[146] to observe the
public festival of his deity by participating actively in the
public offerings, singing, and dancing which occur during the
festive time. The two motivations which Ani accents for such
cultic involvement are the avoidance of the deity's anger
against the cultically negligent, and the enhancement of the
career of the observant sage by the deity "who will magnify the
name of him who *does it*...." In fact, the young man should be

sure that his cultic service is duly witnessed and recorded in writing so as to have proof of his faithful cultic participation.[147]

In iv, 1-4 the experienced sage considers what is to be the proper demeanor of the wise cultic participant, and it is that which should characterize the wise man in any and all circumstances: dispassionate and well-tempered self-control, or, more simply put, 'silence.' Thus the ideal sage, the 'silent man,' should be one's model even in the realm of the cult. Such a decorum of self-control avoids the boisterous loqaciousness and frenzied activity which characterize the 'heated man,' who foolishly believes his passionate and garrulous cultic activities, bordering on the edge of sacrilege, will ensure the attention of the deity, and, concomitantly, the divine favor, but in reality disturb the inner sanctity and peacefulness of the divine abode, thereby resulting in the arousal of the divine wrath. How much more effective, counsels Ani, is the solemn and composed solicitude of the sagacious worshipper who lovingly presents his offering with a silent entreaty before the hidden and secretive deity, sure that "he will do what thou needest, he will hear what thou sayest, and he will accept thy offering..."[148]

Ani, in contrast to his contemporary, the author of "In Praise of Learned Scribes," impresses upon his young son the importance of prompt attention to mortuary provisions in order that he may secure an official's orderly transition to the future life (iv, 14-v, 4).[149] Even a young and non-affluent scribe should be concerned with his future dwelling, for death's messenger comes to all irrespective of age or preparation.

The most extensive section concerning cultic participation occurs in vii, 12-17 in which the young scribe is admonished to make offerings and to prostrate himself in the name of the deity, and yet maintain a discreet distance as a restrained spectator when the veiled image of the deity passes through the public throngs during a holy procession occurring during festival seasons.[150] He reiterates the motivations for cultic observance to be those of appeasement of the divine wrath ("Let thy eye have regard to the nature of his anger") and personal exaltation by the deity of the minor official ("...they are magnified whom he magnifies"). The latter would appeal, of course, to the young scribe in his quest to orient himself within the beneficent spheres of order maintained by the deity, and in his efforts to progress upward within the scribal hierarchy.

Finally, he interjects a perceptive insight concerning the images of the sun god, for the real deity is "the sun which is on the horizon," though through means of cultic activity, particularly the offering of incense, he is able to appear especially during festivals among men in the earthly realm in the images located in the cultic shrines, and, thereby, to effect blessings for the cultic participants.[151] The tension between the multiplicity of images in cultic religion and the customary sapiential understanding of the deity who created and maintains the order of creation is resolved to the satisfaction of this sage, an effort that shows indepth reflection of the sage over certain incongruities in cultic dogmas (cf. Meri-ka-Re, ll. 125f.).

This instruction provides us with ample material to validate the thesis that cult was an important sphere to be analyzed by the sages, and, in this case, participation in cultic rituals and the affirmation of cultic beliefs receive a most definitely favorable emphasis. To Ani, the observant scribe could not only avoid the destructive power of the deity, but at the same time would enjoy his favor which could be tangibly realized in his rise in the scribal ranks. Even the much disputed mortuary religion receives a positive concern, for Ani considered it necessary for the participation of the wise in the future life. But above all, Ani informs us that in the sacral sphere as well as in the spheres of everyday existence, the wise man is to incorporate within his character the decorum of the 'silent man.'

The Instruction of Amen-em-Opet.[152] Another Egyptian sage who provides us with important insights into the cultic sphere of world order is Amen-em-Opet, a high official in the administration of royal estates,[153] who wrote his instruction perhaps as early as the 19th dynasty (13th century, B.C.).[154] Writing expressly for his own son, Hor-em-maa-kheru, a young priestly scribe functioning within the temple of Min, the father seeks to instruct him in the familiar areas of the official or scribal functionary who seeks to orientate himself within the beneficent spheres of world-order overseen by the god of justice by following the model of the "silent man" and by avoiding the destructive behavior of the "passionate man." By faithfully discharging his scribal duties as the deputy of the deity of justice, the young sage can expect to be rewarded with success and prosperity.[155]

As concerns our subject, Amen-em-Opet never directly and explicitly admonishes his young adherent to perform specific cultic duties within the framework of the cultic community, a fact that has led one scholar to remark that the reason is the young priestly scribe would have had that impressed upon him by the very nature of his office.[156] Therefore, Amen-em-Opet is not giving his son cultic instructions, but rather is seeking as a counsellor to impress upon him the correct conduct and behavior befitting a priestly scribe within the realm of the holy.

In keeping with his desire to school his son in the proper decorum within the various spheres of life, he establishes the model for proper behavior within the cultic sphere in the fourth chapter, which, according to Grumach, is a *Pausenkapital*. Thus in terms of structure and content, chapter four is an artistically constructed poem that is placed within two groups of chapters contrasting the "passionate man" (chapters 1-3) to the "silent man" (chapters 4-7).[157] As a result of the sage's literary skills, strophe one of the poem in chapter four concerns the "passionate man," thereby succinctly summarizing the central subject of chapters 1-3, and the second strophe presents his opposite, the "silent man," which provides a summation of the major subject of chapters 4-7.[158]

Wilson translates the chapter as follows:[159]

Strophe I	Strophe II
As for the heated man of the temple	(But) the truly silent man holds himself apart.
He is like a tree growing in the open.	He is like a tree growing in a garden.

In the completion of a moment (comes) its loss of foliage,	It flourishes and doubles its yield;
And its end is reached in the shipyards;	It (stands) before its lord.
(Or) it is floated far from its place,	Its fruit is sweet; its shade is pleasant;
And the flame is its burial shroud.	And its end is reached in the garden.

The two strophes exhibit external, antithetical parallelism as the translation above indicates. The first lines of both strophes denote the two types of persons under consideration and seems, at first glance, to contrast their respective positions concerning the temple: the passionate man is within the temple, whereas the "silent man" is one who holds himself apart. The next two lines of each strophe describe the different areas in which the two trees, metaphorically depicting the two opposite types of people, grow and develop. The final four lines in each strophe present in graphic fashion the contrasting fates which meet each tree: destruction and preservation.[160]

The two major problems confronting the interpretation of the poem involve the meaning and translation of *m ḫntj* at the end of line 2 in Strophe I and *m tḥn.t.* in the second line of Strophe II and the intent of the sage's statements that the "heated man" is within the temple whereas the "silent man" holds himself apart." With respect to the first problem, Posener has summarized the different possible translations: *ḫntj*-- 'courthouse,' 'courtyard of a temple,' 'outside,' 'prematurely,' 'in the open,' 'in an enclosed space,' or, by changing the text to *m hntj(-s)*, 'in the forest'; and *tḥn.t.*--'canal,' 'fertile soil,' 'plot,' and 'garden.'[161] Posener observes that the general idea, of course, is that the first tree grows in an area that ultimately leads to the demise of the tree, whereas the second grows in a place which causes it to flourish. More specifically he argues that perhaps the terms should be understood as a contrast between *endroit sombre* and *endroit ensoleillé*, that is, the position of the "silent man" is preferable because outside the temple he is like a tree that

flourishes in the bright sunshine, a symbolic idea for being
present before the sun god, whereas the position of the tree
representing the passionate man is within the temple which
causes it to die from the lack of sunshine.[162]

Integrally related to this is the problem of determining
the intent of the sage's remark that the foolish, heated man is
inside the temple while the "silent man holds himself apart."
Fichtner's argument is that the "heated man" should be regarded
as the priest or layman who participates actively in the cultic
sphere, whereas, by contrast, the truly wise man does not.
Thus he concludes that the polemic against the cult opposes the
idea of worship as *opus operatum*.[163] But this interpretation
does not consider chapter five in which the "silent man," in
contrast to the "heated man" who is characterized by an in-
satiable greed and therefore finds himself in the precarious
position of those who are swept away by natural disasters,
takes refuge in the temple:

> Alle Schweigenden im Tempel aber,
> die sagen: "gross an Gunstbeweisen ist Re."
> Erfülle dich mit Schweigen, und du wirst das Leben finden,
> und dein Leib wird heil sein auf Erden (7:7-10).[164]

Unless we charge the sage with a contradiction, Amen-em-Opet
must be stating in this latter passage that the position of
the "silent ones" is within the temple where they offer praise
to Re even during times of disaster, and he intimates that such
a response by the "silent" will lead to their preservation from
catastrophe. Thus a more judicious solution to chapter four is
to argue that the sage is prescribing the preferred behavior of
the "silent man" who in his decorum of discretion and his control of his passions behaves in the same manner in the cultic
sphere, while by contrast the "passionate man," whose demeanor
lacks self-control even in cultic activities, falsely believes
that it is proximity to the divine that results in blessing,
when actually, because of his overzealous and boisterous behavior, he is quickly destroyed for disrupting the silence,
order, and sanctity of the divine sphere. The "silent man" in
his religious piety continues to be characterized by discretion
and a submissive faith. Grumach is correct in the observation:

"Das Abseitsstellen des Frommen (6,7) ist denn auch nicht als Gegensatz zum Sein im Tempel gemeint, sondern nur als eine... Verhaltensweise.[165] Thus "holding himself apart" is not a rejection of the cultic duties of the wise in the temple, but rather a criticism of the bawdy, boisterous behavior of the fool within the cult who wrongly believes that such actions will negate the forces of retribution which will bring about his destruction for reasons of unwise behavior both within the cult and without, and an affirmation that the wise actions of the "silent man" both within and without the temple will lead to his good fortune within the sphere of retribution. Blessing may result from proximity to the divine, but it results only by means of wise behavior in the cult and in daily life.

Like his predecessor, Ani, Amen-em-Opet impresses on his young scribe the importance of praying to the sun disc each morning for prosperity and health, resting assured that:

> He will give thee thy needs for this life,
> And thou wilt be safe from terror (X, 13f.).

The admonition concerning prayer occurs at the end of a chapter which contrasts the foolish pursuit of wealth, especially wealth obtained dishonestly, with the pious behavior of the true wise man who realizes that his needs will be met by the sun god who dispenses favor to the one who avoids the pitfalls of greed.

In chapter eight, Amen-em-Opet adds certain motivations to his admonitions pertaining to the control of one's tongue and the avoiding of injurious speech:

> Thou wilt find thy place within the temple,
> and thy provisions in the bread-offerings of thy lord;
> Thou wilt be revered in old age and be hidden (in) thy
>   coffin,
> and be safe from the power of God (X, 21-XI, 5).[166]

Thus the sage obviously supports the importance of mortuary religion, for he who controls his tongue will receive as a reward a lovely grave. His statue will be kept in the temple and sustained by the temple offerings, and in the judgment of the dead he will be preserved from destruction.[167] In his introduction, Amen-em-Opet had indicated his own possession of a tomb.

It would be inaccurate to argue that, in contrast to the older wisdom, Amen-em-Opet has yielded to the influence of popular beliefs and local cults, as has been charged,[168] but rather as we have seen in much of the literature of the sages, the wise believed that cult was an important sphere of world order, and, therefore, cultic devotion should be of concern to the pious scribe. Once more we find a sage who criticizes foolish, overly zealous cultic participation by the "heated man" who regards cultic participation as a guarantee of divine favor, regardless of the manner of life he leads both inside and outside the cultic realm. In contrast, he depicts the discreet behavior of the "silent man" that characterizes his actions even within the sphere of the holy, and it is this behavior that achieves beneficent blessings from the divine, both within the sphere of cultic religion and without.

The Late Dynastic Period and Hellenistic Rule

Introduction. The chain of Egyptian instructions continued unbroken through the periods of Egyptian history in which Egypt fell victim to the immense power of the Persians in the sixth century B.C. and finally to the military power and rule of Alexander and his Greek successors. First, we find "The Instruction of 'Onchsheshonqy" during the period of Persian domination, and then, when the Ptolemies ruled Egypt, "The Instruction of Papyrus Insinger."

The Instruction of 'Onchsheshonqy.[169] Writing during the eclipse of Egyptian civilization and power,[170] a priest of the sun god Re of Heliopolis wrote a rustic instruction intended primarily for Egyptian peasants of the countryside, and not, like his sapiential predecessors, for officials and courtiers of royal position.[171] The range of the subjects covered involves familial relationships, relationships with friends, neighbors, landlords, the conducting and managing of one's affairs, and one's religious obligations. Not only do the various items of the instruction smack of a rural flavor, but, likewise, so do the formal characteristics.[172] First of all, the fact that almost half of the instruction consists of indicative statements conforming to the form of the popular proverb lends itself to a rural origin. Secondly, the instruction is marked by an almost complete omission of any extended motivations for observing the admonitions, again indicating a less erudite audience lacking acutely sharpened tools of reason and an investigative spirit, or, in other words, pointing to an audience which would probably accept without hesitancy the admonitions of the sage. If such an audience is plausible, we are provided not only with evidence that wisdom teaching eventually penetrated the lower strata of Egyptian society, but, in addition, with material concerning the sapiential instruction for the peasant with respect to his cultic duties.

Cultic participation by the peasant is important as the following admonition demonstrates:

> Make sacrifice and libation before God,
> And let the fear of him be great in your heart
>   (Col. 14, 1. 10).

The motivation for cultic involvement is, of course, projected upon the belief that such activity results in the evoking of divine favor:

> Serve[173] your God(?) that he may protect you (Col. 6, 1. 1).

> Wealth is perfected in the service of God,
> The one who causes (it) to happen (Col. 18, 1. 17).

> The master's favourite will act the master,
> if the household do not worship before God (Col. 19, 1. 14).

Besides sacrifice, prayer is also presented as an important act of piety by the sage who insists that persistence in prayer will eventually be rewarded:

> Do not be weary of crying to God,
> for he has his hour for hearing the scribe (Col. 28, 1. 10).

Like many of his sapiential ancestors, 'Onchsheshonqy also demonstrates a funerary interest, for he urges his adherents to be concerned with mortuary preparations, even before the threat of death is imminent:

> Do not delay to get yourself a tomb on the hill;
> You do not know the length of your life (Col. 12, 1. 5).

Finally, the sage is a loyalist to the priestly clerics, for he notes that "the blessing of a temple is a priest" (Col. 8, 1. 18), but he does issue the dire warning to the chief priest against being negligent in his duties:

> Bread is given to the chief priest in return for his
> intercession;
> If he does not intercede he is slain (Col. 24, 1. 11).

Though our sage does not engage in any outspoken critique of cult, he, like many of his sapiential predecessors, does share the view that the cult is most certainly an important area of world order, and therefore should receive due attention from those who desire to integrate themselves within the beneficent spheres of world order.

The Instruction of the Papyrus Insinger.[174] An anonymous sage of the Ptolemaic period (304-30 B.C.) was responsible for the compilation of our final Egyptian instruction, and once more we are provided with material supporting the contention that the Egyptian wise were concerned with cult as an important sphere of world order.

The key concept of this instruction around which the admonitions and proverbs are centered is the idea of *Gleichgewicht* (*p3 dnf*), "balance, equilibrium," which is the guiding principle of world order, and, therefore, of orderly human activity. And though the deity may be inscrutable, beyond the ken of human knowledge and understanding, our sage never allows himself to question the justice of this deity, even though experience may not always support a rigid scheme of retribution at first glance, and he continues to adhere to the ethical standard of *Gleichgewicht* for every human activity.[175]

In the realm of cultic participation, the sage gives cult its due, for, though the deity is inscrutable in his ways, he continues to bless those who are cultically observant:

> 10:1 (Denn Gott) hilft dem weisen Manne, weil er
> (ihm) dient.[176]
> 29:1 Wer seinen Gott morgens in seiner Staat anbetet,
> der wird leben.
> 29:2 Wer seinen (d.h. Gottes) Namen in seinem Munde
> führt während des Unglücks, wird daraus er-
> rettet.[177]

The sage is also a supporter of the mortuary cult and admonishes his followers, even though, paradoxically, their fate and fortune is completely determined by the deity, to make the proper preparations for burial:

> 2:9 Vergiss (aber) das Begräbnis nicht, sei nicht lässig in den (Ehren), die Gott befiehlt.
> 2:10 Das Begräbnis ist in der Hand Gottes, (aber) der Weise Mann trägt dafür Sorge.

In fact God's reward for those who fear him is a grave:

> 2:11 Gottes Gnade für den Gottesfürchtigen ist sein Begräbnis und seine Ruhestätte.

A most interesting social cast is given to the sacrificial cult, and in this way the text is similar to a contemporary Hebrew sage, Sirach. Not only is god pleased by offerings, but in this manner one is able to support the poor who are dependent upon the offerings for sustenance.

> 16:4 Hast du Besitz, dann gib einen Teil Gott, das ist der der Armen.
> 16:1 Brandopfer und Trankopfer sind nützlich wegen der Berwirtung (C.V, d,1:(um) einer Anderen zu bewirten).
> 16:2 Ein Begräbnis ist nützlich, weil man dort bewirtet.

Such a social concern for the poor and the usage of sacrificial offerings for their sustenance is given the stamp of divine authority:

> 16:3 Denn das Herz Gottes wird zufrieden, wenn der Arme vor ihm gesättigt wird.

Thus it becomes obvious that our sage is equally concerned with cultic observance, but his unique contribution is the social concern which he demonstrates and to which he appeals in regard to the offering of sacrifices and gifts to the cult, for such may be used not only for the support of the priests who at times of hardship and religious laxness suffered severely, but also for the socially deprived as well.

Conclusions

On the basis of the above investigation, it becomes obvious that the sphere of cult was of considerable concern to the wise of ancient Egypt. While references to the cult during the period of the Old Kingdom are relatively infrequent, nevertheless, the advocacy of the importance of mortuary religion and service to the divine pharaoh is found in Old Kingdom wisdom literature. Furthermore, Schmid's contention that the attacks against Egyptian cults made by the critical wise of the First Intermediate Period are understandable only if their predecessors had provided sapiential support for the ancient cults of Egypt seems to us a most plausible suggestion.

With the eruption of the volcanic conditions of the First Intermediate Period, the Egyptian sages were divided into two antagonistic camps in their analyses of cultic religion. The critical wise attacked the validity of mortuary religion and service to the divine king, while the pious wise asserted the importance of the Egyptian cults in efforts to re-establish the beneficent orders of the Egyptian state. Even so, the critical strain of Egyptian wisdom continued into later periods as is evidenced by the sapiential "In Praise of Learned Scribes" which continues to castigate the failures of mortuary religion.

The texts dating from the Middle Kingdom take on an especially propagandistic character as loyal support of the scribal officials is urged by the sages for the court, and this flows over into the area of cultic religion as well, since the support of the divine pharaoh in loyal service brings the sage both advancement in the scribal ranks and the blessing of a tomb for continuance into the future life by means of mortuary religion.

The New Kingdom texts, with the noted exception of "In Praise of Learned Scribes," continue the sapiential support of the validity of mortuary religion and urge their recipients to participate in the temple cults of Egypt. However, new emphases are placed on the behavior of the wise in the sphere of the cult, for the pious sage is to be characterized in his cultic behavior by the decorum of the "silent man," and not by the garrulous activities of the "heated man."

The Late Dynastic and Hellenistic texts point to the continuing emphasis of the wise on the importance of cultic religion, as these texts admonish their adherents to continue to support the Egyptian cults and to be concerned with the preparations of mortuary religion.

Throughout the history of Egyptian wisdom literature, it is apparent that, except for periods of disruption and despair, the wise placed their support behind the varieties of Egyptian cultic religion, believing that the Egyptian cults aided in the processes of securing and maintaining beneficent order for the Egyptian state and the sagacious individual. This belief, expressed most often in the general categories of retributive blessing and destruction, was the primary motivation for active participation by the wise in cultic religion.

Finally, present within the Egyptian wisdom texts are a number of developed units of didactic poems, including some which are quite similar to cultic psalms. This indicates that the wise participated in the writing of didactic poems, including genres similar to cultic psalms, a point to which we shall return in Chapter V when we investigate Hebrew didactic poems and wisdom psalms.

CHAPTER II

[1]*Ma'at.* For an examination of *Ma'at* in Egyptian literature, see C.-J. Bleeker, "L'idée de l'ordre cosmique dans
l'ancienne Égypte," *RHPR* 42 (1962), pp. 193-200.

[2]A reference to the creation and establishment of *Ma'at* as
the order of the cosmos by the sun god Re (Siegfried Morenz,
Ägyptische Religion [Stuttgart: W. Kohlhammer, 1960], p. 121).

[3]Ptah-hotep, ll. 84-94: *ANET*, p. 421. Aksel Volten has
pinpointed the essence of the citation in his explanation: "Wir
finden in der eben zitieren Ptahhotep Stelle den ägyptischen
Schicksalglauben klar ausgedrückt. Gott und die Gerechtigkeit,
die mit ihm identisch ist, lenken seit ewiger Zeit die Welt
nach unveränderlichen vorausbestimmten Gesetzen" ("Der Begriff
der Maat in den ägyptischen Weisheitstexten," SPOA [Paris:
Presses Universitaires de France, 1963], p. 79).

[4]E.g., Meri-ka-Re, ll. 131f. (*ANET*, p. 417).

[5]Gese brings this point clearly into focus in his monograph, *Lehre und Wirklichkeit in der alten Weisheit* (Tübingen:
J. C. B. Mohr [Paul Siebeck], 1958), p. 12: "Der Begriff Maat
umfasst zwei für uns unterschiedene Bereiche: die Ordnung des
Kosmos *und* die Ordnung des menschlichen Lebens."

[6]The recognition of the religious basis of wisdom instruction in the concept of order permeating the creation which was
brought into existence by the *Urgott* has caused more recent
wisdom scholars to reject the once prevalent but questionable
view of wisdom as being crassly eudaemonistic and utilitarian
in tenor and purpose, a view represented by Fichtner in his
otherwise useful analysis of the wisdom literature in the ancient Near East (*Die altorientalische Weisheit in ihrer
israelitisch-jüdischen Ausprägung*, BZAW 62 [Giessen: Alfred
Töpelmann, 1933], pp. 75f.). For more judicious assessments of
this essentially religious character of wisdom literature, see
A. De Buck, "Het Religieus Karakter der oudste egyptische
Wijsheid," *NTT* 21 (1932), pp. 322-49; and Hellmut Brunner, "Der
freie Wille Gottes in der ägyptischen Weisheit," SPOA, p. 203.

[7]There is some difficulty in finding an Egyptian word
which corresponds to wisdom. The scribe is referred to as *s33*,
and, therefore, "scribal wisdom" is *s3t*. A more rare word for
wisdom is *ikkw*. The ideal of the Egyptian wise is referred to
as *kbb* ('the cool man') who is characterized by 'silence' (*gr*),
whereas the 'fool' is the *t3w*, or the 'envious' (*'wn-ib*). See
Jean Leclant, "Documents nouveaux et points de vue récente sur
les sagesses de l'Égypte ancienne," SPOA, p. 13.

[8]H. H. Schmid, *Wesen und Geschichte der Weisheit*, BZAW 101 (Berlin: Alfred Töpelmann, 1966), p. 21.

[9]See *ANET*, pp. 3-10, for various creation myths.

[10]The *Urhügel* was symbolized by the pharaonic pyramids and assumed the same hieroglyph as Ma'at: ⬭. In addition, the *Urhügel* was also presented as the foundation of the divine and royal thrones. Consequently, it seems likely that *Ma'at* was also seen to be the foundation of these thrones, symbolizing the concern of the gods and the pharaohs for justice and order (cf. H. Brunner, "Gerechtigkeit als Fundament des Thrones," *VT* 8 [1958], pp. 426-28).

[11]Given demonic characterization as Apophis (cf. *ANET*, pp. 6f.).

[12]*ANET*, p. 372, footnote 9. Through the process of hypostatization, *Ma'at* acquired divine status, though she never seemed to achieve prominence in the Egyptian pantheon. In fact, with the exception of the temple built for her in Karnak by Amen-hotep III, she remained in relative obscurity (Schmid, *Wesen und Geschichte der Weisheit*, p. 20).

[13]ll. 132ff.; *ANET*, p. 417.

[14]H. Bonnet, "Maat," *RÄRG* (Berlin: A. Töpelmann, 1952), pp. 430-34.

[15]H. Frankfort, *Ancient Egyptian Religion*, Harper Torchback (New York: Harper and Brothers, 1940), p. 76 (see Meri-ka-Re, ll. 53f.; *ANET*, p. 415).

[16]"Die Weisheitsliteratur," *Ägyptologie*, HO 1 (Leiden: E. J. Brill, 1952), p. 94. This point is illustrated in Meri-ka-Re, ll. 49-50 (*ANET*, p. 415).

[17]This is especially true in later wisdom (Ani, 8, 3-10; Amen-em-Opet, 22, 5-8; 23, 8-21; 24, 13-18; Papyrus Insinger, 2, 14-20; 30, 23; 32, 18; and 'Onchsheshonqy, 23, 12).

[18]Amen-em-Opet, xix, 16-17 (*ANET*, p. 423). De Buck states in reference to this passage: "Het is een thema, dat ons uit de Bijbelsche Chokma welbekend is, een prediking, dit tot de meest ken merkende trekken dezer chokma behoort: de geringheid en nietigheid van den mensch tegenover God, bij wien allen de wijsheid is en de macht, die over den mensch beschikt naar zijn welbehagen men kent zijn plannen, treft maatregelen, naar over de toekomst vermag hij niets; die is in Gods hand. ("Het Religieus Karakter der oudste egyptische Wijsheid," p. 328). For a discussion of the freedom of God, see Hellmut Brunner, "Der freie Wille Gottes in der ägyptischen Weisheit," SPOA, pp. 103-20.

[19]See "The Prophecy of Nefer-rohu" (*ANET*, pp. 444-46), "The Admonitions of Ipu-wer" (*ANET*, pp. 441-44), "The Protests of th Eloquent Peasant" (*ANET*, pp. 407-41), and "A Dispute over Suicide" (*ANET*, pp. 405-7).

[20]So remarks Morenz: "Mit 'Gott' meinen die Weisheits-lehren das durch Wirksamkeit gekennzeichnete Wesen, das *mutatis mutandis* dem Urgott entspricht" (*op. cit.*, pp. 27-28). Some scholars have argued for monotheistic tendencies in Egyptian wisdom (Joseph Vergot, "La notion de dieu dans les livres de sagesse Égyptien," SPOA, pp. 159-90; and Eberhard Otto, "Mono-theistische Tendenzen in der ägyptischen Religion," WO 2/2 [Göttingen: Vandenhoeck und Ruprecht, 1955], pp. 99-110).

[21]Meri-ka-Re, ll. 131f. (*ANET*, p. 417).

[22]Sigmund Mowinckel declares: "In the static view of life, kingship is an essential factor in the eternal world order and the basis of all ordered existence" (*He That Cometh* [Oxford: Basil Blackwell, 1956], p. 28).

[23]See the study of H. H. Schmid, *Gerechtigkeit als Welt-ordnung*, BHT 40 (Tübingen: J. C. B. Mohr [Paul Siebeck], 1968). The king's concern for *Ma'at* may be seen in a statement taken from the "Inscription of Vizier Kagemni": "Tut die Sache der Maat dem König denn das, was der König liebt, ist die Maat. Sagt die Sache der Maat dem König, denn das, was der König liebt, ist die Maat" (E. Edel, "Inschriften des Alten Reiches," MIO 1 [1953], p. 213).

[24]Meri-ka-Re, ll. 47f. (*ANET*, p. 415).

[25]*Hu*, *Sia*, and *Ma'at*. Wilson comments: "*Hu*, 'authoritative utterance' or 'creative command,' and *Sia*, 'intellectual per-ception' or 'cognition,' were a pair of related attributes, often deified. As attributes of kingship, they were sometimes linked to *Ma'at*, 'justice' or 'truth.' Kingship thus needed the ability to comprehend a situation, the authority to meet the situation by command, and the balance of equitable justice" (*ANET*, p. 443, footnote 39).

[26]XII, 11f. (*ANET*, p. 443).

[27]ii, 7f. (*ANET*, p. 419).

[28]ll. 119f. (*ANET*, p. 417).

[29]Hor-dedef was a royal prince, though apparently not the crown prince (*ANET*, pp. 419-20).

[30]Amen-em-het boasts: "I was the one who made barley, the beloved of the grain god. The Nile honored me on every broad expanse. No one hungered in my years; no one thirsted therein" (*ANET*, p. 419). Frankfort explains this expression: "The king 'produced barley,' not merely in an indirect way,...but through his own actions--by maintaining Maat, the right order which allowed nature to function unimpaired for the benefit of man!" (*Kingship and the Gods* [Chicago: The University of Chicago Press, 1948], pp. 57-58).

[31] 11. 27f. (*ANET*, p. 445). We have purposefully omitted the responsibility of the pharaoh as concerns cult, since this will be part of our investigation later on. However, Schmid's comment should be underscored: "Die so zentrale Funktion des Maat-Begriffs in kultischen Zusammenhängen zeigt, dass der Ägypter den Kult (zumindest auch) als Teil der Bemühung um die umfassende Weltordnung verstanden hat" (*Gerechtigkeit als Weltordnung*, p. 60).

[32] Faulkner, "The Installation of the Vizier," *JEA* 40 (1955), pp. 22-23.

[33] The ruling pharaoh was regarded as the incarnation of the god Horus.

[34] 11. 640f. (*ANET*, p. 414). Eberhard Otto explains: "Der zentralistische Verwaltungsstaat bedarf auf seiner Aufrechterhaltung eines bestimmten Beamtentyps. Aus der Praxis und Erfahrung wird dieser Typ durch fachliche Ausbildung und charakterliche Bildung geformt. Er muss über ausgedehnte Kenntnisse der Verwaltungspraxis verfügen; er dient in seinem Amt nicht einem bestimmten Herrscher, sondern verwirklicht die Idee der Staats- und Weltordnung, deren Garant, nicht Schöpfer der jeweilige Pharao ist" ("Bildung und Ausbildung im alten Ägypten," *ZÄS* 81 [1956], p. 47).

[35] The god is probably the king, a conclusion drawn by K. A. Kitchen who refers to a variant reading, 'king' ("Studies in Egyptian Wisdom Literature," *OrAnt* 8 [1969], p. 193, footnote 25).

[36] For a discussion of this political instruction, see Hans Goedicke, "Die Lehre eines Mannes für seinen Sohn," *ZÄS* 94 (1967), pp. 62-71.

[37] John Wilson, *The Burden of Egypt* (Chicago: University of Chicago Press, 1951), p. 79. That this was the case may be seen in the position of the massabas of the nobility closely grouped around the pharaoh's pyramid. However, through a democratization process by the time of the New Kingdom even commoners could become Osiris and achieve the gift of eternal life. Also see an early Middle Kingdom text, "The Divine Attributes of Pharaoh," (*ANET*, p. 431): "Fight on behalf of his (pharaoh's) name, and be scrupulous in the oath to him, (that) ye may be free from a taint of *disloyalty*. He whom the king has loved will be a revered one, (but) there is no tomb for a rebel against his majesty, and his corpse is cast into the water."

[38] *ANET*, pp. 431-32.

[39] *ANET*, pp. 432-34.

[40] I, 2f. (*ANET*, p. 434).

[41] *ANET*, pp. 431f. Brunner indicates that the four pairs of famous men who are mentioned are identifiable, with the exception of Ptah-em-Djehuti. Ka-iris is probably Ka-gem-ni, and Nofry is probably Nefer-rohu. All of these wise men ($r\underline{h}$-$y\underline{h}t$) are said to have written "Instructions" and to have predicted the future. This is a puzzling statement, but Brunner explains that in Egypt both "prophecy" and rules of life are based upon an idea of order. In addition, Kha-kheper-(Re)-seneb wrote a lamentation, not any known instruction. Yet Brunner believes that the inclusion of lamentations along with prophecies and instructions seems to be based on the fact that each of the three types of literature contained the *Spruch* (*ts*), and thus can be classified as *Spruchliteratur* ("Die 'Weisen,' ihre 'Lehren' und 'Prophezeiungen' in altägyptischer Sicht," *ZÄS* 93 [1966], pp. 29-35). We would add that it appears that the wise did write lamentations, e.g., the one found in "The Dialogue of a Man Tired of Life with his Soul."

[42] Brunner defines the genre in the following way: "Mit 'Weisheitslehren' bezeichnen wir die Literaturgattung der Werke, die eine Unterweisung eines Lehrers an einen Schüler (oft als Form die eines Vater an seinen Sohn) oder die Fiktion einer solchen Belehrung enthalten. Der Lehrer leitet auf Grund überlieferter Erkenntniss seinen Schüler zu richtigen Verhalten im Leben an" ("Die Weisheitsliteratur," p. 90). Such literature comprised a major part of the literature of the school curriculum. Other school literature included the *Kemyt* ("completion"--a collection of idioms and formulae completed in the eleventh dynasty), "Satire on the Trades," "Sinuhe," "Hymn to the Nile," and possibly Nefer-rohu and certain of the other loyalist teachings. During the New Kingdom, hymns to deities and kings and letters were also studied. Williams remarks: "The words of the ancestors furnished much of the material for instruction. Reading and writing were learned by copying them, and they provided the norms of correct speech. From them too the rules of court etiquette would be imparted as well as the principles of ethical conduct" ("Scribal Training in Ancient Egypt," *JAOS* 92 [1972], p. 217). In addition to literature, the curriculum also included foreign languages, administrative concerns, lists, geography, mathematics, music, and sports (Otto, "Bildung und Ausbildung," p. 42). Otto also points out: "Eigentlich religiöser Schrifttum (Rituale, Kultvorschriften) findet sich in der Schulliteratur bemerkenswerter Weise nicht, wohl aber Hymnen und Anrufungen verschiedener Götter (auch des Königs) in allgemeinerer Form" (*ibid*.). For a comprehensive treatment of education in ancient Egypt, see H. Brunner, *Altägyptische Erziehung* (Wiesbaden: Otto Harrassowitz, 1957).

[43] It should be stressed that wisdom's orientation is both religious and authoritative, for it finds its grounding in the cosmic order established by the creator. It is not simply 'good advice' in contradistinction, say, to law (Morenz, *op. cit.*, p. 125). Rather, wisdom's authoritative call to men demands obedience, and if spurned destruction will occur. The authority is based not only upon the divine order, but also upon the verification of wisdom teaching in the arenas of personal

experience and the experiences of the fathers incorporated in sapiential tradition (Ptah-hotep, ll. 30f.; *ANET*, p. 412). Otto observes: "Es ist so dann der Begriff der Kontinuität hervorzuheben: Das vom Vater oder Lehrer Vertretene und Erbprobte soll der Lehrende annehmen; darin liest eine Guarantie für die ununterbrochene Weiterführung der Weltordnung" ("Bildung und Ausbildung," p. 44). Also see Brunner, *Erziehung*, pp. 130-31.

[44]iii, 17f. (*ANET*, p. 422).

[45]iii, 9f. (*ANET*, p. 421).

[46]l. 545 (*ANET*, p. 414). See H. Brunner, "Das hörende Herz," *TLZ* 79 (1954), pp. 697-700.

[47]See Brian Kovacs, "Is There A Class Ethic in Proverbs"? *Essays in Old Testament Ethics* (New York: Ktav, 1974), pp. 171-90.

[48]For the contrast between the "Heated Man" and the "Silent Man," see Amen-em-Opet, vi, 14, xi, 14f., xiii, 10f.; Ani, iv, 1f.; and "A Prayer to Thoth" (*ANET*, p. 379).

[49]*Die altorientalische Weisheit*, p. 36. Zandee's statement is comparable: "Over cultische plichten wordt slechts zelden gesproken" ("Egyptische Levenswijsheid," *Phoenix* 10 (1964), p. 175).

[50]We are following the chronology in the text by William Hallo and William Simpson, *The Ancient Near East* (New York: Harcourt, Brace, Jovanovich, Inc., 1971).

[51]An English translation has been made by A. H. Gardiner, "The Instruction Addressed to Kagemni and his Brethren," *JEA* 32 (1946), pp. 71-74.

[52]In addition to Gardiner's translation and study, one should consult Walter Federn, "Notes on the Instruction to Kagemni and his Brethren," *JEA* 36 (1950), pp. 48-50; A. H. Gardiner, "Kagemni Once Again," *JEA* 37 (1951), pp. 109-10; Elmar Edel, "Inschriften des Alten Reiches. II. Die Biographie des k3j-gjnj (Kagemni)," *MIO* 1 (1953), pp. 210-26; and especially, Alexander Scharff, "Die Lehre für Kagemni," *ZÄS* 77 (1941), pp. 13-21.

[53]For a recent translation, see *ANET*, pp. 419-20. Scholarly examinations of the instruction include: Georges Posener, "Le début de l'enseignement de Hardjedef," *RE* 9 (1952), pp. 109-17; Emma Brunner-Traut, "Die Weisheitslehre des Djedef-Hor," *ZÄS* 76 (1940), pp. 3-9; Helmut Brunner, "Ein weiteres Djedefhor-Zitat," *MDAIK* 19 (1963), p. 53; and Hans Goedicke, "Ein Verehrer des Weisen *DDFḤR* aus dem späten Alten Reich," *ASAE* 45 (1958), pp. 35-55. The fame of Hor-dedef is seen in the numerous references to him and his instruction in later literature (cf. "In Praise of Learned Scribes," *ANET*, p. 432; and "The Song of the Harper," *ANET*, p. 467). Goedicke also points to evidence for a cult of *Ddfḥr* by the First Intermediat Period (*op. cit.*).

[54]Brunner-Traut, *op. cit.*, p. 5. Ironically, according to the Intef Song and "In Praise of Learned Scribes," Hor-dedef's hopes for immortality by means of mortuary religion were dashed by the destruction of his tomb.

[55]Thus Posener observes: "L'auteur montre...le désarroi de l'homme devant l'antinomie entre la vie et la mort et rappelle que la tomb assure l'immortalitié. La garantie matérielle de la survie est celle de l'époque où vit Hardjedef; le point nouveau et intéressant est que le problème de la vie et de la mort se pose de son temps, et trouble déja les esprits. À la Premiere Période Intermediaire, l'écralement des monuments funéraires ancien montre la fragilité du *credo* de l'Ancien Empire..." (*op. cit.*, p. 115). This concern for proper burial including a tomb and mortuary service is illustrated in "The Story of Sinuhe" (*ANET*, pp. 18-22; 11. 190-200). Si-nuhe was a courtier who fled Egypt at the death of Amen-em-het I, perhaps because of his fear of being implicated in some palace intrigue. After becoming quite successful in Asia, the successor, Sen-Usert I (1971-1928 B.C.), writes to Si-nuhe, urging him to return to Egypt: "Recall thou the day of burial, the passing to a revered state, when the evening is set aside for thee with ointments and wrappings from the hands of Tait. A funeral procession is made for thee on the day of interment, a mummy case of gold, with head of lapis lazuli, with the heaven above thee, as thou are placed upon a sledge, oxen dragging thee and singers in front of thee, when the dance of the *muu* is performed at the door of thy tomb, when the requirements of the offering table are summoned for thee and there is sacrifice beside thy offering stones, thy pillars being hewn of white stone in the midst of (the tombs of) the royal children. It should not be that thou shouldst die in a foreign country. Asiatics should not escort thee. Thou shouldst not be placed in a sheepskin when thy wall is made. This is (too) long to be roaming the earth. Give heed to *sickness*, that thou mayest return." Also see 11. 300-310 where Si-nuhe, having returned to Egypt, tells of his tomb being constructed, his mortuary priests, his necropolis garden, and his statue overladen with gold. He boasts that "there is no poor man for whom the like has been done."

[56]For a survey of the major emphases in mortuary religion, see Morenz, *Ägyptische Religion*, pp. 192f.

[57]For an English translation, see *ANET*, pp. 412-14. Among recent scholarly studies dealing with this instruction, see A. Dobrovits, "Sur la structure stylistique de l'Enseignement de Ptahhotep," *AcAnt* 16 (1968), pp. 21-37; and Gerhard Fecht, *Der Habgierige und die Maat in der Lehre des Ptahhotep*, MDAIK 1 (Glückstadt: J. J. Augustin, 1958).

[58]*Das Werden der Altägyptischen Hochkultur* (Heidelberg: Carl Winter, 1953), p. 464.

[59]*Ibid.*, p. 460.

[60]Fecht, *op. cit.*, pp. 43-44.

[61]1. 639; *ANET*, p. 414. Also see 11. 32, 199, 229, 393, 545, and 588.

[62]For discussions of the dogma of the divine king, see Ivan Engnell, *Studies in Divine Kingship in the Ancient Near East* (Oxford: Basil Blackwell, 1967), pp. 4-15; H. Frankfort, *Kingship and the Gods*, pp. 15-214; H. W. Fairman, "The Kingship Rituals of Egypt," *Myth, Ritual, and Kingship* (Oxford: At The Clarendon Press, 1958), pp. 74-104; and Morenz, *Egyptian Religion*, pp. 33f., 85. With respect to the cultic worship of the Pharaoh, there is no doubt that the dead kings were the recipients of cultic worship like other Egyptian deities, though there is some dispute as to whether or not kings were worshipped while still alive (S. A. B. Mercer, *The Religion of Ancient Egypt* [London: Luzac and Co., 1949], pp. 253f.).

[63]For a survey of this historical period, see Sir Alan Gardiner, *Egypt of the Pharaohs* (New York: Oxford University Press, 1966), pp. 67ff.

[64]The text has been translated into English in *ANET*, pp. 405-7. This piece of Egyptian wisdom literature has elicited more response than any other piece with the exception of Amenem-Opet. R. J. Williams has provided a brief overview of the studies which were written before 1962 ("Reflections on the Lebensmüde," *JEA* 48 [1962], pp. 49-56). Among the more important studies which should be consulted are Emma Brunner-Traut, "Der Lebensmüde und sein Ba," *ZÄS* 77 (1944), pp. 18-29; Alfred Hermann, "Das Gespräch eines Lebensmüden mit seiner Seele," *OLZ* 34 (1939), pp. 345-51; "Review of Siegfried Herrmann, *Untersuchungen zur Überlieferungsgestalt Mittelägyptischer Literaturwerke,*" *OLZ* 54 (1959), pp. 251-53; Siegfried Herrmann, *Untersuchungen zur Überlieferungsgestalt Mittelägyptischer Literaturwerke,* DAWBIO 33 (Berlin: Akademieverlag, 1957); Günter Lanczkowski, "Der 'Lebensmüde' als antiosirianische Schrift," *ZRGG* 6 (1954), pp. 1-18; Émile Suys, "Le dialogue du désespéré avec so âme," *Or* 1 (1932), pp. 57-74; Gertrud Thausing, "Betrachtungen zum Lebensmüden," *MDAIK* 15 (1957), pp. 262-67; Raymond Weill, "Le livre du 'Désespéré,'" *BIFAO* 45 (1947), pp. 89-154; R. O. Faulkner, "The Man who was Tired of Life," *JEA* 42 (1956), pp. 21-40; Jean S. F. Garnot, "La vie et mort d'après un texte égyptien de la haute époque," *RHR* 127 (1944), pp. 18-29; and Hans Goedicke, *The Report about the Dispute of a Man with his Ba* (Baltimore: The Johns Hopkins Press, 1970).

[65]See Morenz, *Egyptian Religion* (London: Methuen and Co., 1973), pp. 183f.

[66]A. Hermann correctly classifies the piece as wisdom literature ("Review of Siegfried Herrmann," p. 262). The most obvious sapiential elements include the form of the *Streitgespräch*, the Ba's assuming the role of a wisdom teacher when he admonishes the man to heed his instruction, the Ba's admonition and two parables (11. 66f.), the theme of the loss of world order, and the position of the man as a 'wise man' (*rh jh.t*).

[67]This is in striking contrast to Hor-dedef's positive admonitions concerning the mortuary cult.

[68]Hermann, "Das Gespräch," p. 348; and Weill, *op. cit.*, p. 114. Thausing agrees: "Der Konflikt liegt in dem erwachenden Rationalismus und einem religiösen Zweifel an den Grundfesten ägyptischen Glaubens, in einem Zweck an der Magie der Bestattung und der Weiterexistenz im Jenseits" (*op. cit.*, p. 264).

[69]Lanczkowski, *op. cit.*, pp. 1-2.

[70]Louis Žabkar, "Ba," *Lexikon der Ägyptologie* 1 (1973), pp. 588-98.

[71]Cf. Frankfort's discussion of these views in *Ancient Egyptian Religion*, pp. 88f.

[72]See "A Song of the Harper," *ANET*, p. 467.

[73]Williams, *op. cit.*, p. 52.

[74]Brunner-Traut, *op. cit.*, p. 7.

[75]Cf. the discussion above.

[76]Brunner-Traut, *op. cit.*

[77]Williams, *op. cit.*, p. 52.

[78]S. Herrmann has argued that the Ba would not be destroyed by the fire, and as proof he refers to a coffin text translated by Otto, "Die beiden vogelgestaltigen Seelenvorstellungen der Ägypter," *ZÄS* 77 (1941), p. 80: "Ich habe meinen Ba nach mir geschaffen, um ihn wissen zu lassen, was ich wusste. Er soll nicht verbrennen mit meiner Leiche. Er soll nicht von der Türhütern des Osiris aufgehalten werden."

[79]Translating *ihm* "to urge," "to incite" (Weill, *op. cit.*, p. 120), rather than "delayest" (John Wilson, *ANET*, p. 405).

[80]Weill, *op. cit.*, p. 133.

[81]*Ibid.*

[82]This strophe may be taken as an indication that the traditional wise had always considered cult to be an important part of world order.

[83]The following views are representative of the major ones offered by scholars concerning the conclusion: Williams concludes the Ba is urging the man to suicide, since a speedy death will allow the two of them to quickly enter the future life in the mode of the Ba (*op. cit.*, p. 56); Wilson believes the soul is won over to the man's position of suicide and is willing to share the man's fate (*ANET*, p. 407, footnote 27); A. Hermann accepts the position that the man's traditional view of the future life finally convinces the Ba ("Das Gespräch," p. 351); and most intriguing is the conclusion of Weill who argues that the Ba's extreme position is modified by a vacillation which

allows the possibility that he may be wrong in completely denying a future existence, a vacillation which would avoid offend-
ing the pious orthodox (*op. cit.*, pp. 137-38).

[84]Thausing argues that the Ba's position is one of complete denial of any type of future life (*op. cit.*, p. 267),
while Williams argues that the Ba believes in the existence of
a future life by means of the Ba, but not by means of mortuary
religion (*op. cit.*).

[85]Such a relief is on the north wall of a passage leading
from the tomb's outer hall into the inner shrine of the tomb of
Nefer-hotep. The relief pictures a priest, wife, and squatting
harper near a table laden with food. Below this scene was the
engraved song (see Miriam Lichtheim, "The Songs of the Harpers,"
JNES 4 [1945], p. 178).

[86]Lichtheim, *op. cit.*, pp. 178f., regards most of the Harper Songs which she examined to be derived from and intended
for the mortuary cult, while Edward Wente, in a study of Harper
Songs done after Ms. Lichtheim's article, and after new Harper
materials had come to light, argues that the songs were secular
i.e., used at secular banquets ("Egyptian 'Make Merry' Songs
Reconsidered," *JNES* 21 [1962], pp. 118-28).

[87]J. A. Wilson, "A Song of the Harper," *ANET*, p. 467.

[88]Lichtheim, *op. cit.*, pp. 200-201. She argues that the
one found in Papyrus Harris 500 is different from the others
she examined both in tone and spirit, and therefore concludes
that the origin is best to be seen as that of the skeptical
wisdom tradition being formulated at this time. We would agree
with her classification for the following reasons: the incorporation of various sapiential admonitions which are given
validity by the addition of motivation clauses; the same skeptical attitude toward mortuary religion found in the "Man who
was Tired of Life"; references to the two great sages of the
Old Kingdom (Imhotep and Hor-dedef) coupled with what appears
to be a direct repudiation of their admonitions to participate
in mortuary religion, though this is only a guess with respect
to Imhotep, since his instruction has not been discovered; and
finally the sapiential structure of the song. The refrain
around which the structure is developed is an admonition followed by two sayings. The admonition sums up the content of
the second strophe, while the two sayings provide the thesis
for the first strophe. Cf. our chapter on Israelite Wisdom
Psalms.

[89]Lichtheim, *op. cit.*, p. 200.

[90]Cf. Koh. 3:21-22.

[91]English translations include: *ANET*, pp. 441-46; A. H.
Gardiner, *The Admonitions of an Egyptian Sage* (Leipzig: J. C.
Hinrichs, 1909); and R. O. Faulkner, "The Admonitions of an
Egyptian Sage," *JEA* 51 (1965), pp. 53-62. Among the better

scholarly literature, one should consult: R. O. Faulkner, "Notes on 'the Admonitions of an Egyptian Sage,'" *JEA* 50 (1964), pp. 24-36; Siegfried Herrmann, "Prophetie in Israel und Ägypten. Recht und Grenze eines Vergleichs," VTSup 9 (Leiden: E. J. Brill, 1963), pp. 47-65; Eberhard Otto, "Weltanschauliche und Politische Tendenzschriften," pp. 111-19; John van Seters, "A Date for the 'Admonitions' in the Second Intermediate Period," *JEA* 50 (1964), pp. 13-23; and Siegfried Herrmann, *Untersuchungen zur Überlieferungsgestalt Mittelägyptischer Literaturwerke*, pp. 8-36.

[92]The literary genre of this piece has been assessed as prophecy (Wilson, *ANET*, p. 441), wisdom (Gardiner, *op. cit.*), and *Auseinandersetzungliteratur* (Otto, *Der Vorwurf an Gott* [Hildesheim: Gerstenberg, 1951]) which incorporates a *Streitgespräch* of men with the god who has allowed his creation to be disrupted. S. Herrmann (*op. cit.*, p. 60) points out that this piece is not an 'inspired' text of a so-called charismatic prophet who speaks for god (as with the literature of the Hebrew prophets), and is much closer to wisdom literature than sacral literature. However, it is not just a collection of admonitions: "Viermehr muss der neue Charakter dieser Literatur verstanden werden aus der geschichtlichen bewegten Umbruchsperiode, wie sie nach dem Ende des Alten Reichs die erste Zwischenzeit unter Einschluss der Herakleopolitenzeit darstellte. Das Aufbrechen neuer Erfahrungen und Horizonte brachte auch neue und universale Formen hervor. Diesem so entwickelten neuen Stil, der aus dem Gegenüber von alter Ordnung und neuer Erfahrungen erwuchs, der sich in den Werken selbst bis zum Dialog steigerte, suchte E. Otto sachlich richtig, wenn auch terminologisch nicht unbedingt schön, in der Wortverbindung 'Auseinandersetzungliteratur' gerecht zu werden." Of course, this type of literature can be found in the critical wisdom literature in Egypt, Mesopotamia, and Israel.

[93]Scholarly consensus dates the "Admonitions" in the First Intermediate Period. However, for a recent attempt to place the piece within the Second Intermediate Period, see John van Seters, *op. cit.*

[94]"Ah, would that I had raised my voice at that time--it might save me from the suffering in which I am" (VI, 5f.).

[95]"WHY REALLY, crocidiles (*sink*) *down because of* what they have carried off, (for) men go to them of their own accord...." (II, 12). In an expression of overwhelming despair, the sage utters a wish that the entire human population would cease to exist: "Ah, would that it were the end of men, no conception, no birth. Then the earth would cease from noise, without wrangling" (VI, 1).

[96]For a discussion of the literary structure, see Gardiner, *op. cit.*

[97]*ANET*, p. 443, footnote 44.

[98]Translation by Faulkner, "The Admonitions," p. 55.

[99]II, 6; *ANET*, p. 441. Unless indicated otherwise, the other quotations of the text are taken from *ANET*.

[100]VII, 2f.

[101]VI, 6f.

[102]Faulkner translates this as "altar," or "offering stone" ("Notes," p. 28).

[103]XI, 1f. Faulkner remarks: "All the paragraphs opening with 'Remember' except the first, appear to refer to the performance of the ritual by the king, an act essential to the well-being of the land" ("The Admonitions," p. 60).

[104]The text is corrupt at this juncture, and thus it is difficult to know exactly who is the subject, both here and at the end of XI and the beginning of XII. We have accepted the argument of Otto that it is Re, the creator and the one who was to maintain the order of creation ("Weltanschauliche und Politische Tendenzschriften," pp. 131f.). Contrast this attack on the creator to the hymn found in Meri-ka-Re, ll. 131f.

[105]Otto, *op. cit.*

[106]The king's negligence in the sphere of cult is so apparent that even his officials are deceitfully enriching themselves by means of the offerings: "Behold, the king's men thrash around among geese, which are presented (to) the gods instead of oxen" (VIII, 10f.).

[107]XII, 11f.

[108]For an English translation, see *ANET*, pp. 414-18. Among the scholarly investigations of this instruction, one should consult H. Brunner, "Ein weiteres Djedefhor-Zitat," MDAIK 19 (1963), p. 53; "Die Weisheitsliteratur," pp. 99-102; Siegfried Herrmann, *Untersuchungen zur Überlieferungsgestalt Mittelägyptischer Literaturwerke*, pp. 54f.; William McKane, *Proverbs*, OTL (London: SCM Press, 1970), pp. 67f.; Rudolf Anthes, *Lebensregeln und Lebensweisheit der alten Ägypter*, Der Alte Orient 32 (Leipzig: J. C. Hinrichs), p. 17f.); A. Scharff, *Der historische Abschnitt der Lehre für König Merikarê*, SBAW 8 (C. H. Beck, 1936); and Aksel Volten, *Zwei altägyptische politische Schriften*, Analecta Aegyptiaca 4 (Copenhagen: E. Munksgaard, 1945).

[109]Scharff, *op. cit.*, p. 8, points to ll. 140f. and argues that Khety was the father to whom the instruction was attributed (also see ll. 109f.).

[110]For the formal characteristics of the instruction genre, see Brunner, "Die Weisheitsliteratur." Such a stylistic device of communications with the dead is comparable to the "letters to the dead" (see Volten, *op. cit.*, p. 83). Another sapiential instruction purported to be from a dead pharaoh is "The Instruction of King Amen-em-het" (*ANET*, pp. 418-19). See

G. Posener, *Littérature et politique dans l'Égypte de la XIIe Dynastie* (Paris: Librairie Ancienne Honoré Champion, 1956); and A. De Buck, "The Instruction of Amenemmes," *Mélanges Maspero*, Orient Ancien 1 (Le Caire: Imprimerie de l'Institut Français d'Archéologie Orientale, 1935-38), pp. 847-52.

[111]Volten, *op. cit.*, p. 85.

[112]11. 119f. Also see 11. 69f. Such a frank admission demonstrates the depths to which the dogma of the divine, infallible king had plummeted.

[113]11. 46f.

[114]1. 139. The idea supports the cultic view of a judgment of the dead following death, and indicates that when the king is judged there should be no accusers to testify against him. The idea of a reckoning of the pharaohs before a divine tribunal is discussed in detail in 11. 53f., and is similar to the 125th chapter of "The Book of the Dead" (*ANET*, pp. 34f.). Volten remarks concerning this passage in Meri-ka-Re: "Der Inhalt der Schrift wird hiermit kurz und genau angegeben. Sie lehrt, wie der König Merikarê das Reich gerecht regieren soll, damit er im Jenseits, wenn er seinem Vater begegnet, ohne Allage beim Totengericht freigesprochen werden kann" (*op. cit.*, p. 85). Throughout this Instruction, it is apparent that even the pharaoh is subject to the ethical laws of the creator deity (see Eberhard Otto, "Weltanschauliche und politische Tendenzschriften," *Ägyptologie*, HO 1 [Leiden: E. J. Brill, 1952], p. 115).

[115]The pharaoh was regarded as the ideal wise man who should develop according to this instruction an ability to speak well (11. 31f.), study the wisdom of the ancient savants, incorporate the virtue of patience, and learn how to avoid evil (11. 35f.) in order that he might meet the expectations incorporated in the affirmation: "The (Lord of) the Two Banks is (already wise) when he comes forth from the womb" (11. 115f.).

[116]11. 63f. For a discussion of the significance of this passage, see Schmid, *Gerechtigkeit als Weltordnung*, pp. 59f. He remarks: "Die so zentrale Funktion des Maat-Begriffs in kultischen Zusammenhängen zeigt, dass der Ägypter den Kult (zumindest auch) als Teil der Bemühung um die umfassende Weltordnung verstanden" (p. 60).

[117]A similar admonition and motivation is found later: "Act for the god, that he may act similarly for thee, with oblations which make the offering-table flourish and with a carved inscription that is what bears witness to thy name. The god is aware of him who acts for him" (11. 129f.).

[118]11. 78f.

[119]This passage seems to suggest that each pharaoh should respect the tombs of his predecessors whether or not they were of his dynasty. Perhaps the civil wars that plagued Egypt

during this period were even extended to the destruction of an opposing dynasty's tombs (see Volten, *op. cit.*, p. 89).

[120] ll. 127f. This may be a quotation of Hor-dedef (see H. Brunner, "Eine neue Entlehnung aus der Lehre des Djedefhor," *MDAIK* 14 [1956], pp. 17-19).

[121] This may refer to the practice of inscribing one's just deeds upon the walls of one's tomb (see Schmid, *Wesen und Geschichte der Weisheit*, pp. 44f.).

[122] The dangers of cultic ritual without righteous living are indicated by the wise of the ancient Near East, but such criticism does not lead them to withdraw from cultic participation, except in very disruptive situations. Morenz makes this clear when he states concerning this passage: "Es wird auf die Gefahr des Kultus hingewiesen, nicht er selbst in Frage gestellt. Daher bezieht die Weisheitsliteratur, der es um rechts Verhalten im ganzen Menschenleben geht, den Kultus in ihre Weisungen ausdrücklich ein" (*Ägyptische Religion*, p. 104). This section also deals with the worshipping of the image of the deity when it is moved in cultic procession (ll. 125f.), a point to be considered in more detail later. However, the passage includes a discussion of the *Deus absconditus*, and while the hidden god at times may reveal himself in the form of an image in the processional march, and at such times should be worshipped, Meri-ka-Re is to remember that this hidden god continues to oversee the world and is well aware of the actions of men which he recompences accordingly. Thus the problem of a deity being associated with an image receives sapiential reflection, and the conclusion is not a rejection of the cultic dogma of a deity being present in an image, but rather an explanation that the deity is not limited to the presence of the image, but rather knows the hearts of all men (ll. 132f.).

[123] For an excellent discussion of the Middle Kingdom, see John Wilson, *The Culture of Ancient Egypt* (Chicago: The University of Chicago Press, 1951), pp. 125-53.

[124] For a recent transcription, collation of texts, textual notes, and translation, see Wolfgang Helck, *Der Text der Lehre Amenemhets I. für seinen Sohn*, Kleine Ägyptische Texte, 1 (Wiesbaden: Harrassowitz, 1969). Also see *ANET*, pp. 418-19, for an English translation. For scholarly literature on Amen-em-het, see A. De Buck, "La composition littéraire des Enseignements d'Amenemhet," *Muséon* 59 (1946), pp. 183-200; "The Instruction of Amenemmes," *Mélanges Maspero* 1, Orient Ancien (Le Caire: Imprimerie de l'Institute Français d'Archéologie Orientale, 1935-38), pp. 847-52; Alan H. Gardiner, "The Earliest Manuscripts of the Instruction of Amenemmes I," *Mélanges Maspero*, pp. 479-96; H. Grapow, "Die Einleitung der Lehre des Königs Amenemhet," *ZÄS* 79 (1954), pp. 97-105; Battiscombe Gunn, "Notes on Ammenemes I," *JEA* 27 (1941), pp. 2-6; G. Posener, *Littérature et politique dans l'Égypte de la XIIe Dynastie* (Paris: Librairie Ancienne Honoré Champion, 1956); and Rudolf Anthes, "The Legal Aspects of the Instruction of Amenemhet," *JNES* 16 (1957), pp. 176-91.

[125]The piece should be regarded as coming from a deceased Pharaoh (see Posener, *op. cit.*, pp. 66f.; Grapow, *op. cit.*, pp. 97f.; and Helck, *op. cit.*, pp. 12f.), and not as a text presented at the occasion of Sen-Usert's becoming a co-regent, ten years before his father's death (Gardiner, *op. cit.*, p. 495; and Rudolf, *op. cit.*, pp. 185f.).

[126]De Buck compares this instruction to "Letters to the Dead" ("La composition littéraire des Enseignements d'Amenemhet," p. 189).

[127]For an eclectic text, transliteration, and translation, see K. A. Kitchen, "Studies in Egyptian Wisdom Literature--I, 'The Instruction by a Man for his Son,'" *OrAnt* 8 (1969), pp. 189-208. Also see Hans Goedicke, "'Die Lehre eines Mannes für seinen Sohn,'" *ZÄS* 94 (1967), pp. 62-71; and Posener, *Littérature et politique*.

[128]Goedicke, *op. cit.*, p. 94.

[129]R. J. Williams, "Literature as a Medium of Political Propaganda in Ancient Egypt," *The Seed of Wisdom* (Toronto: University of Toronto Press, 1964), p. 27.

[130]Kitchen remarks: "The promises of advancement and material advantage, the references to the humble surpassing the great and to the last being first, plus the immediacy of achievement ('within a lifetime'), are all a powerful appeal to the *petites gens* and the have-nots, to win their support" (*op. cit.*, p. 197).

[131]A variant reading is "the king." Kitchen suggests that the variant demonstrates which deity was in mind, at least to one copyist (*op. cit.*, p. 193, footnote 25).

[132]Such service may have included the cultic worship of the living king (see Morenz, *Egyptian Religion*, p. 85).

[133]This instruction was found on the stele of Sehetep-ib-Re at Abydos. The translation we have utilized is that of John A. Wilson, *ANET*, p. 431.

[134]The hymnic character of this instruction is most important, for it is another indication that the wise were familiar with cultic genres and, if the occasion arose, could utilize them in the literary formation of their writings. The combination of these genres is comparable to Hebrew wisdom psalms.

[135]Williams argues: "It was addressed to the high functionaries and members of the nobility by some important personage, probably the vizier" ("Literature as Propaganda in Ancient Egypt," p. 25).

[136]Williams contends that the piece was originally created by an earlier sage, possibly vizier Ptah-em-Djedhuti who was among those praised in the panegyric Papyrus Chester Beatty IV

(cf. *ANET*, pp. 431-32), and then appropriated by this later official (*op. cit.*, pp. 25-26).

[137]Posener (*Littérature et politique*, p. 120) observes: "La vénération du souverain prend ici le caractère d'une religion évoluée; l'auteur vent que le culte royal soit fait à la fois de piété personnelle et des pratiques extérieures de confiance aussi bien que de crainte. La foi monarchique suppose une forme de prosélytisme, et cette action incombe aux dignitaires du régime." This cultic emphasis, centered around the worship of the divine pharaoh, is one of the distinctive marks of the Egyptian sages' attitude towards cult. The same is true for the cultic concern of the Egyptian wise with mortuary religion and the continuance of one's being by the orderly transition to the afterlife.

[138]Cf. sapiential onomastica (A. H. Gardiner, *Ancient Egyptian Onomastica*, London, 1947).

[139]For a discussion of this period, see Wilson, *The Culture of Ancient Egypt*, pp. 166f.

[140]An English translation is found in *ANET*, pp. 431-32. Hellmut Brunner provides not only a German translation, but also a valuable analysis of the text, especially in the context of efforts made by Egyptologists to define the nature and scope of wisdom literature ("Die 'Weisen,' ihre 'Lehren' und 'Prophezeiungen' in altägyptischer Sicht," *ZÄS* 93 [1966], pp. 29-35).

[141]Children, especially a "son-he-loves," and lector priests were deemed essential according to mortuary religion for the continuance into the future life, since they both were needed to provide the proper burial and to ensure the reading of the ritual texts that would magically provide for the continuing needs of the deceased.

[142]A suggestion by Wilson, *ANET*, p. 432, footnote 2, for "the back of a stone."

[143]Paintings and reliefs on the walls of tombs were deemed important in mortuary religion for depicting the important activities and the position of the deceased during his earthly life, and were to ensure him of the continuance of such a state in the future life. "The pictures summed up the content of the dead man's life on earth. They had to be at his disposal in the same way as the offerings of food and clothing" (Morenz, *Egyptian Religion*, p. 202). In addition, mortuary texts were placed on the walls of the pyramids or on the face of the sarcophagus as inscriptions (Pyramid Texts) in the Old Kingdom, put in the coffins of private individuals from the First Intermediate Period (Coffin Texts), and written on papyrus scrolls and buried with the mummy from the time of the New Kingdom (The Book of the Dead) (*ibid.*, p. 227). These included "liturgical lists" of various provisions and materials deemed essential for the future existence, so that through the magical power of the recitation of these texts by the deceased, he could continue to exist independently of any lector priest or descendants (*ibid.*, pp. 209, 229).

[144]Translations have been made by Wilson, *ANET*, pp. 420-21; Émile Suys, *La Sagesse d'Ani*, Analecta Orientalia 11 (Rome: Pontifical Biblical Institute, 1935); and Aksel Volten, *Studien zum Weisheitsbuch des Anii*, Det. Kgl. Danske Videnskaberneg Selskab. Historisk-Filologiske Meddelelser 23 (Copenhagen: Levin and Munksgaard, 1937).

[145]Volten lists the following areas of concern in Ani: religious duties, obligations to parents, obligations as an honorable man, friendship, relations to superiors, hospitality and help for the poor, behavior towards one's enemy, civic responsibility, and diligence in scribal training (*op. cit.*, p. 57).

[146]In this case, the 'son' of Ani, Khonsuhotep, appears to have been his real son (vii, 18f.).

[147]The recording process "might well imply that only such persons as were recorded in writing on temple rolls were accorded the privilege of direct participation in the festivities of the god" (Alan Gardiner, "A Didactic Passage Re-examined," *JEA* 45 [1959], p. 15).

[148]Morenz refers to Urk., IV, 99, which speaks of the image's sanctity and hiddenness: "Less accessible (*ḏsr*) than that which is in heaven, or secret than the affairs of the nether world, more (hidden) than the inhabitants of the prime-val ocean." He later explains that the power of the deity makes contact extremely dangerous, and, therefore, the sanctity of "the Other" must be observed by strict precautions which maintain segregation. For example, the deity's image was concealed in deep darkness and approached and handled only by the properly initiated priest (*Egyptian Religion*, pp. 94, 99). Anthes remarks concerning the devotion of the scribe in this passage: "Aus solchem persönlichen Verhältnis zu Gott erwächst die innere Frömmigkeit und die Betonung einer Sittlichkeit, die ihren Massstab nicht in der äusseren Ordnung als solcher, sondern unmittelbar in dem Willen Gottes findet" (*Lebensregeln und Lebensweisheit*, p. 28). This section is important, since it combines an affirmation of the cultic dogma of sacred space with sagacious behavior.

[149]Cf. Hor-dedef and Meri-ka-Re. By the time of the New Kingdom, even the lowly scribe could hope for a future life, as is evidenced in the "Book of the Dead" (see C. J. Bleeker, *The Religion of Ancient Egypt* [Leiden: E. J. Brill, 1969], pp. 47-48).

[150]Morenz explains that the deity's image was brought out into the antechambers of the temple during processions, though it seems to have remained concealed, and was probably veiled as it was carried on its portable shrine (*op. cit.*, p. 94). Thus the young scribe should not be foolish enough to inquire concerning its visible form nor should he press close to the deity in an effort to "see for himself" and thereby profane the sanctity and mystery of the divine image. This effectively

demonstrates Ani's acceptance of the cultic dogma of the sacred character of the holy which should not be profaned, lest destruction to the guilty one occur.

[151]"God, the Distant One, is made present in the image by the daily service, and during the festival the deity 'appeared,' i.e., its image left the sanctuary and, borne by the priests in a shrine...upon a barque, went out among the crowd" (Morenz, op. cit., pp. 88-89). The reference by Ani to the sun god as the real 'god of this land' is probably a reference to Amon-Re, the national deity of the Egyptian empire, whose prominence rose with that of the Theban 18th dynasty. He is "mysterious of form, glistening of appearance, the marvelous god of many forms...his soul is in heaven, his body is in the West, and his statue is in Hermonthis, heralding his appearances...One is Amon, hiding himself from them...no gods know his true form... He is too mysterious that his majesty might be disclosed, he is too great that (men) should ask about him, too powerful that he might be known. Instantly (one) falls in a death of violence at the utterance of his mysterious name, unwittingly or wittingly. No (other) god knows how to *call him* by it, the Soul who hides his name, according as he is mysterious" (A hymn to Amon from the 19th dynasty, *ANET*, pp. 368-69). Yet Amon's national prominence also went hand in hand with the fact that he was "the linchpin between national ritual and popular piety," and the object of the devotion of royalist and commoner alike (Morenz, op. cit., pp. 104-6). Thus Ani's own piety and theological reflection flows from the cultic circles of the New Kingdom which exalt devotion from Amon-Re.

[152]A recent textual examination, translation, and commentary has been written by Irene Grumach, *Untersuchungen zur Lebenslehre des Amenemope*, Münchener ägyptologische Studien 23 (München: Deutscher Kunstverlag, 1972). For English translations, see *ANET*, pp. 421-24; and F. L. Griffith, "The Teaching of Amenophis, the Son of Kanakht," *JEA* 12 (1926), pp. 191-231.

[153]H. Brunner, "Die Weisheitsliteratur," p. 106. Among the duties of Amen-em-Opet was "setting up the divine offerings for all the gods," probably indicating a regulation of types and quantities of sacrifices to be given to each deity.

[154]An early date has been proven by the discovery of a broken, though unpublished, ostracon by Černý in the Cairo Museum which contains parts of 3, 8-4, 10, and which dates from the late 21st dynasty, indicating that it had been known for some time, and possibly originated as early as the 19th dynasty (see Ronald J. Williams, "The Alleged Semitic Original of the Wisdom of Amenemope," *JEA* 47 [1961], pp. 100-06). Such a discovery undercuts the extensive arguments of Drioton that the Hebrew instruction in Proverbs 22:17-24:22 was the original from which the "Instruction of Amen-em-Opet" was partially written ("Le Livre des Proverbes et la sagesse d'Amenemope," *Sacra Pagina* 1 [Gembloux: Éditions J. Duculot, 1959], pp. 228-421).

[155]This may be noticed in the introduction and the first chapter.

[156]R. Anthes, *Lebensregeln und Lebensweisheit der Alten Ägypter*, p. 29.

[157]Irene Grumach, *op. cit.*, pp. 44f. Anthes goes even farther to suggest that the poem, the only one in the entire instruction, has the general function of poems placed in larger works, and that is to summarize the main point of the entire work; in other words, the poem is a condensation of the instruction (cf. the poem in Sinuhe and the four poems in "The Dialogue of a Man Tired of Life with his Ba"). ("Die Funktion des vierten Kapitels in der Lehre des Amenemope," *Archäologie und Altes Testament* [Tübingen: J. C. B. Mohr (Paul Siebeck), 1970], pp. 9-18).

[158]*Ibid.*

[159]*ANET*, p. 422.

[160]Georges Posener, "Le chapitre IV d'Aménémopé," *ZÄS* 99 (1973), pp. 129f.

[161]*Ibid.*, pp. 130ff.

[162]*Ibid.*, p. 133.

[163]Fichtner, *Die altorientalische Weisheit*, p. 38.

[164]Translation by Grumach, *op. cit.*, p. 49.

[165]*Ibid.*, p. 45.

[166]Translation by Griffith, *op. cit.*, p. 206.

[167]Grumach, *op. cit.*, p. 73. The statue of the deceased was often placed in his tomb, in a chamber behind the funerary chapel, or at times in the temple, and it was in the statue that the Ka of a man was believed to take his residence (Morenz, *Egyptian Religion*, p. 204). Frankfort observes that "a statue, properly identified with the dead man by an inscription and magically animated by the 'opening of the mouth' ceremony, could replace the body if it should be damaged by decay or violence" (*Ancient Egyptian Religion*, p. 93).

[168]Griffith, *op. cit.*, p. 230. For a rejection of the idea of older wisdom as secular and profane and later wisdom as more religious and superstitious, see A. De Buck, "Het Religieus Karakter der oudste egyptische Wijsheid," *NTT* 21 (1932), pp. 322-49. He states, for example, that both Amen-em-Opet and Ptah-hotep are permeated by a religious spirit: "de gelijkenis in toon en stemming is onmiskenbaar" (p. 339).

[169]The text, transliteration, and translation have been published by S. R. K. Glanville, *Catalogue of Demotic Papyri in the British Museum*, Vol. II. "The Instructions of 'Onchshe-shonqy," (London: The British Museum, 1955).

84

170Glanville places the piece in either the 5th or 4th
century B.C. (*op. cit.*, p. XI), and B. Gemser agrees that the
date is not pre-fifth century ("The Instructions of 'Onchsheshonqy and Biblical Wisdom Literature," VTSup 7 [Leiden: E. J.
Brill, 1960], p. 106). However, B. H. Stricker places the
origin in the Saite Dynasty ("De Wijsheid van Anchsjesjonqy,"
JEOL 15 [1933], p. 11).

171Glanville, *op. cit.*, p. XIV.

172McKane, *Proverbs*, p. 122; and Gemser, *op. cit.*, p.
115.

173Glanville believes that the word *šms* may indicate
'worship' in this context (*op. cit.*, p. 70, footnote 76).

174For the transcription and translation of Papyrus Insinger, see P. A. A. Boeser, *Transkription und Übersetzung des
Papyrus Insinger*, Oudheidkundige Mededeelingen 3 (Uit 'Srijksmuseum van Oudheden Te Leiden, 1922). In addition, Volten has
translated the Papyrus Carlsburg which contains the same contents as Papyrus Insinger, and he compares the two texts in
chapters One and Two (*Das Demotische Weisheitsbuch* [Kopenhagen:
Einar Munksgaard, 1941]).

175"Das Gleichgewicht...ist das Prinzip der ganzen Weltordnung" (Volten, *op. cit.*, p. 128).

176All of the quotations are from Volten's translation.

177Another interesting point concerning prayer and theology is made in the warning intimated in 28,15. One who is "far
away" (presumably in another country) finds to his dismay that
his gods and his prayer are likewise "far away," suggesting
that travel to foreign destinations is made hazardous by the
absence of one's gods, a cultic belief present when Egypt was
not in an imperial position.

CHAPTER III

THE VIEWS OF CULT IN MESOPOTAMIAN WISDOM LITERATURE

A. *The World View of Mesopotamian Wisdom Literature*

Before turning directly to the task of delineating and
analyzing the views of cult in the Mesopotamian Wisdom Literature, a succinct summary of the world view of the Mesopotamian
sages will serve as an introduction.[1]

Wisdom and the Cosmos

In the myth of "Inanna and Enki: The Transfer of the Arts
of Civilization from Eridu to Erech,"[2] one finds listed on four
occasions over one hundred elements of creation, each of which
was constituted and regulated by a *me*, best regarded as a cosmic law which, acting in concert with the other cosmic laws,
provided the force which originates, integrates, and regulates
a particular element of the natural and societal spheres of
world order.[3]

> The Sumerian theologians adduced what was for them a
> satisfying metaphysical inference to explain what
> kept the cosmic entities and cultural phenomena,
> once created, operating continuously and harmoniously
> without conflict and confusion; this was the concept
> designated by the Sumerian word *me*, the exact mean-
> ing of which is still uncertain. In general, it would
> seem to denote a set of rules and regulations as-
> signed to each cosmic entity and cultural phenomenon
> for the purpose of keeping it operating forever in
> accordance with the plans laid down by the deity
> creating it.[4]

Since these cosmic laws were considered to have originated at
the time of creation and became, as it were, the glue which
held together the various elements of nature, civilization, and
society in an eternal continuum, the purpose and function of
wisdom was not only to reflect these cosmic laws in ideology
and practice, but, at the same time, was to maintain and actually promote these divinely ordained laws, and thereby maintain
and promote the harmony of the universe, the gifts of civilization, and the institutions of society, all of which were believed established by the gods.

The sages of ancient Mesopotamia shared the mythological
emphasis placed on world order, and considered it their primary
duty to observe its cosmic laws and to translate them into the
language of the various sapiential genres, oral as well as
written, which then could be used as instructive guidance for
the orientation of the wise man's life within the spheres of
world order so that he might come within the beneficent powers
of the cosmos, and consequently experience the rewards of a
life spent in harmony with the universe. Such an understanding
is succinctly stated in the following proverb: "Whoever has
walked with truth generates life" (1. 1).[5]

Wisdom, also an element of civilization governed by its
own *me* according to the myth of "Inanna and Enki," was considered to be of divine origin and was given by the gods to enable
the sage to observe world order and the rules which governed
the cosmos, to incorporate them within the wisdom sayings, to
live according to the sapiential precepts, and to integrate his
life within the beneficent spheres of world order established
and regulated by the gods.

The Mesopotamian sages proceeded to build upon this concept of world order a structure of retribution whereby various
gods were believed to oversee the smooth functioning of the
spheres of world order by ensuring that the harmony of the integrated *mes* was maintained.[6] Thus the righteous wise who observed and followed the cosmic and societal laws were rewarded,
but the foolish wicked who perverted the eternal orders were
punished and destroyed. Success or failure, life or death,
depended upon the following of the cosmic rules of nature,
civilization, and society. Since the cosmic laws originated
with the gods and must be maintained and followed for the preservation of order, sin was viewed as the transgression of
these divine laws and the failure to carry out the responsibility of maintaining the divine order, such as a king's arbitrar-
ily robbing his own people or his failure to establish a just
judiciary. This system of retribution involved the belief that
a particular action or thought led to a prescribed result,
though it was not automatic or self-governing, but rather was
directed by various gods consigned the duty of overseeing the

integrity of the system. A typical example of retribution is found in the "Counsels of Wisdom" and concerns the responsibility of individuals to provide for the poor:

> Give food to eat, give date wine to drink;
> Grant what is asked, provide for and honour.
> In this a man's god takes pleasure,
> It is pleasing to Shamash, who will repay him with
> favour (ll. 61-64).[7]

The arguments of the Friend in "The Babylonian Theodicy" share this understanding:

> The rogue who has acquired wealth (in a manner) which
> is against the will of the gods is persecuted by a
> murderer's weapon.
> Unless you seek the will of the god, what success can
> you have? (ll. 237f.)[8]

Of course, the sages of Mesopotamia were deeply disturbed by the breakdown of world order and the integrally connected failure of the system of retribution, so painfully obvious during times of national, natural, and even personal disasters which were exceedingly difficult to explain on the premise of some retributory system. Several approaches were offered. The difficulty was often placed at the feet of the gods who were held responsible for creating evil and even for acting wickedly and capriciously. At best they were deemed inscrutable. In the myth concerning Inanna and Enki, there were *mes* to govern 'falsehood,' 'strife,' 'fear,' etc.,[9] thus implying that the gods were responsible for the operation and regulation of evil and that destruction and evil were made a part of the created order. A congruent idea was advocated by the Friend in "The Babylonian Theodicy" who argued that the gods made men evil by nature, and therein was the answer for humanity's wicked behavior.

> Narru, king of the gods, who created mankind,
> And majestic Zulummar, who dug out their clay,
> And mistress Mami, the queen who fashioned them,
> Gave perverse speech to the human race.
> With lies, and not truth, they endowed them for ever.
> (ll. 276-280).[10]

In times of despair the gods themselves were considered to act wickedly and capriciously whether it be in the destruction

of mankind for disturbing their restful peace,[11] or in their
collusion with the wicked designs of evil men. This is charged
by the complainant in "I Will Praise the Lord of Wisdom":

> My slanderer slanders with god's help;
> For the...who says, "God bless you,"
> death comes at the gallop.
> While he who utters a libellous cry is
> sustained by his guardian spirit. (ll. 95-97).

Others concluded that the gods and their will are inscrutable, and, therefore, have left man in the dark recesses of an
unenlightened spirit, not knowing whether his actions will result in blessing or destruction at the hands of the gods:[12]

> What is proper to oneself is an offence to one's god;
> What in one's own heart seems despicable is proper to
> one's god.
> Who knows the will of the gods in heaven?
> Who understands the plans of the underworld gods?
> Where have mortals learnt the way of a god? (Tablet
> I, ll. 34-38).[13]

Another explanation was that man had no intuitive sense of
sin, and thus was unable to know whether his actions were
wicked or righteous:

> Mankind is deaf and knows nothing.
> What knowledge has anyone at all?
> He knows not whether he had done a good or a bad
> deed.[14]

And finally, the denial of a universe permeated by order
and ruled according to the rule of just retribution is presented in the "Dialogue of Pessimism."[15]

Wisdom and the Gods[16]

As mentioned above, the gods were believed responsible for
the establishment of world order as part of the creative process
by the originating of various *mes* and for the maintenance of
world order by means of overseeing a system of retribution, established in order to assure the harmonious functioning of the
various spheres of world order (nature, society, and civilization). Generally speaking, the sages viewed the gods as just
and moral; especially is this true of the Babylonian wise.
However, during periods of disaster, this moral and ethical

character of the gods was questioned and at times even blasphemously denied. The responsibility for the continuation of
world order according to a system of just rewards and punishments is most noticeable in the "Advice to a Prince":

> If he (i.e., the prince) does not heed the justice of
> his land, Ea, king of destinies will alter his destiny
> and will not cease from hostilely pursuing him (11.
> 2-3).[17]

The deity usually singled out as the one who oversees the
sphere of just retribution is the sun god (Akk. Shamash; Sumerian Utu).

> Do not slander, speak what is fine.
> Speak no evil, tell what is good.
> Whoever slanders (or) speaks evil,
> As a retribution the god Shamash will pursue after
> his head.[18]

In their conception of the gods, the wise considered a
number of deities to be the gods of wisdom, though it was primarily Enki (Akk. Ea) who, as the god of wisdom, ordered the
world in creation according to the designs of his wisdom, presented to mankind the gifts of artistic skills and handicrafts,
and provided man with divine wisdom so that the laws of world
order could be observed and the spheres of world order maintained.[19] The other gods of wisdom most often mentioned are
Nisaba, the mistress of scribal writing, and Nabu who, as the
divine scribe, was the patron deity of the scribal profession.[20]

Believing that the great gods, like their earthly counterparts, the king and the ruling house, were too preoccupied with
important matters to be overly concerned with the petty needs
of individuals, the Mesopotamian savants projected the idea of
a personal deity, usually a minor god, who, as the center of
individual devotion, provided safety and protection against the
demonic forces and evil magicians, believed to be possessors of
powers to afflict one with suffering and even death.[21] Thus
finding himself in dire distress, the individual could appeal
to his personal deity who would intercede on his behalf before
the great gods. Such a personal deity is frequently mentioned
in the wisdom literature. For example the sufferer in "I Will
Praise the Lord of Wisdom" bemoans his wretched condition in
terms of the abandonment of his personal deity:

> My god has forsaken me and disappeared,
> My goddess has failed me and keeps at a distance.
> The benevolent angel who (walked) beside me has
> departed,
> My protecting spirit has taken to flight, and is
> seeking someone else (Tablet I, ll. 43-46).[22]

Subsequently, the demonic forces are given free reign to afflict the lamenter. Only the inducement of the deity's return
will result in the sufferer's restoration to health and prosperity.[23]

Wisdom and the King

According to Mesopotamian literature, society, its political and social institutions, was ordained by the gods to be a
major sphere of world order, and consequently was regulated by
societal *mes*.[24] As such, the society of the Mesopotamians was
regarded as the microcosm of world order, and the responsibility for the maintenance of societal order was given to the
royal institution. In fact kingship, itself ordained and
governed by a number of *mes*, was considered to have been "lo-
wered from heaven" for the specific purpose of maintaining order in Mesopotamian society.[25] Individual kings proclaimed the
contention that they were specifically selected by the high god
to rule and to maintain order within the state as his unique
representative.[26] In a song to An which included a Prayer for
Lipit-Ishtar, the following occurs:

> Höchster Herr, allen vorangehend,
> der die vollkommenen me gewaltig gemacht hat,
> ältester der Herren!
> Alle me hat er (An) strahlend erscheinen lassen--
> die Götter des Himmels sind (darob) zu ihm gegangen.
> Des (Himmels) Regeln hat er recht gefügt--
> im Himmel und auf Erden beugt sich ihm jeder.
> In höchstem me, in...,
> hat das Königtum, das teure,
> Lipitištar, Enlils Sohn,
> der grosse An zum Geschenk gemacht.
> An ist gross, der strahlend erscheinende Gott ist gross--
> des gewaltigen An Stütze ist König Lipitištar.[27]

The kings are thus chosen by the gods to establish and maintain
the societal sphere of world order in the areas of warfare,
legal justice, and cult, with the result being that of procurin

for the state victory in warfare, peace, and a prosperity usually described in terms of the fructification of nature.[28]

The ability to accomplish such beneficent results was credited to their reception of the gift of divine wisdom.[29] In fact certain kings even extended their claim to divine wisdom to include initiation within the scribal crafts, and, as such, were the patrons of the wise and their literature. Ashurbanipal, the founder of the famous library of Nineveh, proclaims in a self-exaltation:

> I, Ashurbanipal, laid hold upon the wisdom of Nabu, penetrated into all (the intricacies) of the art of writing, as practiced by all kinds of craftsmen...[30]

Wisdom and Mankind

The insecurity of the human condition pervades the spirit of Mesopotamian literature in general, an insecurity due to many different historical, geographical, and existential factors. The tumultuous course of Mesopotamian history certainly yielded itself to this deep sense of insecurity, as did geographical conditions such as the turbulent character of the Tigris and Euphrates rivers and the easy accessibility of the area to invaders. The vulnerability of human life to the ravages of death in its many forms--disease, famine, warfare-- contributed to the agonizing realization of the dreadful dilemma of human existence. This insecurity is reflected in the thoughts of the wise, including the beliefs that death was the inescapable lot of mankind,[31] that the nether world was a wretched and dreadful abode of the dead, that the gods were at times inscrutable[32] and capricious deities who could bring suffering and destruction at any time,[33] that the powers of demons and evil magicians were ever present to afflict the living,[34] that the gods determined the fate of man who was subsequently unable to alter it,[35] and that man was often unable to ascertain his sin and thus incapable of rectifying the situation in order to be saved from destruction.[36]

Even though the limitations and uncertainty of human existence were well recognized and often bemoaned by the wise, nevertheless, the quest for at least a restricted certainty was undertaken. Affirming that the world was constituted by a system of world-order regulated by a complex of integrated cosmic laws, the wise ascribed to the belief that the ultimate purpose of human activity and behavior was to reflect these eternal dictates. By successfully integrating himself within the beneficent spheres of world order, the wise man could expectantly hope for success, prosperity, and even longevity. Thus wisdom was seen as providing a limited measure of certainty in a very insecure world, and the wise devoted themselves to its articulation and to follow its observations and dictates. Only the fool gave no concern to the divinely constituted structure of world order, disregarded the seriousness of obeying its cosmic rules and the sapiential sayings incorporating these rules, and consequently met sure destruction.[37]

In their quest for security in human existence, the wise recognized the limitations of wisdom based on reason and experience, and often sought out the wise cultist and magician whose revealed insights into the mystery of human existence and the will of the gods could further one's attempts to find a secure existence. The wise shared the idea that security in life was impossible apart from giving consideration to the will and the needs of the gods, for was not the purpose of the creation of mankind to faithfully execute the divine cultic demands in order to provide for the needs of the gods?[38] And through such cultic observances, especially to one's protective deity and his consort, one could at least hope for the divine favor.[39] Thus the Friend in the "Babylonian Theodicy" argued a commonly accepted sapiential observation:

> He who waits on his god has a protecting angel.
> The humble man who fears his goddess accumulates wealth. (ll. 21-22).
> Seek the kindly wind of the god,
> What you have lost over a year you will make up in a moment. (ll. 241-42).[40]

And the "Counsels of Wisdom" adds: "Sacrifice prolongs life," and "He who fears the Anunnaki extends (his days)" (ll. 144-147).[41] Failure to care for the needs of the gods through the offerings of sacrifices and gifts led to suffering and death. The sufferer in "I Will Praise the Lord of Wisdom" protests that he is suffering "like one who has not made libations to his god, nor invoked his goddess at table" (Tablet II, 11. 12-13).[42] Even magic was resorted to during times of distress which were attributed to the actions of demons, as evidenced by the same sufferer who turns to diviners to determine the reasons for his plight so that rectification of his situation might be initiated (Tablet II, 11. 50f., 108f.).[43]

Wisdom and the Sages

The wise of ancient Mesopotamia were primarily scribes who functioned within the service of the two great social and economic institutions of Mesopotamian society: the palace and the temple, and ranked in importance from minor scribes with perfunctory and minor duties to officials of great importance such as royal counsellors or the king's secretary, thus exercising tremendous positions of power. Training for scribal service was provided in the scribal schools attached to the palaces and temples throughout Mesopotamia which not only provided the young sages considerable expertise in the carrying out of the economic, administrative, and bureaucratic tasks of the palace and temple but also became centers of the creation and transmission of Mesopotamian culture, including, of course, wisdom literature. Most students who passed through these schools proceeded into careers as scribes, officials, and bureaucrats of the palace, temple, and large aristocratic estates, but a few became teachers and scholars who continued to function within the sphere of the school.[44]

The wisdom literature was then the promulgation of the sages functioning within the wisdom schools, and included the following sapiential genres: proverbs, fables and parables, folk-tales, miniature essays, riddles, *Edubba* compositions, wisdom disputations, practical instructions, satirical dialogues, precepts, and "righteous sufferer" poems.[45] It is an accepted point of modern scholarship that these were written in order to incorporate the observations of the wise concerning the salient features of world order and were taught to successive generations of scribal aspirants not only for the purpose of teaching the technical scribal crafts of reading, writing, and literary creativity, but even more importantly to demonstrate the proper direction of life and the correct orientation of a wise man to the spheres of world order which were controlled by the eternal *mes*. The hope was that the young scribe would attune himself to the harmony of world order and discover a successful, rewarding, and extended life. Every conceivable area of nature, existence, civilization, and society was subjected to sapiential scrutiny and interpretation, for each was considered to be constituted by the eternal dictates established by the gods, and through the appropriation of wisdom these laws could be discovered and placed within the conceptual categories of sapiential thought.

The sapiential concern to analyze and describe the tenets of world order can best be explained in terms of how the sage conceived himself as a wise man. Ideally speaking, the sage, first of all, conceived himself to be a functional extension of the royal institution, and thus it was his task to contribute to the royal task of establishing and maintaining cosmic and societal order, whether he served as a scribe, lawyer, court historian, architect, priest, or sheep counter. Thus the royal tasks of promulgating law-codes, maintaining and regulating cultic temples and rituals, and training and leading into battle the cohorts of soldiers were delegated to and carried out by the total hierarchy of scribaldom which considered itself as the functional extension of the royal task of creating and maintaining societal order. Such royal service elicited from the wise exclamation of the majesty and greatness of the king who established and maintained the microcosm of world order.[46]

Yet, the sage also conceived of himself as the functional extension of the gods of wisdom and order who established and supervised the continuance of the complex of the *mes*. Therefore the sages were considered to be the recipient of a divine commission to aid the gods in the maintenance of world order by means of their specific professions, their literary activities which sought to harness the power of the dictates of cosmic order, and their own sagacious behavior in every sphere of human existence. To enable them to achieve their task, they were equipped with divine wisdom by the gods of wisdom.[47]

B. *The Views of Cult in Mesopotamian Wisdom Literature*

Having surveyed the basic ideas of the sages in Mesopotamia, especially the view that world order is permeated by a complex of cosmic, societal, and cultural laws, it becomes our
task to determine whether or not these sages demonstrated a
concern for the realm of the cult and its rituals and laws. In
other words did the sages view cult as an important area of
world order which necessitated sapiential observation and participation, or was this an area left to the priests, whereas
the sages were content to concern themselves only with the
secular spheres of existence and reality?

Sumerian Wisdom Literature

The Sumerian "Man and his God."[48] Writing perhaps as
early as the Third Dynasty of Ur (2,000 B.C.),[49] a Sumerian
sage of the *Edubba* wrote a reflective discourse concerning a
young Sumerian wise man who, in spite of his own wisdom and
righteousness, underwent the excruciation and inexplicable
trauma of emotional and physical suffering which included the
contempt of his fellow Sumerians, the demonic attack of his
body in the forms of physical torment and disease, and the displeasure of his ruler, all of which were believed occasioned by
the abandonment of the youth by his personal deity, thus expos-
ing him to the onslaught of these misfortunes.[50] The major
thesis of the poem has been succinctly described by Kramer:

> The main thesis of our poet is that in cases of
> suffering and adversity, no matter how seemingly
> unjustified, the victim has but one valid and
> effective recourse, and that is to glorify his god
> continually, and keep waiting before him until he
> turns a favorable ear to his prayers.[51]

Throughout the poem the sage, speaking in the first person, continues to assert that he is wise and righteous:

> The young man--he uses not his strength for evil *in*
> the place of deceit (l. 10).
> I, the wise, why am I bound to the ignorant youths?
> I, the discerning, why am I counted among the ig-
> norant? (ll. 42f.).

As the poet develops the thesis of the poem, he suggests a number of reasons as to why the youth may be suffering. First, the youth points the finger of accusation towards his personal deity whose abandonment has provoked the misfortune and suffering he was experiencing, and though the deity's justice is never attacked directly, the youth makes implicit his blame of the deity[52] as being responsible for his current state of suffering:

> You have doled out to me suffering ever anew, (1. 30)
> ....
> The man of deceit has conspired against me,
> (And) you, my god, do not thwart him,
> You carry off my understanding.
> The wicked has conspired against me
> Angered you, stormed about, planned evil. (11. 38f.).

This questioning of the deity's failure to destroy the wicked does not come forth from an alienated spirit, for the youth continues to lament to his deity to deliver him from his distress. He further advocates the generally accepted idea concerning fate, that perhaps his suffering has been decreed by the gods as part of his fate: "On the day shares were allotted to all, my allotted share was suffering" (1. 45). Finally, the common dogma that suffering results because all men are evil by nature is proposed:

> They say--the sages--a word righteous (and) straight-
> forward: "Never has a sinless child been born to its
> mother,...a sinless *worker* has not existed from of
> old" (1. 101f.).

Therefore, the sage cannot be truly a "righteous sufferer," for all men are created by nature to be wicked, and thus deserve punishment from the gods.

The question as to why the gods created man to be evil by nature is never raised, nor are the gods attacked for having made man evil. But most important for our own investigation is the observation that the poem is a reflection over the lament process in which a sage wonders, questions, and searches for answers to his problems from the grab-bag of theological acumen but finds his only answer in the continuing efforts to lament his plight before his personal deity in the hopes that the god would have his inexplicably aroused anger soothed and would

eventually correct his situation. And this is exactly what
happens:

> The man--his bitter weeping was heard by his god,
> When the lamentation and wailing that filled him had
> soothed the heart of his god for the young man,
> The righteous words, the artless words uttered by him,
> his god accepted,
> The words which the young *man* prayerfully confessed,
> *Pleased* the..., the *flesh* of his god, (and) his god
> withdrew his hand from the evil word,
> ....
> He turned the you(ng *m*)*an's* suffering into joy
> (ll. 117f.).

Thus it is through the offering of penitential prayer that the
young man is eventually rescued by his deity, an obvious cultic
ritual and theological understanding.[53]

Sumerian Proverbs. The Sumerian proverbs have been critically investigated by Gordon and Jacobsen[54] who have provided
translations of two collections of proverbs, most of which
originated in the scribal quarter of Nippur during the Old
Babylonian Period.[55] Gordon has argued that the proverbs were
collected for use in the *Edubba*,[56] and one may well imagine
that they were used in teaching the language, thought, and
proverbial forms of the Sumerian sages to scribal initiates.
As one might expect, the proverbs cover a broad range of topics,[57] but, because of the limitations inherent in this rather
truncated sapiential form, it proves difficult to elicit any
detailed information from them with respect to observing attitudes and concepts of the Sumerian wise.

These proverbs prove to be of only limited value with respect to our investigation, since one finds only scattered references to matters of cult, most of which bear out Gordon's
observation that such references "are almost entirely incidental."[58] The only proverb which might be indicative of the importance of cult is 1. 70:

> (The people of) a city--their hymns; a kid--its (being
> used for purposes of) extispicy.[59]

This proverb may imply that ingrained within the order of the
cosmos is the law that a society structured in the form of a
city-state has the duty of cultic service to its gods, the

owners and protectors of the city-state, even as young lambs
used in the sacrificial cult find their proper function in being used for extispicy, one of the most important means of ascertaining the will of the gods.[60]

A number of proverbs exude quite a different spirit.
These are the proverbs which, with rather pointed satirical
barbs, lampoon the *Kalû*-priests because of their pretentious
self-importance.[61] Notice the following translations and ex-
planations by Jacobsen:

> The *Kalû*-priest, if he is engendering a (lit. 'his')
> son, (will say): "may he build cities as I do, may
> he give life to the nation as I do"! (2. 99).

Here the priest is ridiculed for his incredible boast that by
means of his cultic service he establishes and preserves city-
states.[62]

> As the saying goes: If the *Kalû*-priest slips as he
> is sitting down, (he will immediately say): "it is
> a visitation from (lit. 'a thing of') my mistress
> Inanna: far be it from me that I may rise"! (2. 100).

> As the saying goes: If the grain-boat of the *Kalû*-
> priest sinks for him, he will stand on dry land,
> (saying): "O Enki! In what you are robbing me of,
> may you take pleasure" (2. 103).

These two proverbs, of course, aim a satirical blow at the pretentious priest who attributes divine import to every incidental
matter, regardless of how trivial or disastrous.[63] The *raison
d'être* for these proverbs is never expressed, and thus they remain humorous, but enigmatic. But since the *Kalû*-priest was
the most important cultic official and was even found frequently
in important governmental positions,[64] the sages have used satirical humor as a weapon to attack a professional class within
Sumerian society for its pretentious and pompous self-esteem.
This suggests, of course, that all areas of life as well as
every social class are open to the critical analysis of the
wise, including socially and cultically prominent groups, if
those groups possess attributes which are subject to the stamp
of foolishness or incorrect behavior according to the standards
of the wise. Even social groups considered by the society as
sacrosanct lost such a holy aura when observed by the sages.

In conclusion it is interesting to note that proverbial materials rarely provide substantive references to cultic faith and practice. And, as we shall see, references to cult are usually found in other genres, especially "righteous sufferer" poems and instructions.[65]

Akkadian Wisdom Literature

Advice to a Prince.[66] This sapiential text, dating between 1,000-700 B.C., consists of omen-patterned counsels to a Babylonian ruler concerning the legal privileges guaranteed to citizens of three ancient Babylonian cities: Nippur, Sippar, and Babylon.[67] The counsels articulate the king's responsibility in maintaining social justice in general and in recognizing the legal rights of the citizens of these ancient cities.[68] If the king fails to maintain justice, and, more specifically, if he tries to abrogate the divinely established and guaranteed privileges granted to the citizens of these three cities, then the entire Babylonian pantheon[69] will strike in concert against the king. For example,

> If he does not heed the justice of this land, Ea, king of destinies, will alter his destiny and will not cease from hostilely pursuing him. (2-3).

The final omen-like admonition, found in lines 55-59, concerns the king's responsibility for the maintenance of the Babylonian cults, a responsibility which gave him the power to establish *corvée* labor gangs for temple building projects and various kinds of temple service.[70] However, due to the legal privileges enjoyed by the citizens of the three cities, they were exempted from the *corvée* gangs of the king. The punishment to be directed against the king for forcing these citizens to participate in the labor gangs is interesting for our concerns, since the punishment involved the great gods abandoning "their dwellings in their fury" and "not entering their shrines." Such a threatened punishment directed against the king paralleled the cultic understanding that the temple was regarded as the dwelling place of the god of the city whose very presence insured the protection and prosperity for the city-state.[71]

The acceptance of this cultic dogma is an indication that the traditional wise supported the understanding that the cult played a crucial role in Mesopotamian life, for its practices secured divine blessings for society.[72]

The Counsels of Wisdom.[73] One of the best known instructions in Mesopotamian wisdom literature is "The Counsels of Wisdom" which dates probably from the Cassite rule of Mesopotamia (1600-1200 B.C.).[74] The piece consists of 160 lines which are divided into ten different sections, each of which contains admonitions with respect to a single topic. Lambert lists the following sections and their topics:

(a) 19-25 Avoidance of bad companions
(b) 26-30 Improper speech
(c) 31-... Avoidance of altercations and pacification of enemies
(d) ...-65 Kindness to those in need
(e) 66-71 The undesirability of marrying a slave girl
(f) 72-80 The unsuitability of prostitutes as wives[75]
(g) 81-... The temptations of a vizier
(h) ...-134 Improper speech
(i) 135-147 The duties and benefits of religion
(j) 148-... Deception of friends[76]

The most important section for our own scrutiny is section (i) which deals with the cultic duties that a sage is expected to perform:

Every day worship (*kit-rab*) your god.
Sacrifice (*ni-qu-u*) and benediction (*qi-bít pi-i*) are the proper accompaniment of incense (*qut-rin-ni*).
Present your free-will offering (*šà-giš-gurₑ-ra-a*) to your god,
For this is proper toward the gods.
Prayer (*su-up-pu-u*), supplication (*su-ul-ul-u*), and prostration (*u la-ban ap-pi*)
Offer him daily and *you will* get your reward.
Then you will have full communion with your god.
In your wisdom study the tablet.
Reverence (*pa-la-ḫu*) begets favour,
Sacrifice (*ni-qu-u*) prolongs life,
And prayer (*ù tés-li-tú*) atones for guilt.
He who fears the gods (*pa-liḫ ilīmeš*) is not slighted by.(..)
He who fears the Anunnaki extends (his days).[77]

This section contains four admonitions (ll. 135, 137, 139-140, and 142) concerning the responsibility of the sage in the area of cultic offerings and prayer. The deity who should be the

recipient of the sage's cultic worship is primarily one's personal deity,[78] and as can be discerned from the text, the motivations for cultic participation are those based upon the desire for a "reward," "favour," and "longevity." In other words,
one who pleases his deity by offering the proper sacrifices is
able to gain the favor of the deity resulting in his protection
and blessing. Other motivations for cultic participation include "communion" with one's own deity and the "atoning for
guilt."

This text testifies openly to the concern of the wise for
proper cultic participation, especially as concerns one's own
personal deity, since that deity was believed to possess protective powers which could divert the attacks of evil forces
and the power to bless with prosperity and long life his observant worshippers. As the wise of Mesopotamia sought to find
security within reality, they believed that the cult was an important way of achieving that security. Only the fool and the
skeptic reject cultic duties.

Counsels of a Pessimist. One of the most interesting instructions from Mesopotamia is the instruction entitled by
Lambert "Counsels of a Pessimist," because of the content that
bespeaks a pessimistic resignation with respect to the evanes-
cent character of human existence and activities.[79] The text,
broken in several places, is terse, and, due to what appears to
be a truncated form, may have been originally part of a larger
work.[80]

The first ten lines discredit the illusion of permanence
sometimes attached to human life and the activities in which
men engage themselves, with the concluding lines observing:

> (Whatever) men do does not last for ever,
> Mankind and their achievements alike come to an end.
> (ll. 9-10).

With this rather futilitarian depiction of the limitations of
human existence and capabilities, the author begins to suggest
what may provide at least some limited security in existence.
First, some security in human existence may be found in the
protection of one's deity who is responsible for one's

conception in the womb and who will continue to provide a
shield against demonic and other evil forces, but only as long
as one remains observant in his cultic devotion directed towards the needs of his god:

> (As for) you, offer prayers (*su-pe-e šu-taq-rib*) to
> (your) god,
> Let your free-will offering (*šagigurû*) be constantly
> before the god who created you (ll. 11-12).

And since the sage has stressed the fleeting brevity of human
life and accomplishments, he encourages his audience to be
cultically observant in the hopes that a pleased god and his
consort will grant one with offspring, through whom a limited
form of immortality is obtained:

> Bow down (*kan-šá-ta-ma*) before your city goddess
> that she may grant you offspring (l. 13).

Then the sage moves into other areas of human activities
in which his audience should be engaged, activities which at
least provide the necessities for human existence: being concerned to care for one's crops and domesticated animals which
provide the basis for human existence.

Finally the sage admonishes his audience to banish the destructive forces of misery and suffering, choosing to rejoice
rather in the reality of being alive (ll. 14-22). Though the
last section concerning the banishment of misery is fragmentary,
the sage apparently counsels his followers to dispense with
fear and anxiety caused by "dreams," since the true origin of
such dreams comes from "misery and suffering." What may be involved in this admonition is a veiled attack levelled against
the cultic understanding of dreams within the sphere of divination, for dreams were, of course, considered to be the portents
of future events, and were a way of determining the future, if
properly interpreted by priestly officials. Our sage takes a
strikingly modernistic view of dreams, appearing to scoff at
the cultic concern for dream interpretation, and writes them
off as the product of misery and suffering. The cure for
dreams, especially those that appear to be terrifying, is to be
contented and happy.[81]

Once again we are confronted with concerns for cultic involvement in Mesopotamian sapiential literature, in this case
in an instruction by a sage who recognizes the limitations of
human existence and accomplishments and seeks to give his audience what he considers to be the primary means of accomplishing at least some security in a rather insecure reality. He
chooses the double paths of cult and sapiential instruction.
By being cultically observant one may continue to enjoy the
protective guidance of one's personal deity and his consort,
and even be rewarded with offspring who are the primary means
for achieving "immortality" in Mesopotamian literature. But
the sage is not cowered by the importance of the cultic institution, for one of its most sacred dogmas and practices is
scoffed at: the practice of the interpretation of dreams. Our
sage presents a psychological explanation of dreams instead of
a theological one.

The Shamash Hymn.[82] A number of psalms in ancient Mesopotamia have been considered wisdom psalms, a conclusion based
primarily on content and the occurrence within the body of the
psalms of a number of sapiential forms.[83] Among these is the
lengthy hymn to Shamash, the god of justice in Babylonian wisdom.[84] Thematic and form-critical arguments for including the
psalm among the literary creations of the wise are as follows.
As noted earlier, Shamash plays a central role in the theology
of the wise as the overseer of retribution, and this is the major theme of the psalm:

> You give the unscrupulous judge experience of fetters,
> Him who accepts a present and yet lets justice mis-
> carry you make bear his punishment.
> As for him who declines a present, but nevertheless
> takes the part of the weak,
> It is pleasing to Shamash, and he will prolong his
> life. (11. 97-100).[85]

In addition to the common wisdom theme of Shamash as the one
who maintains order by means of retribution, there is the presence of a typical wisdom form: an instruction dealing with dis-
honest and honest merchants.[86] Further, the absence of any
reference to incantation indicates that it is not written as a

cultic incantation.[87] Thus, while the form of the entire psalm
is comparable to that of a hymn, the sapiential motif of Shamash as the overseer of justice and the instruction concerning
merchants lead us to argue for the classification of the text
as a wisdom hymn.

If the psalm has been correctly evaluated as a part of
wisdom literature, then we have another important text demonstrating the concern of the wise for cultic participation.
First, the psalm itself breathes of cultic piety issuing forth
in a hymn praising the god of justice, and the context, if not
the cult, very possibly could be the wisdom school. Secondly,
there are several references to cultic worship of Shamash as
the god of justice, which demonstrate that the wise supported
and participated in the sun god cult.[88] Among the specific
cultic devotions to Shamash are sacrifice and especially the
monthly festival in his honor which consisted of libations of
beer and celebrated his maintenance of justice and his deliverance of the righteous. Furthermore, Shamash is primarily the
deity to whom the wise present their laments in the hope that
he will remove their distress:

> You observe, Shamash, prayer, supplication, and
> benediction,
> Obeisance, kneeling, ritual murmurs, and prostration.
> The feeble man calls you from the hollow of his mouth,
> The humble, the weak, the afflicted, the poor (ll.
> 130-33).

Finally, Shamash is approached in the cultic sphere because of his role as the revealer of fate and fortune in the
sphere of divination, especially in the science of omenology,
demonstrating that some of the wise regarded highly this cultic
practice for ascertaining the will of the gods.[89]

> You grant revelations, Shamash, to the families of men,
> Your harsh *face* and fierce light you give to them.
> You manage their omens and preside over their
> sacrifices,
> To all four points of the compass you probe their
> state.
> So far as human habitations stretch, you grant
> revelations to them all (ll. 149-53).

The Babylon Theodicy.[90] The absence of a just social order and the subsequent vitiation of any perceptible principle
of retribution functioning within the spheres of reality are
the central concerns in one sapiential "contest," issues which
lead the author to place in the mouth of one of his contestants
the suggestion that the gods themselves are responsible for
human wickedness, thus leading to the title of this piece of
contest literature: "The Babylonian Theodicy." This sapiential
writing is difficult to date precisely, though the formal
structure is more easily perceived, being an acrostic poem
divided into twenty-seven stanzas of argumentation between two
sages, a "righteous sufferer" and a "friend," who represent
respectively the assault of the critical wise against the major
bulwarks of sapiential tradition and the pious, traditional
wise who defend fortress wisdom against their more critical
colleagues. Interestingly enough, the acrostic spells what
presumably is the name and profession of the author of the dialogue: "Ich, Saggil-kinam-ubbib, der Beschwörer, bin ein Verehrer von Gott und König."[91] Thus we find a wise priest questioning the validity of his own profession.

This disputation between the two wise is initiated by the
"sufferer's" own existential predicament: in spite of his righteousness, wisdom, and cultic piety, he has been abandoned by
his personal deity and has become the object of demonic attack
and social oppression. The "friend" represents the views of
traditional wisdom by staunchly arguing that world-order and
the integrally connected principle of retribution are operative
within the structure of reality which is maintained by the gods
who ensure that the wicked fool is punished, but that the pious
and righteous wise man is rewarded:

> He who waits on his god has a protective angel,
> The humble man who fears his goddess accumulates
> wealth. (II, 21-22).

While the "sufferer" may be impatient with the process, in due
course, argues the "friend," retribution will be effectuated
for him, if he remains pious and wise, whereas the wicked fool
will certainly be destroyed "before his time."[92]

By contrast, the "sufferer" counters both from his own experience and from his own observations of reality that such an understanding of reality shared by the "friend" is totally absurd. He has been pious and wise, and yet calamity has accompanied his every step:

> My strength is enfeebled, my prosperity has ended,
> Moaning and grief have blackened my features (VI, 29-30).

Such catastrophes in spite of his personal piety and wisdom coincide with the natural world and its incongruities as well as the general tenor of society:

> The Onager, the wild ass, who filled itself with ..(.)
> Did it pay attention to the giver of assured divine oracles?
> The savage lion who devoured the choicest flesh,
> Did it bring its flour offering to appease the goddess's anger?
> (.)..the nouveau riche who has multiplied his wealth,
> Did he weigh out precious gold for the goddess Mami?

In fact, our sage contends that the pious, cultic observer is actually impoverished for his piety while the impious is enriched.[93] The "sufferer," to the obvious chagrin of the "friend," even considers discarding adherence to traditional wisdom piety, affirming that he will ignore religious observations and disobey social standards, choosing to exist as an impious social vagabond and criminal.[94] Finally, he not only condemns the gods for being responsible for not maintaining a just and fair system of retribution, but attacks the tolerance of and even participation in social injustice by the masses which lead not only to a denigration of themselves, but also to the very suffering of those who, like himself, are pious and just (XXV).[95]

The "friend," cognizant of his failure to prevail against the adamant position of the "sufferer," does advance his argumentation several steps in his responses to his critical friend. He concedes that the concept of "fate" may explain the reason for the suffering of some and the success of others, but adds that attempts to discover reasons for the specific determination of fate and fortune are defeated by the inscrutability of

the gods and their will.[96] Such a solution to the problem of
the righteous "sufferer" is merely suggested and never tena-
ciously advocated either by the "friend" or the "sufferer."
The "friend," in an effort to concoct a reasonable response to
the accusation made by the "sufferer" against the masses for
social injustice, censures the deities who created mankind, for
they have created mankind to be wicked by nature:

> Narru, King of the gods, who created mankind,
> And majestic Zulummar, who dug out their clay,
> And mistress Mami, the queen who fashioned them,
> Gave perverse speech to the human race.
> With lies, and not truth, they endowed them for
> ever (XXVI, 276-80).

The poet who places such a view of human nature within the
mouth of his pious and traditional sage never seems to realize
the full implications of his suggestion, for if valid, anthropological and consequently societal order would be impossibili-
ties. This idea may aid the "sufferer" in his efforts to understand why he is the object of social oppression, but it
would certainly make wisdom's search for "order" an impossible
quest. We are left with many ponderables concerning the sage's
thesis, but the absence of extrapolations leaves us with no
concrete solutions.

The response of the "sufferer" is difficult to ascertain
in the final section. He seems to have had his anguish somewhat alleviated by the suggestion of the "friend" that the
gods, at least the ones who created mankind, are ultimately
responsible for the perversity of mankind, and thus the "sufferer" does not merit the social oppression by which he has
been victimized. He also gains some solace, it seems, by having found a wise friend who may commiserate with his suffering
and who well knows he is free of personal guilt. Strangely
enough, the "sufferer" does not abandon his piety, but rather
adjures his personal deity and his consort to return their
protective presence, and concludes with the hymnic adulation of
Shamash, the shepherd who "guides the peoples like a god."
Perhaps we should conclude that the "sufferer" can accept the
suggestion that the blame for the perversity of man rests with
the gods, but Shamash, the god of justice, seems to be absolved

of any complicity, and his function as the god of justice is affirmed. Thus the "sufferer" finds his only recourse to be that of hoping for his eventual salvation by the god of justice.[97]

As has been indicated above, the major contention between the two sages concerns the spheres of cultic piety and righteousness. The author of the contest paints the picture of the traditional sage who bows in cultic adoration before the gods, and especially before his own personal deity and consort, with the expressed motivation being that cultic piety leads to reward, whereas cultic negligence leads to destruction.[98] While righteous behavior is also mentioned, it is primarily cultic piety and its supposed rewards that stand at the heart of the contest.[99]

The "sufferer," on the basis of personal experience, including his own observations concerning nature and society, is depicted as one who contends that cultic piety does not bring the garland of success and prosperity, but, and here is an obvious case of hyperbole, may actually lead to the destruction of the pious. Nor does the disregard of cultic participation bring the punishment of the culpable, for such people actually enjoy a happy and prosperous life. As a result, he avows on one occasion that he will completely disregard cultic observances. Yet as indicated above, the final position of the "sufferer" is not one of promethean defiance, but rather is that of one who prays for the return of his protective deities and continues to hope that the god of justice, Shamash, will find him pious and just and will reward him accordingly. In this sapiential writing, the structure of cult with its principle of reward and punishment was cracked but did not crumble. The poet could see no alternative to that of a renewed avowal of piety by the "sufferer."

I Will Praise the Lord of Wisdom.[100] The best known "righteous sufferer" poem in Mesopotamian literature is *Ludlul bēl nēmeqi*, "I Will Praise the Lord of Wisdom," written during the "Dark Ages" of Mesopotamian history, the Cassite Period,[101] either by the "sufferer" himself, *Šubši-mešrê-šakkan*,[102] or

more probably by an unknown sage utilizing the common autobiographical style of poetic fiction.[103]

In this excellent literary creation, the "sufferer" is
characterized as a feudal lord who rules a city for a Cassite
sovereign,[104] and who is beset by numerous catastrophes, including his social and political plummeting from the position
of feudal lord to that of slave, the animosity of his former
Cassite overlord, the treachery of his former courtiers, the
contempt of his fellow men, the abandonment by his relatives
and former comrade, and the onslaught of demonic forces believed
responsible for his bodily ills, all of which were occasioned
by the inexplicable desertion of his personal deity. Thus the
key issue is the inexplicable abandonment of the noble by his
personal deity, a desertion which has resulted regardless of
the feudal lord's exact observance of cultic responsibilities.
Since retribution was a time-honored dogma in Mesopotamian wisdom and cult, the "sufferer," whose thoughts are bound to such
a dogma, is at a loss to explain the god's desertion and the
subsequent catastrophes occasioned by such a divine action.
The poem becomes then an anguished wrestling with the dogmas of
retribution and the justice of the personal deity which seem
controverted by the sage's human experience.

The flow of the contents may be summarized as follows. In
Tablet I the opening is a hymn in praise of Marduk as the wise
and powerful deity whose anger brings destruction, but whose
mercy by contrast extends the healing powers of salvation to
one in dire distress. After an unfortunate lengthy break in
the text, the poet then presents the disconsolate state of the
feudal lord who, because of the desertion of his deity, has
suffered from what appears to have been a successful treacherous plot of court intrigue which resulted in the Cassite king's
anger and the lord's subsequent removal from office. Further
disasters included enslavement of him and his family and the
hostility and contempt of the city's populace, his relatives,
and even his former confidant. In his distress he turns to
diviners and exorcists whose magical activities were sought in
order to obtain either a solution to his problem or soothing
comfort.

Tablet II proceeds to present the worsening of the man's position, this time due, not to human treachery, but rather to demonic powers who have afflicted his body with insufferable torment; all this, in spite of his faithfulness in the observance of cultic rites and loyalty to the Cassite ruler. This leads him to surmise that the retributive standards of the gods must actually be the opposite of those of men, or at the very best, the gods have hidden themselves in the dark clouds of inscrutability, impervious to human understanding. Even so, the tablet concludes with what seems to be a wistful belief in his coming deliverance.

In Tablet III, the description of the salvation of the noble is depicted, as Marduk, his personal deity, apparently has had his anger assuaged by means of exorcism and the lament This seems to be the implication of the appearance of four rather enigmatic persons in the four described visions who are presented apparently as exorcists and incantation priests. The demonic forces are dispelled, he successfully negotiates a river ordeal, and Marduk's protective powers once again engulf him.

Tablet IV(?) presents the redeemed sufferer proclaiming the great salvation of Marduk to his fellow Babylonians and performing his thanksgiving sacrifices in the Esagil before Marduk and his consort.

The central issue which dominates the author's thinking is, of course, the general problem of the "just sufferer," i.e why an individual who has been rigorously precise in his cultic loyalties and duties to the gods, especially his own personal deity, and unswerving in his feudal fealty to his Cassite sovereign, suddenly finds himself abandoned by the encompassing protective power of his deity, consequently is cast into a position of suffering, and made the object of contempt. The critical issue of theodicy never reaches the impassioned and blasphemous stage of Joban anger, but certainly the issue is viewed with a questioning perplexity.[105]

The closest the sufferer comes to presenting an accusation against the moral justice of the gods is his articulation of the idea that his own predicament and his failure to understand

why results from the impossibility of forcing upon divine will
and activity humanly conceived standards of justice and moral-
ty:

> What is proper to oneself is an offence to one's god,
> What in one's own heart seems despicable is proper
> to one's god. (Tab. II, 11. 34-35).

Such an idea, if accepted, would negate the basic affirmation
of wisdom that human standards of justice, resulting from sa-
iential understanding and experience, are reflective of divine
tandards, or, in other words, of the divinely established sys-
em of just order that permeates the universe. He proceeds
urther into the theological realm in his questioning about his
wn predicament and muses that perhaps the gods are inscrutable,
herefore making it an impossible task for man to determine the
ivine will and to make this the basis for human behavior that
eads to security in human existence:

> Who knows the will of the gods in heaven?
> Who understands the plans of the underworld gods?
> Where have mortals learnt the way of a god?
> He who was alive yesterday is dead today (Tab. II,
> 36-39).

If the will and actions of the gods are either inscrutable
r not susceptible to the measurements of human standards of
ustice, there would remain two defiant alternatives to the
ufferer as he contemplates his course of action. One would be
ne complete rejection of the sapiential and cultic idea that
thically conceived behavior and cultic participation lead to
ecurity in human existence, an idea based on the dogma of the
ustice of the gods and thought to be taught by means of both
upernatural and natural revelation, and a return to a more an-
ent and manipulative view that cultic participation has the
otential of appeasing the wrath of malicious, capricious gods
d that by providing for their needs the gods are obligated to
lp the sufferer.

The second defiant alternative would be a total abandon-
nt of the quest for understanding based upon an accurate per-
eption of the divine will, a repudiation of cultic participa-
on, and a turn to completely anthropological concerns. Yet

our sage finally chooses a third, more traditional course of
action by which the marriage of sapiential ideas of order with
cultic processes for the appeasement of divine wrath through
the ritual and theology of the lament process is intensely
questioned, but not annulled. He chooses to continue to affirm
his faith in the justice of the gods and to lament for deliverance from Marduk, hoping that his present torment would be alleviated and ultimately his plight answered.

Enigmatically, Marduk is presented as delivering the sufferer from death, and, it is possible that the sufferer was
restored to his former position as is implied in the Commentary

> Besides the River, where the judgment of the people
> is decided,
> My brow was shaved and my slave mark removed.
> I proceeded along the Kunus-dadru Street--redeemed!
> ....
> He who has done wrong in respect of Esagil; let him
> learn from my example!
> It was Marduk who put a muzzle on the mouth of the
> lion who was eating me.
> Marduk despoiled my pursuer of his sling and turned
> aside his slingstone (ll. l-r).

Therefore, the author apparently is satisfied with the eventual
salvation of the nobleman, and never articulates any reasons
for the suffering of the feudal lord, apparently advocating the
position that eventually deliverance will come to the faithful
devotee who maintains his decorum of obedience even when on the
brink of the abyss.[106]

If we may include this reflective poem concerning the
lament's ritual and theology among the Mesopotamian wisdom
literature,[107] then the importance of this text for our quest
to determine the views of the wise concerning cult cannot be
overestimated. The central protestation of the sufferer has
been that he has faithfully performed his cultic duties, and,
therefore, is undeserving of his god's desertion and the subsequent misfortunes which have afflicted him. Thus his defense
rests primarily upon an advocacy of his continued cultic loyalty.

In Tablet II, after lamenting his inexplicable abandonment
by his deity and the resulting suffering, he protests that such

suffering should come only to the fool who had been frivolous
with respect to cultic obligations to be performed on behalf of
his deity:

> When I look behind, there is persecution, trouble.
> Like one who has not made libation (*tam-qí-tum...*
> *uk-tin-nu*),
> Nor invoked his goddess at table,[108]
> Does not engage in prostration (*ap-pi*), nor takes
> cognizance of bowing down (*šu-kin-ni*);
> From whose mouth supplication (*su-up-pe-e*) and
> prayer (*tés-li-ti*) is lacking,
> Who has done nothing on holy days (*u₄-mu ili*), and
> despised sabbaths (*eš-še-ši*).[109]
> Who in his negligence has despised the god's rites,
> Has not taught his people reverence and worship
> (*pa-la-ḫu ù it-ʾu-du*),
> But has eaten his food without invoking his god,
> And abandoned his goddess by not bringing a flour
> offering (*mas-ḫa-tu*),
> Like one who has grown torpid and forgotten his lord,
> Has frivolously sworn a solemn oath by his god,
> (like such an one) do I appear (II, 12-22).

On the contrary, the sufferer constructs a picture of himself as a faithfully meticulous cultic devotee:

> For myself, I gave attention to supplication (*su-up-
> pu-ú*) and prayer (*tés-li-ti*).
> To me prayer (*tés-li-ti*) was discretion, sacrifice
> (*ni-qu-u*) my rule.
> The day for reverencing the god (*u₄-mu pa-la-aḫ
> ilⁱmeš*) was a joy to my heart;
> The day of the goddess's procession (*u₄-mu ri-du-ti
> diš-tar*) was profit and gain to me.[110]
> The king's prayer (*ik-ri-bi šarri*)--that was my joy,[111]
> And the accompanying music became a delight for me.
> I instructed my land to keep the god's rites (*mêmeš*),
> And provoked my people to value the goddess's name.
> I made praise for the king like a god's,
> And taught the populace reverence for the palace
> (II, 23-32).

It is at this instant that the frustration of the sage
over the failure of these actions to obtain release from his
misfortunes leads him to question whether these cultic actions
which had been considered by the wise to be right and efficacious were exactly the opposite of what the gods considered as
just and proper:

> I wish I knew that these things were pleasing to
> one's god!
> What is proper to oneself is an offence to one's god,
> What in one's own heart seems despicable is proper
> to one's god (ll. 33-35).

Thus he calls into question the idea of the justice of the gods
and the value of cultic duties, questioning the revelation upon
which they were supposedly based:

> Who knows the will of the gods in heaven?
> Who understands the plans of the underworld gods?
> Where have mortals learnt the way of a god? (ll.
> 36-38).

This questioning of the belief that the gods demanded
cultic participation, coupled with the reflection that perhaps
the gods are inscrutable, strike at the heart of Babylonian
religion which stressed that cultic obedience was a revealed
demand of the righteous gods, a teaching buttressed by the traditional wise, and that cultic obedience produced the divine
reward of security in human existence. Furthermore, the sage's
attack on the inability of the clergy (including his own cultic
profession) to determine the causes of the lord's predicament
and to resolve his problems by means of divination and exorcism
cast doubt upon the effectiveness of the priestly office and
questioned the validity of the cultic claim that divination revealed the divine will (Tab. I, ll. 51-52; II, ll. 6-9, 110-
11).[112] These disclaimers of the validity and efficacy of cult
would have been a devastating blow to cult and its support by
the wise had the poem ended abruptly following such outbreaks
against the strictures of sapiential teachings concerning the
cult. However, the poet offers the sufferer no other recourse
than to continue to resort to diviners and exorcists and to
continue to offer his lament in an effort to remedy his situation. And finally, such persistence pays off, for Marduk,
through, it seems, the activities of the priests and the lament
process has his anger assuaged, the sufferer is delivered from
his terrible situation, and he is restored to his former glory.

Finally, if Tablet IV(?) is a part of the original poem,[11]
then we see the noble in the traditional cultic role, presenting himself along with his sacrificial offerings in the Esagil

before Marduk and his consort in thanksgiving, praising the
wise Marduk for his salvation, a cultic activity which should
be an example to all. Thus, this would be connected with the
opening hymn of thanksgiving to Marduk for his powers of salvation.[114]

This piece of literature is best seen as a serious questioning of the cultic theology and ritual of the lament-
thanksgiving process which was based upon the ideas of the
justice and mercy of the gods, the belief that this process was
revealed by the gods, and the ability of the clergy to discover
the reasons for divine chastisement and to effect the appeasement of divine wrath. This cultic response to suffering had
been supported by the traditional wise who counseled their adherents to engage in the lament-thanksgiving process when afflicted by suffering ("The Babylonian Theodicy" and "Man and
His God"). While the cultic process is seriously questioned by
our poet, in the final analysis, he offers the suggestion that
the only recourse for the one afflicted by suffering is the
traditional, cultic one.[115]

Dialogue of Pessimism.[116] The sages in Mesopotamia were
intimately involved in efforts to determine which human activities provided the sources for meaning in human existence. One
such sage produced a reflective dialogue, usually named the
"Dialogue of Pessimism," in which he set forth an examination
of human activities which had been judged by the wise as providing the basis for meaningful existence. And he comes to the
depressing conclusion that each of these esteemed activities
could not be deemed intrinsically good and as a valid basis for
meaningful existence, since every advantageous result issuing
forth from such an activity has its adverse counterpart.[117] In
other words the nature of each activity had the potential two-
edged sword of good and evil results.[118] The activities listed
in the nine strophes of the dialogue include in order of their
appearance in the writing: prestige, sumptuous dining, leisure
time, family, power, love, religion, business activities, and
patriotism. And unfortunately each has its own potential for
devastating consequences.

In each strophe, a nobleman enthusiastically announces a course of action deemed worthwhile and as that which provides meaning in human existence, and his slave, in turn, sets forth a proverbial reply which buttresses the positive values of such a pursuit. The nobleman then abruptly changes his intention and announces he has rejected pursuing such an activity, whereupon the sagacious slave[119] responds again with proverbial observations pertaining to the possible adverse results.

Having negated the positive value of each activity deemed capable of providing meaning in human existence, the slave suggests in answer to the master's query, "What, then, is good"?: "to have my neck and your neck broken and to be thrown into the river is good." Thus suicide is the only activity that can be deemed as "good." This suggestion is supported by the sage in the appending to his answer two impossible questions taken from other Mesopotamian literature:[120]

> Who is so tall as to ascend to the heavens?
> Who is so broad as to compass the underworld?

The point of the impossible questions is to demonstrate that human knowledge is severely limited and that it is impossible even for a sage to ascertain whether an activity, even a treasured one, may provide meaning in life, and whether or not it should be pursued, seeing that the reverse of what is desired may result. With no orderly reality to be perceived or to become the basis for meaningful pursuits, the wise man is faced with an existence in torment, alienation, and a despair that can be remedied by the only activity deemed "good": suicide. When the master probes the slave to determine if the slave has answered seriously, he tells the slave that, if such were true, then he will put the slave to death first, a testing to which the slave responds in striking fashion. He suggests that the absence of meaning would so engulf the despondent master that he too would choose quick self-destruction.[121]

The section dealing with cultic participation (53-61) is the one germane to our investigation. As is obvious from the analyses of other sapiential texts, cult was regarded by the traditional wise as an area to be observed and followed, for it was a primary way of gaining some security in a rather precarious existence. Divine favour was believed to provide a shield of protection around the pious cultic devotee, keeping him from the powers of evil and surrounding him with divine beneficence. After all, the gods had created mankind for the specific purpose of providing for divine needs, needs which could be met in cultic offerings and participation by the pious. And their own justice would certainly make them bless the just cultist.

But in the "Dialogue," as one might already have presumed, a different picture of cult emerges. In the typical way that the dialogue is structured throughout, the master announces his intention to engage in making a sacrificial offering to his personal deity,[122] having just commanded, first of all, his slave to provide him with water for purification before engaging in the rites. The slave in typical fashion then supports the course of action by quoting a proverb intended to affirm the inherent value in cultic participation:

> The man who sacrifices to his god is satisfied with
> the bargain:
> He is making loan upon loan.

This saying supports a cultic dogma that cultic activity results in the deity being placed in debt to the worshipper, and that he must reciprocate with a desired reward. Then the groundwork is laid for the rejection of this commonly accepted dogma. The master in typical fashion abruptly changes his mind and informs his servant that he will not participate in cultic sacrifice to his deity. The slave responds once more with a proverbial reply stressing that sacrifice results in the deity's constant hounding of the master "like a dog" which realizes its complete dependence upon man. Thus the reply contends that the gods cannot exist apart from human devotees, and yet their constant demands for sustaining cultic service negate any advantages which might accrue to the cultically observant in the form of divine pleasure and blessing.[123] The absurdity of cultic religion suggested here is that it makes the deity completely dependent upon the man, a dependence too bothersome to tolerate.[124]

This dialogue demonstrates that some of the critical wise
of the ancient Near East did question and even blatantly attack
cultic religion during periods of skepticism and doubt precipitated by catastrophic experiences which destroyed the confident
assertion of the existence of a beneficent world order. But
this piece of wisdom literature not only swings the execution-
er's axe against the neck of cultic religion, but also against
other activities usually deemed good and meaningful for human
existence, demonstrating that it is not simply religion that is
singled out for attack, but the entire gamut of sapiential activities within the sphere of human existence.[125]

Conclusions

As we conclude our examination of the views of the Mesopotamian wise concerning cultic religion, it becomes apparent
that the insecurity of Mesopotamian life had two important consequences for the Sumerian and Akkadian sages. The first was
the significant emphasis placed upon cultic religion by the
wise in the obvious attempt to channel the protective powers of
the gods into the arenas of political and individual existence.
Thus, the pious wise in Mesopotamia in their search for certainty in life admonished their adherents to be cultically observant, not only with respect to the state gods, but even more
importantly with respect to one's personal god and goddess.
The personal god and goddess were believed to provide the individual savant who was faithful in his cultic duties with
blessings, security, and protection against the demonic forces.
Also implicit in the sapiential teaching concerning cult is the
acceptance of the cultic dogmas of the divine origin of the
cultic institution and the cult as the vehicle for the knowledge
of the divine will. Such traditional, pious wise were the authors of "The Shamash Hymn" and the "Counsels of Wisdom."

However, the second consequence of this pervading insecurity so noticeable in Mesopotamian society and literature was
the outcry of the sages against both the justice of their gods
and the effectiveness of cultic religion during periods of
political and/or individual distress. Not only was the justice

of the gods placed under critical scrutiny, but so were the failures of cultic religion to provide the security so desperately wanted by the sages. The cultic institutions and practices which came under most of the criticism included divination, exorcism, and the cultic lament. The crescendo of the criticisms rises from an almost inaudible murmur found in the Sumerian "Man and his God" to the deafening roar found in "The Babylonian Theodicy" and "I Will Praise the Lord of Wisdom." Yet, while cultic religion is severely questioned as regards its effectiveness and validity, these critical sages do not abandon their allegiance and loyalty to the cult. The sufferers are presented as continuing their cultic efforts to obtain release from their suffering, and only the sufferer in "The Babylonian Theodicy" is still continuing his cultic efforts to be redeemed when the text ends. However, as pertains to divination, "The Counsels of a Pessimist" implies a rejection of the cultic understanding of dreams, choosing rather a psychological explanation.

Only one Mesopotamian wisdom text completely castigates and even ridicules cultic piety, and this is the "Dialogue of Pessimism" which lays bare the absurdity of the complete dependence of the gods upon their human worshippers and concludes that the constant demands of the gods for cultic service negates any advantages which might accrue to the worshippers. However, it must be pointed out that the same text overturns the other accepted values of Mesopotamian society.

Finally, we also have noted that the Mesopotamian sages participated in the writing of long didactic poems, most of which are similar to cultic genres. These include the "Shamash Hymn," "Man and his God," and "I Will Praise the Lord of Wisdom." This gives us evidence that the sages of the ancient Near East participated in the writing of poetry similar to cultic psalms in order to express their worship of the gods. Whether or not these were intended for cultic service is difficult to say, though the "Shamash Hymn" may have been, especially for his public festival.

CHAPTER III

[1]A brief historical survey of wisdom thought and literature is found in W. G. Lambert, *Babylonian Wisdom Literature* (Oxford: At the Clarendon Press, 1960), pp. 1-20.

[2]Translated by S. N. Kramer in *Sumerian Mythology*, rev. ed. (New York: Harper and Brothers, 1961), pp. 64ff.

[3]The Akkadian equivalents for *me* are *parṣu, mešaru,* and *kettu* (cf. E. I. Gordon, *Sumerian Proverbs* [Philadelphia: The University of Pennsylvania, 1959], p. 309; E. A. Speiser, "Authority and Law in Mesopotamia," *Authority and Law in the Ancient Orient*, JAOS Supplement 17 [1954], p. 12; and Helmer Ringgren, *Word and Wisdom* [Lund: Hakan Ohlssons Boktryckeri, 1947], pp. 53f.).

[4]S. N. Kramer, *The Sumerians* (Chicago: The University of Chicago Press, 1963), p. 116.

[5]Gordon, *Sumerian Proverbs*, p. 41. Gordon suggests concerning the proverb: "That is, perhaps, a man who lives in accord with the universally recognized 'cosmic and immutable truths' will be able to obtain for himself all the good things in life." Cf. "The Babylonian Theodicy," 1. 142 (BWL, p. 73); and "I Will Praise the Lord of Wisdom," Tab. II, 1. 29 (BWL, p. 41).

[6]This is argued throughout "The Advice to a Prince," BWL, pp. 110-15. Also compare the Sumerian proverb: "A boat bent on honest pursuits sailed downstream with the wind; Utu has sought out honest ports for it" (1. 8, *Sumerian Proverbs*, p. 84).

[7]BWL, p. 103.

[8]*ANET*, p. 603.

[9]Kramer, *The Sumerians*, p. 125.

[10]BWL, p. 89.

[11]"The Atrahasis Epic," *ANET*, p. 104.

[12]BWL, p. 35.

[13]Cf. the time honored proverb quoted in the Sumerian Job: "They say--the sages--a word righteous (and) straightforward: Never has a sinless child been born to its mother,...a sinless *workman* has not existed from of old" (ll. 101f.; *ANET*, p. 590).

[14]*OECT*, CI. 43. Translated by Lambert, BWL, p. 16.

[15]BWL, pp. 139-40, especially ll. 70f. For a discussion of the questioning of the justice of god, see Wolfram von Soden, "Das Fragen nach der Gerechtigkeit Gottes im Alten Orient," MDOG 96 (1965), pp. 41-59.

[16]As we have noticed in Egyptian Wisdom Literature, the Mesopotamian wise also often refer to deity by using the generic term 'god' (Sumerian *dingir*, Akk. *ilu*), and when an individual deity is specified, he is usually the god of justice, the sun god (Utu, Shamash).

[17]BWL, pp. 112-15. The crediting of the gods with high moral qualities can be traced back to Sumerian theology as Kramer (*The Sumerians*, p. 123) and H. Ringgren (*Religions of the Ancient Near East* [Philadelphia: The Westminster Press, 1973], p. 51) argue.

[18]"The Shamash Hymn," BWL, pp. 121-38.

[19]Ringgren, *Religions of the Ancient Near East*, p. 8.

[20]Cf. Bruno Meissner, *Babylonien und Assyrien*, II (Heidelberg: Carl Winters Universitätsbuchhandlung, 1925), p. 324.

[21]Gordon, *Sumerian Proverbs*, p. 307.

[22]BWL, p. 33.

[23]Cf. the Sumerian "Man and His God," *ANET*, pp. 589-91; and "The Babylonian Theodicy," BWL, pp. 71f.

[24]Kramer, *The Sumerians*, p. 116.

[25]"The Sumerian King List," *ANET*, p. 264; and "Etana," *ANET*, p. 114.

[26]Schmid, *Gerechtigkeit als Weltordnung*, pp. 24-28.

[27]SAHG, Nr. 20, pp. 102-5. Schmid comments concerning this list: "Damit vereint der König alle me in sich, er hat die me von Himmel und Erde inne, er thront in hohem me und vollzieht sie" (*Gerechtigkeit als Weltordnung*, p. 65).

[28]The most detailed wisdom text dealing with the responsibilities of the king in terms of societal justice is "Advice to a Prince," BWL, pp. 110-15. Other sapiential texts point to a similar conviction:
The opulent nouveau riche who heaps up goods
Will be burnt at the stake by the king before his time
("Babylonian Theodicy," BWL, p. 75, ll. 63-64).
The command of the palace, like Anu's is sure.
Like Shamash, the king loves righteousness and hates
evil. (ll. 4-5, K4160+13184; BWL, p. 234).
Cf. ll. 1-3, K4160+13184, BWL, p. 234; "The Assyrian Collection," iv, 9-16, BWL, p. 232.

[29]Shulgi makes the claims: "Endowed with wisdom by Enki am I," and "The wise scribe of Nidaba am I" (ll. 12, 19; "The Shulgi Hymn," *ANET*, p. 585).

[30]D. D. Luckenbill, *Ancient Records of Assyria and Babylonia* (Chicago, 1926-27), no. 767. See the references mentioned in Adam Falkenstein, "Der 'Sohn des Tafelhaus,'" *Die Welt des Orients* 1 (1947), pp. 172f.

[31]The well known speech of the ale-wife, Siduri, poignantly expresses this divinely determined fate of mankind:
 Gilgamesh, whither rovest thou?
 The life thou pursuest thou shalt not find.
 When the gods created mankind,
 Death for mankind they set aside,
 Life in their own hands retaining (Tablet X, Old
 Babylonian Version, ll. 1f.; *ANET*, p. 90).
Cf. "The Babylonian Theodicy," ll. 16-17, BWL, p. 71; and "Counsels of a Pessimist," BWL, p. 109, ll. 9f.

[32]See Prov. 1. 30, 1. 38, 1. 183 (Gordon, *Sumerian Proverbs*, p. 309).

[33]See "I Will Praise the Lord of Wisdom," Tablet II, ll. 33f.

[34]*Ibid.*, ll. 50f.

[35]See, e.g., "The Babylonian Theodicy," BWL, p. 87, ll. 260f.

[36]*Ibid.*, p. 16.

[37]Cf. "The Shamash Hymn," *ibid.*, pp. 121-38.

[38]See "The Creation Myth," *ANET*, p. 68, Tablet VI. Marduk proclaims:
 Blood I will mass and cause bones to be.
 I will establish a savage, man shall be his name.
 Verily, savage-man I will create.
 He shall be charged with the service of the gods
 That they might be at ease.

[39]Lambert cogently argues: "There was no distinction, such as we tend to make, between morally right and mutually proper. The god was just as angry with the eating of ritually impure food as with oppressing the widow and orphan. His anger would be appeased no less with the ritual offering than with a reformed life" ("Morals in Ancient Mesopotamia," *JEOL* 15 [1957/58], p. 194).

[40]BWL, pp. 71, 85.

[41]*Ibid*, p. 105.

[42]*Ibid.*, p. 39.

[43] *Ibid.*, pp. 41, 45.

[44] For studies on scribes and scribal schools, one should see Bruno Meissner, *op. cit.*, pp. 324f.; A. Leo Oppenheim, *Ancient Mesopotamia* (Chicago: The University of Chicago, 1964), pp. 235f.; "The Position of the Intellectual in Mesopotamian Society," *Daedalus* 104 (1975), pp. 37-46; Kramer, *The Sumerians*, pp. 165-248; "Schooldays: A Sumerian Composition Relating to the Education of the Scribe," *JAOS* 69 (1949), pp. 199-215; Benno Landsberger, "Scribal Concepts of Education," *City Invincible* (Chicago: The University of Chicago Press, 1958), pp. 94-123; Adam Falkenstein, "Die babylonische Schule," *Saeculum* 4 (1953), pp. 125-37; B. Landsberger, "Babylonian Scribal Craft and its Terminology," Abstract in *The Proceedings of the 23rd International Congress of Orientalists* (Cambridge, 1954), pp. 123-26; W. G. Lambert, "Ancestors, Authors, and Canonicity," *JCS* 11 (1957), pp. 1-14; Harmut Schmökel, *Das Land Sumer*, 3rd ed. (Stuttgart: W. Kohlhammer, 1962), pp. 96f.; and J. J. A. van Dijk, *La sagesse suméro-accadienne* (Leiden: E. J. Brill, 1953), pp. 21-28.

[45] Those listed by Gordon, "A New Look at the Wisdom of Sumer and Akkad," *BO* 17 (1960), pp. 122-52.

[46] See the references mentioned in Falkenstein, "Der 'Sohn des Tafelhaus,'" pp. 172f. For example, in the Lipitishtar Hymn (*TCT*, XVI 87 VI 5-7): "Deinen Lobpreis möge er (=der Tafelschreiber) im Tafelhaus nicht enden lassen"! (*ibid.*, 185f.

[47] See the schoolboy text translated by Kramer ("Schooldays: A Sumerian Composition Relating to the Education of a Scribe," ll. 74f.) in which the teacher says to his scribal protégé:
May Nidaba, the queen of the guardian deities, be your guardian deity.
May she show favor to your *fashioned* reed.
May she take all evil *from* your hand-copies.
....
I will give speech to you, will decree (your fate).
Verily your father and (mother) will support you *in this* matter,
As (that) which is Nidaba's, as that which is thy god's,
They will present offerings and prayers to her.
Nidaba, the queen of the place of learning, you have exalted.
O Nidaba praise!

[48] For the translation, see *ANET*, pp. 589-91.

[49] S. N. Kramer, "Man and his God," VTSup 3 (1955), p. 170.

[50] The poem has been classified as a "righteous sufferer" poem in regard to content (Gordon, "A New Look at the Wisdom of Sumer and Akkad," p. 149). We would prefer to use the classification "A Reflective Poem Concerning the Lament" or Gese's "Paradigm of an Answered Lament" (*Lehre und Wirklichkeit in der*

alten Weisheit (Tübingen: J. C. B. Mohr [Paul Siebeck], 1958), for the poem reflects over the thought of the cultic lament, and is similar to the structure of the lament (see SAHG, pp. 183f.).

[51]S. N. Kramer, *From the Tablets of Sumer* (Indian Hills, Colorado: Falcon's Wing Press, 1956), p. 148.

[52]The god concerned is the sufferer's 'personal' god.

[53]As we shall see in Chapters IV and V, the traditional wise in Israel were also involved in writing reflective poems concerning the lament (cf. the opponents of Job and Psalm 73).

[54]E. I. Gordon, *Sumerian Proverbs* (Philadelphia: The University Museum, 1959). Jacobsen's materials are found in the same book, pp. 447-87.

[55]Gordon, *Sumerian Proverbs*, pp. 3, 23, 24.

[56]*Ibid.*, p. 18.

[57]Gordon has a useful catalogue of subjects mentioned in the two collections on pp. 285-323.

[58]*Ibid.*, p. 310.

[59]*Ibid.*, p. 76. However, see the alternative translation of Jacobsen: "The songs of a city are its fortune-tellers" (pp. 460-61).

[60]Gordon, *op. cit.*, p. 76.

[61]So argues Jacobsen, p. 482. Gordon has suggested that the *Kalû*-priest is lampooned because of his being a eunuch and a devotee of the goddess Inanna, reasons which help in explaining why these proverbs are written mainly in the Emesal dialect, usually reserved for speeches of women and goddesses (*op. cit.*, pp. 13-14, 310).

[62]Jacobsen, p. 482.

[63]*Ibid.*, pp. 483-84.

[64]Gordon, *op. cit.*, p. 310.

[65]This is the same in Hebrew Wisdom Literature as we shall see in Chapter IV.

[66]BWL, pp. 110-15, 316-17.

[67]*Ibid.*, pp. 110-11.

[68]Oppenheim indicates that this legal status was referred to as *kidinnūtu*, 'status of being under the aegis of the *kidinnu*,' a term which "denotes an object placed at the gateway

of such a city as a symbol of divine approval and protection which safeguarded the status of the citizens" (*Ancient Mesopotamia*, pp. 120-21).

[69]The gods mentioned are Ea, Shamash, Marduk, Enlil, Anu, Era, Addu, and Nabû.

[70]Oppenheim, *op. cit.*

[71]*Ibid.*, p. 108.

[72]See Edouard Dhorme, *Les religions de Babylonie et d'Assyrie*, Mana 2 (Paris: Presses Universitaires de France, 1945), pp. 174f.

[73]Once more the translation is found in BWL, pp. 96-107.

[74]*Ibid.*, p. 97. Other instructions include the "Instructions of Shuruppak," a section in the "Shamash Hymn," and "Counsels of a Pessimist."

[75]Among the prostitutes a wise man was to avoid in marriage was a temple harlot (*ḫa-rim-tu*) whose devotion to a god did not prevent the ingraining of an irreverent spirit concerning her new husband or a continuation of her profession after marriage. This demonstrates that the wise were not entirely favorable of those professional priests and priestesses who devoted their bodies to the fertility cults. For a discussion of temple harlots, see Dhorme, *op. cit.*, p. 213.

[76]Two general terms for worship which are used are *kit-rab* and *pa-la-ḫu*. Terms for sacrifice include *ni-qu-u* ("bloody sacrifice") and *ša-giš-gurš-ra-a* (interpreted by Lambert as a "free-will offering"), while the words for prayer are *qi-bit pi-i, su-ul-lu-u, su-up-pu-u, la-ban ap-pi*, and *tés-li-tu*. Finally the term for incense is *qut-rin-ni*. For a discussion of these cultic actions and the different terms, see Dhorme, *Les religions de Babylonie et d'Assyrie*, pp. 225f.

[77]BWL, p. 96.

[78]Other references to the personal deity are ll. 59 and 63.

[79]Lambert, BWL, pp. 107-9.

[80]*Ibid.*, pp. 107-8. The date is impossible to determine specifically, argues Lambert, who sets the rather broad limits of the First Dynasty of Babylon to the library of Ashurbanipal.

[81]For a study of dreams in Mesopotamia, see Oppenheim, *The Interpretation of Dreams in the Ancient Near East*. Our sage's scoffing at the theological interpretation of dreams should be compared to the remarks of Koheleth (5:1-7) and Sirach (31:1-8).

[82]Translation by BWL, pp. 121-38. For a study of the Shamash hymns and prayers, see P. Anastasius Schollmeyer, *Sumerisc babylonische Hymnen und Gebete* (Paderborn: Ferdinand Schöningh, 1912).

[83]Extensive work needs to be done in the area of sapiential psalms in Mesopotamian literature along the lines established by Lambert and von Soden (see the latter's "Der grosse Hymnus an Nabû," *ZA* 66 [1971], pp. 44-71). Von Soden has argued that this psalm was not written primarily for use in the cult, but rather was a confessional hymn written by a scholarly poet for a learned audience (*ibid.*, p. 48). A number of sapiential writings were dedicated in hymnic fashion to the gods of wisdom and order, as may be seen in the conclusions of a number of wisdom texts (e.g., see "Nisaba and Wheat," BWL, p. 173; and Kramer, "Schooldays," p. 213).

[84]For another discussion of this hymn, see F. M. Th. Bohl, "De Zonnegod als de Beschermer der Nooddruftigen," *JEOL* 8 (1942), pp. 665-80. Bohl comments concerning Shamash as the defender of right and justice: "Hij is de god, die bij zijn dagelijkschen loop over den hemel alle ongerechtigheid bespeurt en het moreele en sociale evenwicht op aarde handhaaft" (*ibid.*, p. 666). Lambert has divided the poem into the following sections:

1- 20	Shamash as the giver of light
21- 52	The beneficent care of Shamash
53- 82	Shamash as the source of all revelation and the caretaker of the needy
83-127	Shamash as the overseer of justice by means of retribution
128-148	The presence of Shamash even in remote spheres
149-155	Shamash as the one who grants revelations
150-166	The monthly festival of Shamash
167-173	(lines not in context)
174-183	Renewal of praise for Shamash as the giver of light

Cf. "The Babylonian Theodicy," BWL, p. 89, l. 297; and "I Will Praise the Lord of Wisdom," BWL, p. 46, l. 120.

[85]Cf. "The Babylonian Theodicy," BWL, p. 89, l. 297; and 'I Will Praise the Lord of Wisdom," BWL, p. 46, l. 120.

[86]Found in the section dealing with Shamash as the overseer of justice by means of retribution (ll. 83-127). The proverbial observation is sometimes bolstered by the motivation clause that such "is pleasing to Shamash" (ll. 100, 106, 119).

[87]C. D. Gray, "A Hymn to Shamash," *AJSL* 17 (1901), p. 130.

[88]Prayer stands out in this hymn as the most important cultic ritual. The terms used for prayer are *su-up-pa-a*, *su-la-a*, *ka-ra-bi*, while the gestures used in praying, especially in offering laments (Dhorme, *Les religions de Babylonie et d'Assyrie*, p. 250) are *šu-kin-na* ("obeisance"), *kit-mu-su* ("kneeling"), *lit-ḫu-šu* ("ritual murmurs"), and *la-ban ap-pi* ("prostration"). Other cultic rituals include *ni-(q)i-i* ("sacrifice") and *sir-qi* ("libations"). Two terms for cultic worship which are used are *pal-ḫa* and *i-dal-lal*.

[89]For a discussion of omenology, see Oppenheim, *Ancient Mesopotamia*, pp. 210f. More recently, Glendon Bryce has discussed omen-wisdom in Mesopotamia and attempts to argue certain Israelite proverbs (19:10, 16:30, 9:12) are related to the form and content of certain Akkadian omens. He concludes that these Hebrew omen-proverbs may argue for the existence of priestly sages in Israel ("Omen-Wisdom in Ancient Israel," *JBL* 104 [1975], pp. 19-37).

[90]The translation is in BWL, pp. 63-91, and *ANET*, pp. 601-4.

[91]B. Landsberger, "Die babylonische Theodizee," *ZA* 43 (1936), p. 34. The date is extremely difficult to establish. Lambert suggests a time between 1400 and 800 B.C. (BWL, pp. 66-67).

[92]See VI; XX, 219-220; XII, 239-42. The position of the "friend" is paralleled in proverbial literature: "When you have seen the profit of reverencing (your) god, you will praise (your) god and salute the king" (BWL, p. 233; The Assyrian Collection, IV, pp. 24-26).

[93]VII, 70-71:
> Those who neglect the god go the way of prosperity,
> While those who pray to the goddess are impoverished and dispossessed.

[94]XIII, 133-43:
> I will abandon my home.(.........)
> I will desire no property.(.........)
> I will ignore my god's regulations and trample on his rites.
> I will slaughter a calf and....food,
> I will take the road and go to distant parts.
> I will bore a well and let loose a flood,
> Like a robber I will roam over the vast open country.
> I will go from house to house and ward off hunger;
> Famished I will walk around and patrol the streets.
> Like a beggar I will (....) inwards (........)
> Bliss is far away..(........)

[95]XXV, 265-75. Buccellati, "Tre saggi sulla sapienza mesopotamia--III, La teodicea: condanna del'abulia politica," *OrAnt* 11 (1972), pp. 162-63. Cf. D. J. Wiseman, *Assyria and Babylonia*, CAH 2, chap. 31 (Cambridge: Cambridge University Press, 1965), p. 38. Wiseman suggests that the theodicy may "reflect a conflict of political and religious ideologies caused by the times of economic stress resulting from the Aramaean incursions. There is evidence that this text, in its present form, was composed by Saggil-kinam-ubbit, a scholar of Babylon contemporary with the Aramaean usurper Adad-apal-iddina."

[96]XXIV, 254-64.

[97]Buccellati has observed that the only two possibilities for the "sufferer" are either a complete denial of social, religious, and cultural values (XIII) or humility and an imploring of his "friend," his personal gods, and Shamash to help and comfort him (XXVII) (*op. cit.*, p. 162). Cf. Gray, "The Book of Job in the Context of Near Eastern Literature," *ZAW* 82 (1970), p. 258; and J. J. Stamm, "Die Theodizee in Babylon und Israel," *JEOL* 9 (1952), p. 103.

[98]As is the case in most Mesopotamian wisdom literature, the primary emphasis is placed upon one's protective deity and his consort.

[99]Cultic terminology used by the author includes terms for worship (*pa-li-iḫ*, *a-dal-lal*), cultic rites (*par-ṣ(i)*, *pi-il-u-de-e ili*, and *ma-si-šu*), prayer (*su-up-pe-e*, *il-la-ba-an ppi*, and *te-mi-qi*), flour offering (*mas-ḫat-s(u)*), offerings *nin-(d)a-ba-a*), and prescribed offerings (*sat(tu)kkē^e*).

[100]For the translation, see BWL, pp. 21-62. However, the lost introduction consisting of a hymn has been published by E. Reichty ("Two New Fragments of Ludlul Bel Nemeqi," *Or* 28 [1959], p. 361-63), and is now found in the translation in *ANET*, p. 596.

[101]BWL, p. 21. Gray specifically dates the piece around 1500 B.C. ("The Book of Job in the Context of Near Eastern Literature," p. 254), while W. von Soden argues for a 12th century dating ("Das Fragen nach der Gerechtigkeit Gottes im alten Orient," MDOG 96 [1965], p. 49).

[102]BWL, p. 51; Tablet III, 1. 43.

[103]W. von Soden, "Zur ersten Tafel von Ludlul bel nemeqi," O 10 (1953), p. 8.

[104]Lambert argues: "One may conjecture that *Šubši-mešrê-ukkan* was a feudal lord ruling a city for the Cassite monarch" (BWL, p. 22).

[105]Lambert makes the observation: "To the pious writer it as blasphemy openly to charge Marduk with the injustice of allowing his devoted servants to suffer... Unlike Job the author of *Ludlul* was not free to debate the question openly because of its blasphemous implications" ("The Literary Structure, Background and Ideas of the Babylonian 'Poem of the Righteous Sufferer,'" *Akten des vierundzwanzigsten Internationalen Orientalisten-Kongresses München* [Wiesbaden: Franz Steiner Verlag, 1959]).

[106]Cf. the Sumerian "Man and his God."

[107]The major problem in including this poem within the sphere of wisdom literature is the question of determining its genre. It certainly is closely similar to the Psalm of Thanksgiving, for it includes a hymnic introduction concerning Marduk

and his power to rescue the needy (I, lf.), a description by
the sufferer of his former state of suffering (I-II) and his
subsequent deliverance by Marduk (III), and his thanksgiving to
Marduk and his consort in the temple which involves his procla-
mation to others of Marduk's great power to save. Kuhl does
argue that it is a *Dankgebet* ("Neuere Literaturkritik des
Buches Hiob," *ThRu* 21 [1953], p. 299). Oppenheim seems to imply the same (*The Interpretation of Dreams in the Ancient Near
East*, Philadelphia: The American Philosophical Society, 1956,
p. 217). Lambert suggests that it is much like a dramatization
of an incantation ("Literary Structure," p. 147). Gese has
considered the poem as an example of "The Paradigm of an Answered Lament" (*Lehre und Wirklichkeit*). Van Dijk has argued,
however, that the poem was not intended for the cult, but rather should be regarded as a reflective poem seeking to deal
with the critical problem of one who suffers unjustly, and in
this way differs from psalms of confession which are efforts to
persuade a deity to change his attitude towards a penitent and
act to deliver him (*op. cit.*, p. 119). We tend to accept Van
Dijk's arguments and classify the writing as a sapiential reflective poem concerning the theology and ritual of the lament-
thanksgiving process. We shall meet similar poems in the Hebrew Psalter, especially Psalm 73, and, of course, in the Dialogues of Job.

[108]Lambert argues 11. 13 and 19 refer to a cultic meal
(BWL, p. 289).

[109]*eš-še-ši* is the monthly offerings and rites (Dhorme,
op. cit., p. 235).

[110]For a discussion of the cultic procession, see Dhorme,
op. cit., pp. 243f.

[111]For examples of prayers for the king, see SAHG, pp.
279f.

[112]The various priests, diviners, and exorcists who are
named by the poet as being unable to help the sufferer, at
least initially, are the *bārû* ("diviner"), the *šā'ilu* ("dream
priest"), the *mašmaššu* ("incantation priest"), the *zaqīqu*
(possibly an "astrologist"), and the *a-ši-pu* ("exorcist"). See
Tablet II, 11. 6-9, and 110-11. The four enigmatic figures who
appear to the sufferer in four dreams include an exorcist in
dream two, an incantation priest in dream four, a young woman
who is suggested by Lambert to be an *entu*-priestess (BWL, p.
22), and the young man in dream one whose identity and function
remain unknown since his message is lost (Tablet III, 11. 1f.).
For discussions of these priests and the *entu*-priestess, see
Dhorme, *op. cit.*, pp. 206f. For a discussion of divination in
general, see Oppenheim, *Ancient Mesopotamia*, pp. 206-27.

[113]Lambert argues that this tablet is either Tablet V or
perhaps not even a part of the original poem (BWL, p. 30).

[114]The description of the redeemed nobleman's thanksgiving
in the Esagil is filled with cultic detail (Tablet IV(?), 11.
76f.).
(   )..which in my prayers (*tés-li-ti-ia*)..(.......)
(With) prostration (*la-ban ap-pi*) and supplication
(*ut-ni-ni*) (....) to Esagil.
....
In the "Gate of Pure Water" I was sprinkled with
water of purification (*me-e te-lil-te aš-ša-li-iḫ*),
....
In the "Gate of Exuberance" I kissed the foot of
Sarpanitum (*še-ep ṣar-pa-ni-tum an-na-šiq*).
I persisted in supplication and prayer (*su-pe-e ù
te-me-qí*) before them,
Fragrant incense (*qut-rin-na*) I placed before them,
I presented an offering, a gift, accumulated donations
(*ir-ba ta-'-ti igisê eta-an-du-te*),
I slaughtered fat oxen (*le-e ma-re-e*), and butchered
fattened sheep (*sap-di*),
I repeatedly libated honey-sweet beer (*at-ta-naq-qi
ku-ru-un-nu du-uš-šu-pá*) and pure wine (*karāna (i)l-lu*).
....
(..). libation (*tam-qi-ti*) I made their hearts glow,
....
(I..). oil, curds, and choicest grain (*el-la ḫi-ma-tú
ṭuḫ-di aš-na-an*).
(.......).....the rites of the temple (*parṣi bīti*).
Lambert has suggested reading *šapsu*, "fattened sheep," instead of
sap-di in line 94 (BWL, p. 301). For a translation and study
of Mesopotamian laments and thanksgiving hymns, see SAHG.

[115]A comparable text concerning a just sufferer who continues to offer a lamentation to his god who finally announces
a speech of salvation to the sufferer is A04462 (J. Nougayrol,
"Un version ancienne du 'juste souffrant,'" *RB* 59 [1952], pp.
239-50). Also see R. S. 25.460 (Jean Nougayrol, Emmanuel
Laroche, Charles Virolleaud, and Claude F. A. Schaeffer, *Ugaritica* 5, Mission de Ras Shamra, 16 [Paris: Imprimerie Nationale,
1968], pp. 266f.).

[116]For the translation, see BWL, pp. 139-49.

[117]The date can be no earlier than the beginning of the
Iron Age (1,200 B.C.), since there is a reference to an 'iron
dagger' in 1. 52 (Jean Bottéro, "Le'Dialogue Pessimiste' et la
transcendance," *RTP* 16 [1966], p. 7).

[118]The most frequently encountered interpretation is the
one which regards the piece as essentially a pessimistic,
skeptical, philosophical tractate that negates all value to
human activity. See Thorkild Jacobsen, "Mesopotamia," *The Intellectual Adventure of Ancient Man* (Chicago: University of
Chicago Press, 1946), p. 218; S. Langdon, *Babylonian Wisdom*
(London: Luzac and Co., 1923), p. 68; and G. B. Gray, "Job,
Ecclesiastes, and a New Babylonian Literary Fragment," *ET* 31
[1920], p. 441). Lambert (BWL, p. 141) adds to this

interpretation the feeling that perhaps the piece is written by a disturbed mind in a state of morbid depression. Bottéro accepts the pessimistic interpretation, though he combines this with a satirical attack on proverbial wisdom as the basis for human activity, since, as the slave so adroitly demonstrates, a proverbial response can be made to support both a decision to act or a decision to refrain from acting (*op. cit.*, p. 15). G. Buccellati has followed Bottéro's interpretation, though he stresses the repeatedly found polarity of thought that occurs in this piece which is frequent in wisdom literature in general: "il leitmotif del Dialogo è la polarità." By this he means that due to the multiplicity of sapiential experiences, the wise constructed "the science of opposites" whereby the results of a particular activity were weighed against each other in an attempt to discover if the activity were worthwhile or not ("Tre saggi sulla sapienza mesopotamica, II. Il Dialogo del Pessimismo: la scienze delgi oppositi come ideale sapienziale," *OrAnt* 11 [1972], pp. 92f.). A completely different interpretation has been presented by E. A. Speiser who refers to the dialogue as a satirical farce enacted before an audience by two performers and meant primarily to entertain. Therefore, the piece should not be regarded as serious pessimism ("The Case of the Obliging Servant," *JCS* 8 [1954], pp. 98-105). For a rebuttal of Speiser's arguments, see Lambert, BWL, pp. 139f.

[119]The slave is presented as a wise man who can support both a decision to act or not to act by means of proverbial sayings. Bottéro's precise argument that this dialogue attacks sentence wisdom as the basis for making decisions deserves careful consideration, though we believe that something more than an attack against sentence wisdom is involved, and that is an all out attack of wisdom's claim to perceive world order and the sapiential doctrine of meaningful action based on the dictates of order.

[120]Cf. "The Gilgamesh Epic," *ANET*, p. 79; Tablet III, iv, ll. 3f.

[121]Bottéro, *op. cit.*, pp. 15f.

[122]The deity with which the nobleman is concerned is typically his personal deity (cf. ll. 55, 56, 58, 60, 61).

[123]Jacobsen presents the interpretation of the slave's response to the master's determination to refrain from cultic observance: "in other words, 'be uppish with the god'; let him feel that he depends upon you for service, for prayer, and for many other things, so that he will run after you, begging you to worship him" (*op. cit.*, p. 217). However, since the other responses of the slave to the master's decision not to pursue an activity involve the slave's listing of the disadvantages of the action, we would go farther by suggesting that the slave is bolstering the decision not to sacrifice by showing that the deity's constant demands for cultic worship to meet his needs produce far more bothersome troubles than any reward the deity might provide the master. In fact, there may be implicit the denial that the gods are capable of any action, good or bad. If this be true, why worship them?

[124]The idea of the dependence of the gods upon human service is common in Mesopotamian literature (e.g., see the recounting of the flood story in "The Epic of Gilgamesh," Tablet XI, lines 158f.; *ANET*, p. 95). See Dhorme, *op. cit.*, pp. 221f.

[125]The cultic rituals mentioned include purification before engaging in cultic service and sacrifice (*niqâ ana ili-ia lu-pu-uš*). The general term for cultic rites is also used: *par-ṣi.*

CHAPTER IV

THE VIEWS OF CULT IN ISRAELITE WISDOM LITERATURE

A. *The World View of Israelite Wisdom Literature*

Before initiating our quest to discover the views of the
Israelite sages with respect to the realm of cult, we should
set forth certain broad guidelines which speak to the views of
reality as perceived by the Hebrew sages.

Wisdom and the Cosmos

As we have found in other ancient Near Eastern wisdom literatures, so it is that the Israelite wisdom literature speaks
of the creation as being permeated by an all-embracing cosmic
order, צדקה, which served as the cohesive force holding together the various components of created order in a well-
integrated, harmonious whole.[1] Thus each natural phenomenon
had its own particular place, function, time, and norms regulating its existence within the complex of cosmic order.
Sirach speaks of cosmic order in 16:24-28:

> The works of the Lord have existed
> from the beginning by his creation,
> And when he made them,
> he determined their divisions.
> He arranged his works in an eternal order,
> and their dominion for all generations;
> They neither hunger nor grow weary,
> and they do not cease from their labors.
> They do not crowd one another aside,
>   and they will never disobey his word.[2]

Thus the task of the wise man became that of observing
this complex of natural phenomena held in an orderly continuum
in order to perceive their interrelated unity and to deduce
from them the divine norms which governed their harmonious
functioning within the order of the cosmos. By observing and
consequently placing these cosmic dictates into the major forms
of sapiential language, the sages obtained the basis for guidance in the living of a wise and orderly existence in harmony
with the other natural phenomena. For once the sage by means
of his wisdom[3] discovered his own place, function, and time

within the gamut of cosmic order, he then had the means to
achieve harmony with the structure of creation.

The Israelite wise also perceived this order in terms of
justice, thus making an ethical category the permeating force
which held in concert the various phenomena of the cosmos, and
they did not view order as cold, amoral, and indifferent to
just and righteous behavior of men. Therefore, we find intimately connected with the idea of cosmic order the idea of
retribution in which orderly, wise behavior of men led to their
experiencing of blessing, whereas the disorderly, foolish behavior of the wicked led to their destruction, for the maintenance and continuous functioning of world order depended upon
conformity to the dictates of an ordered reality, and consequently those who were ignorant of or rebelled against these
cosmic norms were led by their own wicked behavior to destruction.[4]

Also in their perception of cosmic order, the wise attributed to צדקה the characteristic of beneficence, for cosmic order contained within its structure the generating force of
blessing for those who followed the dictates of reality and,
therefore, lived in harmony with the cosmos. In general then,
the cosmos in its structured order was not hostile or alien to
human existence, but, on the contrary, was structured for the
beneficence of orderly existence. Even wicked and evil things
should not be so judged, says Sirach, for things like the vi-
per's fang have their purpose in the punishment of wicked men.
Thus the sage remarks in 39:25-27:

> From the beginning good things were created for good
> people,
>   just as evil things for sinners.
> Basic to all the needs of man's life
>   are water and fire and iron and salt,
> And wheat flour and milk and honey,
>   the blood of the grape, and oil and clothing.
> All these are for good to the godly,
>   just as they turn into evils for sinners.

Of course, the Hebrew sages believed that God was the
creator of reality and the one who arranged the elements of the
cosmos into a just, well-integrated complex, knitted together
by order. The deity achieved this orderly cosmos by means of
his own wisdom. Thus in Prov 3:19-20 one sage proclaims:

> The Lord by wisdom founded the earth;
> > by understanding he established the heavens;
> By his knowledge the deeps broke forth,
> > and the clouds drop down the dew.

Because it was wisdom that enabled the deity to structure cosmic order, wisdom became the key to human cognition of cosmic order and the norms which regulated cosmic phenomena.[5] Thus those who become possessors of wisdom have the means by which to understand the interworkings of cosmic order, to analyze the divinely instituted cosmic laws, and to achieve the basis for orderly existence within the cosmos, for the wise man is empowered to know his own place, function, and time within the spheres of order.

Wisdom and God

The sages held to the theological affirmation of God as the creator deity who in his creation established order as the permeating force of cosmic reality, and, as we shall see momentarily, of society and mankind as well. Thus, theologically speaking, God as creator is the central view of God in the thinking of the sages.[6]

Because order was given the basic connotation of justice, the wise also considered the deity to be characterized by justice and to function as the just overseer of his creation by means of the principle of retribution. It was he who maintained the just functioning of reality and who blessed or destroyed those who lived within his creation according to their behavior. Thus in the first speech of Eliphaz, this traditional sage remarks to Job in 4:7-9:

> Think now, who that was innocent ever perished?
> > Or where were the upright cut off?
> As I have seen, those who plow iniquity
> > and sow trouble reap the same.
> By the breath of God they perish,
> > and by the blast of his anger they are consumed.

Of course, when order was no longer perceived by the wise, and when the dogma of retribution was controverted in the arena of human experience, the theological structure of the wise began to crumble. In Israel we find this crisis following the

decimation of the state when voices are raised against the concepts of just order, retribution, and theodicy. Thus wisdom
enters into its crisis stage, and the critical wise devastate
the sapiential heritage of their ancestors. Job and Koheleth
no longer are able to perceive a just order permeating reality,
nor are they able to validate the principle of retribution.
And in theological terms God is still perceived to be the creator, but he either is stripped of the mask of righteousness
(Job), or becomes the *Deus absconditus*, hidden to human understanding, but certainly a power to be feared (Koheleth).[7]

Wisdom and Society

The Israelite sages also perceived society to be divinely
constructed and provided with norms for its institutions. In
other words, the creator deity permeated society with societal
order, thus making the Israelite society the microcosm of world
order. The divine ordering of society may best be seen in the
institution of kingship, for the royal institution was established by the creator for the primary purpose of maintaining
societal order in the areas of law, the military, fertility,
and cult.[8] The purpose of kingship in terms of maintaining
societal order may be seen in several wisdom sayings which
speak of the king's throne as founded upon order (צדקה). Hellmut Brunner has argued that these sayings found in Prov 16:12
and 20:28 are paralleled in certain Egyptian texts which point
to the pedestal of the royal throne as the *Ürhügel* upon which
the creator deity stood when he created the world and established *Ma'at* as the constitutive order of reality. In fact,
the same hieroglyph is used for *Ma'at* and the royal pedestal.
Brunner believes such texts in Egypt and Israel point to a commonly shared view that the royal institutions had the primary
responsibility for maintaining order within their respective
societies.[9]

The divine gift which enabled the king to maintain societal
order was the charismatic endowment of wisdom. A number of
texts point to this, including the legendary account of Solomon's request for and reception of the gift of wisdom from God:

> Give thy servant therefore an understanding mind to
> govern this thy people, that I may discern between
> good and evil; for who is able to govern this, thy
> great people.[10]

A similar text is found in Isa 11:1-11 in the depiction of the
ideal king who is described as one who rules justly by means of
certain charismatic gifts, among which is the "spirit of wisdom."

Therefore, the ideal of a just and orderly society is an
intimate part of the views of the wise, and it is kingship,
divinely ordained and guided by the divine gift of wisdom, that
must insure the order of Israelite society, and that leads the
society into a beneficent relationship with the cosmos.

Wisdom and Mankind

The sages of Israel also come to speak of anthropological
order, often referred to in terms of "the way" or "the path"
which those who sought to live in harmony with the beneficent
spheres of world order were to follow. This anthropological
order contained divinely instituted norms which were to regu-
late the behavior of the followers of wisdom. Those who followed the dictates of orderly existence, whether they concern
the correct behavior with respect to the proper social etiquette or whether they involve the ethical responsibility of
caring for the impoverished and destitute, were considered to
belong to one of two anthropological categories which the wise
constructed: the religio-ethical category of the righteous
(צדיקים). However, those who, either by ignorance or willful
disdain, failed to follow the norms of sagacious behavior were
placed within the religio-ethical category of the wicked (רשעים)
who by means of their own actions were planting the seeds for
eventual destruction and removal from society. But those who
possessed wisdom had the key to understand the norms for correct anthropological behavior, and thus may develop the proper
decorum which leads to their own well-being. Thus one sage ex-
claims in Prov 3:13-18:

> Happy is the man who finds wisdom,
>   and the man who gets understanding,
> For the gain from it is better than gain from silver
>   and its profit better than gold.
> She is more precious than jewels,
>   and nothing you desire can compare with her.
> Long life is in her right hand;
>   in her left hand are riches and honor.
> Her ways are ways of pleasantness,
>   and her paths are peace.
> She is a tree of life to those who lay hold of her;
>   those who hold her fast are called happy.

Wisdom and the Sages

Though we find manifold expressions of the wise with respect to many of their concerns, unfortunately they rarely speak of themselves, their professions, their tasks, and the institutions to which they may have belonged. This reticence, inexplicable as it may seem, is especially true of the sages who functioned within pre-exilic society. We find them speaking about the court, farming, legal jurisprudence, and, as we shall argue, even the cult, but are we to conclude that this makes them royal courtiers, farmers, judges, and priests? Furthermore, may we say that the wise could legitimately be described as a movement with a common profession and a commonly shared *Standesethik*? This may be the case, but it remains for broad and penetrating assessments by scholars who heretofore have too easily acquiesced to impressive theories concerning the profession and function of the wise, but which are often devoid of textual evidence.[11] Thus in seeking any possible description of the pre-exilic wise in ancient Israel, we shall have to step outside the boundaries of wisdom literature, if that is possible in a time when "everything under the sun" reeks of wisdom ideas, language, and influence.

In examining certain non-wisdom texts such as the Joseph Narrative, the Succession Document, the Deuteronomistic redacted Books of Kings, and the prophetical books of Isaiah and Jeremiah, we are presented with depictions of sages who found their primary locus in the royal court where they functioned a a professional class of royal bureaucrats, counsellors, military generals, judges, and diplomats; in other words they are

presented as the "Men of the King." As such, they were delegated the tasks of serving as agents of the king in carrying
out his divine commission to establish and protect societal order within the Israelite kingdom. This is true with respect to
Joseph, Ahithophel, Hushai, the wise woman of Tekoa, the wise
woman of Abel of Bethma'acah, the wise mentioned in Isaiah and
Jeremiah, and Baruch, the scribe of Jeremiah, who was an intimate associate of the royal officials in Jerusalem. But again
we are depending upon non-sapiential texts for such a depiction
of the wise, though in approaching these texts, we would argue
that supportable evidence should be indicated that will contra-
dict the depiction of the pre-exilic sages as "Men of the King,"
rather than arguing that because the sages themselves do not
speak of their own duties and functions we must maintain a
skeptical view of depictions in non-sapiential texts.

If the pre-exilic sages found their locus in the royal
court, and again the evidence for such is non-sapiential, it is
plausible that the training of such sages took place within the
context of a royal school, though here we move from the realm
of limited evidence to that of non-existent evidence, making
the theory of royal schools pure speculation.[12] Even so, comparable literature from the other cultures of the ancient Near
East was composed within the milieu of schools which were also
used for the training of bureaucrats and officials, and it does
seem reasonable to suggest that for the practical functioning
of the kingdom of Israel, and, early on, even a small but important empire, trained officials were necessitated, and it
would seem plausible to suggest that such training occurred
within a royal school which was partially responsible for the
creating of wisdom literature.

We are on more steady ground when we come to examine certain sages of the late post-exilic period, for in this time we
find sages who are obviously no longer functionaries of a non-
existent royal institution, but rather, at least with regard to
Sirach, teachers in a school with circles of disciples, though
whether or not such schools were connected to the central temple is impossible conclusively to say. Yet it may be reasonably

argued that the sages, at least by the time of Sirach, found a new locus to replace kingship, and that was the torah, for the law of God became the possession of the wise who were concerned with its proper interpretation and formulation into rules for sapiential existence.

Now it is interesting, in this connection, to point to the Chronicler's interpretation of Ezra, for he makes this Jewish official who functioned as the Minister of Jewish Religion in the Persian empire a "scribe of Torah."[13] One could conceivably see in this depiction of Ezra the model of the post-exilic sage, at least in the eyes of the Chronicler, and certainly this would correspond with the picture we have of Sirach. Once more, however, the purpose and function of the sage is to extend the orders of reality into the social and anthropological spheres, only in the case of the post-exilic sage, this is done by the study of torah and the following of its dictates by his society. In other words, society is to be based on the correct norms of orderly existence found embedded within the torah of God.

B. *The Views of Cult in Israelite Wisdom Literature*

Proverbs 1-9

Introduction. Proverbs 1-9 is one of eight major collections[14] found within the Book of Proverbs,[15] and contains diverse types[16] of sapiential materials, including instructions,[1] wisdom poems,[18] and different kinds of proverbs,[19] redacted in a compact collection and introduced by a superscription in 1:1 which translates: "The Proverbs of Solomon, Son of David, King of Israel."

Until recently, it was commonly asserted that this collection and its contents were the latest proverbial material, appearing in the late Post-Exile.[20] Such an assertion has been based on the following arguments. The first argument involves the appearance of what were described as rather lengthy forms in the collection, and, since it had been assumed that there was a gradual development from simple, laconic forms (e.g., the one line proverb) to more developed ones, this superabundance

of developed, lengthy forms supported a late origin.[21] The
second argument centers on certain theological ideas which were
believed appropriate for the Post-Exile: the personification of
wisdom, thought to betray Greek influence, the role of wisdom
as mediator between man and a transcendent deity, the appearance of wisdom as a prophetess, evidence of the growing nationalization of wisdom, including the stress on the "fear of the
Lord," and the close relationship of the collection to Sirach
in forms and theology.[22] The third argument centers on the
language and style of the collection which was said to have
been influenced by Greek literature, especially as pertains to
the length of sentences,[23] and by Deutero-Isaiah, Deuteronomy,
and the Deuteronomistic redaction.[24]

However, recent scholarship has dismissed as erroneous or
at least has questioned many of these arguments used to but-
tress a post-exilic dating. The form-critical argument is
based upon the erroneous assumption that there is a slow and
perceivable development of forms from more simple to more complex ones, and upon the failure to recognize that Proverbs 1-9
contains ten "instructions," a form which existed in Egypt as
early as the period of the Old Kingdom.[25] The occurrence of
wisdom poems in this collection cannot be adduced as evidence
for lateness, since comparable poems are present in much older
ancient Near Eastern wisdom sources, and since, as we shall
demonstrate in Chapter V, the Israelite wise were writing wisdom poems in the pre-exilic period. In addition, Christa
Bauer-Kayatz has argued cogently that the wisdom figure in
Proverbs 8 and 9 is influenced neither by a prophetic model nor
by Greek hypostatization, but rather by the speeches of Egyptian goddesses, especially divine *Ma'at*, and, since Egyptian
influence was most prevalent during the Solomonic period, it is
probable that such speeches could occur during this very early
period.[26] In addition, she demonstrates that the assumed influence by the prophets upon the wisdom literature could just
as well be reversed, i.e., the wise may have influenced the
prophetic language and thought.[27]

The theological argument involving the idea that personification and hypostatization are late developments ignores

other examples of personification and hypostatization in Israelite literature coming from the pre-exilic age: the personification of Israel as the bride of Yahweh and of death (e.g.,
Ps 49:15f.), and the hypostatization of the angel of the Lord
at least as early as E (Gen 21:17, 31:11; and Ex 14:19).[28]
Furthermore, the transcendent deity in Proverbs 1-9 conforms
completely to the general picture of deity in wisdom thought,
that is, the deity is primarily a transcendent creator and
guarantor of retribution, and not the Lord of Salvation History.
Added to this is the counter theological argument which observes the absence of salvation history themes in the collection which are present in Sirach and the Wisdom of Solomon.
The idea that the collection is late, since it exudes a deeper
sense of piety as may be seen in the stress on "the fear of the
Lord," overlooks or conveniently excises the occurrences of
such a phrase in the other proverbial collections (10:27; 14:
26, 27; 15:16; etc.), and is based upon the disputable thesis
that the early wise were non-religious, secular, career-
oriented, statesmen who functioned with a radicalized intellectual empiricism, and who would not tolerate doctrinaire, chau-
vinistic theologies.[29]

The question of dating does have some consequence for our
investigation, since the references to cult in this collection
could be argued to be the result of a post-exilic spirit which
includes a growing awareness of nationalistic emphases which
would encompass cultic concerns supposedly not in evidence in
earlier wisdom. Since most of the arguments for a post-exilic
dating can be negated, we tend to accept a pre-exilic dating
following the arguments of Bauer-Kayatz, and would add other
arguments including the absence of aramaisms, salvation history, and an emphasis upon Torah as the source of wisdom.[30] It
is especially striking that there are no references to Torah in
this section in view of the probable thesis that in Ezra one
finds a model of the fifth century sage whose primary role is
study and interpretation of Torah, the true source of wisdom
according to Sirach (39:1).

Proverbs 3:9-10. The third instruction in Proverbs 1-9
(3:1-12)[31] is an instruction given to schoolboys to incorporate

145

within their hearts "the fear of the Lord"[32] which involved
subjection of will, reverence, piety, and trust in the deity
who is the ultimate source of wisdom, for he was believed to
guide the god-fearer in the correct course of behavior that
would result in blessing and well-being.

This instruction includes an admonition for cultic participation in vv. 9-10:

Honor[33] the Lord with your prosperity and with the
first fruits of all your produce,[34]
So that your barns will be filled with grain,[35] and
your wine vats will burst with new wine.

The form of vv. 9-10 is that of the admonition (v. 9), followed
by two consequential clauses stating the benefits derived from
adhering to the admonition.[36] The content involves the participation in the presentation of "first fruits" to the Lord, an
activity taking place during the major agricultural festivals
(Unleavened Bread--the barley harvest; Weeks--the wheat harvest; and Tents--the vintage harvest).[37] The cultic understanding of the presentation of first fruits to the cultic officials
in the holy place sees the offering not as a gift to the deity,
but rather as a desacralization of the agricultural produce
which belonged in its entirety to the deity, and was therefore
sacred. By returning to the deity the first, and presumably
the best, of the crop the remainder was desacralized and subsequently could be used for profane consumption.[38] The presentation of first fruits was also a part of Israelite social
legislation, since the first fruits were to be eaten by cultic
personnel who served in the cultic centers.[39] In addition it
is well known that during these agrarian festivals taking place
in Israel during the cultic year the community celebrated and
re-experienced the benefits of salvation history which were associated with these festivals perhaps as early as the time of
the tribal federation.[40]

The motivation for participation in the presentation of
the first fruits given by our sage is that of blessing which
will come to the participant as a result of his cultic observance,[41] a blessing in the form of increased harvests and agricultural yields, and as such was given a wisdom intonation

involving the principle of retribution, or what the Germans term *Tun-Ergehen-Zusammenhang*, the idea that a particular deed leads to a certain result, a process that is controlled and overseen by the deity.[42] By observing the sage's admonition, the wise student will incorporate himself within the beneficent spheres of cosmic, social, and cultic order established and maintained by the deity for the blessing of the righteous. While it is impossible to determine if the sage is concerned either with the cultic understanding of first fruits as desacralization, the celebration of salvation history during the agrarian festivals, or with the social concern for cultic personnel, what is obvious is that the sage and his students are seen as functioning members of the cultic community.[43]

The Strange Woman. The complex of material centering on the controversial motif of the "Strange Woman" has significance for our investigation, especially so if Böstrom's thesis that she is to be identified as a devotee of a fertility goddess possesses cogent argumentation.[44]

The "Strange Woman" occupies the central position of concern in four instructions (2:1-22, 5:1-23, 6:24-35, and 7:1-27) and one didactic poem (9:1-6, 13-17). In each case she is described as a seductress whose sexual promiscuity leads to the entrapment of wisdom students, and the result of such a liaison is grimly depicted as "death." According to the wise teachers, the avoidance of such a liaison and the dreadful consequences to which such an affair leads rests in the devotion of the young students to wisdom which, at times, also is personified as a beautiful seductress and as a fertility goddess, though the intended contrast between the "Strange Woman" and wisdom is that the latter leads to life.

In approaching this complex of sapiential material, the primary concern is to identify as specifically as possible the "Strange Woman," no easy task in itself as may be concluded from the many differences of opinion among wisdom scholars[45] and the fact that adultery, prostitution, and fertility rites were lumped together in the Israelite literature, presumably since the three different subjects were activities involving

illicit sexual behavior. The "Strange Woman" has been interpreted as an Israelite or foreign adulteress,[46] prostitute,
fertility priestess, or devotee of a fertility goddess (Anat,
Astarte, Ishtar); as a prostitute-magician mentioned in the
Maqlu series of Assyrian oaths;[47] and as a literary personification of folly who is contrasted to the personification of
wisdom. Let us begin our attempts to identify this rather perplexing figure by examining each individual pericope devoted to
this enigmatic female.

The first mention of the "Strange Woman" (אשה זרה and
נכריה)[48] is found in the second instruction, 2:1-22, which involves a teacher admonishing his students to seek wisdom, for a
successful quest will preserve them from the menace of evil men
and the "Strange Woman." In this instruction, the "Strange Woman" is described as possessing "seductive speech" (אמריה
החליקה), as one who "deserts the husband of her youth" (העזבת
אלוף נעוריה), and as one who "forgets the covenant of her god"
(ואת-ברית אלהיה שכחה). Such a description best fits an Israelite adulteress who is unfaithful to her husband, and thus
breaks the covenant commandment prohibiting adultery. It is
possible, however, to regard the "Strange Woman" in this context as a married Israelite woman who either has turned to
prostitution in order to support herself or has become a fertility devotee or priestess who, as a sacral functionary, is
supported within the structure of the community of the cult by
receiving her share of the offerings. A cultic dimension of
adultery could be strengthened by the possible translation of
v. 18:

> For her temple[49] bows[50] down to Mot,
> And her courts[51] to the Rephaim.[52]

But the terms for "prostitute" (זונה) and "sacred harlot"
(קדשה) are not found, thus making the identity of the "Strange
Woman" in this context as a prostitute or temple harlot only a
suggestive possibility.

The eighth instruction (5:1-23) is devoted entirely to the
"Strange Woman" who is described as one whose "lips drip honey"
and whose "mouth is smoother than oil," metaphors which succeed

not only in depicting in seductive terms an enticing woman, but also in describing the seductress in literary images which are associated with the specific types of payment made to prostitutes and temple priestesses.[53] Once more a liaison with her leads the young fool to death, a fate that is given a certain vividness in v. 5, an old crux, which we argue is best translated:

> Her sexual organs descend upon Mot,
> Her aroused vagina embraces Sheol.[54]

If the "Strange Woman" is a paid prostitute in this context, then vv. 7-11 would refer to the young man's wasting of his life's resources in the misspent life of a profligate who squanders the resources of his family which are enjoyed by those outside his familial social unit. However, if one should regard her as a fertility prostitute, then בית נכרי should be translated "Strange Temple" (v. 10), and פתח ביתה (v. 8) as "door of her temple." Finally, the "strangers" who are the recipients of the young man's wealth and labors could be regarded as sacred functionaries within a fertility cult. But again we are speculating, for the text contains nothing that would allow us to decide whether she is to be regarded as a prostitute for hire or as a temple priestess.

We are more fortunate in the ninth instruction (6:20-35), most of which concerns the "Strange Woman," for in this case she is easily identified as an Israelite adulteress, since she is referred to as an אשת רע ("a neighbor's wife"),[55] an אשת איש ("another's wife"), and a אשה נאף ("an adulterous woman"). Furthermore, a description of the wrath of a cuckolded husband is presented (vv. 29-35). Finally, the price paid to a prostitute (זונה), "a loaf of bread," is contrasted to the price an adulterer must pay, namely his life (v. 26).

Thus far a cultic interpretation of the "Strange Woman" has been difficult to prove, but in the tenth instruction, 7:1-27, we find material more conducive to a specifically cultic identification. In this instruction, the teacher instructs the young student to cultivate a love for Mistress Wisdom (v. 4) who will preserve him from the seduction of the "Strange Woman" (v. 5).[56]

Verses 6-7 present a difficult textual problem, for, depending on which textual tradition one follows, these verses
describe either "Mistress Wisdom" or the "Strange Woman." In
following the MT, which has the first person (אבינה, נשקפתי,
אשנב, ביתי), one could conclude that wisdom is personified as
a fertility goddess who is observing the seduction of a young
man, a wisdom student. However, if one follows the textual
tradition represented by the LXX and the Syriac translations,
which have the third person (תרא, נשקפה, אשנב, ביתה), then one
would find in vv. 6-7 a description of the "Strange Woman."

The intriguing description of this one "who looks out the
lattice of the window" is paralleled by a number of Phoenician
ivory plaques found in Samaria, Arslan Tash, Nimrud, and
Khorsabad which depict a fertility goddess looking through the
lattice of her window, as well as by the παρακυπτουσα of Cyprus.[57] Thus there is good evidence to support the position
that vv. 6f. refer to a sacral priestess or a devotee of a fertility goddess who dresses in her sacral garb and takes to the
streets in order to induce a young man to join her in fertility
rites.[58]

Verses 14-15 seem to support this interpretation. The
woman says to the young man:

> I must offer communion sacrifices,
> Today I shall have fulfilled my vows.[59]
> Consequently, I have come forth to meet you,
> To seek you out, and I have found you.

The woman indicates that she is in the process of presenting
communion sacrifices, a type of sacrifice practiced in Israel
and in Canaan which had as its purpose the ritualistic binding
together of deity and communicants by means of a communion repast in which the deity, priestly officials, worshipper, and
guests share (Lev 17:11-21, I Sam 9:11-13, and Jer 7:21).[60] In
Israel after the "devouring" of the fat and intestines by the
deity, certain pieces were presented to the cultic officials,
and the remainder was eaten at home by the one making the offering and by the guests who are invited. That the meal at
home was a sacral repast is seen in the fact that the participants had to be in a state of ritual purity. Furthermore, a

specific type of communion sacrifice was the votive offering, involving the fulfillment of a vow after the deity had ful- filled his part of the obligation by granting the worshipper's request, and as such, with respect to the meal, the sacrifice had to be eaten on the day the sacrifice took place and on the following day, since whatever remained following that time be- came defiled and could not be eaten. Thus the woman has made a vow with her deity, and is now in the process of fulfilling her obligation by offering a communion sacrifice and participating in a communion meal.

It appears, however, that her fulfillment of the vow in- volves also the engaging in fertility rites. Such fertility rites in Canaanite religion appear to have followed communion sacrifices (Ex 32:1-6; Num 25:1f.), and thus her statement to the young man to come home with her to engage in sexual inter- course is not only simple adultery, but rather is an invita- tion to participate with her in fertility religion. McKane has objected that, while the woman does seem to be a devotee of a fertility goddess, vv. 19-20 indicate that her husband is away from home, and therefore she seeks to engage a young man in an adulterous affair.[61] However, we would suggest that it appears that her husband is a merchant, since he has "gone on a long journey" with "a bag of money," and he is engaged in business pursuits during the time of the "waxing of the new moon," deemed a propitious time for successful business activities. And he is going to return at כסא, the "full moon," a day con- sidered to be a time of "good fortune" and thus most advantage- ous for difficult and dangerous travel back home.[62] Further- more, the period of the "waning of the moon" during the lunar cycle was to be a time of cessation from business activities.[63] Also it is possible that the sacred time in which she is en- gaged in her cultic activities is that of the "New Moon," the time when the moon makes its first appearance in the heavens, and, of course, a sacred time celebrated in Israel and in Canaan.[64] In order to participate in the culmination of her sacral activities and to fulfill her vow, she needs a male partner, since her husband is away from home engaged in mercan- tile pursuits. So her statement concerning her husband's

absence need not be seen as an attempt to engage in sexual activity objectionable to her husband, since even the marriage of
temple prostitutes seems to have been common enough to require
legislation, and since sacred fertility rites were seen as acceptable within the cultic sphere even for those who were married.

Finally the ghastly description of the fate of those who
had succumbed to her propositions seems to be a close reflection of the slaughter of men by the goddess Anat in Canaanite
myth.[65]

Thus we would argue, then, that the woman in all likeli-
hood is a devotee of an ancient Near Eastern fertility goddess,
and is seeking to entice a young Israelite student into joining
with her in the sexual worship of her goddess within the context of a communion repast. Consequently, this admonition involves not only a warning against illicit sexual behavior, but
also specifically warns against participation by the wise in
fertility religion.

The poem in chapter 9 contrasts Dame Wisdom (Strophe I,
vv. 1-6) with Dame Folly, though both are depicted as fertility
goddesses engaged in cultic activities. The poem is among the
best artistically structured poems in Israelite wisdom literature, consisting of two strophes exhibiting external parallelism. Each strophe has 6 lines (12 hemistichs), and each line
possesses 3 + 3 meter.[66] In Strophe I, Dame Wisdom builds her
seven pillared temple which is located on the acropolis of the
city, prepares her cultic festival intended to initiate her new
sanctuary, and then sends forth her priestesses to invite new
cultic adherents to her festive meal. Those who accept the invitation will leave simpleness and gain insight, and as a result will find life.

This depiction of Dame Wisdom, coupled with similar texts
in 8:1-21 and 8:22-31, borrows heavily in terms of form from
first person speeches attributed to certain ancient Near Eastern goddesses who engage in self-praise (Inanna, Ishtar, Ma'at,
Isis).[67] However, are we to assume that wisdom is an actual
goddess to be worshipped, or is this either an example of the
hypostatization of wisdom in which a former attribute of Yahweh

is now given independent, personal existence, or of literary personification?[68]

With regard to the mythological theory that regards wisdom as an actual goddess, there is no doubt that the form of the speech of wisdom in chapter 8 is heavily influenced by the form of divine speeches, especially Egyptian goddesses, nor is there any doubt that the characteristics attributed to wisdom in these texts are borrowed from descriptions of ancient Near Eastern goddesses of fertility and wisdom.[69] Further, gods and goddesses of order and wisdom in the ancient Near East were certainly the recipients of sagacious worship, and this was especially true with respect to *Ma'at*.[70] Furthermore, Sirach's later reference to wisdom as one who dwells in "the assembly of the Most High," presumably as a goddess (chapter 24), and the description of wisdom as the "consort" of Yahweh in the Wisdom of Solomon (chapters 6-9) give further support to the mythological theory. Finally, W. F. Albright[71] has argued that these texts have been heavily influenced by non-extant Canaanite texts devoted to a Canaanite goddess of wisdom; an interesting theory, but unfortunately based upon meager evidence. Albright's contention is based upon references to El as "wise" in the Baal Cycle (*ANET*, p. 133), and upon a broken Aramaic text in Ahikar which seems to suggest that wisdom dwells as a goddess in heaven (vii, 95f., *ANET*, p. 428).

While the mythological theory is most attractive, we cannot support it, and choose rather to regard this as a bit of demythologizing or perhaps as literary mythologizing in which mythological ideas and symbols are used, but are not to be taken literally. For example, Deutero-Isaiah does this in the connection of the Red Sea tradition with the creation myth (Isa 51:9-11). Furthermore, the parallel texts in the Wisdom of Solomon could hardly be seen as an example of a goddess of wisdom in Israel, since the author is a rigid monotheist.

The second theory concerning the depiction of wisdom in chapter 9 is that offered by Ringgren, among others, who suggests that this text is an example of an hypostatization of an attribute of Yahweh. In this process wisdom is then an attribute of Yahweh which begins to assume its own distinct personal

existence, eventually is considered a functionary within the
divine council of Yahweh, and even takes on divine existence as
a goddess.

Finally, a number of scholars[72] have championed the position that wisdom is personified as a goddess in chapter 9, a
position that gains added merit when it is conceded that wisdom
is personified as a prophetess in 1:20-33. Furthermore, one
finds many parallel examples of literary personification in the
Bible: Jeremiah's and Hosea's personifications of Israel as the
bride of Yahweh and, even more similar to our passage, Ezekiel's
rather graphic depiction of Jerusalem and Samaria as unfaithful
lovers of Yahweh who became sacred prostitutes (Ezekiel 23).
In following this argument, wisdom would then be seen as a literary personification, and the language and symbols are those
of the fertility goddesses. Thus wisdom is personified as a
fertility goddess in order to present her as an enticing alternative to the "Strange Woman."

We tend to accept the last theory, and thus regard wisdom
personified as a fertility goddess, especially since Dame Wisdom sends forth her maidens not to entice people to participate
in fertility rites, but rather to be schooled in sapiential
nourishment. Thus we have here an example, not of a wisdom
goddess initiating her cult within the confines, say, of a wisdom school, but rather the utilization of mythological language
and symbols in order to give poetic expression to a sapiential
concept: through devotion to and a seeking of wisdom, one finds
life and the source of life, Yahweh.[73] Even as cultic religion
was perceived by Israel's priests to serve as the sphere of
mediation between the holy deity and profane man so that man
could approach the realm of the holy and enjoy the resulting
blessings, so the wise utilize cultic and mythological language
to speak of wisdom as the mediator between a transcendent deity
who ordered creation and the followers of wisdom. A similar
process is at work in 1:22-33 where wisdom is personified as a
prophetess embodying the revelatory word which confronts and
redeems man from ignorance, non-being, and destruction, and
leads him to Yahweh.

Furthermore, the adaptation of mythological and cultic language to describe the concept of wisdom is an excellent example of von Rad's musing concerning what is at work when the wise apparently use cultic language and ideas. The process in this case involves the effort by the wise to give poetic vividness and aesthetic attractiveness to the concept of wisdom in order to emphasize ideas which existed within the structure of their own ideology.[74]

The second strophe found in vv. 13-18 of chapter 9 involves, we would argue, a similar process in which "folly" (כסילות) is personified as a fertility goddess, for she is found enthroned in her temple located on the acropolis of the city and calls out to those who pass by to participate with her in a sacral meal involving fertility rites. In contrast to the life which Dame Wisdom offers her devotees, "Folly's" temple is presented as the gateway to the realm of the dead ruled by Mot and the Rephaim. The sapiential idea of folly is given poetic, mythological form by utilizing the imagery of a fertility goddess.

Now it seems rather striking to notice that in these descriptions of personified wisdom, folly, and the "Strange Woman," we have the sages utilizing the basic mythological characteristics of ancient Near Eastern fertility goddesses who were said to be goddesses of love and life, jealousy and death (war), and, at least as concerns Ishtar, wisdom. Yet only goddess wisdom truly leads to love and life, whereas folly and her devotees: the prostitute, the adulteress, the fertility devotee, and the fertility goddesses lead to death.

In conclusion, it is apparent that the "Strange Woman" is a rather motley figure who includes the adulteress, the prostitute, the fertility devotee, the fertility goddess, and finally the personification of folly as a fertility goddess. This fusion of different types seems most comparable to a similar blending together of the same types in the prophetic literature where they are again lumped together in an indistinguishable maze. What they share is obvious: sexual deviation from accepted socio-religious behavior, a deviation that appears to the Israelite sage to be the epitomy of folly[75] and the pathway to death. An avoidance of the "Strange Woman" includes a rejection of any type of illicit sexual behavior, including participation within the structure of fertility religion.

But the warning against cultic involvement in the fertility religions known to the Israelites is not based upon sacral law issuing forth from the Yahwistic polemic against the Canaanite and Mesopotamian fertility cults, but rather upon the sapiential ethos in which certain sexual relationships were completely rejected as being out of step with the righteous order of society expressed in social mores and customs. Finally, it seems most probable that such a warning against participation in illicit sexual relationships, including fertility rites,[76] would stem from the sapiential disdain of any activity in which passions were given free rein. Thus, for example, ecstatic religious behavior would characterize the "heated man," but not the true sage, the "silent man."

Proverbs 10-31

Sacrifice[77] *and Prayer.*[78] In the second[79] and fifth[80] major collections of Proverbs, the wise refer to the cultic acts of sacrifice and prayer: 15:8 (sacrifice and prayer), 15:29 (prayer), 17:1 (sacrifice), 21:3 (sacrifice), 21:27 (sacrifice), and 28:9 (prayer). And though admittedly these references are few in number, they should provide us with additional insight in the attempt to analyze the views of the Israelite wise concerning cultic religion.

The first mention of cultic ritual occurs in 15:8:

The sacrifice of the wicked is an abomination to the Lord,
But the prayer[81] of the upright obtains his favor.

The form of the saying is an antithetical, literary proverb[82] consisting of two stichoi, the most common form found in the first subdivision of the second collection (10-15). Gerhard von Rad has commented concerning this type of saying:

One can see that the contrasts are sharply opposed. But the endless possibility of variation in this literary form consists in the fact that these contrasts are not, in fact, precise opposites. What is said is not simply the opposite of what has gone

> before--that is, tautologically, with the elements
> completely reversed--that would be tedious. The
> antithesis has, in fact, a relative independence as
> a statement, while it turns the thought that has
> already been expressed, very freely into its oppo-
> site. In each case we have simply one possible
> opposite among many.[83]

Furthermore, such a saying, which is concerned with contrasting
the cultic involvement of the wicked with that of the righteous, certainly is evidence of serious theological reflection
by the wise concerning cultic participation in general and concerning what is or what is not acceptable cultic worship to
Yahweh.

In this proverb are we to conclude that the wise are contrasting two different cultic activities, i.e., sacrifice and
prayer, and therefore are stating that sacrifice is rejected by
Yahweh but prayer is accepted, or rather is the contrast emphasizing the radically different character of two opposing groups
as they participate in cultic worship, and that it is the character of the worshiper which makes a cultic activity acceptable
or unacceptable to Yahweh?[84] In our opinion, the emphasis is
not upon the contrast of two different cultic activities, sacrifice and prayer, but rather upon the character of the cultic
participants.[85] Cultic participation by the wicked, those
people whose behavior is immoral, disorderly, and not in tune
with the social dictates of the God of order, is cultically unacceptable, and instead of producing the desired results--the
obtaining of the blessing of the deity--actually is rejected as
'abhorrent.' However, the cultic participation of the upright,
those whose social and moral behavior is in accordance with the
demands of Yahweh, is judged acceptable to Yahweh, and thus the
blessings flowing through the channel of the cult may be obtained.[86] After all, the proverb does not read: "Sacrifice is
an abomination to Yahweh, but prayer obtains his favor," but
rather both nouns have qualifying genitives--"the sacrifice of
the wicked" and "the prayer of the upright."

That the antithesis is not contrasting sacrifice and
prayer also may be deduced by the recognition that sacrifice is
considered to have been accompanied by liturgical prayer uttered

by a priestly functionary who identifies the worshipper and describes the nature and purpose of the sacrifice (cf. II Chron 29:27f.; Dt 26:1f.). In fact, many of the psalms have been regarded as liturgical texts read during cultic services. This is especially true of the lament-thanksgiving service when sacrifices are accompanied by psalms of lament and thanksgiving.[87] The implication of this is that the reference to sacrifice and prayer in this antithetical proverb is the result of the variation of language typical of such proverbs and of the effort common to the wise to include, as much as possible, the totality of a particular activity, in this case the cultic activity of sacrifice and prayer.[88]

Furthermore, an examination of the word for 'sacrifice' (זבח) deserves close attention. זבח may refer to 'sacrifice' in general, i.e., any type of sacrifice, though in early cultic traditions it may refer to a specific type of sacrifice, the 'communion' or 'peace' offering.[89] If the more specific nuance of the term is intended in the proverb, then we have a concern with the communion sacrifice which, as discussed earlier, has as its primary intent the establishing of a communion between cultic personnel, the worshipper, his invited guests, and the deity as they participate in a cultic meal at a sanctuary. Such cultic participation was considered to result in the 'well-being' of the participants, a state indicated by a synonym for this sacrifice, שלם. The observation of the wise would indicate, then, that such a communion and subsequent state of well-being is impossible for the 'wicked.' In addition, according to cultic tradition a communion sacrifice could not be offered by a sinner, since he had to offer a sacrifice of expiation which did not include any communion meal.[90] Only those who had not disturbed the sacral and moral orders of the cultic community were allowed to participate within the framework of a communion sacrifice and meal.[91] Such a proverb, then, would correspond to the understanding of the priestly creators of ritual and sacral law.

That the wise were well aware of priestly sacral law also seems apparent in the usage of priestly terms which designated

158

whether or not a cultic activity was acceptable to Yahweh. תועבה is found in cultic traditions to describe social and cultic practices which were considered morally repugnant or cultically abhorrent to Yahweh,[92] while רצון is a designation made by a priest who, after examining a cultic offering or activity, declares it is acceptable.[93] Statements to the effect that the priests were concerned with proper ritual, whereas the wise were concerned with the moral and social character of the worshippers, may be rejected out of hand when one sees in certain "Entrance Liturgies" (Psalms 15, 24) and in the Holiness Code (especially chapter 19) that members of the sacral community had to exhibit moral character. In the "Entrance Liturgies" those seeking to participate within the sphere of cult were allowed entrance to the holy only if they could deny any complicity in wrongdoing. Certainly, the emphasis of the wise in this proverb is on the character of the cultic participants, not on whether a sacrifice met the proper ritual requirements. That was for the priests to decide, but it is apparent that the priests were just as concerned with the moral integrity of the worshippers.[94]

The second reference to cultic activity is found in 15:29:

The Lord is far from the wicked,
But he hears the prayer of the righteous.

The form of this saying is also an antithetical, literary proverb consisting of two stichoi in which the emphasis is placed upon those who may have access to the realm of the holy, and, therefore, may benefit from the fortune-working sphere of cultic blessing. While the cultic terms for 'approaching' Yahweh (קרב, נגש) are not present in the saying, the occurrence of their opposite, רחוק, should be noted. In Ex 24:1-2 (J), only Moses is allowed "to draw near" (נגש) to God on the Mount, whereas Aaron, Nadab, Abihu, and the seventy elders had to stand from afar (מרחק). Similarly in Ex 20:18f. (JE) the congregation at Mt. Sinai stood from afar (מרחק), whereas only Moses 'drew near' (נגש). Therefore, in this proverb the point is made that only the righteous enjoy access to Yahweh, whereas the wicked do not. Such an access is concretely described in

terms of the cultic act of prayer which Yahweh 'will hear,' a
term usually implying 'with favor' (Num 20:16, Dt 33:7, and I
Kgs 8:45).

The prayer of the righteous is an important motif in many
Old Testament traditions, and involves the idea of being able
to approach the deity with a petition that will be granted a
favorable response. Abraham's intercession for Sodom (Gen 18:
22f.) and for Abimelech (Genesis 20), Job's intercession for
his opponents (42:7f.), and the petition of a righteous lamenter (Psalms 7, 17, etc.) are examples of the importance placed
upon the prayer of the righteous. That the wise shared this
concept is evident in this literary saying.

In 17:1 we have a 'Better' saying[95] which speaks of cult:

> Better is a dry morsel with quiet than a temple[96]
> filled with sacrificial feasting and contention.

In a 'Better' saying, two points are compared with a decision
being made by the wise that one is preferable to the other. In
such a comparison the judgment is made even more striking by
the fact that what is judged preferable is often rather meager
and undesirable in and of itself ('a dry morsel,' a 'little'--
Prov 16:8, 'reproach'--Prov 27:5), whereas that which is judged
less preferable often is in and of itself bountiful, pleasur-
able, desirable ("a temple filled with sacrificial feasting,"
"large income"--Prov 16:8, "love"--Prov 27:5). Yet what makes
that which is undesirable or meager more preferable than that
which by itself would seem desirable or bountiful is due to the
practice by the wise of appending qualifying adjectives and
phrases which provide the limits of a particular context or
condition.

Thus the point is not that a 'dry morsel' is more desirable than a sacrificial feast, but rather quiet solitude in
one's meager repast is far preferable to sumptuous cultic dining taking place in an atmosphere of strife. The saying should
not be taken as a lambast of the wise against cultic activities
occurring in the temple, but rather as an emphasis upon the
supreme desirability of tranquility, even with certain limitations, to strife, even in the best possible surroundings.

Again, it should be noted that the purpose of a communion
sacrifice followed by a communion meal was to achieve communion
between the participants and the deity and to establish harmony
and well-being, so that strife in such a context is the opposite of what was intended in the ritual.[97] Such a text demonstrates that the wise were quite aware of cultic theology and
were in accord with it.

A second 'Better' saying that involves a reference to cult
is 21:3:

> The establishing of righteousness and justice is
> more acceptable[98] to the Lord than sacrifice.

It is, of course, possible to regard this saying as a polemic
against the cultic practice of sacrifice, and, therefore, as
evidence of a tension existing between the wise and the practitioners of cultic ritual. However, some of the edge is taken
off this argument when one realizes that it is conceivable that
the clause, "the establishing of righteousness and justice,"
may have been taken from a priestly torah in which only those
who "establish righteousness and justice" and are judged צדיק
may enter into the sacred place to participate in cult. Ezekiel utilizes such a priestly torah which contains in the introduction the statement: ואיש כי-יהיה צדיק ועשה משפט וצדקה. Then
follows a list of cultic, moral, and social sins which one must
not be guilty of committing in order to be judged צדיק, one who
"establishes righteousness and justice."[99] Only after a denial
of such sins and a receiving from the priest a declaration of
being a צדיק may one enter into the cultic realm in order to
participate in cultic activities.

Yet, this is not to deny that in a scale of values the
wise were more praiseworthy of the establishing and maintaining
of cosmic and societal order by means of 'orderly' behavior
than of sacrifice. But it is not inconceivable that the priests
were of the same opinion. In fact, one who was judged רשע was
not allowed to participate in cult, and, if found guilty of
certain 'unforgiveable crimes,' deliberate crimes which could
not be removed by ritual atonement, he was removed from the
sacral community and even put to death (see Leviticus 20).[100]

One should also recognize that a 'Better' saying does not necessarily judge what is less valued as intrinsically bad, but
that with which it is compared is of more value.[101]

Finally, the term for 'sacrifice' once again is זבח, and,
if it is given the more specific meaning of 'communion sacrifice,' then we have additional evidence that the wise were well
aware that those not judged to be צדיק by the priest could not
participate in a communion ritual.

The final proverb in the second collection which refers to
sacrifice is 21:27:

> The sacrifice of the wicked is an abomination,
> How much more so[102] when he brings it with an evil
> design.

This saying is a comparative, literary proverb which utilizes
according to von Rad the argument *a maiore ad minus* ("if here,
then how much more there"),[103] an argument in which the observation made in the first stichos takes on added import when the
condition or circumstance pointed to in the second stichos is
appended. In this proverb the wise once more are familiar with
the cultic pronouncement of "abomination" with respect to the
sacrifice of the wicked, but add that it is even more abhorrent
when brought with an evil design, i.e., to obtain the aid of
the deity in a wicked activity or to be foolish enough to try
to receive the divine blessing while engaged in wickedness.

It is interesting to observe that the word translated
'evil design,' זמה, is found in cultic traditions to refer to,
in most cases, sexual sins which are judged to be "abominations"
(תועבות) to Yahweh.[104] Since both תועבה and זמה are used in
this proverb, it is conceivable that the wise are again utilizing cultic language and the specific cultic meaning which that
language conveys, and, as a result, are in agreement once more
with their priestly colleagues.[105]

The only reference to prayer in the fifth collection occurs in 28:9:

> He who turns his ear from the hearing of instruction,
> Even his prayer is an abomination.

This saying is the most simple of the sayings and does not exhibit any obvious parallelism, though it is quite similar to

certain participial laws in the legal codes.[106] The term *tôrâh* could be regarded as either sapiential instruction or priestly law. If the latter is the case, then the wise have again agreed with their priestly colleagues that worship, in this case prayer, is judged to be abhorrent to Yahweh if the worshipper is not 'obedient' to the priestly instruction. If the sapiential instruction is intended, then the wise would indicate that there is a close relationship between obedience to wisdom instruction and cultic prayer.

The image of 'not hearing' is a common one in sapiential literature. Ptah-hotep argued:

> To hear is of advantage for a son who hearkens. If hearing enters into a hearkener, the hearkener becomes a hearer. (When) hearing is good, speaking is good. Every hearkener (is) an advantage, and hearing is better than anything that is, (and thus) comes the goodly love (of a man). How good it is when a son accepts what his father says! Thereby *maturity* comes to him. He whom god loves is a hearkener, (but) he whom god hates cannot hear. It is the heart which brings up its lord as one who hears or as one who does not hear. The life, prosperity, and health of a man is his heart...[107]

In Egyptian wisdom texts the heart was considered to be that organ which received the sapiential instruction and then initiated wise actions. A fool was dubbed as a man who was "without heart." The Israelite wise appeared to have borrowed this expression, as Solomon, for example, in I Kings 3 prayed for a 'hearing heart' in order to receive the divine wisdom that would enable him to rule as a just king and judge.[108] The point in the proverb is that one who does not obey sapiential instruction, thus devoid of a 'hearing heart,' is incapable of acting wisely, and, therefore, is in no position to petition or make requests from Yahweh in the form of prayer, for only a wise and righteous individual is able to do so.

The Vow. The second and seventh collections each contain a reference to the cultic vow: 20:25 and 31:2. 20:25 may be translated:

> It is a snare for a man to declare impetuously: "It is sacred,"
> And to reflect only after making his vows.

The form of the saying is a synthetic, literary proverb in which the second stichos extends the thought of the first. The proverb makes the judgment that, before one obligates himself to a vow, he should engage in a careful, judicious process of examination to determine whether or not he is capable of fulfilling his obligation to the deity.[109]

A vow usually involves a bargain with the deity in that, if the deity grants one's petition, then the petitioner will fulfill a particular vow that he has made.[110] In the course of making a vow, one announces that the promised activity, commitment, or possession is 'holy' (קדש), i.e., it is to be set apart for divine service or usage if the deity grants his petition. In declaring something 'to be holy,' it is then transferred from the sphere of the profane to the sacral realm. A good example of a vow is that of Absalom who vows to sacrifice to God at Hebron, if he is returned to the good graces of David (II Sam 15:7f.). The most common situation for the vow within the sphere of the cult was during the lament in which the one lamenting vowed to do something for God, most often to return to the sanctuary in order to offer up a thanksgiving sacrifice accompanied by a thanksgiving psalm, if God would deliver him from his distress (cf. Pss 56:12-13 and 66:13-15).

The best known example of a hasty and rather foolish vow was the one made by Jepthah in Jg 11:30-39 who vowed to sacrifice as a burnt offering the first one to meet him from his house as he returned from the hoped for military victory over the Ammonites, and, of course, to his dismay, this 'one' turned out to be his own daughter.[111] Such an incident also shows the extreme seriousness of the obligation that one has to fulfill a vow, for failure to do so met with destruction from the deity.[112]

It should be noted that the wise in this proverb are not counseling their adherents to refrain from making vows, but rather are stressing that, before any vow is made, considerations of the seriousness of the vow and especially of the matter of being able to carry out the pledge should be made. Again we find the wise in harmony with priestly traditions concerning the vow:

> When a man vows a vow to the Lord, or swears an oath
> to bind himself by a pledge, he shall not break his
> word: he shall do according to all that proceeds out
> of his mouth (Num 30:2).

> When you make a vow to the Lord your God, you shall
> not be slack to pay it; for the Lord your God will
> surely require it of you, and it would be sin in you.
> But if you refrain from vowing, it shall be no sin
> in you. You shall be careful to perform what has
> passed your lips, for you have voluntarily vowed to
> the Lord your God what you have promised with your
> mouth (Dt 23:21-23).[113]

The second reference to the vow occurs in 31:2:

> What my son? What son of my womb?
> What, son of my vows?

The reference to "son of my vows" reflects the common cultic
practice of a woman who, devoid of male offspring, makes a vow
committing her to a particular obligation if the deity grants
her a son. The best example is that of Hannah who "devotes"
Samuel to cultic service in Shiloh in fulfillment of her vow
(I Sam 1:1f.).

The Sacred Lots.[114] The priestly consultation of the oracle by means of the casting of sacred lots referred to as *Urim*
and *Thummim* is mentioned in the second collection in 16:33:

> From the breastplate the lot is cast,
> But the decision is from the Lord.

Again we have an antithetical, literary proverb emphasizing a
theological reflection of the wise concerning a cultic activity.
The sacred lots were the possession of the chief priest who apparently kept them in the breastplate (חשן) attached to the
ephod, a priestly garment (I Sam 2:18, 28). When a decision
from Yahweh was desired, the priest would cast forth the lots,
and the answer to a yes or no question would be made. Such a
mechanical means of obtaining an oracle of Yahweh was in practice until after the time of David when it seems to have been
replaced by the prophetic oracle. The next reference to the
sacred lots occurs during the time of Ezra and Nehemiah when
again they appear in the possession of the priests, perhaps
coinciding with the "death" of prophecy in the Post-Exilic
period.[115]

Once more we find the wise functioning as critics of the
popular misunderstanding of cultic activities by emphasizing
that the lots have no magical power in and of themselves, but
rather it is Yahweh who acts in giving the decision (מש‎פט), a
view most probably shared by the priests themselves.[116]

Cultic Language in Proverbs. We have mentioned already in
other contexts the noticeable usage of cultic language by the
wise, and it appears in the previous cases that cultic language
by the wise at times coincides with cultic meaning associated
with that language, but not always. Without pretending to be
comprehensive in considering this complex problem, one more example of the possible usage of cultic language by the wise
needs to be examined. The case in point is 16:6:

> Iniquity (עון) by means of steadfast love and faith-
> fulness is expiated (יכפר),
> And in the fear of the Lord there is a turning away
> from evil.

The first stichos of this synthetic, literary proverb has been
regarded by a number of scholars as a polemic against the cultic idea that sin is atoned for only by means of cultic sacrifice, whereas the wise, using cultic language ("atonement,"
כפר), have argued that it is the steadfast love (חסד) and faithfulness (אמת) of an individual that expiates sin.[117]

However, we prefer to regard the wise once more as critics
of a popular misunderstanding of cultic ritual that would involve the magical conception of sacrifice, that is, that there
is some magical power within the ritual itself that automatically expiates the sins of the worshipper.[118] They do this by
stressing an idea certainly current in non-wisdom traditions
that it is the 'steadfast love' and 'faithfulness' not only of
the worshipper but also of Yahweh which cause him to act to remove the guilt of sin (cf. Ex 32:30, and esp. 34:7f.). Von Rad
cogently observes that according to cultic tradition expiation
by sacrifice is 'a saving event,' meaning that Yahweh acts to
remove the guilt of the worshipper offering the sacrifice.[119]
He acts to remove sin because of his "steadfast love" for his
people and "faithfulness" to his promise to forgive sins which
commit him to act, and not because of any magical power unleashed in the sacrifice that would force him to do so.

Job (The Narrative)

Introduction. That the Joban Narrative was originally an independent didactic narrative which had its own rather protracted as well as complex development separate and apart from the poetic Job is a position which has been accepted by the large majority of modern students of Job.[120] However, exactly how that development may be traced out by means of traditio-historical research does not receive such unanimity.[121] It does appear that the legend had its origin in a non-Israelite wisdom setting, probably in Canaan,[122] if Sarna's analysis proves correct,[123] eventually made its way into Israelite sapiential traditions, and received its final redaction in the early post-exilic period before being inserted by the Joban poet into his own work.[124] The narrative was used by the poet to provide a framework for his own writing and as a popular drawing card, though it is doubtful that the story was intended to furnish any theological contribution to the poet's own very different creation.

The sapiential character of the legend may be seen, first of all, in regard to wisdom terminology: Job's description as one who was "blameless (תם) and upright (ישר)" (1:1; cf. Prov 2:21, 28:10, 29:10), and as one who "feared God and turned away from evil" (1:1; cf. Prov 3:7, 14:16, 16:6); and the description of Job's wife as one of the "foolish women" (2:10; cf. Prov 9:13). Secondly, one also notices the presence of sapiential forms: the casting of the tale into the form of a didactic narrative (cf. Mesopotamia: "The Legend of Ahikar," "Tale of the Poor Man of Nippur," and "The Three Ox-Drivers from Adab"; Egypt: "Lament of the Eloquent Peasant," "The Prophecy of Neferrohu," "Sinuhe," and "The Tale of Two Brothers"; and Israel: possibly the "Joseph Story");[125] elements from the *Streitgespräch*, including the missing disputation between Job and the three friends and the judgment of Yahweh (cf. Akkadian fables);[126] and the proverb in 1:21 (cf. Koh 5:14). Thirdly, a number of sapiential themes run throughout the narrative: theodicy, Job's refusal to speak rashly (cf. Prov 19:11), the idea that God knows the 'hearts' of men (cf. Prov 15:11), retribution, and the emphasis upon the prayer of a righteous man (cf. Prov 15:8).

If we are correct in regarding the narrative as sapiential in origin and character, then the references to Job's cultic devotion will provide us with additional insights into the views of the wise concerning cultic religion.

Cultic Devotion. In the "Prologue" Job is characterized as a pious and upright, semi-nomadic patriarch whose piety is exemplified by his scrupulous devotion to cult. The key section pertaining to his cultic devotion includes 1:4-5:

> And his sons would come and celebrate a feast in each one's house on his assigned day, and they would send and invite their sisters to eat and to drink with them. And it would happen when the days of the feast were ended that Job would send for his sons and sanctify them. Then he would rise up early in the morning and offer up a burnt offering for each of them, because he said: "Perhaps my sons have sinned and have cursed God in their heart." Thus Job would do continually.

Since some effort is made to depict Job as a semi-nomadic patriarch, it is important to note that he, like the patriarchal leaders of families and clans, is given the responsibility for serving as the chief cultic functionary, that there is no reference to any priesthood or centralized cultic site, and that the participants are the members of the family.[127]

With regard to the 'feast' celebrated by Job's children, a number of scholars have suggested that the 'feast' is actually a cultic festival, since it lasts for a period of seven days and is consummated by Job's consecration of his sons and the subsequent burnt offerings.[128] In addition, the occurrence of the verb נקף may indicate that it is a cultic celebration, since the verb is found in other cultic contexts to mean "when the cycle of the cultic festivals comes round" (cf. Isa 29:1 and the related noun תקופה in I Sam 1:20 pointing to a cultic festival occurring at "the end of the year"). Furthermore, the statement "to celebrate a feast" (עשה משתה) does have the meaning in two other texts "to celebrate a cultic festival" (I Kgs 3:15, Isa 25:6). However, efforts to be more specific, and to suggest possible specific cultic festivals are more tenuous.

The closest Israelite festival is that of Tabernacles, a
Canaanite agrarian festival borrowed by the Israelites after
settlement in Canaan. This festival occurred at the end of the
year according to one tradition (Ex 34:22), lasted seven days,
and celebrated the harvest of the produce of the threshing
floor, especially grapes and olives.[129] Its joyful character
was enhanced by the drinking of wine and dancing.[130] P added
an eighth day which followed the conclusion of the festival
when the people were to gather together in a "solemn assembly"
(מקרא קדש) to worship and participate in the sacrifice of a
"fire-offering" (אשה, a synonym in P for עלה).[131] The עלה was
also given an expiatory value by P (Lev 1:4).

However, attempts to be too specific as concerns a particular Israelite festival are out of character with the effort of
the narrative to present Job as a semi-nomadic patriarch, and,
therefore, a participant in a primitive cult. The most that
can be said is that it is possible that a festival like Tabernacles influenced parts of the description of the cultic ritual.

On the other hand, there is equally good evidence that the
feast has no religious import whatsoever,[132] as may be argued
from the typical meaning of עשה משתה, "to celebrate a feast"
(non-cultic). Examples of non-cultic feasts where we find the
statement include: marriage (Jg 14:12, 17), hospitality for
guests (Gen 19:3), weaning of a child (Gen 21:8), a birthday
(Gen 40:20), a parity covenant (Gen 26:30), cessation of hos-
tilities (II Sam 3:20-21), sheep-shearing (II Sam 13:23), and a
royal banquet (Est 1:2f.). Furthermore, the seven day period
is also a time period for certain non-cultic feasts (e.g., marriage, Jg 14:12f.). Besides, the emphasis is not directly connected to the seven day period of the feast, but rather is on
the number of Job's sons, and the fact that the feast lasted
seven days may simply be incidental to the fact that this is
the number of Job's sons. It also seems strange that Job's
sanctification of the sons would take place only after the
feast had been concluded, if the feast were considered to be a
cultic festival. Finally, the feasting of the sons in each
one's house seems to be introduced into the narrative in order
to provide the background for the calamitous death of Job's

children in one house, and Job's absence from the feast would
seem strange if the feast had cultic overtones, since he was
supposedly the leader of the cult. Therefore, the evidence for
the feast being a cultic festival is quite inconclusive.

More central to the legend is the emphasis upon Job's cultic piety. Following the feast, Job sends for his sons to come
so that he might "consecrate" (קדש)[133] them in preparation for
the cultic sacrifice (cf. I Sam 16:5).[134] Following this, Job
then rises up early in the morning and sacrifices a burnt offering (עלה) for each of his seven sons.[135] The עלה was a
sacrifice assumed to be borrowed from Canaan, and had the primary meaning of the offering of a 'gift' to the deity, though
it also was attributed atoning powers as well,[136] especially by
means of appeasing the deity's wrath, and would thus correspond
to Job's concern to remove the sin possibly committed by the
sons of cursing God in one's heart. In cultic traditions earlier than P, the עלה was a morning sacrifice (II Kgs 16:15;
Ezek 46:13), and thus parallels the time of Job's offering. In
addition, such a sacrifice is mentioned in the narrative to
correspond to the patriarchal עלות in the Yahwist (Gen 8:20,
22:2f., and Num 23:1f.).

The second section of the folk-tale (the "Epilogue," 42:
8-10) also mentions cultic activities. After Yahweh has judged
Job's remarks to be correct and the statements of the friends
to be incorrect, he commands Eliphaz:

> And now, take seven bulls and seven rams and go to
> my servant Job and offer up a burnt offering on your
> own behalf, and my servant Job will make interces-
> sion for you, for surely I will accept his prayer
> not to punish you for your folly, because you did not
> speak correctly concerning me as did my servant Job.
> And Eliphaz the Temanite, Bildad the Shuhite, and
> Zophar the Naamathite went forth and did according
> to what Yahweh had commanded them, and Yahweh ac-
> cepted Job's prayer. Now Yahweh restored the for-
> tunes of Job when he prayed on behalf of his friends,
> and Yahweh gave to Job all that he had formerly
> possessed twice over.

Two points are of considerable interest to us in this passage: the burnt offering consisting of seven bulls and seven
rams, and the intercessory prayer made by Job. Once again the

sacrifice is a "burnt offering" which is intended in this context to appease Yahweh's wrath so that he will not punish the friends for speaking incorrectly about him.[137] Yet even more significant is the fact that the sacrifice made by the friends, again underlining the patriarchal character of the setting, is accompanied by Job's petition, and corresponds exactly to the cultic practice of offering עלות accompanied by petitions (e.g., Jer 14:12 and I Kgs 3:4f.). This also reflects a common Old Testament idea that the "intercession" of a just and righteous person has tremendous power and influence (Moses: Ex 32:11, Num 11:2, 12:13; Abraham: Gen 18:22f., 20:7f.; and Job, Noah, and Daniel in Ezek 14:12-23).[138] In addition, Job's intercessory prayer is given further theological importance in the narrative by assigning to it the basis upon which Job's restoration by Yahweh is made. Such an emphasis on prayer is common in wisdom literature, and supports the point we have made all along: an emphasis on prayer led to the creation of psalmodic prayers, especially those of the lament-thanksgiving cycle, by the wise.

Job (The Dialogues)

Introduction. The religious and existential torment of a righteous man whose former religious convictions and personal self-identification become shattered by suffering, social ostracism, and a harsh reality reflecting a deity hostile to man is poignantly described by the Joban poet. Since Job is readily recognizable as being part and parcel of the crisis stage of wisdom literature, it will be of interest to determine what are the views of the Joban poet with respect to cult.[139]

The debate over the date of the poetic Job is still continuing, with most scholars opting for a time somewhere between the seventh and third centuries. Our own tendency is to follow the arguments of Fohrer which place the book no earlier than fifth century Palestine.[140]

Just as problematic is the question of the formal structure of the book with scholars supporting the lament,[141] the "paradigm of the answered lament,"[142] legal controversy (*ríbh*),[143] the disputation,[144] and Greek tragedy.[145] One scholar even suggests the book is *suis generis*.[146] The complexity of the issue is understandable, since one can easily discover forms within the structure of the dialogues which belong to the categories of lament, *rîbh*, and disputation. We tend to accept the position of Fohrer that the book best fits the formal structure of the disputation, though certainly laments and elements of the *rîbh* are frequently found.

The Lament-Thanksgiving Cycle. Our major concern, however, is to examine the poet's views of cultic religion, an examination which would be doomed even before being initiated, if we followed the observations of a number of Joban scholars. Humbert, no mean wisdom scholar himself, has commented:

> Une omission est caractéristique dans le livre de Job: l'effacement de la révélation de Dieu dans l'histoire d'Israël et par la Loi, le culte et ses rites.[147]

But as we shall demonstrate, the latter part of this comment is open to question.

In our analysis of the three cycles of debate between Job and his three opponents, a central concern involves what is the proper response to be made with respect to suffering. As becomes obvious throughout the speeches of the opponents, their viewpoint is a traditionally cultic one, indicating that in this regard traditional wisdom, which is represented by the three opponents,[148] is the handmaiden of the Israelite cult.

Suffering to the opponents is an omen that the wrath or at the very least the displeasure of the deity has been incurred by some inadvertent or conscious action or negligence on the part of the one afflicted. This traditional explanation for suffering includes, therefore, the belief that the sufferer has sinned and is being punished by the deity, a viewpoint buttressed by the recurring rhetorical question:

> Can man be righteous before God?
> Can a man be pure before his Creator? (4:17)[149]

A second, less elaborated, explanation is that suffering is discipline or chastisement meant to test the faith of the sufferer who should continue in his steadfast belief that the

deity will soon redeem him from his affliction.[150] Now the
crucial point for our investigation is the cultic response that
Job is counseled to make concerning his suffering, and that
response turns out to be the uttering of a lament in the sanctuary to the deity in which one confesses his sins and pleads
for divine healing.[151] After the lament is offered, according
to cultic ritual and the advice of the opponents, the priest
consults the oracle and returns with the answer as to whether
or not the lament is acceptable to the deity, and, if so, the
worshipper is declared to be צדיק, that is, his 'righteousness'
has returned to him, demonstrating divine forgiveness of the
sufferer's sins. Following that, the deity is presumed to heal
the individual who fulfills his vow to the deity made during
the course of the lament, a vow usually involving the pledge to
return to the sanctuary to offer up a thanksgiving psalm accompanied by a thanksgiving sacrifice before the cultic community during which he extols the deity for his redemptive
powers. It is this cultic response to suffering that the opponents urge Job to make.

In the first speech by Eliphaz, the wise man advises Job:

> As for me, I would seek (אדרש) God,
> And to God would I commit my cause (5:8).

As is well know, דרש is the technical term used to indicate the
worshipper's approaching of the deity who resides in the cultic
sanctuary in order to present cultic worship.[152] If Job would
do so, says Eliphaz, then God would heal him from his affliction and would continue to protect him from destruction (5:17f.).

Bildad's first discourse affirms this counsel of
Eliphaz:[153]

> If you will seek (תשחר) God and make supplication
> (התחנן) to the Almighty,
> If you are pure and upright, surely then he will
> rouse himself for you, and reward you with a
> rightful habitation (8:5-6).

שחר is a term meaning "to seek out God" by means of coming to
the sanctuary with a penitential psalm (Ps 78:34; Hos 5:15),
while חנן means "to implore the favor" of God in the offering
of a prayer of petition in the sanctuary (I Kgs 8:33, 47).

Zophar gives Job the same counsel in his first speech (11:13-15):

> If you set your heart aright, then you will stretch
>   out your hands toward him.
> If iniquity is in your hand, put it far away and let
>   not wickedness dwell in your tent.
> Then you will lift up your face without blemish,
>   you will be secure, and will not be afraid.

The "stretching out of the hands toward God" is a reference to the customary manner of praying in which one extends his arms heavenward with palms turned upward to demonstrate that one's hands are "clean," that is, free of sin.[154] And if God judges one to be so, then the prayer will be answered, one's "face will be lifted up."[155] The image of hands which are judged to be without blemish points to the cultic ritual of the removal of sins by means of washing one's hands in a solution of soap and lye, after which the prayer is offered by the supplicant who demonstrates he has approached the deity without the stain of sin. Eliphaz mentions this ritual in 22:30: "You will be delivered through the cleanness of your hands." Job's response to the ritual is that it would have no lasting effect due to the malicious nature of a capricious deity: "If I wash myself with soap,[156] and cleanse my hands with lye, yet you (God) will plunge me into a pit, and my own clothes will abhor me" (9: 30-31).

In chapter 22, Eliphaz once more advises Job to make this cultic response by indicating that he should first "remove unrighteousness" from his life and then be confident that his cultic devotion will be accepted:

> You will make your prayer (תעתיר)[157] to him, and he
> will hear you; and you will pay your vows...You will
> be delivered through the cleanness of your hands.

The paying of vows refers to the obligation that the one lamenting binds upon himself, if the prayer is answered favorably. Such a vow in the lament involved the worshipper returning to the sanctuary and offering a thanksgiving sacrifice accompanied by a psalm of thanksgiving (see Pss 22:26; 50:14).

The most detailed reference to this cultic response to suffering is made in the Elihu interpolation[158] in 33:18-33.[159]

After describing the typical situation of the sufferer in vv. 19-22, Elihu then delineates the elements of the lament-thanksgiving cycle and counsels Job to engage in the ritual. First of all, Elihu refers to a מלאך ("messenger"), also referred to as a מליץ ("mediator"), who "declares to a man he is upright" (להגיד לאדם ישרו). Irwin has argued, among others, that this may be a reference to a redeemer figure in the council of Yahweh, a figure with parallels in ancient Near Eastern mythology (see 9:32-33, 16:19-22, 19:25-27, and 26:6-7).[160] However, we suggest that the מלאך in this context is a cultic official whose duty it is to examine the would-be supplicant and to declare him to be צדיק, a function indicated by the statement להגיד לאדם ישרו.[161] Furthermore, the priestly official not only acknowledges that the supplicant is צדיק and may petition the deity, but he also makes entreaty[162] on his behalf because he has "found the ransom" (מצאתי כפר). The כפר may refer to a legal or cultic payment to be paid by the supplicant in order to 'redeem his life,' that is, to keep the divine anger from destroying him.[163] Because the כפר has been paid, the priest makes entreaty on behalf of the worshipper, and asks God to act in good faith by removing his affliction and healing him. Following this intercession by the cultic official, the supplicant's lament is said to be accepted by the deity (וירצהו),[164] another cultic term indicating a decision made by a priest that the worship is acceptable to God.[165] Then the supplicant either immediately following the acceptance of the lament or later, after his healing, offers a psalm of thanksgiving praising the deity for his deliverance ("he will see his face accompanied by the cultic joyful shout").[166] In the course of the psalm, he confesses his transgression and praises the deity for not destroying him for the transgression and for delivering him from the hands of death.[167] Finally Elihu urges Job to engage in this cultic response, identifying what he has described as חכמה.

In turning to Job's position with respect to the lament-thanksgiving response to suffering, he mentions that during his former days he, too, was one whose lament had been answered:

> A derision to his neighbor I am become,
> One whose God answered (ענה) when he called (קרא),
> The just and perfect a derision (12:4).

But now he faces the perplexing agony that God refuses to answer his lament with a recognition of his innocence of sin and
to redeem him from suffering. In a blasphemous rage Job denies
he has committed any sin of which he is conscious, and, therefore, he has no reason to "remove wickedness from his tent" and
to confess his sins before the deity in his lament. Thus Job
moves to attack the interpretation of the wise opponents and
priests concerning the lament-thanksgiving cycle, since the
deity has refused to act in good faith and acknowledge his innocence.[168] He accuses God of being a malicious despot whose
superiority to Job rests only in his power, and certainly not
in matters of justice. Job's integrity refuses to permit him
to engage in the sham and pretense of the facade of confession
of sins, especially to a malevolent and capricious God (27:
1-6).[169]

In the Joban poet's reflection on the lament-thanksgiving
process, Milgrom has pointed to an important issue that should
be remembered. Job is one who refuses to accept the cultic
dogma, apparently supported by the friends, that he may be
punished severely for crimes of which he has no recollection,
that is, unconscious sins.[170] This is the reason why he con-
stantly demands from his opponents and God evidence that he has
committed an inadvertent sin of which he is aware (6:24). In
sanctioning the idea of punishment only for inadvertent, conscious sins, Job removes the causal nexus between sin and punishment from the realm of the unconscious violation of taboo.[171]

In chapters 29-31 Job once more demands from the deity a
recognition of his innocence, even though he does not believe
the deity will act justly and redeem him. Again we find him
engaging in the lament process in which his "lament of innocence" is similar to that specific type of lament in the
Psalter, but with one important exception: he expresses no
confident hope that God will redeem him, but rather affirms
that he knows the deity will soon put him to death.

In chapters 29-30, as is common to the lament, Job contrasts the "Then and Now" of his existence. In pictorial pathos, Job painfully recalls his former existence which was characterized by favor with God, wealth, honor, family, and the secure hope for a long and prosperous life, wishing, but never believing, that God would restore him to this former position (29:2). The "Now" is lamented in chapter 30 (ועתה, 30:1), which includes poverty, disgrace, social ostracism so intense that even the dregs of humanity scoff at him, an unbearable agony of mind and body, and, worst of all, his lack of hope that the deity will redeem him: "I cry (אשוע) to you, but you do not answer me (לא תענני)." He bewails being brought to the edge of death by this malevolent deity who has turned against him, ignoring his cry for help in the cultic assembly (30:28b). Finally, in chapter 31, Job not only takes the final and drastic step to prove beyond all doubt his innocence in the "Oath of Innocence," he also uses this process to challenge the deity to a *Streitsrede* in which he could prove that the deity, not he, is the one who is unjust.[172]

God then appears in a storm theophany and responds to Job's lament and his challenge. If Tsevat's analysis is correct, then the point of the Yahweh speeches is to dash to pieces forever the idea that justice is the order permeating reality, and consequently, the principle of retribution.

Since the Joban poet is arguing that the cosmos is ethically neutral and is not responsive to human actions or divine intervention, be they good or evil, the poet is fundamentally damning not only the essence of sagacious ideology, but the very foundation of cultic religion which had been presumed to be the means of garnering the vital forces of nature and of repelling the forces of chaos. Sapiential ethics and cultic religion are stripped of their life-inducing powers. Furthermore, the God who appears to Job "is neither a just nor an unjust god but God."[173] Or as Kluger has cogently perceived, the irrational and malevolent side of God is revealed and is to be accepted by Job.[174] This devastates both the sapiential and the cultic view of God. The entire structure of Israel's cult was built upon the affirmation of the justice of God, and the

Joban poet's repudiation of this motif certainly would demand
the complete re-constitution of cultic theology and the nature
and purpose of cultic ritual.

With such a conclusion, what happens to the cultic response of the lament-thanksgiving? Certainly the cult has been
emasculated. Yet, Job's response appears to be the lament in
which he "repents in dust and ashes" (42:6). But for what reason? Certainly not in the theological understanding of the
lament that a just and merciful deity would redeem the penitent, righteous man. Rather, Job's response takes a new and
daring step: he worships the deity from the perspective of disinterested piety, expecting neither reward for his worship, nor
punishment for his sins. He worships from the position of one
overcome by the mystery and awesomeness of the rational-
irrational deity.[175] Thus the poet is not dispensing with cultic religion, but rather he is seeking to re-structure the cult
upon a new theological and cosmological understanding: God is
ethically neutral and the cosmos is impervious to the moral
quality of human behavior. The only correct basis for cultic
religion is the feeling of awe occasioned by the mysterious
majesty of the divine.

Apostasy: the Unforgivable Sin. In returning to the "Oath
of Innocence," it is interesting that in Job's denial of having
committed sins which were punishable by the verdict of death he
refers to only one cultic crime: apostasy, a crime punishable
by death (31:26-28).[176] In the typical form of the self-
imprecation, Job denies that he has been unfaithful to God by
engaging in astral worship:[177]

> If I have looked at the sun when it shone, or the
>   moon moving in splendor,
> And my heart has been secretly enticed, and my mouth
>   has kissed my hand,
> This also would be a crime worthy of being judged,
>   because I would have been deceitful to God above.

Cults of astral deities were quite common in ancient Near Eastern religions, thus making it difficult to discover which astral deities are of concern in this context. But if the dating
of the poetic book is in the sixth to fifth centuries, the two

deities are probably Shamash and Sin.[178] Furthermore, Job's
denial that his "mouth has kissed his hand" is most certainly
a reference to the Akkadian ideogram for prayer (*ikribu*) in
which the hand touches the mouth. This cultic gesture appears
on the Code of Hammurabi and on other Babylonian and Assyrian
monuments.[179] In addition, McKay's comments give us additional
insight into the crime Job denies he has committed:

> The stars and constellations were often regarded as
> numinous and powerful in magic and astrology and
> could be involved in prayer. Observation of the
> stars and planets therefore played a not inconsider-
> able role in Mesopotamian religious circles.[180]

While Job denies he has committed the sin of apostasy, it may
not be fortuitous that the cultic act he has refrained from
doing is the act of prayer to other gods. This text gives us
additional insight into the views of the Joban poet with respect to cult, and we find him aligned with the traditional
wise in Proverbs 1-9 who admonished against participation in
fertility religion and, as we shall see, with the same counsel
of avoiding apostasy in the Wisdom of Solomon.[181]

Koheleth

Introduction. Koheleth also comes from the legacy of the
critical wisdom tradition, having been written in Hebrew by a
Palestinian sage in third century Jerusalem and placed in the
form of a first person narration.[182] In Koheleth's attack on
the ideological structure of his traditional opponents, we
should find fertile ground for an examination of the views of
the critical wise concerning cult.[183]

As we shall discover, what Koheleth says of cult is grounded in his intense reflections concerning reality, a reality
which he discovers to be inaccessible to the penetrations of
sapiential scrutiny, and, thus, for a sage, devoid of the possibilities for a meaningful human existence. Koheleth's despair over the absence of meaning in human existence results
from his unsuccessful quest to determine a tangible answer to
his central question: מה טוב לאדם בחיים.[184] But, of course, to
the sages such meaning was intimately tied to one's ability to

observe and understand some sort of order of reality which, having been perceived and comprehended, could provide the direction for the sage's own efforts to find his place, function, and time within the scheme of reality. But Koheleth finds no grand, comprehensive order which embraces the spheres of reality, and certainly no 'righteous' order permeating existence as did his traditional counterparts.[185] To Koheleth the severe limitations of human knowledge and understanding which are the result of man's own finite existence and the capricious action of the deity who has placed "confusion, mystery" (עלם)[186] into the human mind make it impossible to perceive any order in reality. Furthermore, existence in an irrational reality is complicated by an inscrutable, arbitrary, capricious deity, capable of and responsible for both good and evil (7:14), the one who is the *Deus absconditus*, incapable of being known, but most certainly to be feared.[187] Such an irrational reality coupled with an inscrutable, and yet terrifying, deity finally lead Koheleth to a total abandonment of the one sapiential dogma to which he tried so desperately to cling, the principle of retribution.[188]

Having denied theological and cosmological meaning, Koheleth turns to a radical anthropocentricity, hoping to find something which could provide man with a meaningful existence, but once again his efforts are futile. Wealth, power, and satiation of human appetites are experienced by the sage and found devoid of any meaning. Even human toil, the endeavor to create something lasting, significant, and noteworthy, provides no meaningful existence in a determined reality where the only actions of any consequence are those of the deity; whereas man's own efforts are reduced to meaningless motion, unguided by a perception of the structure of time, stripped of any potential for significance, and incapable of producing change.[189]

The wisdom tradition, as a result, has become bankrupt, defeated in its attempts to understand an irrational reality and an enigmatic, inscrutable deity, and to find any place and meaningful function for its adherents. Its doctrines have become vanquished in the arena of human experience. The only

certainty that knowledge can produce is the empirical certainty
of death as the common lot of all men.

To Koheleth's question, מה טוב לאדם בחיים, the only 'good'
is centered in a divine gift of joy that enables one to find
some pleasure in his labor and family (2:26, 3:22, 5:18-20,
7:14, 9:7-10, and 11:7), a joy that aids in dulling the torment
of a meaningless existence.[190] Yet even the experience of joy
is problematic, because its reception is dependent not upon
wealth, power, and labor (6:1-9), but rather upon an arbitrary,
incalculable decision by the deity. And the basis upon which
he seems to dispense joy is the enigmatic statement by Koheleth
that he gives joy to those who please him (2:26), and yet the
tragedy of even this one small boon is that one never knows how
to please the deity, unless the answer rests in the repeated
statement by Koheleth that one should "fear god." "Fear of
god" to Koheleth is actual fear, fear of an unknowable power
who has the ability to destroy or to reward, to dispense joy or
to withhold it. Furthermore, "fear of god" to Koheleth signals
the attitude of 'resignation,' resignation to an irrational
reality, to an inscrutable God, to a meaningless existence, and
finally to the inescapable conclusion that, regardless of one's
actions, social position, and character, death is the final lot
of every man.[191]

Koheleth's Views of Cult. Koheleth's views of cult are
found primarily in the form of an instruction concerning cult,
separated from the surrounding materials by a different form,
and occurring in 5:1-7 (Heb 4:17-5:6). A form-critical analysis and translation are as follows:[192]

Sacrifice and Obedience

Admonition (1)
Watch your step whenever you approach
the temple of God,

Motive Clause
(Better Saying)
(For) it is better to draw near to
listen than to offer the sacrifice
of fools,[193]

Circumstantial Clause
(Koheleth's Comment)
Since they have no knowledge of do-
ing evil.

Prayer

Admonition (2)	Be not hasty with your mouth, nor let your heart be quick to utter a word before the deity.
Motive Clause (Proverb)	(Because) the deity is in heaven and you are upon the earth.
Result Clause (Koheleth's Comment)	Therefore let your words be few.
Motive Clause (Proverb)	(Because) a dream comes on account of much activity, and the voice of a fool with many words.

Vow

Admonition (3)	Whenever you make a vow to the deity, do not delay in paying it.
Motive Clause (Proverb)	(Because) there is no pleasure in fools.
Admonition Restated (Koheleth's Comment)	Whatever you vow, pay.
Motive Clause (Better Saying)	It is better that you do not vow, than to vow and not pay it.

Willful Sin

Admonition (4)	Do not allow your mouth to cause you to sin, and do not say before the priest that it was an unconscious sin.
Motive Clause (Koheleth's Comment)	Why should God be angry at your voice and destroy the work of your hand.
Motive Clause (Proverb)	(For) when dreams increase so do vanities and words,
Admonition (Koheleth's Imperative)	But even so, fear God.

As the form-critical analysis demonstrates, Koheleth utilized the style of the teacher in issuing four admonitions, all of which deal with the realm of the cult: sacrifice and obedience, prayer, vows, and willful sin. The admonitions consist of imperatives and prohibitions buttressed by the addition of motive clauses which demonstrate why a particular admonition merits obedience. What is intriguing is the fact that most of the motive clauses are constructed from proverbial sayings and

better sayings. Furthermore, Koheleth's adaptations of traditional material may be seen in the additions of his comments in
strategic places which give us a better insight into his own
expressions concerning cult.

In the first admonition, Koheleth establishes the tone for
the entire unit: "Be careful when you approach the temple of
God."[194] Guarded caution, perhaps even fearful foreboding, is
the proper decorum in the realm of the holy, for the impassioned
fool, the religious ecstatic, will quickly meet his end from
his foolish behavior which arouses the destructive power of the
deity.[195] And it is significant that Koheleth's counsel concerning cultic behavior contains an emphasis only on the negative, destructive side of the sacral realm, and nothing whatsoever of the beneficence believed to be derived from the cult by
priestly traditions. To Koheleth, fear, extreme caution, a
lack of religious passion, and a cool disdain for the frenetic
fanatic remain the proper virtues of the wise cultist.

Koheleth's imperative is supported by a motivation in the
form of a better saying: "(For) to draw near to listen is better than the sacrifice of fools." This saying is quite similar
to the one attributed to Samuel in his castigation of King Saul
in I Sam 15:27--"Behold, to obey is better than sacrifice,"
thus supporting the conclusion that such a saying was commonly
known.[196]

לשמע may be translated either "to listen" or "to obey,"
and though the object of the infinitive is left unstated, it
may well be "instruction" offered by the priest or levite (see
Psalms 15, 24; Ezekiel 18; Leviticus 19). Again we find a contrast being made with sacrifice, and we are faced with the possibility that sacrifice is rejected by Koheleth, especially in
what appears as his own comment appended to the better saying:
"since they have no knowledge of doing evil." It would be possible to regard Koheleth's comment as intimating that sacrifice
is foolish and evil. However, as indicated before, a better
saying does not necessarily imply that one thing is good and
the other is bad, but rather in the value system of the sages
one is to be preferred over the other. Thus, in our case,
"hearing" or "obeying" is to be preferred over the offering of

"the sacrifice of fools." Again it should be noted that sacrifice is qualified by the statement "of fools" who in sapiential
traditions are identified with "the wicked," those who are not
wise and prudent, who do not observe the dictates of the wise,
and who are not followers of "order." Further, Koheleth's comment ("they have no knowledge of doing evil") may be taken to
mean that fools offer sacrifice without having the insight to
know that with respect to their behavior in life they are per-
petrators of evil, transgressors of the dictates of "order,"
and consequently offer a cultic sacrifice which is considered
to be valueless, and, in fact, even compounds their guilt.[197]
Obedience to priestly instruction concerning the צדיק who may
enter the realm of the holy is better than the offering of
sacrifices by fools who disregard instruction. In addition, if
the more specific meaning of זבח ("communion sacrifice") is intended, then Koheleth would be affirming the priestly instruction that such a sacrifice may be offered only by a צדיק, and
not by one who has breached the sacral orders.

The second admonition concerns a warning to the wise with
respect to prayer. Once again a cultic act is viewed with caution, and a warning is issued to avoid imprudent, hasty behavior in the realm of the holy: "Be not hasty with your mouth,
nor let your heart be quick to utter a word before the deity."
This admonition is based on the sapiential ideal of the "silent
man," one who thinks before speaking, in contrast to the "passionate man" who speaks before carefully thinking, and thus
acts foolishly. The motive clause is structured from an antithetical proverb by which Koheleth wishes to emphasize the distance between the inscrutable deity and men: "(Because) the
deity is in heaven and you are upon the earth," a saying which
appears to be taken from Dt 4:29,[198] but with an interesting
twist:

Dt. - יהוה הוא האלהים בשמים ממעל ועל הארץ מתחת
Koh. - כי אלהים בשמים ואתה על הארץ

Thus Koheleth's point concerning prayer is intimately linked to
his theological emphasis upon the deity as a *Deus absconditus*
who is completely hidden from human cognition, indicating his

doubts concerning the cultic dogma of a deity who is revealed in the sanctuary and could be approached and induced to act favorably on one's behalf in the offering of a petition.

Koheleth's addition, "therefore let your words be few," opposes the behavior of the foolish cultist who believes that, by the constant petitioning and repetition of certain "power-laden" formulae, he can induce divine action on his behalf.[199]

Koheleth supports his counsel by the addition of a synonymous proverb: "(Because) the dream comes on account of much activity, and the voice of a fool with many words." This is a most enigmatic saying, and is open to a number of interpretations. Some scholars have suggested that the saying alludes to the activity of the cult prophet (or levitical singer who in the post-exilic period took over the functions of the cult prophet) who, having heard the request of the supplicant, obtains an oracle by means of a dream and then delivers to the worshipper the divine decision.[200] If so, then Koheleth would be lambasting the cultic prophet who believes he has knowledge of the inscrutable deity, which to Koheleth is inconceivable. Scott has suggested that the first part of the proverb is quoted only for the sake of completeness and that Koheleth's emphasis is on the latter part: he is counseling the cultic participant to avoid excessive speaking in the sanctuary.[201]

However, in our opinion, Koheleth is alluding to the reason that one is in the sanctuary to offer the prayer: he has been the recipient of a terrifying dream which he has taken as a divine warning from the deity of punishment for some misdeed. That such dreams were considered to be omens of warning to the wise is indicated in Job 4:12f. and 33:14f. The terrified person would then come to the cult to present his lament, or to relate his dream to a cult prophet whose function it was to interpret the meaning of such dreams. Indeed, Koheleth's point is that a dream follows much activity, עְנְיָן, used by Koheleth with the negative connotation of the wearisome "task" of men who live in a world in which toil and activities pursued have no meaningful significance or ability to produce change. Rather such actions are simply motion. The reason, then, for one's dream is his meaningless toil, for a dream is neither a

warning of divine displeasure nor connected to the so-called
science of omenology in which dreams were seen to be signs of
specific, future events. This is compared in the proverb to
the observation that only a fool is extremely loqacious and
even in the cult speaks unendingly in the false hopes of obtaining divine aid. The proper decorum is a prudent silence.[202]

Koheleth's third admonition contains a warning against
hasty vows: "Whenever you make a vow to the deity, do not delay
in paying it." In this admonition Koheleth warns the wise not
to avoid making a vow completely, but rather to consider carefully the obligation before being bound by it.[203] In the making of a vow, prudence enables the wise man not only to avoid
making an unwise vow, but at the same time causes him to realize the folly of making a vow and not fulfilling it: "(Because)
there is no pleasure in fools." This proverbial statement
demonstrates the extreme displeasure of the deity with respect
to those who do not fulfill their vows. חפץ is often found
with respect to whether or not someone or some action is
"pleasing," "acceptable," to the deity (I Kg 10:9, II Sam 15:
26, and Ps 22:8).

Koheleth's own addition to the saying is an emphatic imperative: "Whatever you vow, pay." A vow is to be taken as a
serious obligation. He underlines his imperative with a better
saying: "It is better that you do not vow, than for you to make
a vow and not pay it." The same attitude concerning the vow is
found in cultic traditions, demonstrating that in this regard
Koheleth is in agreement with the priests.[204] Even to Koheleth,
the vow is a serious cultic obligation, once it is made, and
failure to carry out the vow places one in a precarious situation (cf. Prov 20:25).

Koheleth's fourth admonition has been interpreted in different ways, since it is a rather enigmatic admonition: "Do not
allow your mouth to cause you to sin, and do not say before the
priest that it was an unconscious sin." Generally, Koheleth
scholars have regarded the prohibition as connected to the earlier admonition concerning the vow, and consequently interpret
it to be a warning against hasty vows which cannot be paid when
the "priestly official" comes to collect payment, for the result is punishment by the deity.[205]

However, we choose to suggest another possibility. The two-fold prohibition in v. 6 marks the beginning of a new admonition, and it would seem redundant simply to repeat what had earlier been said. Rather the admonition concerning foolish speech appears to involve the "willful sin" in which one commits a sin willfully and with full awareness of the fact that his action is wrong. Thus the first part of the prohibition warns one not to commit a willful sin, and the second warns one not to compound one's guilt by lying to the "priestly official" by saying that it was a שגגה, that is, an inadvertent or unconscious sin. The מלאך, we would suggest, is the priest who gives instruction to the worshippers to determine those who are צדיקים and may participate in cult.[206] According to Koheleth, one should not commit a willful sin, and then try to pass it off as a שגגה to the priest. A willful sin could not be forgiven in the cult, and punishment, at times even destruction for serious sins, had to be borne by the sinner.

Such punishment is pointed to by Koheleth when he adds his own comment as a motive clause in the form of a question: "Why should God be angry at your voice and destroy the work of your hands." מעשה to Koheleth is the major source for "joy," the one thing in life that makes living tolerable (e.g., 3:22). Thus such a foolish action, in which one commits a willful sin and then compounds his guilt by trying to say it was only an inadvertent or unconscious sin, profanes the holy, results in the wrath of the deity, and consequently leads to the destruction of the major source of joy. "Joy" or "satisfaction" is the motivation for Koheleth's entire ethic.

Koheleth once more buttresses his admonition with a proverbial saying that is rather enigmatic: "(For) when dreams increase, so do vanities and words."[207] Once again Koheleth seems to suggest that after the reception of omens there is a tremendous flurry of cultic activities by frenetic fools who foolishly believe that their frenzied behavior in the cult will influence the deity to act on their behalf, activities which Koheleth finds foolish not only because they oppose the ideal model of sapiential behavior, but also because destruction is the punishment for foolish behavior in the cult. Further,

Koheleth rejects the notion that cultic behavior can influence an inscrutable, capricious deity to act beneficently on one's behalf.

Koheleth adds his final comment to the instruction, "But even so, fear God." In terms of the structure of the entire instruction, the final statement refers back to the initial statement of "watching one's step," indicating that 'fear of God' in this context intimates that extreme caution and a fearful foreboding should characterize the wise man when he enters the realm of the cult.[208] Much of what takes place in the cult may be foolish, ecstatic behavior, even meaningless, and in addition, the opposite of what is desired may result: destruction by the deity. Though Koheleth does not admonish his students to avoid cultic participation, he, nevertheless, warns them of the potential for destruction and advises them to exude in the cult wise, prudent behavior. Furthermore, the idea of divine beneficence through the channel of cult is never mentioned, for Koheleth's worldview would never allow an affirmation of any means, even the cultic institution, to influence in a positive way a hidden, enigmatic, capricious deity. The only actions which affect the deity in the cultic realm are foolish ones which may arouse the divine wrath and bring punishment to the fool.

In Koheleth's attack of the pious wise in chapters 7 and 8, there is another reference to cult occurring in 8:10 in the context of Koheleth's reflecting over the abuse of justice and the lack of any retributory principle:

> Subsequently I saw the wicked draw near (to worship),[209]
> For they would come and go from the temple,[210]
> And would be praised[211] in the city where they had
>   acted thus.
> This also is vanity.

Koheleth despairs over the lack of justice in a world that permits praise of the wicked for their pompous show of cultic devotion and that does not bring punishment to them for their wickedness.

In 9:2, Koheleth refers to cultic activities in the context of despairing over the shroud of darkness which engulfs

humanity with respect to knowledge of divine activity. Furthermore, he reflects over the affirmation by the traditional
wise that the wise and their deeds are under the beneficent
care of the deity, and adds sarcastically that if God does
watch over the wise and their deeds, it is impossible to know
whether it is because God loves them or hates them. Then Koheleth comments with respect to the righteous-wise:

> All that is before them is vanity.[212] Because to
> everyone there is the same fate: to the righteous
> as well as the wicked, the good and the bad,[213] the
> clean and the unclean, the one who sacrifices and
> the one who does not sacrifice, the good and the
> sinner, the one who swears an oath and the one who
> avoids making an oath.

Such a fate, of course, is death. מקרה is an important term in
Koheleth, since the sage pictures a world in which all things
have been determined by the inscrutable deity. Since death has
been determined to be the fate for every man, it makes no dif-
ference, in the final analysis, whether or not one's actions
and behavior are righteous, good, and cultically correct.

In this series of contrasts Koheleth refers to the טהור
and the טמא which in P are terms used to classify respectively
people who are either ritually and ethically pure or stained.
Such a decision was made to determine what, if any, ritual
cleansing had to be observed before participating in the sacred
sphere (see Lev 10:10f.). But with respect to one's final fate,
says Koheleth, it does not matter if one has been considered
ritually and ethically pure and has offered sacrifices or not.
In this text Koheleth is not suggesting that ethical behavior
and cultic observations should be abandoned. But what he observes simply is that death comes to all men regardless of
their character and cultic participation, and this is the
greatest tragedy, the worst 'vanity,' of all.

Sirach

Introduction. In the rather prodigious sapiential composition of Sirach, we are confronted by an extensive amount of
material concerning cult, demonstrating the absorbing interest

of this Palestinian sage in the cultic institutions and practices existing during the Hellenistic period of Jewish history.

While it may well be that Sirach's considerable literary
activity spanned a long period of his life,[214] the final product appears to have been finished sometime between 190 and 175
B.C., a date based on the prologue written by his grandson
which states that he carried his illustrious ancestor's writing
with him when he emigrated to Alexandria during the 38th year
of King Euergetes, most certainly Ptolemy VII, thus placing the
date of the emigration to Alexandria in 132 B.C. Furthermore,
Sirach's eulogy to Simon II, the High Priest who died around
190 B.C., intimates that the heroic figure had recently died
and had been replaced by his legitimate successor, Onias III.
In addition, Sirach's obvious concern for the continuance of
Onias in his office indicates that the sage was aware of the
difficulty the high priest was having, though he demonstrates
no awareness of the removal of Onias shortly after the ascen-
sion to the throne of Antiochus IV who replaced him with his
Hellenizing brother, Jason. Nor does Sirach's writing give any
indication of the severe persecution of the Jews undertaken by
the same Antiochus IV.[215]

Sirach appears to have been a wisdom teacher in a sapiential school in Jerusalem (בית המדרש ,ישבה; 51:23, 29), and possibly was a member of the γραμματετεῖς τοῦ ἱεροῦ mentioned in
one of the royal decrees of Antiochus III (Ant. XII, 138f.).[216]
In fact, his laudative description of the positions and functions of the sage in 39:1-11 could very well be based on his
own scribal career. And it is especially in Sirach that we are
able to note the development of the sage from a royal functionary to a scribe of Torah, a process noticeable in Ezra some two
centuries earlier.[217] What is more, the high-minded savant
even considers himself to be an heir of the prophetic role!

The Identification of Wisdom with Cult. In determining
Sirach's attitudes concerning cult, we should first consider
the hymnic aretalogy of hypostatized wisdom in chapter 24.[218]
In this most important composition, wisdom is hypostatized as a
member of the divine court of the Most High, and in her

cosmological function is presented as coming forth from the
mouth of God during creation in order to permeate the expanse
of the created cosmos. Furthermore, she is then appointed as
the ruler (משלתי) over every people and nation, though in her
search to find a permanent resting place, she took up her abode
in Israel, a point illustrating in good fashion Sirach's obeisance to *Heilsgeschichte*.

But even more important for our concerns is Sirach's identification of cosmological wisdom with the Israelite cult.

> In the holy tent I served before him,
> And subsequently in Zion I was established.
> In the beloved city likewise I took my rest,
> And in Jerusalem was my dominion.
> So I took root among an honored people,
> In the portion of Yahweh, his inheritance.

In this most important section of the aretalogy, the process of
the nationalization of cosmological wisdom is most noticeable,[219]
but, what is more, the process of nationalization is part and
parcel of the Israelite cultus, demonstrating in this manner
Israel's special claim to and intimate relation with true, divine wisdom, in contrast to the claim of other nations, especially the Hellenists.[220]

In pursuing an investigation of chapter 24, it is interesting to take cognizance of Sirach's portrayal of wisdom's
thriving in Israel, for included is a metaphorical depiction of
wisdom's emitting of the aroma of spices and fragrances used in
the incense of the incense altar as well as in the holy oil
used to anoint the tabernacle, ark, other various cultic paraphernalia, and the priests.[221]

This identification of wisdom with cultus is derived from
the sage's investigation of Torah which he also identifies with
wisdom: "All of these are the book of the covenant of God Most
High, the Torah which Moses commanded us" (v. 24). This text,
then, provides us with the basis for our understanding of
Sirach's intimate involvement in and devotion to Israel's cultic institutions and practices.

Cultic Orders in "The Praise of the Fathers." In his
panegyric to the "pious" (חסדים) heroes of Israel's past, an

apologetic effort designed to emphasize the virtues of illustrious men of Israelite tradition over against the attractive forces of Hellenism, Sirach is most concerned with illustrating Israel's unique claim to wisdom by stressing the covenants of the Davidic dynasty, the Aaronic priesthood, and the Zadokite high priesthood, and the importance of the Israelite cultus. These emphases result from his efforts to defend Israelite religious faith and tradition during the precarious times of the late third and early second centuries.[222]

In a perusal of this eulogy, Sirach may be seen most certainly as a loyalist to the priestly institution of the post-exilic cult, and especially to the office of the high priest.[223] The panegyric to Aaron in 45:6-22 demonstrates his devoted loyalty to the Aaronic priesthood, and this devotion is apparent even more when it is realized that Aaron's eulogy is three times as long as that given to Moses. According to this eulogy, Aaron was singled out "from among all living" and from the tribe of Levi in order to possess the priestly prerogative in the Israelite cultus, a privilege formally sealed according to Sirach in a legal statute valid for all times (חק עולם). Following a description of the magnificent apparel of Aaron, based on the P material in Exodus 28, Sirach underlines the tradition that only Aaron and his descendants possess the right to wear such clothing, and, concomitantly, to possess the priestly office. And indicating his concern for the continuation of cult, Sirach interjects that their tâmîdh offering should continue to be made. The tâmîdh was the offering of burnt sacrifices which was made twice each day (see Ex 29:38-42, Num 28:2-8, and Lev 6:2-8).[224]

In reaffirming the authority of the Aaronic priesthood, Sirach points to the ordination of Aaron by Moses, thus aligning the authority of Moses with the "sons of Aaron." Sirach follows this by indicating that the ordaining of Aaron was authoritatively perpetuated by "an everlasting covenant" (ברית עולם) which extended to his descendants as well, affirming that only they are "to minister to the Lord and to serve as priests and to bless his people in his name" (v. 15). The specific priestly functions of the Aaronic priesthood outlined by the

the sage include the blessing, the *tâmîdh* offering, sacrifice,
incense as a "memorial portion" (אזכרה), offerings intended to
make atonement (לכפר) for the people, and the instruction of
priestly testimonies and statutes (מצות חק ומשפט) of the Torah.

Once again the sage defends the privilege of the Aaronides
against any challengers to their office, by referring to the
rebellion of Dathan, Abiram, and Korah. The rebellion of Korah
is presented in P as a challenge to the priestly privilege of
the Aaronides by the leader of the levites, "outsiders," who
were consumed by the wrath of the Lord, proving again the Lord's
support of the Aaronic claim to the priestly office (Numbers
16-18).

Sirach concludes by underscoring the priestly right to
support by the people by means of first fruits and sacrifices,
adding that the priests have no "inheritance" (נחלה) or "portion" (חלק), except in Yahweh himself.[225]

The panegyric to Aaron not only demonstrates Sirach's
loyal support of the priesthood and his concern that the
priesthood continue to perform its important cultic duties (v.
14), but also demonstrates his desire to defend the exclusive
claim of the "sons of Aaron" against encroachment by other
groups, especially non-Aaronic levitical families whose wish to
function as full-fledged priests of the altar and not as secondary cultic officials in subjection to the Aaronides is well
documented in post-exilic literature.

Sirach's support of the Zadokite right to the office of
the high priest is demonstrated in his panegyric to Phinehas,
"the son of Eleazar" who "ranked third in greatness." Sirach's
extollment of Phinehas is based primarily on Num 25:10-13 in
which Phinehas is given "a covenant of peace" (ברית שלום), interpreted by P as "a covenant of perpetual priesthood" for him
and his descendants. This was given to Phinehas according to P
because of his "zealous" action to remove foreigners from the
holy congregation by putting to death an Israelite and his
Midianite wife. This was considered an act of "atonement" and
was done to appease the wrath of God who had inflicted a destructive plague upon the people because of the defilement
caused by foreign elements.

Sirach paraphrases this material from P, but adds that this covenant included the giving to Phinehas and his descendants the office of "high priesthood" forever (כהונה גדולה עד עולם). The import of this statement by Sirach is that he supported the Zadokite and, more specifically, the Oniad claim to the office of high priest over against other Aaronic families, especially the Tobiads.[226] The Zadokites had controlled the Jerusalem priesthood during the pre-exilic period, and during the exilic and post-exilic periods had begun to trace their lineage back to Phinehas and Eleazar (I Chr 5:30-34; Ezra 8:2) in their rivalry with another group claiming Aaronic descent through Ithamar. The final solution of this rivalry is indicated by the Chronicler during the third century when all descendants of Aaron finally possessed the legitimate claim to priesthood, though the descendants claiming the Aaronic lineage through Eleazar-Phinehas were in the dominant position. And apparently because Eleazar and Phinehas were seen by P to be the successors of Aaron to the high priest's office, control of this important office was in the hands of the Zadokites.

Sirach's obvious concern to support the Zadokite-Oniad privilege should be understood within the tumultuous struggles concerning the office following the death of Simon II whose son became embroiled in political controversy and eventually was removed from office by Antiochus IV and replaced first by Jason, the brother of Onias, and later, following the removal of Jason, by Menelaus, a Tobiad, who outbid Jason for the office.[227]

Following his eulogy to Phinehas, Sirach adds a comparison between the Davidic and the Aaronic covenants:

> And also there is his covenant with David, the son of Jesse of the Tribe of Judah. The heritage of sacrificial fire before his glory is the heritage of Aaron to all his descendants.[228]

Perhaps Sirach's main intent is to stress the authority and claim to perpetuation of the Aaronic covenant by putting it on an equal basis with the Davidic covenant which was "forever." But it is conceivable, since the statement is preceded by material concerning the high priest, that Sirach is intimating that the ideal theocratic rule of the chosen includes the civil rule of the king descended from David and the religious rule of the high priest, and, therefore, is suggesting that the duties of the priesthood belong in the realm of the cult and not in the pursuing of civil power that had been the case off and on during the post-exilic period, especially during the reign of Simon II, and accordingly led to the embroilment of the sacral office in political turmoil.[229]

Sirach concludes this section relating to the priesthood by addressing to the priesthood of his day an admonitory blessing:

> And now, bless the good Lord, the One who crowned you
> in Glory.
> And may he give to you a wise heart in order to judge
> his people with righteousness,
> In order that your goodness might not be forgotten,
> and your power might continue throughout all
> generations (v. 26).[230]

Once again, Sirach assumes his role of teacher, and exhorts the priesthood of his own day to exhibit in their judgment of the people wisdom and righteousness that their privilege might always continue.[231]

But certainly the longest and most laudative eulogy is devoted to Simon II, the High Priest who had died shortly before the completion of Sirach's writing (50:1-26), and who represents the climatic conclusion of Sirach's "Praise of the Fathers." The dates for Simon's rule as high priest are inconclusive, but roughly may be placed between 220 and 190 B.C. Simon's prominence in Sirach's composition results not only from the tremendous power and prestige of the high priest, but also from the sage's concern to insure the continuity of the Zadokite-Oniad high priesthood which was coming under extreme pressure during the rule of Simon's successor, Onias III, who finally was removed by Antiochus IV some time after 175 B.C.[232]

Sirach points to the accomplishments of Simon in vv. 1-4 which included the repairing and fortification of the temple and city, the construction of a reservoir, and his saving of the people of Jerusalem during the Ptolemaic-Seleucid war which culminated in the victory of the Seleucids. Such a description of his accomplishments most probably is related to the

beneficial decrees of Antiochus III, the victorious Seleucid
king, who rewarded the Jews for their support during the war,
especially in their aiding his taking of the citadel in Jerusalem.[233] The decree granting a number of favors to the Jews
is summarized in a letter from Antiochus III to an official
named Ptolemy and included: the provisions for the rebuilding
of Jerusalem, the allowing of inhabitants who had fled the city
to return, money for temple supplies, tax-free lumber for the
repair of the temple, the exemption of the inhabitants of Jerusalem from taxation for three years and thereafter a reduction
in taxes by one-third, the exemption of the *Gerousia*, the
priests, the temple scribes, and singers from certain taxes,
the freeing of Jewish slaves and prisoners of war and the returning of their property, and, most importantly, the allowing
of the Jews to "live according to their ancestral laws."[234]
According to Tcherikover, the last item included not only the
Law of Moses and various religious traditions, but also the
maintenance of political institutions and social organizations.
Furthermore, he argues that Antiochus III thus gave royal rati-
fication to the theocracy which included the religious and
civil rule of the high priest over Jerusalem and Judea, a rati-
fication probably resulting from Simon's leadership of the
Gerousia which went forth to greet the new conqueror they had
openly supported.[235]

Sirach then turns to what appears to be a firsthand account of the role of the High Priest in his most important
religious function, presiding over the "Day of Atonement" (5-
21), and gives an extended depiction of the radiant glory of
the High Priest in his magnificent clothing, metaphorically
said to make the entire sanctuary shine brilliantly (vv. 5-
11).[236] Sirach follows with a description of the liturgy including the attending priests and their functions, the sacrifice, the libation, the sounding of the trumpets for a remembrance, the prayer of the people, the singing of the singers,
and the blessing of the people by the high priest which included the uttering of the divine name.[237]

Finally, Sirach concludes his "Praise of the Fathers" with
a doxology in which he asks God to grant wisdom and peace to

the Jews of his own day, and, most important for our purposes, asks a blessing for Simon and his descendants in the office of high priest:

> May his steadfast love be confirmed for Simon,
> And may he establish for him the covenant of Phinehas.
> So that one will never be cut off from him and his
> offspring all the days of heaven.[238]

Once more we have evidence of Sirach's concern for the continuance of the legitimate succession of the Zadokite-Oniad high priesthood in the face of a gathering storm of controversy surrounding this most important office.

One other group of cultic personnel mentioned by Sirach is that of the singers. Sirach, obviously following the Chronicler, ascribes the establishment of the guilds of the singers in the temple to David who was himself a singer of psalms of praise to God (47:8f.). As indicated before, he also mentions the singers in the liturgy of the Day of Atonement (50:18). But in contrast to the Chronicler, Sirach appears relatively unconcerned with the levitical singers, probably since he places himself in support of the Aaronic priesthood over against the continued efforts of the levites to assume priestly functions.[239]

Cultic Rituals: Sacrificial Offerings, Ritual Washings, and Fasting. We have already referred to the sacrifices and offerings mentioned by Sirach in his eulogies to Aaron, Phinehas, and Simon. With respect to Sirach's own emphases pertaining to the participation of the wise in cultic worship, by far the most important material is contained in his instruction dealing with the cult in 31:21-32:26 (Gk. 34:18-35:20) which in terms of forms contains admonitions, proverbs, rhetorical questions, and a short didactic poem:

Sacrifice and Oppression

A sacrifice (זבח) of oppression is an evil burnt
   offering (עולה),
And the offering (קרבן) of the wicked is not pleasing
   (לרצון).
The Lord will not be pleased with the burnt offerings
   (עולות) of the wicked,
And transgression is not atoned with many sacrifices
   (זבחים).

A son who sacrifices (זבח) before his father,
Offers (מקריב) an offering (קרבן) from the property
   of the poor.
The bread of the destitute is the life of the poor;
And one who deprives a worker of his wage, spills
   his blood.

Worship and True Repentance

One builds and another tears down.
What will they gain when they toil?
One blesses and another curses.
Whose voice will the Lord hear?
One who is purified after touching a dead body and
   touches it again,
What will he have gained by his ritual washing (רחיצה)?
Thus, a man fasts (צם) for his sins,
And once more goes and commits the same sins.
Who will hear his prayer (תפלה),
And what will he have gained for having humbled himself?

Sacrifice Equated with Righteous Living

He who keeps the Law (תורה) offers many offerings (קרבן).
He who sacrifices peace offerings (שלמים) heeds the
   commandment (מצוה).
He who does kindness, offers fine flour (סלת),
And he who establishes righteousness, sacrifices (זבח)
   a thank offering (תודה).
To turn from evil is pleasing (רצון) to the Lord,
And forgiveness is to turn from unrighteousness.

Sacrifice and the Fulfillment of Torah

Do not appear before the Lord empty-handed,
Because all these things are on account of the commandment (מצוה).

The Sacrifice of the Righteous

The offering (קרבן) of the righteous anoints the altar,
And it is a pleasing odor (ריח ניחוח) before the Lord.
The cereal offering (מנהה) of a righteous man is
   pleasing (תרצה),
And its remembrance (אזכרה) will not be forgotten.

Worship and the Cheerful Giver

Glorify the Lord with a bountiful heart,
And do not diminish the offering of your hand
   (תרומת יד).
In all your deeds make your face cheerful,
And with joy devote the tithe (מעשר).
Give to him according to his gifts to you,
With a bountiful heart and according to your ability.
Because God is one who repays;
Seven-fold he will return to you.

Worship and Oppression

Do not offer a bribe because he will not accept it,
And do not trust in a sacrifice (זבח) of oppression.
Because he is the God of justice,
And he does not show partiality.
He will not show partiality with respect to a poor man,
But the supplication (תחנוני) of a distressed man he
will hear.
He will not abandon the cry (צעקה) of an orphan,
Nor the widow when she increases her complaint.
Do not the tears run down her cheek,
As she bewails those who made them fall?
An acceptable plaint will receive respite,
And a cry (צעקה) is a cloud of solitude.[240]

In this extended instruction concerning cult, it is quite
apparent that Sirach is most conversant with the different
types of sacrificial offerings: תודה, שלמים, קרבן, עולה, זבח,
תרומת יד, מנחה, סלח and אזכרה. In addition, he refers to
prayer (צעקה, תחנון, תפלה), fasting (צם), ablution (רחיצה), and
the tithe (מעשר). But even more important for our concerns are
his usages of cultic language in speaking of acceptable or unacceptable worship, the social concerns he expresses for the
poor and the oppressed, his emphasis upon the intent of the
worshippers, and finally his comments that one should be observant, cultically speaking, because of such being commanded in
the Torah, and that righteous conduct is equal to ritual observance.

First of all, Sirach utilizes the language of the cult
when he assesses whether or not a cultic observance is acceptable to the Lord. The technical cultic terms for "pleasing"
and "not pleasing" (לרצון, לא לרצון) are found in 31:22, 23;
32:5, 9. This coupled with Sirach's acquaintance with the major types of sacrifices demonstrate the sage is well acquainted
with cultic language and terminology.

Even more important for our investigation is the evident
concern Sirach possesses for the poor and oppressed which is
connected with whether or not cultic offerings are acceptable.
If an offering is made at the expense of the poor and oppressed,
then it is declared unacceptable to the deity (21:21, 22, 24,
27; 32:15). Furthermore, Yahweh is depicted as a righteous
judge who cannot be bribed with sacrifices offered by powerful

oppressors (32:14f.). Rather he is seen as the champion of the oppressed who, upon hearing their cry of distress, will rouse himself forth to destroy the wicked. Such a concern for the poor and oppressed is found throughout this sapiential composition, and certainly points to Sirach's defense of the poor and oppressed against the powerful aristocracy, including both Jews and the foreign ruling class (see 32:23).[241]

In like fashion to his sapiential ancestors, Sirach also demonstrates an obvious concern with the character of the worshipper, since worship offered by the wicked is valueless, unacceptable to Yahweh (31:21-22), whereas the offering of the "righteous anoints the altar, and is a pleasing odor before the Lord" (32:8).[242] Also in this regard, Sirach lambasts the cultic participation of the sinner who, having participated in rituals such as fasting or ablutions (31:30-31), immediately commits the same sinful action for which he has sought forgiveness.

The motivations pointed to by Sirach for involvement in cultic worship include the simple answer that such is commanded in the Law, the principle of retribution (he who gives to the Lord will be rewarded many times over the price of his offering), and the desire to achieve forgiveness (atonement) for one's sins and to become "pleasing" to the deity.

Finally, the most striking element is Sirach's equating righteous behavior with cultic devotion, since both achieve the same end: forgiveness and acceptance by the deity (33:1-3). This should not be interpreted to mean that Sirach exalts righteous actions over cultic participation, but rather that he places them both on an equal plane in his depiction of sapiential piety. The true wise man, therefore, is righteous and cultically observant, and to distinguish between the two is a dichotomy completely foreign to Sirach's understanding.[243]

Cultic Rituals: Prayer and the Lament-Thanksgiving Cycle. As was the case in the cultic sensitivities of the traditional wise in Job and Proverbs, prayer in Sirach also appears as the primary cultic act, especially prayer in terms of the lament-thanksgiving cycle. And Sirach is no exception to this general

observation, for the second century sage not only mentions
prayer in numerous places, but even includes several of his own
complete prayers in his final composition (22:27-23:1-4, 36:1-
17, and 51:1-12).

In his praiseworthy description of the ideal wise man in
39:1f., Sirach accentuates prayer as the chief cultic action of
the wise (יעתיר‎, תפלה‎, יתחנן‎). The wise man offers prayer to
God for his sins (cf. 21:2), an important part of the penitential lament, and then, depending upon the acceptance of the
prayer by the deity (ירצה‎), the wise man will be filled with
the "spirit of insight," (רוח בינה‎), which will enable him to
"pour forth words of wisdom," and "he will give thanks (ויורה‎)
to the Lord in prayer, or, in other words, will offer a thanksgiving psalm for God's reception of his lament. A number of
points should be noted in this passage. First, the true wise
man is one who participates in prayer, the primary cultic act
of the pious wise which is probably related to the ability of
the wise to speak well and to the fact that the genres of prayer were most probably learned in wisdom circles.[244] Second,
Sirach, when he speaks of prayer, as is the case here, is generally referring to the lament-thanksgiving cycle. Finally,
the passage refers to the "prayer for wisdom," another type of
prayer appearing in sapiential literature (cf. Wis. of Solomon
9 [cf. I Kings 3], Sir. 37:15 and 51:13-14, 19).

It is evident from Sirach's numerous references to prayer
that he is intimately concerned with the character of the one
who prays, and places serious stress upon obedience to Torah.
If one is obedient to Torah, his prayer will be answered (3:5).
In addition, Sirach teaches that one who is not forgiving
should not expect to have his prayer accepted and his own sins
forgiven (28:1f.). The prayers of the poor and oppressed receive, according to Sirach, special consideration by the deity,
underlining the social and historical circumstances in which
Sirach lived. And Sirach disdains the meaningless repetition
of prayer formulae as uncharacteristic of sapiential behavior
(7:14).[245]

In a brief instruction concerning prayer, specifically in
terms of the lament and thanksgiving, Sirach admonishes his
pupils:

> Turn to the Lord and abandon iniquities.
> Make entreaty (התחנן) before him and diminish the
> cause of stumbling.
> Who is able to praise the Lord in Sheol?
> In place of the living, who give forth praise?
> Thanksgiving (תודה) ceases for the dead as for one
> who never existed.
> The one who is alive and well will praise (יודה)
> the Lord.

The point of the instruction is that the sinner should engage
in a penitential lament before he dies, for Sirach grimly reminds his audience that it is impossible to utter a thanksgiving for divine deliverance, once one has descended to the
depths of the underworld.

One of the most intriguing sections concerning prayer,
especially as regards the lament, is found in chapter 38 which
seeks a solution to a new problem posed by the presence of the
Hellenistic physician.[246] Does the pious Jew seek out the
physician, or does he forego a consultation and depend solely
upon divine healing from Yahweh, the divine physician? Sirach
seeks a middle ground in this dispute and counsels his audience
to consult a physician when ill, since, Sirach suggests, God
has created the physician, his profession, and the medicine
which he dispenses, and thus the physician has his divinely
appointed place and function in the order of reality.[247] Furthermore, the pious physician will pray to the deity for aid in
making the correct diagnosis and for the divine healing of his
patient. God is seen, then, as one who acts to heal the sick
through means of the Hellenistic physician. Even so, Sirach
does not discard the ancient, religious convention of the lament ritual, for the sick are also counseled to offer a lament
to the deity for healing, accompanied by the confession of sins
and an offering of the proper sacrifice (ניחוח אזכרה) and of
oil (v. 11). Thus Hellenistic science and Israelite faith are
entwined by Sirach.

As mentioned previously, Sirach has included three rather
lengthy prayers of his own in the final composition: 22:27-
23:4 ("A Prayer for Self-Control"); 33:1-13, 36:16-22 (Eng.
36:1-17, "A Lament for the Deliverance of the Nation"); and
51:1-12 ("An Individual Thanksgiving for Deliverance from Sin
and Death").[248]

The first prayer, "A Prayer for Self-Control," embraces the desire of the wise man to become the ideal "silent man" by mastery of his passions and especially his tongue:

> Oh that he would place a guard over my mouth,
> And a seal of prudence upon my lips,
> Lest I fall because of them and my tongue destroy me.
> God, my father and Lord of my life,
> Do not allow me to fall on account of them.
> Oh that they would put a whip to my thoughts,
> And a rod of discipline to my mind,
> That they might not pardon my iniquities,
> And pass over my transgressions,
> That my iniquity might not be multiplied,
> And my transgressions increased,
> Lest I fall before one who hates me,
> And my enemy rejoice over me.
> Oh God my father and Lord of my life,
> Do not abandon me to their counsel.
> Do not give me precipitant eyes,
> And keep far from me a wanton heart.
> Do not allow lustful flesh to entice me,
> And do not allow an impudent soul to rule over me.

The second prayer, "A Lament for the Deliverance of the Nation" (33:1-13, 36:16-22), is a communal lament set most probably against the background of a Judah ruled by the Greeks, and, placed on the lips of Sirach, reflects the sapiential emphasis of the efficacious intercession of the righteous, wise man who hopes to persuade the deity to restore his nation to former prominence.[249]

> Save us Oh God of all,
> And place the fear of you over all the nations.
> Move against a foreign nation,
> So that they may see your mighty deeds.
> As you have been sanctified by means of us before them,
> So exalt yourself by means of us before our eyes,
> So that they may know what we have known:
> That there is no God besides you.
> Renew a sign, and repeat a miracle,
> Make glorious your hand and strengthen your strong right
>   hand.
> Arouse your anger and pour out your wrath.
> Subdue the adversary and drive out the enemy.
> Hasten the end time and enjoin the appointed time.
> For who says to you, "What are you doing?"
> In burning anger let the survivor be consumed,
> And let those who oppress your people find destruction.
> Smite the head of the temples of Moab,
> The one who says, "There is no one but me."
> Gather all the tribes of Jacob,
> And let them inherit once again as in former days.

Have mercy upon the people called by your name,
Israel whom you have entitled 'first-born'.
Have mercy for your holy city,
Jerusalem the place of your rest.
Fill Zion with your splendor,
And your sanctuary with your glory.
Give testimony to your deeds at the beginning,
And establish the prophecy spoken in your name.
Give a reward to those who await you,
And let your prophets be trustworthy.
You will hear the prayer (תפלה) of your servants,
According to your delight for your people.
So that all the ends of the earth may know,
That you are the God of the world.

Again notation should be made of the identification of the communal lament with 'prayer' (תפלה).[250]

The third prayer, "An Individual Thanksgiving for Deliverance from Sin and Death," is placed near the end of the final composition (51:1-12). Its authenticity has been disputed by some, but without convincing evidence.[251] The form is a typical individual thanksgiving, and presents Sirach's prayer of thanksgiving to the deity for delivering him from the destructive forces of sin and death.

I will praise you, Oh God of my salvation.
I will thank (אודך) you, Oh God of my father.
I will tell of your name, Oh refuge of my life,
Because you have redeemed my soul from death.
You have spared my flesh from the pit,
And from Sheol you have delivered my soul.
You have set me free from the defamation of people,
From the scourge of the evil report of foreigners,
From lips of rebellious lies.
Before those who stood by, you were my helper,
According to your abundant steadfast love.
You have delivered me from the snare of the watchman
    of the precipice,
From the hand of those seeking my life,
From many sorrows,
From the straits of destructive flames which had
    surrounded me,
From a flaming fire which burned out of control,
From the deep womb of my mother,
From deceitful lips, and those who were foolish liars,
And from the arrows of a deceitful tongue.
For my soul had drawn near to death,
And my life to Sheol below.
And I turned, but there was no one to help me.
And I looked about for someone to sustain me, but
    there was no one.
Then I remembered the mercy of my Lord,
And his eternal steadfast love,

> The one who delivers those who trust in him,
> And the one who redeems from every evil,
> Then I raised my voice from the earth,
> And I cried out from the gates of Sheol.
> And I exalted my Lord, you my father,
> Because you are the mighty one of my salvation.
> Do not abandon me on the day of sorrow,
> On the day of devastation and desolation.
> I will praise your name continually,
> And I will remember you in prayer (תפלה).
> Then the Lord heard my voice,
> And he gave ear to my entreaty.
> He redeemed me from every evil,
> And he delivered me on the day of sorrow.
> On account of that I will give thanks (הודיתי), and
>   I will praise,
> And I will bless the name of the Lord.

Once more the obvious equation between this thanksgiving psalm and prayer is made, and demonstrates support for the position we have argued: the wise were involved in the writing of psalmodic prayers, a point that will be of primary concern in the following chapter.

Didactic Hymns.[252] In addition to laments and thanksgivings, hymns also appear in the repertoire of Sirach's literary accomplishments: 1:1f., 4:11-19, 24:1-29 (hymns concerning wisdom), 16:24-17:14, 39:12-35, and 42:15-43:33 (creation hymns).[25] That the wise of Sirach's day participated creatively in the writing of hymns may be concluded from his statement in 15:9-10:

> A hymn of praise is not fitting in the mouth of a
>   wicked man,
> Because it has not been accorded to him by God.
> Rather a hymn should be uttered by the mouth of a
>   wise man;
> And the one who masters it, will teach it.

Thus Sirach attaches divine inspiration to the production of hymns by the wise, since to Sirach, the ability to write hymns is a gift from the deity. Furthermore, Sirach testifies to the usage of the hymn by the wise in instruction, probably meaning that the genre of the hymn as well as certain didactic hymns were taught to their pupils. The best example of a didactic hymn written by Sirach is a beautifully structured creation hymn placed in 39:12-35.

Introductions

Sapiential Introduction	Again I have reflected, and I shall speak, And like the full moon, I have become full. Listen to me, Oh innocent ones, and sprout forth Like a rose planted by streams of water. And send forth fragrance like frankincense, And like a lily send forth blossoms.
Hymnic Introduction	Give forth your voice and sing praise, And bless the Lord for all his deeds. Ascribe greatness to his name, And praise him in a hymn of praise (תהלה). In songs accompanied by the lyre and stringed instruments, And then shall you say with a shout:
Proverbial Thesis	Every deed of God is good, And every need (צורך) will be supplied in its time (עת).

Strophe I

A

God as Creator and Savior	According to his command he arranged in order the heap of waters, And at the utterance of his mouth its reservoir. Its lowest regions he passes through according to his desire, Even as no restraint is placed on his salvation.

B

Retribution: God as Savior of the Just	The activity of every one is before him, And nothing is hidden from his eyes. From everlasting to everlasting he observes; Is there any limit to his salvation? There is nothing too small and insignificant for him, And there is nothing more marvelous and strong than he.
Disputative Refrain: Thesis Restated	Do not say, "What is this for"? Because everything has been selected for its need (צורך). Do not say, "This is worse than that." Because everything will be powerful in its time (עת).

Strophe II

B¹

Retribution: God as Destroyer of the Foreigners	His blessings overflow like the Nile, And like a river drenches the dry land. Thus the nations will inherit his rage, As he turns fresh water into salt. His paths are straight to the upright, Just as they are crooked to the foreigners.

1. Explanatory Expansion of B¹

Creation of Good Things	Good things were apportioned to the good from the beginning, As both good and evil were to the evil. Basic for every need (צורך) of a man's life are Water and fire, iron and salt, Wheat flour, milk, and honey, Wine, oil, and clothing. All these are good for the good, Yet they are turned to evil for the wicked.

2. Explanatory Expansion of B¹

Creation of Evil Things	There are winds which have been formed for judgment. And in their wrath they move mountains, And at the time (עת) of consummation they will pour out their power, As they soothe the spirit of their creator. Fire and hail, calamity and pestilence, These also have been formed for judgment. The teeth of the wild beast, the scorpion, the venomous serpent, And the sword of vengeance to destroy the wicked.

A¹

God as Creator of Destruction	All these things have been created for their function (צורך). And they will be mustered in the storehouse, and at the proper time (עת), They will leap forth when he commands them. And according to their statute, they will not rebel against his word.

Conclusions

Sapiential Conclusion	Therefore from the beginning I have taken counsel, And I have reflected and in writing have deposited it.

Proverbial Thesis	Every deed of God is good, And every need (צורך) will be supplied in its time (עת).
Disputative Refrain: Thesis Restated	Do not say, "This is worse than that." Because all will become powerful in its time (עת).
Hymnic Conclusion	Now with all your heart give forth praise, And bless the name of the Holy One.

The structure of this didactic hymn is the artistic work
of a master craftsman. Following two 6 hemistich introductions,
a sapiential and a hymnic one in following the nature of the
didactic hymn, Sirach states the thesis over which he is reflecting in his hymn in the form of a proverb: "Every deed of
God is good, and every need will be supplied in its time." The
body of the didactic hymn consists of two strophes, consisting
of two major parts: A, B and B[1], A[1] which are in chiastic arrangement and demonstrate external antithetical parallelism.
A and A[1] each have four hemistichs, while B and B[1] each have 6
hemistichs. Strophe II contains two explanatory expansions,
each possessing 8 hemistichs and demonstrating external antithetical parallelism. Strophe I and Strophe II both are concluded by a refrain which is disputative in form,[254] and the
content effectively restates the proverbial thesis: "Do not
say, 'What is this for?' Because everything has been selected
for its need (צורך)"; and "Do not say, 'This is worse than
that.' Because everything will be powerful in its time (עת)."
Note that the major key words, צורך and עת, are repeated in this
two-part refrain. Finally, in the conclusions, both a sapiential and a hymnic conclusion are presented, paralleling the
two-fold introduction, and the proverbial thesis is stated once
more: "Every deed of God is good and every need (צורך) will be
supplied in its time (עת).

The key words placed in strategic positions throughout the
didactic hymn are צורך ("need," "function") and עת ("time"), and
occur in the proverbial thesis, stressing Sirach's major point
that every part of creation has its proper place, function, and
time for existence within the created order. Sirach reflects

over this proverb, and uses it in his attempts at validating
the justice of God[255] which had been maligned especially by
Koheleth and probably by certain opponents of his own period.[256]
Thus he argues all things are good, and frees the deity of complicity in evil by stating that good things have been merciful-
ly supplied for the righteous, whereas the evil, though they
may at times enjoy the same blessings of good, eventually will
see them turn to evil. Furthermore, even evil things which God
has created have a just and good purpose, and that is, they are
constructed as tools of judgment, sent by God to punish and destroy the wicked at the proper time. This is their function
(צורך), and God determines the time (עת) for them to work their
mission of destruction against the wicked. Thus he disputes
his opponents who question why an apparently evil thing exists
or who dare to call one element of creation worse than another.

But most important for our concerns, besides the obvious
point that the wise wrote didactic hymns, is the manner in
which the hymn has been conceived and constructed by our sage.
He has taken a simple proverb, reflected upon it (see v. 32),
and has built his didactic hymn around it. Such should provide
us with the key to unlock the mysteries of didactic poetry and
wisdom psalms in the coming chapter.

The Vow. Sirach also includes among his writings concerning the cult a short instruction pertaining to the vow in which
he alludes to the extreme seriousness of the obligation to
which one binds himself in the vow making procedure.

> Do not withhold from paying your vow (נדר).
> And do not wait until you are dead to be justified.
> Before you vow, give serious consideration to your vow,
> And do not be one who tempts his Lord (18:22-23).

Sirach includes his teaching with respect to the vow in the
context of careless and rash speech, and, like his sapiential
predecessors, regards hasty vows to be the result of foolishness. He discredits the fool who makes a vow before seriously
considering its consequences. In addition, he is most concerned that his wise pupils fulfill their vow once it is made,
intimating that destruction comes to those who foolishly linger

in paying it.[257] Sirach also disdains the effort to use the
vow as a bargaining process in which one hopes to seduce the
deity into fulfilling one's request by making an enticing bargain.

Urim and Thummim. Sirach places the sacred lots back in
the hands of the priests, indicating that they are in use in
his day, and also places their oracle-obtaining power in high
esteem (see 45:10, and 33:3, Grk.). He states:

> A man of understanding will trust in the law;
> For him the law is as dependable
> As an enquiry by means of Urim.

Holy Times. Besides the lengthy description of the most
important fast day in the Israelite calendar, the Day of Atonement, Sirach also refers to holy seasons in two other important
places. In his eulogy pertaining to David, he praises the august king for "giving glory to the pilgrimmage festivals
(חגים)," and for "arranging in order the appointed times
(מועדים)."[258] Perhaps this reflects David's making Jerusalem
the central sanctuary where pilgrimmage would be made for the
major festivals (47:10).

Secondly, Sirach speaks of holy times in a rather intriguing section which deals with the contrasts of opposites which
are present in reality: good and evil, life and death, the sinner and the pious man, and the blessed and the cursed (36:7-15).
Sirach's explanation for the existence of sacral seasons is
given in response to the question: "Why is one day deemed better than another when all the daylight in the year is from the
same source, the sun?" Sirach's response, which demonstrates
not only his pious faith but also his usage of the "science of
opposites," is that distinctions between holy times and ordinary days were made by the wise Lord. Certain days he made
"festival times" (מועדים), and "blessed and hallowed" them,
whereas some days were made to be ordinary calendrical days
(literally, "days for counting"). Using this as his base,
Sirach moves on to explain the divinely appointed opposites
elsewhere in reality, and especially the divinely determined
behavior and lot of all men.[259]

The Temple. Sirach's devotion to the temple is obvious.
We have already pointed to his placing of wisdom in the "holy
tabernacle" (משכן קדש), his references to the service in the
temple by the high priests in 45:24 and 50:5, and the singers
in the temple organized by David (47:13). Sirach also praises
the Judean kings in their various roles with respect to the
building and reforming of the temple and its cultus. An allu-
sion is made to Josiah's reformation of the cultus in the Jerusalem temple (49:2), and Zerubbabel and Joshua are praised for
their efforts in the rebuilding of the temple (49:11-12).

In two places (33:18, 49:6), Jerusalem is referred to as
the "city of the sanctuary (קרית קדש)," the first of which is
found in the "Lament for the Deliverance of the Nation." In
this prayer, Sirach calls for divine intervention on Israel's
behalf on the basis of the temple in Jerusalem, the place of
the divine abode. This underlines Sirach's devotion to the
temple and the Jerusalem cult and his desire that the temple
cultus should continue to be a revered institution in the Jewish nation.[260]

The Attack Against Illicit Cultic Practices. Sirach castigates divination (קסם), omenology (נחש), and the interpretation of dreams (חלומות) in 31:1-8, categorizing them as folly
(הבל) and delusions of the mind, and judging them to be out of
step with the concerns of torah and wisdom.[261]

His statements concerning dreams are interesting, since
they may be compared and contrasted with Koheleth.[262] Like the
pious wise in Job, Sirach gives credence only to those dreams
which are sent from the Most High as a warning (v. 6), thus indicating that such dreams should be considered as warnings of
coming destruction for sinful actions. Otherwise, dreams are
to be avoided as part and parcel of the processes of divination, which Sirach attacks, not because they are forbidden cultic practices (תעבות ליהוה), but because they are foolishness.

In 30:18-20, Sirach speaks of health, which he considers
to be a divine gift that should be cherished, for without
health the good things of life cannot be enjoyed, especially
since illness may eventually plunge one into the depths of

death's cold stream. To illustrate his instruction concerning
health, he uses a comparative proverb and a rhetorical question, both of which deride idolatry. In an idol satire similar
to that of Second Isaiah and to the Wisdom of Solomon, Sirach
indicates that good things given to one whose lips are sealed
in death is like an offering (תנופה) made to an idol (גלול).
Then he asks, "What good is such to the idols (אלילי) of the
nations who neither eat nor smell?"

The rejection of idolatry is not based on cultic prohibition (Ex 20:4f.; Dt 27:15), but rather on the sapiential observation that an idol has no propensity for the consuming of the
offering. It is like the dead man who no longer possesses the
capacity to eat and drink. We shall return to this matter in
the Wisdom of Solomon.

Conclusion. In characterizing Sirach's interest in the
institutions and rituals of the Israelite cult, we find no sym-
pathy for remarks made by Pfeiffer and others that the sage did
not consider cult as central to his religious understanding,
and that "rites and ceremonies *per se* are really insignificant
and ineffective."[263] On the contrary, Sirach regards cultic
religion as an essential and important part of both Israel's
religious heritage and the wise man's own religious devotion.
To regard cultic religion otherwise would be incongruous with
the sage's own teachings and religious piety.

The Wisdom of Solomon

Introduction. Our final investigation is centered on the
Wisdom of Solomon, written by an Alexandrian Jewish sage during
the first century B.C. when Alexandria was the leading cultural
center for Greek Hellenism in the Near East,[264] a fact that il-
luminates the form and shape of this piece of sapiential literature.[265]

During the lifetime of this sage, anti-Judaism in an incipient, intellectual form developed in the polemical writings
of Hellenistic authors, including Hecataeus of Abdera, Mnaseas,
Posidonius, Apollonius Molo, Apion, and Democritus, literature
which sought to discredit the religious and national heritage

of Judaism and to break its resistance to syncretism. Atheism
(absence of idols, monotheism), barbarisms, nefarious cultic
practices including murder, philosophical obtuseness and absurdity, and the worship of a golden ass were among the accusa-
tions levelled against the Jews by these and other writers.

Not to be upstaged, Jewish men of letters responded with
the creation of a body of apologetic and missionary literature
aimed at repelling the literary thrusts of the Hellenists, and
even at times at converting the Hellenists themselves. This
literature included Josephus, Pseudo-Aristeas, Aristobulus, The
Wise Menander, the Sibylline Oracles, IV Maccabees, Pseudo-
Phocylides, Artapanus, Philo, and the Wisdom of Solomon.[266]
This literature not only served its purpose in the defense of
Judaism to its "cultured despisers," but, in addition, had the
subsequent result of leading to "a more systematic, logical, and
metaphysical presentation of Judaism to the Hellenistic
World."[267]

Yet the assault from without was equalled by the crisis
from within, as Jews of the period were coming to question the
validity and importance of their heritage as well as the deity
their fathers had worshipped for centuries.[268] This crisis of
faith which had burst forth like raging waters from a disinte-
grated dam during the period of the Babylonian conquest and
captivity once again reached flood-stage during the period of
Hellenistic rule, both in terms of the soft and enticing wooing
of the promiscuous maiden of culture and in the brutal club of
Antiochus Epiphanes. Of the many different responses to the
crisis of Hellenism made by the Jews of the Hellenistic period,
from obeisance to the Greek gods of beauty, culture, philosophy,
and religion to fiery rebellion and warfare, we find our sage
choosing a middle road which stressed the validity of the religious, national, and cultural heritage of the Jewish past, but
yet at the same time presented it in the new garment of Hellenistic thinking, literature, and language.

Thus our sage saw his task to be the defense of Judaism
against the literary assault of Hellenistic authors, primarily
in Alexandria, and, in addition, the representation of the faith

of the fathers to Jews who, suffering from the intellectual
persecution of the Hellenists and the inward crisis of faith
during the Hellenistic period, began to respond to the allure-
ments of Hellenistic culture, Greek philosophy, the mysteries,
and the sensual and aesthetic appeal of idolatry.

The Attack Against Foreign Religions. Among the weapons
in the arsenal of our Alexandrian sage, one of those most frequently used was the polemic, for our sage rests not as a cir-
cumspect defender, but, on the contrary, becomes the abrasive
attacker. Such a weapon is used in his critique of pagan religions which were attracting Jewish converts, and to which some
of the Hellenistic opponents adhered. Thus his incisive criticism is motivated not only by the quest to oppose the conver-
sion of Jews to these religions, but at the same time he uses
the weapon of the opponents who had attacked the foolishness
and the less savory aspects of Jewish religion.

The frontal assault made by the sage against the major
pagan religions of his period is found embedded in the extensive midrash on the traditions of *Heilsgeschichte*,[269] and is
contained primarily in the inclusive section comprising chapters 13-15, though other material is found in 11:15-26 and 12:
3-11. The structure of the section has been analyzed by Gilbert as follows:

    13: 1- 9 - Philosophical Religion: The Religion of Nature
    13:10-19 - The Idolatrous Wood-Cutter
    14: 1-10 - The Idolatrous Sea-Farer
    14:11-31 - The Invention of Idols and the Origin of
               Immorality
    15: 1- 6 - The Faithfulness of Israel
    15: 7-13 - The Idolatrous Potter
    15:14-19 - The Religion of Egypt[270]

As we shall see, our sage attacks in general four kinds of
religion: the worship of animals by the Egyptians, the worship
of nature by the philosophers, the worship of fertility by the
Dionysian mystery cult, and the worship of idols by idolators.

Egyptian Religion: The Animal Cults. The most scathing
attack of our sage against pagan religions is leveled against
the veneration of animals in the ancestral Egyptian cults. The
gods in Egypt were conceived to be not only in anthropological

form but, as was the case with most religions of the ancient
Near East, also in animal form as well, for the Egyptians saw
an intimate relationship between their deities and certain,
mysterious, powerful, and 'wise' animals which came to represent symbolically these same characteristics in certain gods,
though at times they were taken to be the abode of the gods and
even the gods manifest in physical form.[271] Thus we find Anubis
associated with the jackal, Hathor with the cow, Bast with the
cat, Thoth with the baboon and the ibis, Re with the Mnevis bull,
Ptah with the Apis bull, and so forth. Documentation of the
association of the gods with certain animals is attested as
early as the beginning of the Old Kingdom, and the practice obviously continued into the Hellenistic period as well. For
example, the Apis bull continued to be regarded as the incarnation of Osiris, and upon death its soul journeyed to heaven
where it was united with Osiris, forming Osiris-Apis, more commonly known as Serapis. Under Ptolemy I, a Serapeum was established at Alexandria. He brought the statue of Serapis from
Pontus to Alexandria, and introduced there the cult of Serapis
who became identified with Dionysus, Alexander, and finally the
Ptolemaic dynasty.[272] Furthermore, Herodotus makes reference
to cultic rites in honor of cats, dogs, crocodiles, etc.[273]
Consequently, when the Alexandrian sage attacks Egyptian animal
worship he attacks not only a dead religious practice of the
past, but also a vital religion of his own time.

The verbal assault of this sage is most harsh against what
he considers to be the most detestable form of religion of his
time: animal worship practiced by the hated Egyptians in Alexandria.[274] He criticizes animal worship in three different
places, seeming never content with an earlier emphasis, and
thus returning once more to enforce upon the minds of his audience the horrid features of such a religion: 11:15-26, 12:23-27,
and 15:18-16:1.

His first criticism of animal veneration occurs in 11:15-
26 which is placed in the context of the plagues sent to punish
the Egyptians but to bless the Israelites who were not affected
by these plagues and were allowed release from Egypt as a result
of them. The plagues provided our sage his first opportunity to

cast aspersion on the religion of Egypt, being a concrete example of what to our author appeared to be a verification of the principle of retribution in its most specific sense: one "is punished by the very things by which he sins." The irony is that the Egyptians who worshipped "foolish reptiles and worthless animals" (ἐθρήσκευον ἄλογα ἑρπετὰ καὶ κνώδαλα εὐτελῆ) were punished by such animals in the second, third, and fourth plagues which, according to P, included frogs, gnats, and fleas.[275] Yet the sending "of multitudes of irrational animals" was not only seen as a verification of the dogma of retribution, an example of the blessings of Israel as opposed to the cursings of Egypt, and as proof of the sinfulness of animal worship, but had the additional function of pointing to the mercy of the Jewish God who certainly had the power to send terrible means of destruction, such as bears, lions, and even more horrible unknown beasts to destroy the Egyptians, but instead sent the plagues of these animals as a warning to them to turn from their sins, especially the sin of animal worship. Thus the mercy of God is stressed even for those who practice the most detestable of all forms of religion: animal worship.

The second passage which berates the veneration of animals is found in 12:23-27, when once more our sage develops similar lines of thought with respect to the folly of animal worship. Again he stresses that the Egyptians in the plagues were punished by means of the same animals they had venerated, but he adds that the punishment of this type was sent in order that the Egyptians might be forced to recognize the true God. Two other reasons are stated as to why the Egyptians worshipped despicable animals: folly and unrighteousness. Thus sin, unrighteousness, and foolishness are the reasons men err in worshipping detestable animals instead of the true deity.

The final reference to Egyptian animal worship concludes the section on pagan religions: 15:8-16:1. Utilizing the philosophical argument of beauty, the Alexandrian sage attacks the Egyptians who worship, not beautiful animals, but the most disgusting of all the animals in terms of their ignorance and repulsive form. Again he emphasizes the principle of retribution in its most specific sense, though he adds in this pericope

that the veneration of animals has led to the failure of the
Egyptians to praise God and, as a result, to receive his blessing.

   Mystery Religions: The Cult of Dionysus. The popular
Hellenistic mystery cult centered around the god Dionysus also
fell beneath the bludgeon of the Alexandrian sage in two pericopes: 12:3-11 and 14:23-26. The first ostensibly is directed
toward the religion of the Canaanites: "those who dwelt of old
in thy holy land." This section follows the discussion of
Egyptian animal worship and the extended statement concerning
the mercy of the deity directed toward even the Egyptians, and
has the same purpose of illustrating the mercy of God to pagans
in Israel's dim past, for God also destroyed the Canaanites
little by little instead of catastrophically in one blow in
order to give them "a chance to repent." But, our sage adds
that God still gave them such an opportunity even though he
knew that, being "an accursed race from the beginning" (cf.
Gen 9:20f.), they would never repent. Furthermore, God's reticence to destroy them totally rested in his mercy and was not
due to weakness or intimidation by other weak or non-existent
powers.

   But most important for our concerns is the listing of the
cultic practices of Canaanite religion: "detestable practices,"
"sorcery," "unholy rites," "the merciless slaughter of children," and the "sacrificial feasting on human flesh and blood"
which is offered "from those who are in their own ranks," including not only the worshippers themselves but also their
children. These practices become the apologetic basis for the
conquest tradition, according to our sage, for God willed to
punish them for their horrible religious rites by means of the
conquest of Canaan. While our writer appears concerned to describe the horrible religious practices of a vanquished people
of the past, his concern to speak to his own contemporaries in
Alexandria may be gathered from his description of the Canaanite rites in terms of a contemporary, ecstatic, fertility religion devoted to the god of fertility and immortality, the Greek
god Dionysus. This has been cogently argued by Gill who

indicates that while the Canaanites may have on occasion practiced child sacrifice, there is no evidence for the eating of
human sacrifices, which, instead, would have been offered as
burnt sacrifices. Furthermore, in his comparison of this passage with the writings of the poets Euripides and Aeschylus
concerning the Dionysian cult, Gill readily demonstrates that
the Alexandrian wise man had borrowed his ideas and description
of the Canaanite cult mostly from the writings of the Greek
poets in their description of the Dionysian Mystery.[276]

Dionysus was identified with Osiris in Hellenistic Egypt,
a rather easy process, since both were fertility gods and gods
of immortality.[277] This deity became the center of one of the
most popular mystery cults in the Hellenistic world and was
widespread in Egypt. It appealed to the individual, and especially to women, though eventually it came to be associated
with the Ptolemaic ruler cult. The myth of Dionysus involved
the general themes of the dying and rising vegetation deity including the death of the god, his body being torn to pieces,
his limbs scattered and eventually gathered by a deity, and the
miraculous revival of the god, a point indicated also by his
name which literally means "twice born." The cult promised to
its adherents the blessings of fertility and, even more important, the gift of immortality, for they could share in the vital powers of their god. The rites of the cult included orgi-
astic fertility practices; the inducing of the ecstatic state
by means of music, dancing, gleaming torches during the noc-
turnal meetings, and intoxication by wine; and enthusiasm, the
process by which the god was believed to dwell within the body
of the effeminate high priest during the rituals.

The Greek poets attacked the cult for its Bacchanalian
practices which were said to include sacrificial murdering and
feasting on the bodies of the victims, usually opponents of the
cult or a child of a female participant,[278] though one has to
admit some scepticism, since sacrificial, religious meals of
the flesh and blood of sacrificial animals in which the god was
believed to have manifested himself may have been the basis for
the possibly misinformed charge of sacrificial murder and feasting on human blood. Christianity was the object of a similar

charge during the period of the ancient church. Yet the eating of the flesh and blood of the cultic animal is an indication of the attempt to gain the god's powers of fertility and immortality for the worshipper.

Now it becomes apparent that the sage's description of the Canaanite cult has been influenced by the Greek poets who described the mystery cult of Dionysus, giving us evidence that our sage wished to use the condemnation of the ancient cult as a pretext for making an attack on the religion of Dionysus of his own day. And he warns his audience that it is only the mercy of God, not fear or impotence, that keeps him from completely devastating the practitioners of this cult in Alexandria.

The second reference to the Dionysian cult is found in 14:23-26 where the sage lists the horrible crimes of those who "celebrate secret mysteries": murder of children, adultery, theft, debauchery, etc. The context for this list is his condemnation of idolatry which he argues is the basis for and origin of all sins. We shall elaborate on this in a moment. But the major point of our sage is that fertility religion deserves to be severely condemned because of immorality.

Philosophical Religion: The Worship of Nature. In 13:1-9 the wise man critiques the philosophical cult of nature, primarily the Stoic view of cosmic monotheism, or pantheism, in which the Stoic πνεῦμα ("world-soul," "Zeus") was seen to be the divine, cosmic, and ethical power of generation and force which permeated all reality. Thus the references by the sage to "fire," "wind," and "air" are references to aspects of the Stoic world-soul. His referring to "the stars and the turbulent water" comes from the Stoic idea that the divine sea provided the nourishment for the heavenly bodies.[279]

The sage criticizes philosophers, and most especially the Stoics, for their deification of nature, a criticism which uses the Aristotelian teleological argument that includes the point that the craftsman is to be known by and yet differentiated from the ordered work which he constructs.[280] The beauty and order of nature resulted in the philosophical worship of nature, but our author critiques such worship for failing to draw the conclusion that the craftsman who created such order and beauty must be himself superior to his creation. He then utilizes the Platonic argument of analogy in v. 5 to underscore his point that the philosophers should have been able to perceive the creator by the process of contemplation in which one makes an analogy between the "greatness and beauty of created things" and their creator who, because he is the artisan of nature, should have been discovered by the philosophers and differentiated from that which he created.[281]

The limitation of this religion of the philosophers is caused by their identification of the unifying order of the cosmos, which they referred to as ὁ αἰών, with the Lord himself. Rather, the true deity, δεσπότης, is the artisan of creation, the God to whom our sage refers as ὁ ὤν, the Septuagint's translation of Yahweh in Ex 3:14.

Philosophical religion receives a good deal of respect from our sage who himself was schooled in the major Greek philosophical traditions, for he says that though they are "not to be excused," they are "little to be blamed." The most exalted form of pagan religion to our sage is philosophical religion, though even this religion receives an incisive critique. But it is commendable when compared to the horrors of animal worship and idolatry.[282]

The Religion of Idolatry. By far the most extensive critique of pagan religions is that of idolatry.[283] This material covers 13:10 through 16:1, and may be divided into the following units: 13:10-19 ("The Idolatrous Wood-Cutter"), 14:1-10 ("The Idolatrous Sea-Farer"), 14:11-31 ("The Invention of Idols and the Origin of Immorality"), 15:1-6 ("Faithful Israel"), 15:7-13 ("The Idolatrous Potter"), and 15:14-16:1 ("The Religion of Egypt").[284]

The first section devoted to the attack of idolatry occurs in 13:10-19, "The Idolatrous Wood-Cutter,"[285] and involves primarily an extensive description of a wood-cutter who, having cut down a tree in order to fashion a useful vessel for his needs, uses the chips for firewood, and, finally, with a piece

of scrap, useful for no good purpose, fashions an idol. Following this, the sage points to the foolishness of the artisan
who then devotes himself to the worship of the idol, and makes
requests which the idol is incapable of granting. The irony
should be duly noted in the series of contrasts made by the
sage who speaks concerning these requests and the subsequent
inability of the idol to fulfill them: the requesting of possessions, marriage, and children from that which is lifeless,
of health from that which is weak, of life from that which is
dead, of aid from that which is inexperienced, of a prosperous
journey from that which cannot take a step, and of prosperity,
success, and strength from that which is impotent. Ironically
the idolatrous wood-cutter asks of an idol that which only he
himself is capable of having and doing, for he possesses life.
The folly of idolatry rests in the worshipping of that which a
man himself has created and which is far inferior to the man
himself.

The second unit concerns "The Idolatrous Sea-Farer" in
14:1-10 who places a wooden idol on the prow of a ship and
prays for protection to "a piece of wood more fragile than the
ship which carries him."[286] The purpose in the building of a
ship was the "desire for gain," in contrast to the folly of
making an idol which can serve no useful purpose. The sage
then presents a contrast between the fragile idol and the providence (πρόνοια) of God which has given to the ship a "path in
the sea" and eventually steers the ship safely into port by
means of the science of navigation. The building of a ship and
the science of navigation are beneficently established within
the structure of reality and given the guidelines of wisdom.
Thus wood put to a wise and orderly fashion in ship-building
and navigation has a good and useful purpose within the ordering of reality.

The guidance of the ship by providence receives an example
from Jewish religious tradition in Noah and the Ark, but in
good sapiential form, for the guiding salvation of the Ark of
Noah was implemented by his "righteousness" that was brought to
a state of blessing by means of the proper use of wood, whereas
the "pride" of the giants of Noah's age brought them to

destruction. In contrast, wood put to an unrighteous, improper use, such as in the building of an idol, is "cursed" along with the one who is responsible.[287]

Finally he speaks concerning the principle of retribution, and the destruction of those, accordingly, who are idolators along with their idols.

The third unit, occurring in 14:11-31 ("The Invention of Idols and the Origin of Immorality"), is perhaps the most interesting as well as the most important of all the idolatry pericopes, for it develops two lines of thought: idolatry as the precipitating cause of all immorality (vv. 12, 22-31) and the explanation of the origins of idolatry--the worship of a statue in commemoration of a dead child (vv. 15-16) and the development of the ruler cult (vv. 17-21).

Comparable to the attempt of Euhemerus to explain the origins of the gods in terms of a hero and benefactor cult,[288] our sage seeks to explain the origins of idolatry in two different ways: the statue commemorating a dead child and the statue in honor of a sovereign. The dead child explanation may very well have been borrowed from sources which explained the Dionysian cult as arising from the grief of the father expressed over the death of Dionysus, an influence which may be argued on the basis of v. 15 which refers to "secret rites and initiations" (μυστήρια καὶ τελετάς) practiced in honor of "a dead human being" (νεκρὸν ἄνθρωπον).[289] Other possible allusions may be to the deification of children by the Ptolemies, including the dead daughter of Ptolemy II.[290]

The second explanation of the origin of idolatry is the practice of venerating idols because of zealous devotion and patriotism shown to the image of an absent ruler who lived in another city or country, veneration which finally develops into a full-blown ruler cult.[291] The development of the Ptolemaic ruler cult in Alexandria, the capital of the Ptolemaic empire, is explained by our sage in terms of the zealous devotion and patriotism of the people of the empire directed towards the image of an absent ruler. The skilled image maker, in his desire to flatter the king, fashions a statue so beautiful that its aesthetic appeal leads eventually to cultic veneration, or in the sage's terms, the "entrapment of mankind."[292] Finally, the idol itself is referred to as a deity. One should not ignore the contrast between the self-designated divine rulers and the ideal just king, Solomon (7:1f.), who is presented as stressing his own mortality and human frailties.

The second major line of thought developed in this unit by the sage is the idea that idolatry is the father of immorality, for those who worship idols are accused of throwing off every restraint and practicing every conceivable wickedness.

After contrasting people who have been seduced by the charms of idolatry with Israel which remained faithful to God in 15:1-6, the sage in 15:7-13 presents a critique of "The Idolatrous Potter." In the condemnation of the potter who makes a clay image, the sage lambasts one who knowingly fashions that which is lifeless, in contrast to himself, for he possesses the breath of life. He also levels the charge of profiteering against the idolatrous potter who is engaged in his craft for the primary motivation of avarice and greed.[293]

Finally, the sage attacks the idolatry and animal veneration of Egypt (15:14-16:1), and in this section catalogues the frailties and incapacities of idols which cannot see, breathe, hear, feel, and walk, and which are manmade and dead. And he again stresses the foolishness of one who worships that to which he is infinitely superior.

Prayer. While the primary cultic concerns of our sage lay in the gladiatorial combat between Jewish monotheism and pagan religions, he, like his Israelite sapiential ancestors, extols the cultic practice of prayer. His first reference to prayer occurs in 7:7 in the Solomonic section (chapters 7-9) in which Solomon is obviously presented as the ideal, just, though human, king who is led to greatness by means of wisdom in contrast to the Ptolemaic rulers who had claimed the status of divinity. In an obvious development of I Kgs 3:3f., the sage presents Solomon as one who, having acknowledged his mortality and human birth, prays to God, receives the gift of wisdom, and in the following verses, is blessed because of her with knowledge, prudence, prosperity, honor, the ability to judge, and, most important, immortality.

A second reference to prayer occurs in 16:28-29 in the context of the presentation of the story concerning the beneficent gift of manna to the children of Israel, and from such our sage draws the admonitory conclusion that those who are to be blessed by God in a comparable manner "must rise before the sun to give thanks, and must pray at the dawning of light." Thus he refers to thanksgiving prayer in similar fashion to his sapiential predecessors.

The sage also presents for us a well-structured prayer involving the request of King Solomon for wisdom which was mentioned in 7:7.[294] The concentric structure of the prayer has been analyzed by Gilbert who points to the request of wisdom from the divine as the reoccurring theme found in vv. 4, 10, and 17.[295] The content of the prayer is based primarily on I Kgs 3:5-15, though ideas added by the sage include the emphasis upon the impotence of human wisdom as compared to the divine wisdom which, when given, guides one in the proper directions of life, and the dominion of man led by wisdom to rule over creation. Finally, in the Solomonic material, the sage refers to Solomon's prayer as including the command to build the Jerusalem temple and the altar, adding that such was to be a copy of the holy tent, and in this manner affirming the P tradition concerning the temple as a copy of the tabernacle.[296]

The Passover. Since the emphasis of the midrash on *Heilsgeschichte* is placed on the Exodus and Wilderness traditions, it is no point of amazement that the sage refers to the first Passover in 18:6-9, and bases his comments on Exodus 12. The context for this text is the discussion of the sage's belief that the same means of punishing the wicked becomes the means for the blessing of the righteous. Thus the plague of the death of the first-born is a terrible punishment for the detested Egyptians, but it results in God's blessing for the righteous who not only are spared the devastating results of the plague, but also achieve their deliverance as a consequence.

The reference to the cultic ritual of the Passover includes the offering of sacrifice, the agreement to follow the divine law (νόμος), and the singing of the praises of the fathers. The sacrifice obviously refers to the pascal lamb, the hymns probably to the *Hallel* psalms which according to Pes. 117a were sung on Passover,[297] and the divine law concerning the sharing of both good fortune and dangers probably refers to the institution of the Passover as a cultic law to be followed henceforth, regardless of the circumstances.[298] This last point possibly is an exhortation and demonstrates that this sage is appealing to sacral law as the basis for celebrating this familial festival in Alexandria.

Aaron, the High-Priest. Finally, in the references to the Wilderness tradition, the sage refers in 18:20-25 to the High Priest Aaron who, according to P, made intercession during the devastating plague inflicted by God because of the "murmuring of the people" against Moses and Aaron which followed the terrible end of the Levitical rebellion led by Korah. In the P account of the story, Aaron takes a censer and fills it with fire from the altar and produces incense in order to make atonement for the people. Such an action was credited with stopping the devastating plague.[299]

Our sage refers to this story by presenting Aaron as a "blameless" man whose major tools were "prayer and intercession."[300] Thus, in the frequently developed theme of the power of the intercession made by the just and righteous man, Aaron brings the plague to an end. The emphasis is placed upon his accomplishment of this task by his "word" (λόγος), and not by "force of arms," for Aaron appealed to God on the basis of oaths and the covenants of the fathers, a common practice in prayers to initiate a favorable divine response. Finally, the sage also points to the robe,[301] the diadem, and the four rows of stones found on the breastplate of the high priest and stresses that these stopped the plague of the "destroyer."[302] This fascination with the priestly apparel of the high priest is comparable to other Jewish writers, including Sirach as we mentioned earlier.[303] But to this sage the emphasis is not placed on the sacrosanct character of the high priest that allows him to come into contact with the holy and to make intercession through ritual, but rather on the intercessory power of the just man which can effectively turn away the destructive powers of divine punishment. This is a typically sapiential interpretation.

Conclusion. The cultic concerns of the sage of Alexandria rested primarily in his attack of pagan religions, which is certainly not an entirely new interest in Israelite wisdom,[304] for as we have seen, the warnings against fertility religion in Proverbs 1-9, Job's oath incorporating his refusal to participate in Mesopotamian astral worship, and Sirach's brief criticism of idolatry indicate that the wise before him were concerned with opposing religious apostasy as well. The significance of this should not be overlooked in terms of our investigation, for this demonstrates that Israel's wise, and we should probably include the wise in the states of Mesopotamia and Egypt, were not tolerant, or unconcerned, men of the world who placed themselves above the disputes of religious provincialism and controversy, a point which casts some doubt on the thesis of an international body of sages whose ideology was cosmopolitan in nature, spirit, and practice.

Conclusions

On the basis of our analyses of the major Israelite wisdom literature, it may be concluded that the Hebrew sages considered cultic religion to be a significant topic for sapiential reflection. As the traditional wise studied the various compartments of world order overseen by a just deity, they concluded that the cult had its own very important place within the structure of cosmic and social order. The spheres of nature and cult were seen to be intimately entwined by the sagacious teacher in Prov 3:9-10 who instructs his students that righteous observation of the cultic law to give to God the first fruits of harvest will lead to increased yields. The close relationship of the social order and the cult is obvious in a number of sapiential texts, including the frequent categorization of cultic acts as "pleasing" or "abominable" on the basis of the socio-ethical behavior of the cultic participant in Proverbs 10-31 and Sirach.

The traditional wise also believed that the principle of retribution functioned within the sphere of the cult, a dogma which led them to caution their adherents to participate in the realm of the cult as wise cultists, exuding the sapiential traits of the "silent man," and to avoid the foolish cultic behavior of the "heated man" whose behavior would lead him to destruction (Proverbs 10-31, Koh 4:17-5:6).

It is also extremely important to note that the Israelite sages often enter into an attack against foreign religions, especially fertility cults and the cults of astral deities, a point that indicates that these wise were not tolerant religionists whose possession of a worldly *savoir-faire* would cause them to dismiss as provincial the polemics of the Yahweh cult. Yet they do not condemn foreign religions and warn against participation in these cults by Israelite sages merely on the basis of sacral law, but also from their own sapiential perspectives.[305]

The Israelite wisdom literature also bespeaks of a critical wisdom tradition which strikes at the theological foundations of cultic religion. The twin concepts of a just order permeating the cosmos, society, and religion and of retribution established and overseen by a just deity are soundly thrashed by Job and Koheleth. While the poetic Job emasculates cultic religion by denying to it the power to influence either nature or deity, nevertheless, the poetic book still ends in an apparent affirmation of the importance of cultic piety. However, cult is no longer to be based on the ideas of order and retribution, but rather on the magnificence of the *mysterium tremendum*. Koheleth, also denying the validity of order and justice, chooses to speak only of the destructive, not the beneficent, side of the holy which is experienced by the frenetic fool, and finally concludes that, in view of the ultimate fate of all men, death, strict cultic observance or the disdain of cultic participation ultimately is a meaningless issue.

Finally, it is obvious that the Hebrew sages participated in the writing of extensive units of poetry, including many pieces which are most similar to cultic genres. This fact provides us with the basis for our next investigation: the wisdom psalms and didactic poetry.

[1]For an indepth study of order, see Hans Heinrich Schmid, *Gerechtigkeit als Weltordnung*.

[2]Cf. Job 38-42; Proverbs 8; Sirach 16 and 38; and Wis 7: 15-22.

[3]A working definition of wisdom is extremely difficult to fabricate as any reading of the major scholarly literature will attest. However, we shall suggest the following three-faceted definition. First, wisdom may be perceived as man's search for and ability to perceive order within reality. Second, wisdom is man's search for meaning and self-understanding. The wise man perceived his task to be that of discovering his proper place, function, and time within the order of reality. By finding his place, function, and time, he becomes aware of the meaning of existence for himself and may achieve self-understanding. Third, wisdom is man's quest to master life. Wisdom was considered capable of providing the wise man with the ability to come to terms with reality so that he would know how to act and what to do in every conceivable situation. Among the best definitions of wisdom in current scholarship, see James L. Crenshaw, "Method in Determining Wisdom Influence upon 'Historical' Literature," p. 132.

[4]For an extensive discussion of retribution in wisdom literature, see Klaus Koch, "Gibt es ein Vergeltungsdogma im Alten Testament"? *ZTK* 52 (1955), pp. 1-42.

[5]The affirmation of the sages that wisdom originated with God and was given by the creator to mankind is one element which points to the authoritative stance of wisdom literature, thus disproving the attempts of some scholars to regard wisdom as simply "good advice" which one may or may not follow. For the authoritative stance of wisdom, see James L. Crenshaw, *Prophetic Conflict*, BZAW 124 (Berlin: Walter de Gruyter, 1971), pp. 116-23.

[6]See Walther Zimmerli, "The Place and Limit of the Wisdom in the Framework of the Old Testament Theology," *SJT* 17 (1964), pp. 146-48.

[7]The absence of theological views involving God as the Lord of Salvation History in wisdom literature before Sirach has always been most perplexing. Efforts to view the early wise as secularistic humanists who functioned within an international setting devoid of doctrinaire theologies fail to take into consideration the fact that the concepts of order as justice, God as creator, and God as the overseer of the principle of retribution point to a religious, theological foundation to wisdom thinking, and that the wise of the major cultures of the

ancient Near East, at least with respect to cult, do engage in certain cultic ideas and practices which are unique to their own cultures. We believe that such a problem requires some involved research and reflective thought before any definite conclusions may be drawn.

[8]Schmid, *Gerechtigkeit als Weltordnung.*

[9]"Gerechtigkeit als Fundament des Thrones," *VT* 8 (1958), pp. 426-28.

[10]I Kgs 3:9. The expression for wisdom in this text is literally "a hearing heart." Once more Brunner has undertaken to explain this phrase by means of Egyptian sapiential parallels in which the heart was seen to be the receptacle for wisdom and to initiate wise decisions. A fool was considered to be one who was "without heart" ("Das hörende Herz," *TLZ* 79 [1954], pp. 697-700).

[11]Such important questions have been raised by Crenshaw in his overview of wisdom literature ("Prolegomenon," *Studies in Ancient Israelite Wisdom* [New York: Ktav, forthcoming 1975], pp. 20-22).

[12]Among those who have argued for a school in ancient Israel are D. Dr. Lorenz Dürr, *Das Erziehungswesen im Alten Testament und im Alten Orient*, MVAG 36 (Leipzig: J. C. Hinrichs, 1932); Wolfgang Richter, *Recht und Ethos*, StANT 15 (München: Kösel Verlag, 1966); and Hermisson, *Studien zur Israelitischen Spruchweisheit*, WMANT 28 (Neukirch-Vluyn: Neukirchener Verlag), pp. 97-132. For a cautious critique of the arguments for the existence of wisdom schools, see R. N. Whybray, *The Intellectual Tradition in the Old Testament*, BZAW 135 (1974), pp. 33-43.

[13]H. H. Schaeder, *Ezra der Schreiber*, BHT 5 (Tübingen: J. C. B. Mohr [Paul Siebeck], 1930).

[14]Georg Fohrer, *Introduction to the Old Testament* (Nashville: Abingdon Press, 1968), pp. 318-19. The major sections, discernible by means of the superscriptions with the exception of the last one, are: 1-9 ("The Proverbs of Solomon"), 10:1-22:16 ("The Proverbs of Solomon"), 22:17-24:22 ("The Words of the Wise"), 24:23-34 ("These also are Sayings of the Wise"), 25-29 ("These also are Proverbs of Solomon which the Men of Hezekiah, King of Judah, compiled"), 30 ("The Words of Agur, son of Jakeh of Massa"), 31:1-9 ("The Words of Lemuel, King of Massa, which his Mother taught him"), and 31:10-31 (no superscription).

[15]The life situation for the collections is difficult to ascertain specifically. However, we adhere to the position that the collections were meant for instructional purposes within the locus of court and temple schools, and were used to teach young students the intricacies of sapiential language, style, and forms, giving them exercises in analytical, empirical, and comparative thinking, and indoctrinating them in general sapiential ideas (see Bernhard Lang, *Die Weisheitliche Lehrrede* (Stuttgart: KBW Verlage, [1972], p. 36).

[16]For a recent analysis of sapiential forms, see James Crenshaw, "Wisdom," *Old Testament Form Criticism* (San Antonio: Trinity University Press, 1974), pp. 225-64.

[17]For an analysis of the instruction genre, see Lang, *op. cit.* The instructions found in Proverbs 1-9 are 1:8-19, 2:1-22, 3:1-12, 3:21-35, 4:1-9, 4:10-19, 4:20-27, 5:1-23, 6:20-35, 7:1-27 (*ibid.*, p. 29).

[18]Wisdom poems include the poem structured around an *'ashrê* saying in 3:13-18; the poetic speeches of personified wisdom in 1:20-33, 8:1-21, 8:22-31; the poem contrasting wisdom and folly in 9:1-6 and 13-18; and the hymnic fragment in 3:19-20.

[19]E.g., 9:7, 10, and the numerical saying in 6:16-19.

[20]Roland Murphy, "The Kerygma of the Book of Proverbs," *Int* 20 (1966), p. 4; Georg Fohrer, *Introduction to the Old Testament*, p. 219; and Otto Eissfeldt, *The Old Testament An Introduction* (New York: Harper and Row, 1965), p. 473. Skehan has argued that the author of Chapters 1-9 is the editor of the rest of the Book of Proverbs ("A Single Editor for the Whole Book of Proverbs," *CBQ* 10 [1948], pp. 115-30).

[21]Otto Eissfeldt, *Der Maschal im AT*, BZAW 24 (Giessen: Alfred Töpelmann, 1913).

[22]Among others, see Berend Gemser, *Sprüche Salomos*, HAT 16 (Tübingen: J. C. B. Mohr [Paul Siebeck], 1963), p. 5; and Fohrer, *Introduction to the Old Testament*, p. 219.

[23]*Ibid.*

[24]A. Robert, "Les attaches littéraires bibliques de Prov. I-IX," *RB* 44 (1935), pp. 44-65.

[25]McKane, *Proverbs*, p. 5; Bauer-Kayatz, *Studien zu Proverbien 1-9*, WMANT 22 (Neukirchener Verlag, 1966), p. 3.

[26]Bauer-Kayatz, *Studien zu Proverbien 1-9*, pp. 15f.

[27]*Ibid.*, pp. 119-20. Others have argued that the wise have influenced the prophets: James L. Crenshaw, "The Influence of the Wise upon Amos," *ZAW* 79 (1967), 42-52; Samuel Terrien, "Amos and Wisdom," *Israel's Prophetic Heritage* (New York: Harper and Row, 1962), pp. 108-15; J. Lindblom, "Wisdom in the Old Testament Prophets," *VTSup* 3 (1955), pp. 193-204; and H. W. Wolff, *Amos'geistige Heimat*, WMANT 18 (Neukirchener Verlag, 1964).

[28]See Ringgren, *Word and Wisdom*.

[29]McKane, *Prophets and Wise Men*, p. 48. We are not contesting the thesis that there is a growing nationalization within the structure of wisdom thought that eventually leads to

an embracing of salvation history and the Torah as the only
true source of wisdom. However, we do find ourselves in direct
conflict with the thesis that the early wise somehow were radical empiricists engaged in a statecraft that did not lend itself to doctrinaire theologies. Wisdom is predicated upon what
can be only described as theological affirmations well beyond
the limits of an empirical epistemology. Ideas of a world order with a moral bent made to permeate creation by the creator
deity and of a process of retribution overseen by the transcendent deity are theological affirmations. Further, to characterize the early wise as unconcerned with religion, and, therefore, "fear of God," involves a complete ignoring of certain
texts including the texts cited above from Proverbs which are
pre-exilic, the pious Job of the Old Folktale, and certain historical texts which, if not sapiential, at least are written
with sapiential characters playing key character roles: Joseph
in the Joseph Narrative rises to the position of vizier in
Egypt as the result of his "fear of God" (see G. von Rad, "The
Joseph Narrative and Ancient Wisdom," *The Problem of the Hexateuch* [New York: McGraw-Hill, 1966], pp. 292-300), and the royal novella found in I Kings 3 and originating during Solomon's
reign portrays a humble, pious Solomon whose prayer for wisdom
is answered not only in the gift of wisdom, but also in his
receiving of the blessings associated with the one who is truly
wise. That the latter text originated in the reign of Solomon
can be argued on the basis that it was written along the lines
of an Egyptian political document for the purpose of underpin-
ing the Solomonic claim to the throne (S. Herrmann, "Die
Königsnovelle in Ägypten und Israel," *Wissenschaftliche Zeitschrift Universitäts Leipzig* 3 [1953-54], pp. 51-62; E. Otto,
"Geschichtliche Literatur: Analistik und Königsnovelle," HO 1
[1952], p. 144; and R. N. Whybray, *The Succession Narrative*,
SBT 9 [Naperville, Ill.: Alec R. Allenson, Inc., 1968], p. 100).

[30]It is also possible to regard the final redaction as
post-exilic and much of the contents as originating in sapiential circles several centuries before that.

[31]Lang, *op. cit.*, pp. 29f. According to Lang's analysis,
the form of the instruction includes: 1. the address clothed in
either the vetitive or imperative mood, directed to the "son"
to hear the instruction of the teacher and not to forget or
ignore the instruction, and including on occasion the buttres-
sing of the address by the addition of a motivation clause (vv.
1-2); 2. the main section consisting of a list of admonitions
in the imperative, prohibitive, or vetitive forms, often indi-
vidually coupled with consequential or motivation clauses
stressing the outcome or the reasons behind such admonitions
(vv. 3-10); and 3. the conclusions presented in the third person, indicating the results of wise or unwise behavior (vv.
11-12).

[32]See S. Plath, *Furcht Gottes* (Stuttgart: Calwer Verlag,
1962), pp. 54f.

[33]כבד (Piel) is found in cultic contexts which indicate
that one "honors" the deity with cultic offerings (Isa 43:23,
Jg 13:17).

[34]תבואה is a general term and may refer to "revenue," "income" (Prov 10:16, 14:4) in general, though the probable meaning in this context is "agricultural produce," since "grain" and "new wine" are mentioned in the two following consequential clauses (cf. Ex 23:10, Lev 19:25, 23:39).

[35]שבע, "plenty," "satiety," has often been emended (e.g., BH³) to שבר, "corn" or "grain," on the basis of the LXX (σίτῳ). However, Dahood has pointed to a Phoenician parallel which reads *šb' wtrš*, "grain and new wine" (the Karatepe Inscription III, 7, 9. *Proverbs and Northwest-Semitic Philology* [Rome: Pontifical Biblical Institute, 1963], p. 9).

[36]Roland Murphy, "Form Criticism and Wisdom Literature," *CBQ* 31 (1969), p. 480.

[37]The cultic legislation concerning "first-fruits" is found in the Covenant Code (Ex 23:19), the so-called Ritual Decalogue (Ex 34:26), D (Dt 26:1-11), and P (Lev 23:1-44). General references to "produce" (תבואה), "grain" (שבע), and "new wine" (תירוש) suggest that the three agricultural festivals which involved the offering of various kinds of "first-fruits" are being referred to, and not a specific festival, though of course, the Feast of Weeks was regarded as the festival of first fruits *par excellence*, and was sometimes referred to as בכורים (see Roland de Vaux, *Ancient Israel* 2 [New York: McGraw-Hill, 1965], pp. 490f.).

[38]J. Morgenstern, "First Fruits," *IDB* 2 (1964), p. 270; H.-J. Kraus, *Worship in Israel* (Richmond: John Knox Press, 1966), p. 117; and H. H. Rowley, *Worship in Ancient Israel* (Philadelphia: Fortress Press, 1967), pp. 135-36.

[39]II Kgs 4:42-44, Num 12:44f., Lev 23:20, Num 13:8f. That the wise, most of whom came from the upper stratum of Israelite society, were concerned for the poor and economically deprived in Israelite society has been recognized for quite some time (see Robert Gordis, "The Social Background of Wisdom Literature," *HUCA* 17 [1944], pp. 77-118).

[40]De Vaux, *Ancient Israel* 2, pp. 484f. See especially Dt 26:1-11.

[41]The blessing derived from the observance of the regulations concerning first fruits is also found in a cultic context (Ezek 44:30).

[42]Bauer-Kayatz, *Einführung in die alttestamentliche Weisheit* (Neukirchener Verlag, 1969), p. 30.

[43]Lang comments concerning the third instruction: "Lehrer und Schüler sind selbstverständliche Teilnehmer am Kult Israels" (*op. cit.*, p. 82).

[44]Gustav Boström, *Proverbiastudien*, Lunds Universitets Årsskrift, N. F. Avd. 1, Bd. 30, Nr. 33 (Lund: C. W. K. Gleerup, 1935).

[45]Boström's thesis has found support from rather prominent scholars, including Ringgren, *Word and Wisdom*, and R. B. Y. Scott. *Proverbs. Ecclesiastes*, AB 18 (Garden City: Doubleday, 1965). However, critics of the thesis include Roland Murphy ("The Kerygma of the Book of Proverbs," *Int* 20 [1966], pp. 8f.) and Berend Gemser (*Sprüche Salomos*, pp. 6, 26).

[46]Ani refers to a foreign adulteress who should be avoided by the wise in terms quite similar to the "Strange Woman":
Be on thy guard against a woman from abroad, who is not known in her (own) town. Do not *stare at* her when she passes by. Do not know her carnally: a deep water, whose windings one knows not, a woman who is far away from her husband. "I am sleek," she says to thee every day. She has not witnesses when she waits to ensnare thee. It is a great crime (worthy) of death, when one hears of it... (iii, 13f.; *ANET*, p. 420).

[47]O. Keel, *Feinde und Gottesleugner*, SBM 7 (Stuttgart, 1967). Keel's thesis carries little conviction, as Lang has demonstrated in his arguments. Lang has pointed out that there is no evidence that the woman of the *Maqlu* series is a prostitute, and that "death" in chapter 7 is brought about by illicit sexual behavior and not by magic (*Die Weisheitliche Lehrrede*, p. 94).

[48]Little precision may be gained from word studies of זרה and נכריה. זרה may mean "one who is estranged" from his society (Job 19:15), "stranger" in the sense of one who belongs to another family (Dt 25:5), tribe (Num 1:51), nation (Hos 7:9), and one whose socio-religious behavior transgresses the commonly accepted sanctions of the community. Thus, the "strange woman" in Proverbs could be a foreigner who is an adulteress, a prostitute, a fertility devotee, or a foreign goddess; or an Israelite adulteress, prostitute, or fertility devotee. נכריה is a synonym of זרה and may refer to a foreigner or a foreign group (Dt 17:15, I Kgs 11:1, 8), an Israelite prostitute (Prov 23:27), and a stranger in the sense of one who is unfamiliar (Ec 6:2). For a detailed analysis, see L. A. Snijders, "The Meaning of זר in the Old Testament," *OTS* 10 (Leiden: E. J. Brill, 1954), pp. 1-154.

[49]בית may mean "temple" (I Kings 6, and Ugaritic *bt*).

[50]Reading שחה as coming from שחה, "to bow down" (Isa 51:23).

[51]The possible translation of משגלה as "court" is based on the occurrence of the word in I Sam 17:20 and 26:5, 7 in which the word refers to an encampment with a definite perimeter, thus an enclosure.

[52]The "Rephaim" in Ugarit were not only the "shades" of the dead, but at times were also chthonic deities (John Gray, "The Rephaim," *PEQ* 84 [1949], pp. 127-39).

[53]Ezek 16:19f. UT 49: III:12f., a text celebrating Baal's resurrection, reads:

| šmm. | šmn. | tmṭrn | The heavens rain oil |
| nḫhm. | tlk. | nbtm | The wadis run with honey |

Thus "oil and honey" are intimately connected with fertility religion.

[54]Translating צעדים and רגלים as "feet" and "steps" faces the difficulty of the verb יתמכו, "to embrace." But by regarding these terms as euphemisms the problem is resolved. רגלים has long been recognized as a euphemism for "sexual organs" (cf. Ezek 16:25). צעדים may be translated "aroused vagina" upon the basis of its parallelism with רגלים and its association with Ugaritic ṣġd, "to make an erection" (Aistleitner, no. 2339).

[55]We prefer to follow the LXX and to read רָע as רֵעַ "neighbor" in v. 24, since the latter word is found in v. 29.

[56]It is important to note in this discussion I Kgs 11:1-8 which refers to the wives of Solomon as נכריות for whom he established non-Yahwistic cults. Among the gods Solomon is criticized for worshipping is the Canaanite goddess Astarte, indicating that Solomon participated in Canaanite fertility rites. If Weinfeld's controversial thesis is correct, that is, the Deuteronomistic History was the creation of the sages beginning their work before the time of Josiah, then this Deuteronomistic critique of Solomon for participating in Canaanite religion with his foreign wives may present us with a sapiential illustration of the warning issued by the sages in Proverbs 7 against participating in Canaanite fertility religion (*Deuteronomy and the Deuteronomic School* [Oxford: At the Clarendon Press, 1972]).

[57]The plaques are mentioned by Y. Aharoni, "Beth-Haccherem," *Archaeology and Old Testament Study* (Oxford: At the Clarendon Press), pp. 180f. He also points to a number of texts in the Old Testament (Jg 5:28; II Sam 6:16; II Kgs 9:30) which refer to a queen looking through the window, and to the excavations at Beth-Haccherem in which was discovered a window with a lattice belonging to a royal palace.

[58]The cultic interpretation of the woman as a sacral prostitute of a fertility goddess would be strengthened if the *terminus technicus* for sacral prostitute, קדשה, had been used, though it is true that the general word for prostitute, זרנה, which occurs here is sometimes used to refer to a sacral priestess (cf. Dt 23:17-18). Gray has suggested that the temple prostitute in Canaan seems to have been referred to as 'enst, "pleasant, sociable" (*The Legacy of Canaan*, VTSup 5 [Leiden: E. J. Brill, 1957], p. 57). Now it is well known that the Hebrew word for "woman, wife," אשה, is derived from the same root word as the Ugaritic term for temple prostitute, 'ns, the *nun* having suffered assimilation in אשה (cf. אנשים where the *nun* is maintained). It may not be too difficult to suppose that the description of אשה by the word זרה is the Hebrew method of referring to the Canaanite sacred prostitute so as to use

the Canaanite term for sacred prostitute, and yet to be able to distinguish the term from the ordinary word for "woman, wife." Albright has referred to the cult of Aphrodite παρακυπτουσα in Cyprus (cf. Babylonian Ishtar *kililu*), and associates this with the ivory plaques ("Some Canaanite-Phoenician Sources of Hebrew Wisdom," VTSup 3 [1955], p. 10).

[59]We have regarded the perfect as pointing to an action that in the mind of the woman is as good as done (see R. J. Williams, *Hebrew Syntax* [Toronto: University of Toronto Press, 1967], pp. 32-33).

[60]For discussions of the communion sacrifice, see de Vaux, *Ancient Israel* 2, pp. 417-18; and John Gray, *The Legacy of Canaan*, p. 141. See UH 1, 4; 9, 7.

[61]McKane, *Proverbs*, p. 337. It should be stated that it was a common practice for temple prostitutes to be married (see "Counsels of Wisdom," ll. 72f.; "Middle Assyrian Laws," Tablet A, 40, *ANET*, p. 183; and Hosea's marriage to Gomer).

[62]De Vaux indicates that the day of the full moon, Akk. *shapattu*, was a "day of good omen" in Babylonia, a time when the gods' hearts were appeased (*Ancient Israel* 2, p. 476).

[63]Cf. John McKay, *Religion in Judah under the Assyrians*, SBT 26 (2nd series, London: SCM Press, 1973), p. 115, footnote 87. He refers to texts pointing out that "if one works he will lose his money" and "one may not take an oath nor transact business" during the 14th and 15th of Nisan when the moon begins to wane.

[64]חדש, "New Moon," was celebrated in Israel as may be determined from such texts as Ps 81:4, Ezek 45:17, 46:1-6, etc. The Canaanites also regarded the New Moon as a holy time (see UH 3; Gray, *Legacy of Canaan*, p. 141).

[65]UH 'nt, II, 3f. It is quite obvious that the two sides to the personalities of the goddesses of the ancient Near East, especially Anat and Ishtar, were erotic love and destructive warfare and death. Thus, while the "Strange Woman" may be appealing in a sensual manner, she, like her divine prototype, brings men to destruction. Such a destruction by Anat may reflect human sacrifice in Canaan, though this is debatable. If it did occur, then the idea of such a sacrifice of men is the unleashing of the power of blood necessary to effect the resurrection of Baal from the underworld (see John Gray, *Legacy of Canaan*, pp. 36-37).

[66]Wisdom's house (בית) has been interpreted in a variety of ways: the seven pillars represent the seven planets in Babylonian astrology which points to a connection with the cult of the Queen of Heaven, "Ishtar of the Stars" (Boström, *op. cit.*, p. 160); pillars of a temple similar to the 45 pillars mentioned in the Solomonic temple (I Kgs 7:2-8); Sennacherib's New Year's house at Asshur which had pillars placed in rows of

seven (Meissner, *Babylonien und Assyrien* 1, p. 308); a house of
instruction; a large aristocratic house similar to large Phoenician houses of the late third millennium B.C. which had seven
interior pillars (M. Dunand, "La Maison de la Sagesse," *Bulletin du Musée de Beyrouth* 4 (1940), pp. 69-84); and a temple
similar to the shrine dedicated to the Cyprian Aphrodite which
was called the "Shrine of the Seven-inside-the-Stelae" (mentioned by Albright, "Some Canaanite-Phoenician Sources of Hebrew Wisdom," p. 9, who compares the seven pillars to the seven
menhirs found at Bâb edh-Dhrâ' from the end of the third millennium). We prefer the interpretation that the "house" of
wisdom is a temple, since, in addition to the parallels listed
by Albright, the temple is located on the acropolis (מרמי קרת)
where temples are normally constructed in Israel and Canaan,
the sending out of maidens compares to the sending out of fertility priestesses by a goddess (cf. Ezek 23:24), the sacrifices and the meal prepared by wisdom are probably within the
context of a festival dedicating her new temple (cf. UH 51
which describes the dedicatory festival held by Baal following
the construction of his new temple), and the invitation in v. 5
appears to be almost a verbatim quote from a cultic text from
Ugarit which is found in the context of a cultic meal participated in by the gods of fertility: UT 52, 6--*lḥm. blḥm ay wšty.
bḥmr yn ay.* Furthermore, the offer of "life" to the participants parallels the ideology of fertility religion in which
fertility religion was the means to revitalize the forces of
life of the society.

[67]Cf. Bauer-Kayatz, *Studien zu Proverbien 1-9*; H. Donner,
"Die religionsgeschichtlichen Ursprünge von Prov. Sal. 8, 22-
31," *ZÄS* 82 (1957), pp. 8-18; Burton Mack, "Wisdom Myth and
Mythology," *Int* 24 (1970), pp. 46-60; Gemser, *Sprüche Salomos*;
and Ringgren, *Word and Wisdom*.

[68]For a summary and analysis, see R. N. Whybray, *Wisdom in
Proverbs*, SBT 45 (Naperville, Ill.: Alec R. Allenson, 1955),
pp. 72-104.

[69]Cf. especially Bauer-Kayatz, *Studien zu Proverbien 1-9*,
pp. 76-118; and W. F. Albright, "The Goddess of Life and Wisdom," *AJSL* 36 (1919-1920), pp. 258-94.

[70]Cf. Chapters II and III.

[71]Albright, "Some Canaanite-Phoenician Sources of Hebrew
Wisdom," and "The Goddess of Life and Wisdom." Note especially
the indications by Albright of Canaanite influence on the gram-
mar, syntax, and mythology of chapters 8 and 9.

[72]Among others, see Whybray, *Wisdom in Proverbs*.

[73]McKane, *Proverbs*, pp. 364f.

[74]Von Rad, *Wisdom in Israel*, pp. 187-88.

[75]This seems to be the best explanation of Koheleth's remark in 7:26 when, in seeking to know and to experience folly, he becomes associated with a woman who is described in similar terms to the "Strange Woman" (Ec 7:23-29).

[76]Bauer-Kayatz observes concerning the sages in Proverbs 1-9: "Ihre vordringliche Aufgabe ist es, vor dem Verlassen des rechten Weges, vor dem Abirren in fremde Bindungen, die aus der Verbundenheit mit Jahwe herausführen, zu warnen. Nach unserer Sammlung besteht die Hauptgefahr in der Gemeinschaft mit den Gottlosen, die den Willen Jahwes verachten, in den Verlockungen und Versuchungen, in die sie hineinführen. Speziell der Umgang mit der 'Fremden,' die als Vertreterin des des jahwefeindlichen kanaanäischen Kultus anzusprechen ist, muss ein aktuelles Problem gewesen sein. Das war von der frühen Königszeit an der Fall, begannen doch zu der Zeit durch die engeren politischen Beziehungen zu den Nachbarvölkern die fremden Kulte stärker ihren Einfluss auf Israel geltend zu machen. Vor allem in Jerusalem, dem Mittelpunkt des kultischen und kulturellen Lebens, als ehemaligem kanaanäischem Stadtstaat mit kanaanäischen Heiligtümern und Kulten müssen sich diese neuen Gefahren und Versuchungen ausgewirkt haben. Es ist deshalb leicht begreiflich, dass hier dringende erzieherische Aufgaben gesehen wurden" (*Studien zu Proverbien 1-9*, pp. 137-38).

[77]For detailed studies of sacrifice, one should consult Roland de Vaux, *Studies in Old Testament Sacrifice* (Cardiff: University of Wales Press, 1964); N. H. Snaith, "Sacrifices in the Old Testament," *VT* 7 (1957), pp. 308f.; and the extensive bibliography listed by H. H. Rowley, *Worship in Ancient Israel* (Philadelphia: Fortress Press, 1967), pp. 111f.

[78]Unfortunately, prayer in ancient Israel has not received indepth analyses by many scholars. General treatments to be consulted include: D. R. Ap-Thomas, "Notes on Some Terms Relating to Prayer," *VT* 6 (1956), pp. 225-41; P. A. H. De Boer, *De vorbeede in het Oud Testament*, OTS 3 (Leiden: E. J. Brill, 1943); N. B. Johnson, *Prayer in the Apocrypha and Pseudepigrapha*, SBL Monograph Series 3 (Philadelphia: SBL, 1948); and E. Peterson, "Die geschichtliche Bedeutung der jüdischen Gebetsrichtung," *ThZ* 3 (1947), pp. 1-15.

[79]The second major collection encompasses 10:1-22:16 and has the superscription: "The Proverbs of Solomon." The larger collection has been redacted to include two minor collections, 10-15 and 16:1-22:16. As is the case with all of the collections, this one most probably was put together in a wisdom school and served the function of a textbook for teaching language skills, analytical and synthetic thought, and sapiential ethics. Dating is a major problem, but certainly the references to the court would indicate that at least some of the material originated during the period of the monarchy, though aramaisms suggest that some of the material is post-exilic (cf. Fohrer, *Introduction*, p. 320). Scott's observation is prudently cautious: "Much, perhaps most, of the material...is traditional

and pre-exilic in origin. Some of it belongs to the ageless
popular wisdom which Israel shared with surrounding peoples.
The most that we can say with confidence about the date of Part
II is that it was the fruit of a long process, and reached its
present form probably in the fifth or fourth century B.C."
(*Proverbs. Ecclesiastes*, p. 18).

[80]The fifth collection comprises chapters 25-29 and has as
its title: "These also are the Proverbs of Solomon which the
Men of Hezekiah, King of Judah, copied." The superscription
provides us with evidence that the date for the redaction is
the reign of Hezekiah (715-687/6). This collection likewise
has been redacted to include two minor units, 25-27, with agrarian concerns, and 28-29, with concerns of the court. Cf.
Udo Skladny, *Die ältesten Spruchsammlungen in Israel* (Göttingen:
Vandenhoeck und Ruprecht, 1962), pp. 46f.

[81]When the wise refer to prayer, they use the most general
term, תפלה, which is defined succinctly as "intercession to God
on behalf of oneself or others." Cf. C. G. F. Smith, "Prayer,"
IDB 3 (1964), pp. 857-67.

[82]For a detailed analysis of the Israelite proverb, see
Hans-Jürgen Hermisson, *Studien zur israelitischen Spruchweisheit*, WMANT 28 (Neukirchener Verlag, 1968). Hermisson considers sayings which contain the statement תועבת יהוה to belong to
lehrhaften Sprüche which have the purpose of instructing and
educating, and are not just observations based on everyday experiences (*op. cit.*, pp. 64f.).

[83]*Wisdom in Israel*, p. 28. He notes that over 90 percent
of the proverbs in 10-15 are antithetical.

[84]W. Stärk represents the first position when he says concerning the wise: "Sie individualisieren den Gottesdienst, so
tritt das Gebet an die erste Stelle, und sie erheben das Sitten-
gesetz über die Zeremonie" (*Lyrik*, SAT 3 [Göttingen: Vandenhoeck und Ruprecht, 1911], p. 213). We do not deny that there
is abundant evidence for a 'spiritualizing' and individualizing
process occurring with respect to cultic symbols and rituals,
especially in post-exilic literature (e.g., Psalm 51). However, as von Rad cogently perceives, such a process was not intended to sever the spiritual individual from rituals and symbols, but rather was intended to preserve them by allowing reflective individuals to see in them the possibilities of spiritual and individual meaning, something which most probably was
inherent in the original understanding (*Old Testament Theology*
1 [New York: Harper and Row, 1962], pp. 396f.).

[85]Prayer as well as sacrifice may be equally deceitful and
involve the mere repetition of words in a liturgical form (cf.
Rowley, *Worship in Ancient Israel*, p. 256). Of course, prayer
was conceived of as possessing an inherent power, similar to
the power of the prophetic word and the ritual blessing and
cursing. However, this power is ultimately dependent upon the
volition of the deity who judges the petition while considering
the disposition of the petitioner (cf. A. S. Herbert, *Worship in
Ancient Israel* [Richmond: John Knox Press, 1959], p. 26).

[86]For a detailed analysis of the 'wicked' and the 'righteous' in Proverbs 10-15, see Schmid, *Wesen und Geschichte der Weisheit*, pp. 156f.

[87]This is argued most effectively by Sigmund Mowinckel (*Psalmenstudien* 1 (Oslo. Reprint, Amsterdam: P. Schippers, 1961). De Vaux states: "The hymn-book, or prayer book, of the second Temple is the Psalter" (*Ancient Israel* 2 [New York: McGraw-Hill, 1965], p. 457).

[88]A similar effort to speak of the totality of a practice, idea, relationship, etc., may be seen in another antithetical proverb found in 10:1--"A wise son makes a glad father, but a foolish son is a sorrow to his mother." Now obviously, the point is not that a wise son would please only the father and not the mother, nor that a foolish son would not be a sorrow to his father, but rather the father and mother are mentioned in order to express the totality of the parental relationship.

[89]Helmer Ringgren, *Israelite Religion* (Philadelphia: Fortress Press, 1966), pp. 166f.

[90]We are referring to the אשם and the חטאה sacrifices. Cf. de Vaux, *Ancient Israel* 2, p. 453.

[91]Kraus affirms this point by stating: "The idea and expectation that the meal eaten together will create *communio* is basic to this sacrifice." He further observes that such a sacrifice and meal often take place within a covenant festival (*Worship in Israel*, p. 118). It is not surprising that the sacrifice that is of greatest concern to the wise is the communion sacrifice, since the cultic understanding of this sacrifice corresponds quite well to the concerns of the wise with respect to 'order' and well-being. It should also be stressed that one of the varieties of the communion offering was a תודה, 'thanksgiving offering.' Now it will become more apparent as we proceed that the wise were involved in the writing of two types of psalms, or prayers, and these are the lament and thanksgiving. We shall suggest that when the wise refer to prayer they specifically have in mind their own participation in the creation of cultic literature, especially the sapiential laments and thanksgivings.

[92]Dt 14:3, 17:4; Lev 18:26, 27, 29, etc. Scott concludes: "The term seems to have meant originally what was ritually forbidden." (*Proverbs. Ecclesiastes*, p. 60).

[93]Lev 1:3; 19:5; 22:19, 20, 29; 23:11, etc. It is possible, however, that the Israelite wise have taken these expressions from ancient Near Eastern wisdom language. In the "Shamash Hymn" (ll. 100, 106, and 119) the basis for doing righteous acts is that they are "pleasing to Shamash, and he will prolong his life" (*ṭa-a-bi eli* ^dᶘamaᶘ *balāṭa (ti.la) uttar*). Also see the "Counsels of Wisdom," l. 64. Throughout Amen-em-Opet wicked and foolish actions are not to be done, because they are "the abomination of the god" (xiii:15, xv:20, etc.).

[94]We concur with A. Drubbel who says concerning the proverb: "C'est affirmer nettement que la valeur des sacri- fices est en strict rapport avec les dispositions du sacrifi- cateur" ("Le conflit entre la sagesse profane et la sagesse religieuse," *Bib* 17 [1936], p. 414).

[95]For an analysis of the 'Better' saying, see J. L. Cren- shaw, "Wisdom," pp. 238-39. Crenshaw remarks that the purpose of the saying is "to single out certain kinds of character or conduct as superior to others."

[96]The temple is referred to as בית זבח in II Chron 7:12.

[97]Cf. Amen-em-Opet, ix, 5f. זבחי ריב may be intended to contrast with זבחי צדק, "correct" or "orderly" sacrifices, men- tioned in Deut 33:19, Pss 4:6 and 51:21. One should also no- tice the parallel to זבח ריב found in UT 51:III:17ff. which, in a numerical saying, lists three sacrifices which Baal hates, and one is called a *dbḥ dnt*, 'a sacrifice of contention.' The best and most detailed description of a communion meal occurs in I Sam 2:13f.

[98]נבחר...מן is substituted in this saying for the more common טוב...מן.

[99]Cf. Walther Eichrodt, *Ezekiel* (Philadelphia: Westminst- er Press, 1970), p. 238. It should be admitted that עשה משפט וצדק also occurs in prophetic oracles concerning kingship (Jer 21:12, 22:3, 15). This has led some to argue for a prophetic influence on the proverb. While this is certainly possible, notation of Meri-ka-Re, ll. 128f., should be made: "More acceptable is the character of one upright of heart than the ox of the evildoer."

[100]צדק is a frequent word in cultic contexts. The cultic community was referred to as the צדיקים (Pss 33:1, 142:8, and especially the "Entrance Liturgies," 15:2, 24:5). The doors of the temple are referred to as the שערי צדק (Ps 118:19), and one who entered was referred to as a צדיק (Ps 118:20). Even the priests were to be clothed in צדק (Ps 132:9).

[101]We strongly disagree with Schmid's contention that the 'Better' saying should not be translated "better....than..., but rather should be understood in the exclusive sense "good is...and not..." (*Wesen und Geschichte der Weisheit*, p. 159, footnote 69). One would hardly argue that "to dwell in the corner of a housetop" or that "a dry morsel with quiet" are "good." Rather these can be judged to be only "better" than that which is relatively worse.

[102]אף כי is an emphatic adverbial phrase (Roland Williams, *Hebrew Syntax*, no. 385).

[103]*Wisdom in Israel*, p. 122.

[104]See Lev 18:17, 20:14 (incest), Ezekiel 16 (idolatry described in terms of prostitution, adultery, and fertility rites), and Ezek 22:9; 23:21, 27, 29, 35, 44, 49 (sexual sins including incest, adultery, and fornication). Such sins had no means of atonement and forgiveness according to priestly traditions (cf. Lev 18:29).

[105]This argument is all the more forceful when it is noticed that a person who partakes of a communion sacrificial meal when he is in a state of sinfulness, that is, he has not had his sin atoned, is "to be cut off from the people," that is, to be put to death. For a discussion of the unforgiveable sin, see Victor Maag, "Unsühnbare Schuld," *Kairos* 8 (1966), pp. 95f. Harrelson's point with respect to the cultic understanding of sacrifices is important: "Neither ancient Israel nor the neighboring peoples thought of sacrifices accomplishing their ends automatically. Sacrifices had to be made in the right way. The intention of the heart was important. And the gods either received or refused to receive the offerings, as they saw fit" (*From Fertility Cult to Worship* [Garden City: Doubleday, 1970], p. 46).

[106]Such a close parallel in language between the forms and vocabulary of the wise and apodictic law has been exhaustively examined by Erhard Gerstenberger, *Wesen und Herkunft des 'apodiktischen Rechts*,' WMANT 20 (Neukirchener Verlag, 1965).

[107]*ANET*, p. 414; 11.534f.

[108]H. Brunner, "Das hörende Herz," *TLZ* 79 (1954), pp. 697-700.

[109]Other wise men were equally concerned with avoiding hasty vows and oaths. In the "Counsels of Wisdom" students are counseled:
Beware of careless talk, guard your lips;
Do not utter solemn oaths while alone,
For what you say in a moment will follow you afterwards,
But exert yourself to restrain your speech (BWL, p. 105, 11. 131-34).
Also see Koh. 5:4-6.

[110]Th. C. Vriezen, *The Religion of Ancient Israel* (Philadelphia: The Westminster Press, 1967), p. 95.

[111]For a discussion of the vow, see Yehezkel Kaufmann, *The Religion of Israel* (Chicago: The University of Chicago Press, 1960), p. 319.

[112]A possible meaning of the word לבקר, translated "to reflect," is "to divine" by means of consultation of the entrails of sacrificial animals (cf. II Kgs 16:15) or by consultation of the oracle (Ps 27:4). Such a meaning is also found in the Ugaritic *bqr* (see Virolleaud, "Les nouvelles tablettes de Ras Shamra," *Syria* 28 [1951], pp. 25-27). If this meaning were intended by the wise, then the point would be that it is foolish to make a vow and then to consult the oracle only to discover that one's request was against the will of the deity.

[113]Also see Leviticus 27.

[114]See J. Lindblom, "Lot-casting in the Old Testament," *VT* 12 (1962), pp. 164f. This element of divination points to the Israelite participation, at least in a limited way, in the arts of the diviner. Glendon Bryce has recently attempted to argue for the existence of omen proverbs in Israel, though he neglects to deal with the attack against forms of divination, except lot-casting, made by Sirach in 31:1-8 ("Omen-Wisdom in Ancient Israel").

[115]Ezra 2:62 and Neh 7:65. The best description of the ritual is found in I Samuel 14. The word בסם may be a reference to a decision reached by the casting of lots in Prov 16: 10, since the same word refers to the casting of arrows of divination by the king of Babylon in Ezek 21:21.

[116]Cf. Ex 28:20, especially the statement that Aaron would carry the lots in his breastplate when he appeared before Yahweh. The usage of lots by the priests to obtain oracles is an involvement in omenology by which various signs were indicative of specific, future events. Such an enterprise was bound up with the idea of the laws of a predetermined order. Therefore, the casting of lots resulted in a preindication of the impending results of that order. Yet, the wise argue that this type of omenology has meaning only in its connection with the will of Yahweh who has the freedom to decide independently of any determined causal nexus (see Gese, *Lehre und Wirklichkeit*, p. 48).

[117]E.g., McKane, *Proverbs*, p. 498.

[118]For an examination of popular religion, see J. L. Crenshaw, *Prophetic Conflict*, BZAW 124 (Berlin: Walter de Gruyter, 1971), pp. 24-35.

[119]*Theology of the Old Testament* 1, pp. 21-71.

[120]Georg Fohrer, "Überlieferung und Wandlung der Hioblegende," *Studien zum Buche Hiob* (Gütersloher Verlagshaus: Gerd Mohn, 1963), pp. 44-67; "Zur Vorgeschichte und Komposition des Buches Hiob," *ibid*, pp. 26-43; A. Alt, "Zur Vorgeschichte des Buches Hiob," *ZAW* 55 (1937), pp. 265-68; and Johannes Lindblom, *La composition du livre de Job* (Lund: C. W. K. Gleerups Förlag, 1945), p. 6. This is indicated not only in terms of differences in language and theology, but also by Ezekiel's reference to Job along with Noah and Daniel which indicates that Job was quite well known during the early 6th century B.C. (14:14f.).

[121]Fohrer's traditio-historical investigation of the narrative is the most extensive (see "Überlieferung und Wandlung der Hioblegende" and "Zur Vorgeschichte und Komposition des Buches Hiob"). He points to four stages in the development of the legend before it was used by the Joban poet: Stage One--a pre-Israelite, probably Canaanite original; Stage Two--the early pre-exilic Israelite adaptation of the legend; Stage

Three--the inclusion of certain early exilic vocabulary; and
Stage Four--the inclusion of the Satan material, the influence
of the priestly narrative, and the wisdom redaction during the
post-exilic period.

[122]The rarity of wisdom literature in the Ugaritic dis-
coveries is most perplexing, though some such literature has
been found, including a Joban parallel in Akkadian (R. S. 25.
460). See Jean Nougayrol, Emmanuel Laroche, Charles Virolleaud,
C. F. A. Schaeffer, *Ugaritica V*, Mission de Ras Shamra 16
(Paris: Imprimerie Nationale, 1968), pp. 266f.

[123]"Epic Substratum in the Prose of Job," *JBL* 77 (1957),
pp. 13-25.

[124]That the final redaction before its incorporation into
the dialogues did not occur until the early post-exilic period
is indicated by the references to "the satan" in the council of
Yahweh and by the influence of the priestly narrative style
noticeable in 42:16-17 ("full of days," cf. Gen 25:8, 35:29;
"and Job lived after this 140 years," cf. Genesis 5). See
Fohrer, *Das Buch Hiob*, KAT 16 (Gütersloher Verlagshaus: Gerd
Mohn, 1963), p. 31.

[125]Considerable work needs to be done in the definition
and analysis of sapiential narratives, which is no easy task as
J. L. Crenshaw has demonstrated ("Method in Determining Wisdom
Influence upon 'Historical' Literature," *JBL* 78 [1969], pp.
129-42).

[126]E.g., see the "Dispute between the Tamarisk and the
Date Palm," *ANET*, pp. 592-93.

[127]For a discussion of patriarchal religion, see Rowley,
Worship in Ancient Israel, pp. 1-36; and Alt's classic study,
"Der Gott der Väter," *Kleine Schriften* 1 (Munich: Beck, 1953),
pp. 1-78.

[128]See, e.g., N. H. Tur-Sinai, *The Book of Job*, rev. ed.
(Jerusalem: Kiryath Sepher, 1967), pp. 7f.

[129]For a discussion of this festival, see de Vaux, *Ancient
Israel* 2, pp. 495-502.

[130]This may be seen in this feast in Job where three sisters are invited to join with their brothers in eating and
drinking. The invitation to the three sisters is paralleled,
not only in the Festival of Tabernacles mentioned in Jg 21:19f.
where fertility rites are suggested, but also in Ugaritic cultic festivals which lasted seven days: 2 Aqht II, 26-40; UH 125,
39f. This may be one example of material remaining from the
Canaanite form of the narrative.

[131]See Num 29:12-34.

[132]Fohrer, *Das Buch Hiob*, p. 77.

[133] For a discussion of the rites and meaning of consecration in the Old Testament, see de Vaux, *Ancient Israel* 2, pp. 406f.

[134] Also see Ex 19:10f.

[135] For a discussion of the עלה, see Kraus, *Worship in Israel*, pp. 115f. The 'burnt offering' was common in Ugarit, and an important point is that it was at times accompanied by a lament. In the Aqht legend, one finds:
qrym. af. dbh. lilm
š'ly. dgt ( ) bšmym (1 Aqht, 191-192).
For additional references to *'ly* as a 'burnt offering,' see Aistleitner, *Wörterbuch der Ugaritischen Sprache*, no. 2030.

[136] The atoning powers of the עולה may be seen in Jg 21:4, I Sam 13:9, and Mic 6:6 (see von Rad, *Theology of the Old Testament* 1, pp. 255-56).

[137] The number of animals sacrificed, seven bulls and seven rams, is extremely large, and probably demonstrates the severity of the 'sin' and the extreme wrath of Yahweh. The offering may have been influenced by the offering for the entire community made during the feasts of Passover and Unleavened Bread and Tabernacles in the cultic legislation in Ezekiel (45:21-25). Other possibilities include the preference for the number seven in the narrative, and the possible influence by the offering made by Balaam in the Balaam Cycle in Num 23:1f. as preserved in the Yahwist source.

[138] See Sheldon Blank, "Men Against God," *JBL* 62 (1953), pp. 1-14. Lindblom comments: "La prière d'intercession d'un homme de Dieu en faveur de personnes qui ont commis une faute est un trait charactéristique de la vie religieuse des Israélites. Abraham, Moïse, Samuel, Jérémie et beaucoup d'autre furent de grands intercesseurs auprès de Dieu en faveur de leur peuple" (*La composition du livre de Job*, p. 19).

[139] The crisis stage of Israelite wisdom literature was precipitated by the catastrophes of the exilic and early post-exilic period. For a discussion, see Schmid, *Wesen und Geschichte der Weisheit*, pp. 173f.

[140] Pope tentatively places the book in the seventh century (*Job*, p. xxxvii), Eissfeldt in the fourth century (*The Old Testament*, p. 470), and Fohrer between the fifth and third centuries (*Das Buch Hiob*, p. 42).

[141] Westermann considers Job to be a dramatized lament (*Der Aufbau des Buches Hiob*, BHT 23 (Tübingen: J. C. B. Mohr [Paul Siebeck], 1956).

[142] H. Gese, *Lehre und Wirklichkeit*

[143] Ludwig Köhler, "Justice in the Gate," *Hebrew Man* (London: SCM Press, 1956); and Heinz Richter, *Studien zu Hiob*, Theologische Arbeiten 11 (Berlin: Evangelische Verlagsanstalt, N.D.).

[144]Fohrer, *Das Buch Hiob*, p. 50.

[145]Richard B. Sewall, "The Book of Job," *The Book of Job* (Englewood Cliffs: Prentice-Hall, Inc., 1969), pp. 21-35.

[146]Pope, *Job*, p. xxx.

[147]"Le modernisme de Job," VTSup 3 (1955), p. 159.

[148]H. L. Ginsberg, "Job the Patient and Job the Impatient," *Conservative Judaism* 21 (1967), pp. 16f. In fact, as we shall see in Chapter V, the thanksgiving-lament cycle is most prominent in didactic poetry and wisdom psalms, thus demonstrating the traditional wise affirmed the theology and ritual of this cultic practice, which leads us to conclude that the Joban poet is criticizing the wise who wrote such psalms.

[149]Also 11:2, 14:4, 15:14, and 25:4. Cf. the statement in "The Sumerian Job": "Never has a sinless child been born to its mother,...a sinless workman has not existed from of old" (ll. 101f.; *ANET*, p. 590). 14:4 is especially interesting in that cultic language ('clean' and 'unclean') is used: מִי יִתֵּן טָהוֹר מִטָּמֵא לֹא אֶחָד. Zink has demonstrated that "in Job xiv, 4 the words used are those which occur in the legislation concerning cleanness and uncleanness, and, therefore, have a direct connection with cultic matters." Cf. Dt 12:15, 22, 15:22; Lev 5:2, 13:11f., 15:2f.; and Num 19:13f. This may demonstrate that the traditional wise accepted the cultic idea that ethical and ritual "sins" are the basis for punishment ("Uncleanness and Sin in Job 14:4 and Ps 51:7," *VT* 17 [1967], pp. 354f.).

[150]5:17f.

[151]For an analysis of the lament, see Claus Westermann, "Struktur und Geschichte der Klage im Alten Testament," *ZAW* 66 (1954), pp. 44f.

[152]Dt 4:29, Hos 10:12, Am 5:4, Is 9:12, 31:1, 55:6, Pss 9:11, 22:27, 34:5, 11, and 119:2, 10. See Claus Westermann, "Die Begriffe für Fragen und Suchen im Alten Testament," *KuD* 6 (1960), pp. 2-30.

[153]See Fohrer, *Das Buch Hiob*, pp. 149f.

[154]E.g., Ex 9:28f., I Kgs 8:22, and Isa 1:15. Such a process was also used in the legal context of the ordeal (Dt 21:1-9). See Fohrer, *Das Buch Hiob*, p. 211. Isa 1:15f. speaks of Israelites whose outstretched hands are stained with blood, and, therefore, their prayers are unacceptable. To remove the stain they are to put away evil, be just, and to wash themselves clean.

[155]The "lifting of the face" is an expression for the acceptance by God of one's prayer (e.g., Job 42:8).

[156]Fohrer demonstrates that שלג in this context is not "snow" but rather a soapy solution made from *Seifenpflanzen* (*Das Buch Hiob*, p. 211).

[157]This term, עתר, may indicate a type of prayer which is accompanied by incense (see Ezek 8:11).

[158]The majority of Joban scholars have concluded that the Elihu material is a later interpolation (see W. A. Irwin, "The Elihu Speeches in the Criticism of Job," *JR* 17 [1937], pp. 37-47; and Fohrer, "Die Weisheit des Elihu [Hi 32-37]," *Studien zum Buche Hiob*, pp. 87-107).

[159]See S. R. Driver and G. B. Gray, *The Book of Job*, ICC 14 (Edinburgh: T. and T. Clark, 1921), pp. 291f.; Gustav Hölscher, *Das Buch Hiob*, HAT 17 (Tübingen: J. C. B. Mohr [Paul Siebeck], 1952), p. 88; and Samuel Terrien, "The Book of Job," *IB* 3 (New York: Abingdon Press, 1954), pp. 1138f.

[160]W. A. Irwin, "Job's Redeemer," *JBL* 81 (1962), pp. 217f.

[161]Mal 2:7f. and Koh. 5:6. Such an examination seeks to determine the worshipper's moral and ritual status (see Psalms 15 and 24). That the מליץ is a cultic mediator may be seen in Isa 43:27 where מליצים are paralleled to the "princes of the sanctuary." "One of a 1,000" is a rather enigmatic expression but possibly refers to the various divisions of cultic officials into groups of one thousand as was common in the Chronicler (I Chronicles 23-24).

[162]It seems probable that the priestly official himself offers the penitential psalm for the worshipper.

[163]The כפר is mentioned in Ex 21:30 in a legal context and is the price of 'redemption' paid by one whose crime would cost his life, if a redemption price were not set by the judges to allow the man to "pay for his crime" in lieu of his life. One example of a כפר in the cultic context is the sanctuary tax paid by each male over twenty years of age at the time of the census in order to keep the punishment of the plague, which was believed caused by census-taking, from destroying the people, and thus those who pay are 'redeemed' from destruction (Ex 30: 11f.).

[164]II Sam 24:23, Hos 8:13, and Ex 28:38.

[165]Such a decision probably involved a *Heilsorakel* in which the priest, having consulted the deity, announces 'salvation' to the supplicant (see J. Begrich, "Das priesterliche Heilsorakel," *ZAW* 51 [1934], pp. 81f.).

[166]Driver and Gray, *op. cit.*, pp. 291f. The "Cultic Shout of joy" (תרועה) is made by the cultic singers who sing the psalm of thanksgiving (Ps 27:6).

246

[167]There is no reference to the חדה sacrifice, but it is probably implied (see Pss 107:22, 100:1, and 116:17).

[168]G. von Rad points to Job's realization that he can declare his own innocence, but for his innocence to be vindicated he has to receive the pronouncement of God. In such a recognition, Job's viewpoint is the same as the lamenters' in the "laments of innocence" in the Psalter (see Psalms 7 and 17). "It is interesting to see to what extent Job here is still living among specifically cultic ideas, perhaps to an even greater extent than his friends" (*Wisdom in Israel*, p. 219).

[169]Job argues that God maliciously mistreats even the leaders of society, including the priests, and withholds insight from them.

[170]Jacob Milgrom, "The Cultic $\check{s}^e g\bar{a}g\bar{a}$ and its Influence in Psalms and Job," *JQR* 58 (1967), pp. 115-25.

[171]*Ibid.*, p. 125.

[172]Fohrer, *Das Buch Hiob*, p. 427. For a recent treatment of Job 31, see Fohrer, "The Righteous Man in Job 31," *Essays in Old Testament Ethics* (New York: Ktav, 1974), pp. 1-22.

[173]"The Meaning of the Book of Job," *HUCA* 37 (1966), pp. 73-106.

[174]*Satan in the Old Testament* (Evanston: Northwestern University Press, 1967), pp. 119f.

[175]The reference to the lament-thanksgiving cycle is excellent evidence that the wise reflected on cultic ritual and theology, and at times even rejected some of the basic premises of cultic theology.

[176]Dt 13:6f. The lack of references to sacrifice in the speeches of Job is perplexing, especially when one sees the numerous references to sacrifices in such Joban literature as "I Will Praise the Lord of Wisdom" and "The Babylonian Theodicy." However, it should be noted that the "Sumerian Job" and the sufferer in Nougayrol's text do not refer to sacrifice. While this omission could indicate a similar feeling toward sacrifice found among the people in the time of Malachi and Ezra-Nehemiah, arguments based on silence are unconvincing. One could just as well argue that the cultic piety of Job in the narrative is presupposed in the dialogues, or even accept Rowley's point that Job could not sacrifice the animals he no longer possessed (*Job*, The Century Bible [Don Mills, Ontario: Thomas Nelson and Sons, 1970], p. 10).

[177]Chapter 31 has 16 self-imprecations consisting of the following formal elements: the protasis, consisting of two, sometimes three, parts and introduced by the conditional אם or אם לא which states the particular sin Job is denying, and the apodosis, containing the particular curse which will overwhelm Job if he is lying. Such a series of oaths is comparable to

the one in the 125th chapter of the Book of the Dead in Egypt and to the Babylonian *Shurpu* texts, though the Israelite setting is either the courtroom or the offering of the lament. We have concluded that the specific setting for Job's series of oaths is the offering of a lament in which the lamenter proves his innocence by taking the "oath of innocence" (see Psalms 7 and 17). For studies dealing with the oath, see Sheldon Blank, "The Curse, Blasphemy, the Spell, and the Oath," *HUCA* 23 (1950/51), pp. 73-95; and J. Scharbert, "'Fluchen' und 'Segen' im Alten Testament," *Bib* 39 (1958), pp. 1-26.

[178]McKay, *Religion in Judah Under the Assyrians*, pp. 45f. Our passage is very similar to the Assyrian cult warned against in Dt 4:19.

[179]E. Dhorme, *Les religions de Babylonie et d'Assyrie*, p. 248. See *The Assyrian Dictionary*, vol. 7 (Chicago: Oriental Institute, 1960), pp. 62f.

[180]McKay, *op. cit.*, p. 48.

[181]There are many examples of psalmodic genres in the dialogues besides the lament (cf. Jean Lévêque, *Job et son Dieu* 1, Études Bibliques [Paris: Librairie Lecoffre, 1970], pp. 312f.; and Georg Fohrer, "Form und Funktion in der Hiobdichtung," *Studien zum Buche Hiob*, pp. 68-86). Such texts demonstrate what is intended by the reference to 'songs' among the sapiential creations attributed to Solomon (I Kgs 4:29f.). Gordis has cogently argued: "Poetry in general, and lamentation in particular, constituted an important segment of the wisdom activity which was carried on in ancient Israel by the *Hakhamim* and *Hakhamot*, men and women skilled in the arts of composition" ("Wisdom and Job," *Old Testament Issues* [New York: Harper and Row, 1968], p. 228). We should mention the "Poem Concerning Wisdom" in Job 28 which consists of four symmetrical strophes, each consisting of seven stichs, 3 + 3 meter, and introduced by a refrain in the form of the catechetical question: "But where shall wisdom be found, and where is the place of understanding." Generally, such questions were answered with proverbial replies (Prov 23:2af.; Koh. 2:12, 22f.; 8:1, etc.), but this author argues that the answer is hidden to human understanding and known only by God. Such a well structured poem which has its structure formed around a simple wisdom form provides us with a major clue to the identification and analysis of wisdom psalms in the Psalter.

[182]Robert Gordis, "Qoheleth and Qumran--A Study of Style," *Bib* 41 (1960), pp. 395-410. For an examination of the structure of Koheleth, see Addison Wright, "The Riddle of the Sphinx: The Structure of the Book of Qoheleth," *CBQ* 30 (1968), pp. 313-34.

[183]For a comparison of Koheleth and other ancient Near Eastern critical wisdom literature, see Oswald Loretz, *Qohelet und der Alte Orient* (Freiburg: Herder, 1964).

184See Zimmerli's discussion: "Zur Struktur der alttestamentlichen Weisheit," *ZAW* 51 (1933), pp. 177-204.

185"Il affirme que l'ordre du monde est absurde, arbi-
traire, injuste..." (J. Pedersen, "Scepticisme israelite," *RHPR*
10 [1930], p. 364).

186Reading עָמָל for MT עֹלָם "eternity." See Scott, *Proverbs.
Ecclesiastes*, p. 221.

187Müller comments: "Qohälät's Gott ist Urheber einer
problematisch gewordenen Welt; der *iniator mundi* ist zum *Deus
absconditus* geworden" ("Wie Sprach Qohälät von Gott?" *VT* 18
[1968], pp. 507f.). Crenshaw's analysis of this "fear" of God
in terms of terror is found in his article, "The Eternal Gospel," *Essays in Old Testament Ethics* (New York: Ktav, 1974),
pp. 23-56.

188"Er vermag nicht mehr, das Vorhandensein einer gerecht-
en Vergeltung anzuerkennen" (A. Lauha, "Die Krise des religiös-
en Glaubens bei Koheleth," VTSup 3 [1955], p. 185).

189See H. W. Hertzberg, *Der Prediger*, KAT 17 (Gütersloher
Verlagshaus, Gerd Mohn, 1963), pp. 222f.; and H. Gese, "Die
Krisis der Weisheit bei Koheleth," SPOA, p. 140.

190In contrasting Koheleth to the Joban poet who stresses
that meaning in human existence comes from the encounter with
the divine, Crenshaw remarks: "Qoheleth can find no such meaning anywhere; this author is convinced that life is empty,
vain, profitless. Neither material possessions, human friendship, nor religious devotion alter the fact that nature is op-
pressive, that death is the negation of all good, that God is
therefore untouched by the plight of his creatures. What then
is man to do? Qoheleth advises him to find some pleasure in
wife and children, and to work with dignity, in this way post-
poning death as long as possible" ("Popular Questioning of the
Justice of God," p. 389).

191See Müller, *op. cit.*, p. 510; and Egon Pfeiffer, "Die
Gottesfurcht im Buche Kohelet," *Gottes Wort und Gottes Land*
(Göttingen: Vandenhoeck und Ruprecht, 1965), pp. 133-58.

192See Walther Zimmerli, *Sprüche. Prediger*, ATD 16
(Göttingen: Vandenhoeck und Ruprecht, 1962), pp. 127f.

193Most scholars have translated v. 1b as a "Better Say-
ing" in spite of the absence of the customary טוב (see Gordis,
Koheleth, The Man and His World, 3rd ed. [New York: Schocken
Books, 1968], p. 247).

194The expression Koheleth uses for "temple" is בית האלהים
(see II Sam 12:20; Isa 37:1; etc.).

[195]Cf. Ani iv, 1f. A fearful caution should characterize the cultic participant, since the deity, though inscrutable, is a destructive power with which to reckon, and, therefore, should not be offended. Like the king, he can consume the unwary.

[196]I Sam 15:22   הנה שמע מזבח טוב
Koh.   קרב לשמע מתח הכסילים זבח

[197]Rudi Kroeber, *Der Prediger* (Berlin: Akademie Verlag, 1963), p. 139. A comparable text is Prov 28:9--"He who turns his ear from the hearing of instruction, even his prayer is an abomination."

[198]*Ibid.*

[199]One wonders if Koheleth has in mind wisdom psalms like Psalm 119.

[200]Kroeber, *Der Prediger*, p. 140.

[201]Scott, *Proverbs. Ecclesiastes*, p. 227.

[202]Cf. Ani, iv, 1-4, and the "Counsels of a Pessimist," ll. 14-22.

[203]Hertzberg, *op. cit.*, p. 122.

[204]See Dt 23:22-24 and Num 30:1f.

[205]Mitchell Dahood, "Canaanite-Phoenician Influence in Qoheleth," *Bib* 33 (1952), p. 207. Gordis considers the מלאך to be "the Pharisaic scholar who acts as God's representative in annulling the vow" (*Koheleth*, p. 249).

[206]Mal 2:7f.

[207]The ב we consider to be temporal "when" (cf. Gen 2:4; 4:8); and the ו a waw apodosis, "then." See Williams, *Hebrew Syntax*, no. 440.

[208]See Egon Pfeiffer, *op. cit.*, p. 157.

[209]Reading קרבים instead of קברים, a probable example of transposition of characters.

[210]The temple, tabernacle, and the area surrounding the sanctuary are called מקום קדוש (see Ex 29:31, Lev 6:9, 19, 20, etc.).

[211]Reading with a number of Hebrew mss. and the major versions וישתבחו instead of וישתכחו. For a discussion of the textual difficulties in this passage, see J. C. Serrano, "I Saw the Wicked Buried," *CBQ* 16 (1954), pp. 68-70.

[212]Reading הבל for MT הכל.

[213]Adding with the major versions, with the exception of the Targum, ולרע.

[214]Scott, *Wisdom in Israel*, p. 202.

[215]Martin Hengel, *Judentum und Hellenismus*, WUNT 10 (Tübingen: J. C. B. Mohr [Paul Siebeck], 1969), p. 241. The textual problems posed by Sirach, especially as concern the textual traditions, are perhaps the most complicated in textual-critical research, but due to the general verification of the mss. of the Cairo Geniza by the Hebrew fragments from Qumran and Masada (e.g., see Yigael Yadin, *The Ben Sira Scroll from Masada* [Jerusalem: IES, 1965], p. 1) we have decided to follow the Hebrew text of Moshe Segal, *Sepher Ben Sira Ha-Shalem*, 2nd ed. (Jerusalem: The Bialik Foundation, 1958). For extensive analyses of the textual traditions and problems, see Alexander Di Lella, *The Hebrew Text of Sirach* (London: Mouton and Co., 1966); and H. P. Rüger, *Text und Textform im hebräischen Sirach*, BZAW 109 (Berlin: Walther de Gruyter, 1970).

[216]Hengel suggests that he may have held an important position as a judge or counsellor, or perhaps was even a member of the *Gerousia* (*op. cit.*).

[217]Hengel's comment supports this point when he states concerning the scribe as represented by Sirach: "Der 'Weisheitslehrer' wird zum 'Schriftgelehrten,' indem er seine Wirksamkeit mehr und mehr auf die heiligen Schriften Israels konzentriert" (*ibid.*, p. 247). Also see J. Marböck, *Weisheit im Wandel*, BBB 37 (Bonn: Peter Hanstein, 1971), p. 83.

[218]For an analysis of this hymnic aretalogy, see Marböck, *op. cit.*, pp. 41f. Marböck points to the significance of the passage with respect to wisdom and cult when he observes: "Wenn als Ben Sira die Sophia in 24, 10 als Liturgin darstellt, wird damit der Kult Israels als ein Höhepunkt der Weisheit bezeichnet, die im Dienst vor Gott zu ihrer Vollendung kommt" (p. 65). A comparable text is found in 4:11-19, especially vv. 13-14, which states that those who serve the temple serve wisdom.

[219]See Rylaarsdam, *Revelation in Jewish Wisdom Literature*, pp. 18f.

[220]Sirach is at odds with both the Hellenists and Hellenizing Jews who are denigrating the rich religious heritage of ancient Israel, though Hellenistic influence even on Sirach is noticeable in a number of places (see J. L. Crenshaw, "The Problem of Theodicy in Sirach: On human Bondage," *JBL* 94 [1975], p. 57). In claiming for wisdom a divine origin, and more specifically an origin with the Jewish deity, he opposes the affirmation that philosophy derives from the Greek philosophers (cf. Alexander Di Lella, "Conservative and Progressive Theology: Sirach and Wisdom," *CBQ* 28 [1966], p. 141).

[221]Cinnamon, calamus, and myrrh were ingredients in the anointing oil (Ex 30:23), while gulbanum, onycha, stacte, and frankincense were ingredients of incense (Ex 30:34). See Marböck, *op. cit.*, pp. 74f. He observes from this that "die Gottesdienst Israels ist demnach kostbare Weisheit...."

[222]E. Janssen remarks: "Die besondere Gabe, die das Volk erhält, ist nicht das Land, sondern das Gesetz und vor allem der Kult. Das wird an der Darstellung Aarons deutlich werden" (*Das Gottesvolk und seine Geschichte* [Neukirchener Verlag, 1971], p. 20). For important studies of the "Praise of the Fathers," consult Edmond Jacob, "L'histoire d'Israel vue par Sira," *Mélanges Bibliques André Robert* (Paris: Bloud and Gay, 1957), pp. 288-94; and Robert T. Siebeneck, "May their Bones return to Life! Sirach's Praise of the Fathers," *CBQ* 21 (1959), pp. 411-28. One should also compare this hymn to the Egyptian "In Praise of Learned Scribes." The Hellenists were also fond of writing panegyrics to their great heroes.

[223]See Aelred Cody, *A History of Old Testament Priesthood*, AnBib 35 (Rome: The Pontifical Biblical Institute, 1969), pp. 194f. For a traditio-historical analysis of priesthood, see A. H. J. Gunneweg, *Leviten und Priester*, FRLANT 89 (Göttingen: Vandenhoeck und Ruprecht, 1965).

[224]Sirach's admonition to the priests to continue faithfully their cultic service receives greater poignancy when seen in the clash with Hellenism, and especially when the temple priests under Jason were reported by the author of II Maccabees to be negligent and even disdainful of their cultic duties (II Macc 4:13f.).

[225]See Num 18:8f. This is comparable to Sirach's teaching in 7:29-31 where he emphasizes that the priesthood should be supported by means of the offerings of the people. In this instruction he gives evidence of a social concern for the priests, since the admonitions concerning the priests are followed by a section dealing with almsgiving for the support of the poor (see Solomon Schechter, "A Glimpse of the Social Life of the Jews in the Age of Jesus the Son of Sirach," *Studies in Judaism* [Philadelphia: The Jewish Publication Society of America, 1908], p. 75). In this passage the "honoring of God" is equated with the "honoring of the priests," and Sirach adds that the giving of offerings for the support of the priests is commanded in the law, providing a second motivation for giving. It may well be that during the difficult economic times following the death of Simon II when heavy taxation, for example, became extremely difficult to pay, and when the leading priestly families had grown rather wealthy, temple offerings had slackened, thus making the gentle prodding of Sirach necessary.

[226]See A. Caquot, "Ben Sira et le Messianisme," *Semitica* 16 (1966), p. 66.

[227] II Macc. 4:1f. For a discussion of the Tobiads, see B. Mazar, "The Tobiads," *IEJ* 7 (1957), pp. 137-45, 229-38. Another reference to the "Sons of Zadok" and their divine selection for the priesthood occurs in the hymn in 51:12:i-xvi, verse ix, though the siracide authorship of this hymn has been questioned, for example, by Di Lella, since "it is not contained in any of the versions and does not seem to suit the context." If authentic, Di Lella suggests it was probably excised "from most of the MSS of Sir in order to avoid embarassing the Hasmonean high priests" (*op. cit.*, pp. 101-5).

[228] The Syriac and Greek translations read in place of "the heritage of sacrificial fire before his glory": "the inheritance of the king is from son to son." They probably intended to demonstrate that Aaron's covenant is to all of his descendants, whereas the Davidic covenant is intended for only one descendant at a time.

[229] Segal, *op. cit.*, pp. 316-17. The covenants of David, Aaron, and Phinehas are important to Sirach, since they guarantee the continuation of the central institutions of the people, and, therefore, the people themselves as a nation. Yet Sirach is also concerned that the successors to these covenants as well as the people of Judah remain obedient and faithful to their religious heritage (see P. A. H. De Boer, "בבריתם עמד זרעם" Sirach xliv 12a," VTSup 16 [1967], pp. 25-29).

[230] This text is directed most probably to the entire priesthood, since the plural verbs and pronouns are used. If singular, then it would have been directed to the reigning high priest as Snaith has suggested (*Ecclesiasticus*, CBC [Cambridge: Cambridge University Press, 1974], p. 227).

[231] The text appears to depend upon I Kgs 3:9 which is part of Solomon's prayer for wisdom.

[232] For a discussion of the problematic reign of Onias III and his subsequent ouster, see Hengel, *op. cit.*, pp. 16f., 491f.

[233] So argues Tcherikover, *Hellenistic Civilization and the Jews* (New York: Atheneum, 1959), pp. 80f.

[234] *Ant.*, XII, 139-41. A second document recorded by Josephus (*Ant.*, XII, 145f.) points to specific examples of the carrying out of the King's decree.

[235] Tcherikover, *op. cit.*, pp. 83f. Thus the Jews were treated, politically speaking, as one of the "nations" within the Seleucid Empire and not as "cities" and "princes." Such a political designation allowed the Jews a good deal of self-autonomy (*ibid.*, p. 88).

[236] Cf. Josephus, *Ant.*, 172f., and his description of the high priest's apparel.

[237]See Othmar Schilling, *Das Buch Jesus Sirach*, Herder-B 7
(Freiburg: Herder, 1956), pp. 208f. Lehmann observes that "his
description of the yom kippur ritual does not follow the standard order of the service, probably as Ben Sira 50 is primarily
intended as a poetic homage to the High Priest and as a description of his personal appearance on this day" ("Ben Sira
and the Qumran Literature," *RQ* 3 [1961], p. 119).

[238]The Greek translation has omitted this specific blessing for Simon and his descendants, probably due to the breaking
of the line of Zadokite succession by the time the translation
was made.

[239]For a discussion of the levitical singers in the post-
exilic period, see de Vaux, *Ancient Israel* 2, p. 394.

[240]A short didactic poem pertaining to prayer follows in
32:21-26.

[241]Haspecker argues that Sirach is primarily concerned
with the social and ethical ramifications of cult in this instruction (*Gottesfurcht bei Jesus Sirach*, AnBib 30 [Rome:
Pontifical Biblical Institute, 1968], p. 178).

[242]"Weiter, die Zeremonie hat nur dann einer Wert, wenn
sie sich mit sittlicher Gesinnung verbindet" (Paul Volz, *Weisheit*, SAT 2 [Göttingen: Vandenhoeck und Ruprecht, 1911], p.
212).

[243]Against Robert H. Pfeiffer, *A History of New Testament
Times* (New York: Harper and Row, 1949), p. 375.

[244]See 44:5 in the context of the "Praise of the Fathers"
which speaks of the wisdom of the fathers and adds that they
"investigated psalms (מזמור) according to their rules, and put
parables into writing."

[245]Cf. Koh. 5:2-3.

[246]For a discussion of chapter 38, see Marböck, *op. cit.*,
pp. 160f.; and Haspecker, *op. cit.*, p. 190.

[247]The Chronicler believed that such a consultation of
the physician indicated a lack of faith in the divine healer
(II Chron 16:12).

[248]Of course, it is possible that Sirach has included
borrowed prayers, and has not composed them himself, though we
lean towards the conclusion that he was the original author.

[249]For an analysis of such prayers, see E. J. Bickerman,
"The Civic Prayer for Jerusalem," *HTR* 55 (1962), pp. 163-95.

[250]Cf. Sirach's references in the "Praise of the Fathers"
to Samuel's successful intercession for deliverance from the

254

Philistines (46:13f.), and to those made by the people during
the time of Hezekiah for deliverance from Sennacherib (48:17f.).
These texts intimate Sirach's faith that God will once again
act on behalf of his troubled people.

[251]For a defense of the siracide authorship of this psalm,
see Heinrich Germann, "Jesus ben Siras Dankgebet und die Hodajoth," *ThZ* 19 (1963), pp. 81-87.

[252]For an analysis of this and other forms in Sirach, see
W. Baumgartner, "Die literarischen Gattungen in der Weisheit
des Jesus Sirach," *ZAW* 34 (1914), pp. 161-98.

[253]Also see the Hebrew hymn following 51:12.

[254]For a discussion of the 'disputation' in Sirach, see
Crenshaw, "The Problem of Theodicy in Sirach," pp. 50f.

[255]For an analysis of this and other hymns in Sirach,
especially as pertains to the problem of theodicy, see Crenshaw, *op. cit.*, pp. 51f.

[256]As noted in our discussion of Koheleth, this sage had
argued that the activity of the deity was beyond human scrutiny,
and, therefore, sapiential understanding (3:11, 8:17). And the
cold and hostile world gave no support to the idea of retribution, which Koheleth was forced to denounce.

[257]See Koh. 5:3f. and Prov 20:25.

[258]מועדים "must...have had a rather wide meaning, and it
seems to have been used for all kinds of religious assemblies.
The word חג, on the other hand, was reserved for the three
great feasts of pilgrimage" (de Vaux, *Ancient Israel* 2, p.
470).

[259]Von Rad, *Wisdom in Israel*, p. 267. For his cogent
analysis of 'time' in Israelite wisdom, see pp. 263-83.

[260]The Greek text reads in 51:14: ἕναντι ναοῦ ἠξίουν περὶ
αὐτῆς, "Before the temple I asked for her (wisdom)." But the
Qumran text from cave 11 has instead: באה לי בתרה, "She (wisdom)
came to me in her beauty (or searching)." Delcor prefers the
Hebrew reading ("Le text hébreu du cantique de Siracide LI, 13
et ss. et les anciennes versions," *Textus* 6 [Jerusalem: Magnes
Press, 1968], pp. 31f.).

[261]For a cultic condemnation of divination and omenology,
save for Urim and Thummim and dreams, see Deut 18:10.

[262]See our discussion of Koheleth who also deprecates
"dreams" (5:2, 6). In addition to Crenshaw's study of dreams
("The Problem of Theodicy in Sirach"), see Ernst L. Ehrlich,
Der Traum im Alten Testament, BZAW 73 (Berlin: Alfred Töpelmann, 1953).

[263]Pfeiffer, *op. cit.*, p. 375. Marböck wrongly insists that there exists a duality of conflicting thought in the mind of Sirach concerning cult, for he believes that while Sirach obviously is supportive of cultic traditions and institutions, his criticism of cult, supposedly seen in his insistence on ethical and social intent in the making of offerings, suggests he has been influenced by the prophetic critique of cult (*op. cit.*, p. 87). However, as we have seen repeatedly, the ancient sages in Israel and in the ancient Near East were just as concerned with ethical and social intent in the cult, and, therefore, there is no need to suggest Sirach has been heavily influenced by the prophets in this matter. He is still at home in the sapiential tradition.

[264]The argumentation for an Alexandrian origin includes the composition of the piece in Greek, the usage of the LXX, the existence of a large Greek-speaking Jewish population in Alexandria during the Hellenistic period, the concentration on the Exodus tradition and the anti-Egyptian polemic, an anti-Jewish literature originating in Alexandria, the apologetic response of other Alexandrian Jewish writers, the address of the "rulers" who were probably the Ptolemies living in Alexandria, the condemnation of the Ptolemaic ruler cult, and the author's acquaintance with Hellenistic thought, culture, and literature which flourished in Hellenistic Alexandria. The date is difficult to determine specifically, but in general the usage of the LXX and the reference to the book by later New Testament writers provide the *Terminus a quo* and the *Terminus ad quem*. Other factors include the writer's acquaintance with Sirach, Daniel, and Enoch, and the first century apologetic literature which is comparable to this writing. Thus most scholars have pointed to the first century B.C. as the date. See Peter Dalbert, *Die Theologie der hellenistisch-jüdischen Missionsliteratur unter Ausschluss von Philo und Josephus* (Hamburg-Volksdorf: Herbert Reich, 1954), pp. 71f.; Joh. Fichtner, *Weisheit Salomos*, HAT 6 (Tübingen: J. C. B. Mohr, 1938), p. 5; A. Goodrich, *The Book of Wisdom* (New York: The Macmillan Co., 1913), p. 5; R. H. Pfeiffer, *History of New Testament Times with an Introduction to the Apocrypha*, pp. 326f.; and Joseph Reider, *The Book of Wisdom* (New York: Harper and Brothers, 1957), pp. 14f. The critical text we shall follow is Alfred Rahlfs, *Septuaginta* 2 (Stuttgart: Württembergische Bibelanstalt, 1935).

[265]While the book may be generally classified as wisdom literature due to the presence of sapiential forms (proverbs: 3:11, 6:14, and instructions: 1:1f., 6:1f.) and themes (hymns to wisdom in chapters 6-9, the new role given to wisdom in salvation history, theodicy, and the view of God as creator and overseer of a just cosmic order), it is clear that the Jewish savant has not limited himself to the forms and thought of the Jewish wisdom literature, but has used ideas and forms from Hellenism, including the four cardinal virtues (8:7), the harmony of the elements (chapter 19), a sorites (6:17-20), the argument concerning the knowledge of an artisan by the examination of his works (13:1-5), the stoic idea of a world soul

(1:13), and immortality of the soul (see C. Larcher, *Études sur le livre de la Sagesse* [Paris: J. Gabalda et Cie, 1969], pp. 201f.; and James Reese, *Hellenistic Influence on the Book of Wisdom and its Consequences*, AnBib 41 [Rome: Pontifical Biblical Institute, 1970]). In addition, he has incorporated biblical materials, most especially the Salvation History traditions centering on the Exodus (Georg Ziener, *Die theologische Begriffssprache im Buch der Weisheit* [Bonn: Peter Hanstein, 1956]; and J. Fichtner, "Zur Problem Glaube und Geschichte in der israelitischen-jüdischen Weisheitsliteratur," *TLZ* 76 [1951], pp. 146-50), and the eschatological motifs of his contemporary apocalyptists (Johannes Fichtner, "Die Stellung der Sapientia Salomonis in der Literatur- und Geistesgeschichte ihre Zeit," *ZNW* 36 [1937], pp. 124f.). As concerns the form, Reese has presented good evidence that the genre of the book as a whole is the *logos protrepticus*, "didactic exhortation" (*op. cit.*, pp. 115f.). Structural analyses have been made by A. G. Wright, "The Structure of the Book of Wisdom," *Bib* 48 (1967), pp. 165-84; James Reese, "Plan and Structure in the Book of Wisdom," *CBQ* 27 (1965), pp. 391-99; and Patrick Skehan, "The Text and Structure of the Book of Wisdom," *Traditio* 3 (1945), pp. 2f.

[266]In the period of our writer, an incipient anti-Jewish polemic began in Alexandria, nurtured by antagonism over Jewish privileges (freedom of worship, the legal position in which all Jews were regarded as a part of the Jewish nation and legally governed by the central Jewish authority, and governmental respect of Jewish customs), Jewish opposition to syncretism, rigid social customs, an intense national awareness, and the militancy of the Maccabean rule in Palestine (W. D. Davies, "The Jewish State in the Hellenistic World," *Peake's Commentary on the Bible* [1962], pp. 686-92). The intellectual polemic was Alexandrian, as was the Jewish apologetic and missionary response (Dalbert, *op. cit.*, pp. 14f.). Such a response by Jewish intellectuals included three emphases: monotheism and the evils of idolatry, the spiritual nature of true revelation, and the election of Israel (Davies, *op. cit.*, p. 69). These are found in the Wisdom of Solomon.

[267]Davies, *op. cit.*, p. 32.

[268]Hengel notes that such a religious crisis was common to many religions and faiths of the fourth century and later, and that it led to three results in the Hellenistic period: a sweeping turn to irrationalism and the existence of secrets which were believed answered only through supernatural revelation, the investigation of basic questions of human life such as the fortune of the soul following death and the integration of the individual within the cosmos, and a growing interest in the wisdom of the ancient Near East which seemed to offer instruction in the meaning of life (*Judentum und Hellenismus*, pp. 381f.).

[269]For studies of the Salvation History material in Wisdom as Midrash, see R. T. Siebeneck, "The Midrash of Wisdom 10-19," *CBQ* 22 (1960), pp. 176-82; and Pierre Grelot, "Sagesse 10, 21 et la Targum de l'Exode," *Bib* 42 (1961), p. 49. On the other

hand, Reese argues against the Midrash form and instead perceives the material to be that of the Greek σύγκρισις, "comparison," used for didactic purposes (*op. cit.*, p. 98).

[270]Among the best studies, see Maurice Gilbert, *La critique des dieux dans le Livre de la Sagesse*, AnBib 13 (Rome:
Pontifical Biblical Institute, 1973); Reese, *Hellenistic Influence*, pp. 115f.; and Friedo Ricken, "Gab es eine hellenistische
Vorlage für Weish 13-15," *Bib* 49 (1968), pp. 54-86. For a recent study of the critique of pagan religions by the Old Testament writers in general, see Horst Dietrich Preuss, *Verspottung
fremder Religionen im Alten Testament*, BWANT 92 (Stuttgart: W.
Kohlhammer, 1971).

[271]S. A. B. Mercer, *The Religion of Ancient Egypt*, pp.
227f. Also see Frankfort, *Ancient Egyptian Religion*, pp. 8f.

[272]Tac. Hist., 4, 83. See H. I. Bell, *Cults and Creeds in
Graeco-Roman Egypt* (Liverpool: At the University Press, 1953),
pp. 10f.; and Bonnet, *RÄRG*, p. 816.

[273]Herodotus, II, 65-76. Also see Philo, *Dec.*, 76, and
the Letter of Aristeas, 138.

[274]Cf. Cicero, *Nat. deor.*, III, 15.

[275]Exodus 8.

[276]David Gill, "The Greek Sources of Wisdom XII 3-7," *VT*
15 (1965), pp. 383-86. Gill sees close comparisons in language
and thought between Wisdom and Greek tragedy in this passage
(Euripides, *Orestes*, 814-18, *Medea*, 795-97, *Bacchae*, 72-76,
Heracles Furens, 1183-84; and Aeschylus, *Choephoroi*, 884-86).
He concludes concerning the sage: "When he came to write about
people who slaughtered children for religious rites, he thought
in the categories of the most poignant instances of such things
known to him, *viz.*, the Greek stories" (*ibid.*, p. 385).

[277]For studies of this god and his mystery cult, see W. K.
C. Guthrie, *The Greeks and their Gods* (Boston: Beacon Press,
1950), pp. 145-82; Bell, *op. cit.*, pp. 18f.; Franz Cumont, *The
Oriental Religions in Roman Paganism* (New York: Dover Publica-
tions, 1956), pp. 74f.; and Martin P. Nilsson, *Geschichte der
Griechischen Religion* 2, Handbuch der Altertumswissenschaft 5
(München: C. H. Beck, 1950), pp. 329f.

[278]Thus Pentheus, a king opposed to the cult in Euripides'
Bacchae, was captured and killed by the worshippers, being torn
to pieces by his own mother.

[279]For a comparison between the philosophical religion attacked in Wisdom and Stoicism, see Gilbert, *La critique des
dieux*, pp. 2f.

[280]This is paralleled in Epictetus: "Assuredly from the
very structure of all made objects we are accustomed to prove
that the work is certainly the product of some artificer, and
has not been constructed at random" (*The Discourses*, I, vi, 7).

[281] See Gilbert, *op. cit.*, pp. 28f.

[282] He also argues in 13:1 that since all men are ignorant by nature, even the intellectual reason of the philosophers cannot succeed in coming to a knowledge of God, an achievement made possible not by reason, but by revelation.

[283] Fransen and Duesberg have observed: "C'est que l'idolâtrie est à ses yeux une des manifestations les plus choquantes, les plus éclatantes aussi de cette méconnaissance de Dieu, *agnōsis tou théou*, qui résume pour lui toute folie humaine" (*op. cit.*, p. 821).

[284] The polemic against idolatry had a long and extensive history in the religion of ancient Israel. Harrelson has argued that the prohibition of images in the Old Testament in general has not so much to do with the idea of a fear of controlling the deity's powers, but rather results from the mystery enshrouding the deity and his being which opposed any effort to depict him in any form (*From Fertility Cult to Worship*, pp. 14, 47). Von Rad adds that the prohibition also involves the concept of revelation, that is, the deity chooses when and where he will reveal himself (*Old Testament Theology* 1, pp. 212f.). In *Wisdom in Israel*, pp. 184f., von Rad has stressed that the prohibition initially is part of cultic law, and that it is condemned as a cultic aberration, whereas by the time of Deutero-Isaiah and later, the Wisdom of Solomon, the attack against idolatry is not based on cultic law, but rather is grounded in "an appeal to sound human intelligence." For an extensive discussion of the attack against idolatry in the Wisdom of Solomon, see H. Eising, "Der Weisheitslehrer und die Göttesbilder," *Bib* 40 (1959), pp. 393-408.

[285] Cf. Isaiah 44:9-20, an obvious *Vorlage* for this pericope.

[286] Gilbert has cogently argued for extensive Greek philosophical influence on this passage, especially in regard to the presentation of God as a pilot in order to depict his providence (Ps.-Aristotle, *De Mundo*, 6, 400b, 6f.; Cicero, *Natura deorum*, II, 34, 87; and Philo, *On Providence*, 1, 25).

[287] Gilbert, *op. cit.*, p. 99.

[288] See T. S. Brown, "Euhemerus and the Historians," *HTR* 39 (1946), pp. 259-74.

[289] Gilbert, *op. cit.*, pp. 155f.

[290] See Ricken, *op. cit.*, p. 65.

[291] For studies concerning the development of the Ptolemaic ruler cult, consult L. Cerfaux et J. Tondriau, *Le cult des souverains* (Tournai: Desclée and Cie, 1956); A. D. Nock, "Notes on Ruler Cult," *Journal of Hellenic Studies* 48 (1928), pp. 21-43; and Nilsson, *Geschichte*, pp. 125-74. Ptolemy I took the

first major steps toward the establishment of the ruler cult
when he brought the body of Alexander to Alexandria and initiated a city cult around Alexander, associated Alexander with the
"fraternal Gods," extended the worship of Alexander into a
state cult throughout the empire, and initiated the Serapis
cult (Dionysus, Osiris) in Alexandria. Ptolemy II later deified his parents as the "Savior Gods," gave Alexander a consort, Arsinoe (Philadelphos), and perpetuated the Dionysian
cult of Alexander. In order to establish a cult of living
sovereigns linked to Alexander, he perpetuated the cult of the
"Fraternal Gods" in which he and his wife were worshipped during their lifetimes. Finally, he extended deification to all
the ruling Ptolemies by making them the "Gods who shared the
temples." Ptolemy III claimed descent from Dionysus himself,
while Ptolemy IV placed tremendous stress on such descent and
even put the deity at the head of the gods in Alexandria.
Ptolemy V was finally the first Ptolemy to be enthroned in the
manner of the ancient pharaohs, and eventually the queen became
identified with Isis, the mother goddess.

[292]Gilbert makes reference to a number of sources which
speak concerning the beauty of idols of the gods, especially
the passion aroused by statues of Aphrodite (*op. cit.*, pp.
112f.).

[293]Cf. Demetrius, the idol-maker, in Acts 11:23f.

[294]As concerns content, this prayer is the specific type
of "Prayer for Wisdom" (cf. Sir. 39:5f.).

[295]Maurice Gilbert, "La structure de la prière de Salomon
(Sg 9)," *Bib* 51 (1970), pp. 301-31.

[296]See Exodus 25-31 and 35-40. It should be noted that
hymns and hymnic language and motifs are scattered throughout
the work, especially in terms of the Isis-influenced portrayal
of hypostatized wisdom in chapters 6f. But the most important
passage is 10:20-21 which alludes to the Song of Moses and the
Song of Miriam which were praises to God made possible by Wisdom who "opened the mouth of the dumb, and made the tongues of
babes speak clearly." This intimates that the wise composed
hymns, a point also made by Sirach.

[297]Joseph Reider, *The Book of Wisdom*, p. 208. Cf. II
Chron 30:21 and 35:15.

[298]Against Jaubert who has argued that the reference to
the law is an insertion of the celebration of the covenant by
our author into the celebration of Passover (*La notion
d'alliance dans le Judaisme*, [Paris: Éditions du Seuil, 1963],
p. 355).

[299]Num 16:40f.

[300]Cf., e.g., Job in the epilogue. Jaubert remarks:
"Peut-être n'est-il pas indifférent que l'intercession d'Aaron

s'exerce ici non pas des victimes expiatoires, mais essentielle-
ment par la prière. Tel était le modèle pour la communauté de
la *Sagesse* qui ne pouvait-sans doute! - offrir de sacrifices
sanglants" (*op. cit.*, p. 354).

[301]An allegorical interpretation of the robe is at work
when he sees in the designs on the robe the entire cosmos.
Thus, he seems to present Aaron as a figure of the intercession
of the cosmos on behalf of the righteous (see Jaubert, *op. cit.*,
pp. 353-54).

[302]See Exodus 28.

[303]Also see Josephus, *Ant.*, III, 7, 7; and Philo, *Mos.*,
III, 11-14. Josephus also gave a cosmological interpretation:
the blue vestment symbolized the sky, the girdle the ocean, the
diadem heaven, and the sardonyx buttons on the shoulder the sun
and the moon.

[304]Against Preuss, *op. cit.*, p. 273.

[305]Job's refusal to participate in astral worship appears
to be based on sacral law, especially since the language of
31:26-28 approximates that of Deuteronomistic legislation (cf.
Dt 13:6f.). However, idolatry is not so condemned, but is rejected because it is foolish, contrary to reason. Furthermore,
adultery and illicit intercourse with the Strange Woman are
prohibited, not on the basis of sacral law, but on the basis of
socio-ethical regulations considered by the wise to govern the
wise-righteous community and its members (Proverbs 1-9).

CHAPTER V

DIDACTIC POEMS AND WISDOM PSALMS

A. *Introduction*

Wisdom Psalms in Modern Scholarship

In our final chapter devoted to the analysis of the views
of the wise concerning cult, we shall focus our attention upon
long didactic poems which are embedded in the Psalter. If we
are successful in identifying a corpus of long didactic poems
present within the Psalter, then we shall have additional
material to assess the views of the wise which pertain to the
Israelite cult. What is more, some of the poems may even be
wisdom psalms and as such were intended by their wise authors
to be utilized in cultic services.[1]

The *Gattung* of wisdom psalms has received different assessments from modern scholars, from Ivan Engnell, on one hand,
who has categorically rejected the existence of this classification to Roland Murphy whose studies have convinced him of its
definite existence.[2] Let us first examine the assessments of
leading psalmodic and wisdom scholars with respect to the existence and analysis of this genre, and then move into our own
identification and genre analysis.

Hermann Gunkel, in his *Einleitung in die Psalmen*, gave
some attention to the existence of what he referred to as *Weis-
heitsdichtung* within the Psalter which he discovered possessed
form-critical and thematic characteristics common to Old Testament sapiential writings as well as wisdom literature from the
ancient Near East. Gunkel apparently regarded the following
as products of the sages: Psalms 1, 37, 49, 73, 112, 127, 128,
and 133, while several others, he believed, were influenced to
some degree by wisdom. In terms of methodology, Gunkel was one
of the earliest psalmodic scholars to utilize what has been until now two criteria in the identification of these psalms: the
presence of sapiential language and the existence of wisdom
themes.[3]

A second major psalmodic scholar of this century, Sigmund
Mowinckel, has done a considerable amount of study in the

investigation of wisdom psalms which he classified as "learned psalmography," a corpus of psalms which he believed were "non-cultic" in origin and purpose. This classification of psalms was also identified by Mowinckel on the basis of the presence of sapiential forms ("saying," "proverb," "exhortation") and wisdom themes (theodicy, retribution, the contrast between the righteous and unrighteous). According to Mowinckel's analysis, such psalms were written as "didactic prayers" directed to God, but also were intended to instruct men in sapiential ideas. Mowinckel's classification included Psalms 1, 34, 37, 49, 78, 105, 106, 111, 112, and 127.[4]

The most extensive analysis of wisdom psalms has been made by Herman Jansen who examined sapiential psalms not only in the Psalter but also in a rather broad expanse of later intertestamental literature including the Psalms of Solomon, the Prayer of Manasseh, Sirach, the Wisdom of Solomon, Daniel, Baruch, I, II, and III Maccabees, Esther, Judith, and Tobit. Jansen concluded that the wise were responsible for the creation of the late Jewish psalms in intertestamental literature. Thus, their form and content were transformed by the sapiential writers who gave the originally cultic genres sapiential character and wrote them not primarily for usage in the temple cult, but rather as instructional material for sages within the circles of the wise: the school, temple and synagogue. While Jansen placed his interests primarily in psalms outside the Psalter, he did argue that there were wisdom psalms in the Psalter: 1, 37, 49, 73, 91, 112, 127, 128, and 133 which were written by the sages in the context of a wisdom school located near the temple for the two-fold purpose of cultic devotion and sapiential instruction. And it is from these sages and their wisdom psalms that eventually developed the literary psalms intended primarily for instruction and not for cultic service.[5]

More recently, Gerhard von Rad has investigated a sapiential corpus of psalms which, like Mowinckel, he classified as *Lehrgebete*, a rather general classification based once more upon the presence of sapiential forms and themes within this body of psalms. However, von Rad believed that such a classification lacked the identifiable structure of other major psalmodic genres, so that one could speak of a "classification" only in very general terms. Further, von Rad argued that this corpus emits evidence of the appropriation of the structure, language, and themes of the other major genres which were recast by the sages into sapiential *Gebete*. Thus the sapiential psalm in Tobit 13:1 appropriated the form and language of the hymn, Psalms 1, 34, 37, 49, 73, 111, 112, 119, 127, 128, and 139 used the structure and language of the Torah Psalms, and 49, 73, and 139 were *Problem- oder Reflexions-dichtungen.*[6]

One of the most incisive form-critical studies in the area of wisdom psalms has been done by Roland Murphy. Having recognized the diversity of scholarly opinion as pertains to this sapiential *Gattung*, Murphy set forth distinctive form-critical and thematic criteria for the identification of wisdom psalms. The stylistic and linguistic forms which Murphy regarded as typically sapiential and that were present in a number of psalms included: the *'ashrê* formula, the numerical saying, the better saying, the proverb, the admonition, the address of a teacher to his "son," and the acrostic. Sapiential themes which were present in a number of psalms included: the contrast between the wicked and the righteous, the two ways, the preoccupation with the problem of evil, practical advice as regards conduct, and the "fear of the Lord." Upon the basis of these two criteria, Murphy regarded the following as wisdom psalms: 1, 32, 34, 37, 49, 112, and 128.[7]

James Crenshaw in his study of the major wisdom forms also has included an analysis of wisdom psalms. Beginning with a brief study of wisdom hymns in Proverbs (1:20-33; 8), Job (28), Sirach (24), and the Wisdom of Solomon (6:12-20; 7:22-8:21), he then moves into the arena of wisdom psalms. Noting the disparity which exists among scholars concerning which psalms should belong to this category and referring to the difficulties which beset the scholar in explicitly distinguishing the boundaries between psalms which are actually written by the wise and those which demonstrate sapiential influence in terms of forms and themes, he proceeds to examine possible psalmodic candidates for this wisdom genre and includes: 1, 19, 33, 39,

49, and 104. He points to wisdom influence in 94, especially in vv. 8-11, and in 127. Crenshaw's methodology is the same used by the other major scholars for the identification of wisdom psalms: the presence of wisdom language and themes.[8]

Finally, Kenneth Kuntz has contributed an indepth analysis of wisdom psalms, a study distinguished not only by a thorough summary of past wisdom psalm research, but also by an explicit delineation of methodological criteria and their application to possible wisdom psalms.[9] These criteria include language (rhetorical/form critical elements and vocabulary) and themes. With regard to rhetorical/form critical elements, Kuntz articulates seven which he considers to be primarily, though not exclusively, sapiential: the 'better' saying, the numerical saying, the admonition, the admonitory address to 'sons', the 'ašrê formula, the rhetorical question, and the simile. While he follows the sapiential vocabulary tabulation of Scott[10] and considers this useful as a criterion for any comprehensive effort to identify wisdom psalms, Kuntz nevertheless notes that it should not be "the truly telling element in our attempt to answer the question, 'Which are the wisdom psalms?'" He then moves into the arena of wisdom themes and primarily concentrates on the following four: "(1) the fear of Yahweh and veneration of the Torah, (2) the contrasting life styles of the righteous and the wicked, (3) the reality and inevitability of retribution, and (4) miscellaneous counsels pertaining to everyday conduct." Following his application of these criteria to various candidates for the classification of wisdom psalms, Kuntz concludes the following are products of the wise: 1, 32, 34, 37, 49, 112, 127, 128, and 133.

Kuntz concludes his incisive investigation by briefly considering two different areas: the delineation of literary structures of wisdom psalms and the possible life situations in which they arose. As relates to the first consideration, Kuntz places the wisdom psalms within three subcategories which are based on literary structures: sentence wisdom psalms (127, 128, 133), acrostic wisdom psalms (34, 37, 112), and integrative wisdom psalms (1, 32, 49). Finally, the possible sociological contexts for the psalms are briefly mentioned, and he

suggests possible cultic (temple and synagogue) and non-cultic
(home, street, city gate, court) life situations, though he
concludes that this matter continues to defy specific precision.

Methodology

It should come as no surprise to us that the wise wrote
long didactic poems, some of which are comparable to well known
genres of psalmodic literature, a point that we have made repeatedly throughout the preceding chapters. The long didactic
poems of the wise which we have discussed previously include
the "Song of the Harper," the fourth chapter of Amen-em-Opet
which contrasts the "silent man" and the "heated man," the poem
concerning the inaccessibility of wisdom (Job 28), and the
poetry which is similar to different genres of psalms including
the "lament" of "The Debate of the Man Tired of Life with his
own Soul," the "Shamash Hymn," and the beautiful masterpiece of
Sirach which is a didactic hymn in 39:12-35.

Furthermore, we have repeatedly pointed to a number of
ancient Near Eastern wisdom texts which reflect over the theology and ritual and even appropriate the style and language of
the lament-thanksgiving cycle found in ancient Near Eastern
psalms: "I Will Praise the Lord of Wisdom," Nougayrol's "righteous sufferer" psalm, and "Man and His God" from Mesopotamian
wisdom circles, and from Israel the Dialogues of Job and
Sirach's "A Lament for the Deliverance of the Nation," "An Individual Thanksgiving for Deliverance from Sin and Death," and
"A Prayer for Self-control." These may be intimately connected
to the emphasis upon prayer made by the sages throughout ancient Near Eastern wisdom literature, since the lament and the
thanksgiving are the primary types of "prayers."

That the wise were familiar with and composed psalmodic
literature may be concluded not only from the existence of such
texts in sapiential literature, but also from a Mesopotamian
schoolboy examination text[11] in which a reference is made to
the material over which a novitiate had to be tested, and among
the material to be covered on the examination were psalmodic

genres, probably alluding to the fact that such literature was
used as instructional models in the wisdom schools. Sirach
also says, as we indicated earlier, that hymns were taught in
wisdom circles (15:9-10; cf. Wis. 10:20-21) and in fact demonstrates this by his artistically constructed didactic hymn that
we examined above.

Now our basic problem is first of all to search out and to
analyze possible candidates for the classification of long didactic poems in the Hebrew Psalter. The methodology for doing
so will include not only the above mentioned criteria of the
presence of sapiential forms, language, and themes,[12] but in
addition the methodology of New Stylistics, a method we have
previously used in our investigation of the sapiential structure of Psalm 49.[13] We shall demonstrate that the structure
and the content of some didactic poetry are based upon a simple
wisdom form such as a proverb, riddle, or 'ashrê saying. It is
this form and its contents which provide the foundation for the
development of the structure and content of the long didactic
poem. Thus, as we seek to identify and analyze didactic poems
and wisdom psalms in the Hebrew Psalter, we shall examine sapiential forms, themes, language, and structure.

Life Situation

Before beginning our task, we should speak to the issue of
the life situation of didactic poetry in general, and, more
specifically, wisdom psalms. The life situations in general
for the different kinds of wisdom literature are varied and
most difficult to assess. Christa Bauer-Kayatz has argued for
several different life situations, including the tribe or family, the court, and the school.[14] When we turn to consider
didactic poems, however, most wisdom scholars would seek their
origins in the context of a wisdom school, the existence of
which, however, remains obscured by the lack of explicit evidence, at least with respect to Israelite wisdom literature,
though the abundance of evidence in the ancient Near East
proves beyond question the existence of schools in Egypt and
Mesopotamia, and, in our view, schools of a similar nature must

have existed in ancient Israel as well.[15] Thus von Rad, Mowinckel, and Jansen have argued that the didactic poems, including wisdom psalms, were produced in a wisdom school in
which the wise sought to instruct their students in different
genres of literature, including cultic forms. The eventual
appearance of long didactic poems in the Psalter, so these men
have argued, occurred in the late post-exilic period when
scribes, who were connected with the cult and who were the
final collectors of the Psalter, included some of the poetic
writings of their sagacious ancestors. Consequently, when the
wise, who originally were attached to the court in pre-exilic
times, became scribes of Torah and found their locus in the
post-exilic temple and temple cult, we find them writing and
collecting long didactic poems and, more specifically, wisdom
psalms (cf. Ben Sira).[16] However, the creation of long didactic poems and wisdom psalms, in our opinion, is not simply
limited to the post-exilic period, but some most probably were
written in the pre-exilic age, for it is apparent that similar
writings had existed for centuries in the wisdom traditions of
the ancient Near East, and it would seem that to deny the Israelite wise the capability or interest to write long didactic
poems and wisdom psalms in the pre-exilic period is without
cogency.[17] The late post-exilic dating for the production of
the wisdom psalms by some scholars is predicated on the questionable assumption that the pre-exilic wise were secularists
and became religious pietists only in the late post-exilic
times.[18]

The primary question which should concern us, however, is
whether the sages intended some of their poetry to be wisdom
psalms, written for usage in the cult, or whether the long didactic poems were merely academic exercises and instructional
literature intended for the teaching of sages and schoolboys.
Unfortunately, there is no easy solution to such a difficult
question. Two possibilities lay before us. One is that we
have only long didactic poems, created within the wisdom school
for the instruction of students in the techniques of artistic,
literary composition, as well as for the indoctrination of sapiential ideas, and, as such, do exude, as we shall see, a

spirit in most instances of pious devotion to God as creator, redeemer of the oppressed, requiter of the good and the wicked; in other words the God who oversees world-order. Furthermore, some poems may even reflect over the validity of cultic theology and rituals. Yet, they were not originally intended by their authors for cultic liturgies as were the cultic genres. Their appearance in the Psalter, as indicated above, was due to the activity of scribal redactors.

A second possibility is that these poems are wisdom psalms and were the contributions of the wise to the creation of liturgical literature, intended to be used in the temple worship.[19] It is possible that they were written by temple scribes or sages functioning in the temple school whose training in the wisdom traditions, mastery of sapiential language, and instruction in sagacious ideology led them to write the wisdom psalms.

In our opinion, both possibilities are valid, for, as we shall argue, some of these poems were used to teach literature and ideology to young schoolboys (see Psalms 1, 37, 49, 112, and 127). Other poems (32, 34, and 73), while not intended for use as cultic literature, nevertheless, do reflect over cultic rituals and dogmas, thus providing for us some valuable sources for our analyses of sapiential views of cultic religion. Finally, at least some of these poems are psalms, written by sagacious authors to be used in the cult (Psalms 19A, 19B, and 119). While a precise distinction between non-cultic wisdom poetry and cultic wisdom psalms is a difficult one to make, we shall follow these criteria as we proceed in our analyses: the presence of cultic terms and references (e.g., the cultic shout of joy, the imperatives to the cultic assembly to praise God, references to a choir, and cultic rituals) and the close similarity of the poem to one of the typical cultic genres: the hymn, lament, or thanksgiving. If these elements are present within a poem that appears to have been the product of the sages, then we shall consider it to be a legitimate wisdom psalm, written by a sage for cultic service.

B. *Proverb Poems*

As we identify and analyze long didactic poems, we shall be concerned also with the didactic structure. And, as we shall see, the structure of several didactic poems is developed around a simple saying: a proverb, a riddle, or an *'ashrê* saying. And yet, these simple sayings provide not only the locus for the structural formation of the poem, but, in addition, contain the sapiential thesis over which the poem reflects and then seeks to develop and extend into several areas of sapiential thought.[20] The first such category of long didactic poems then is the Proverb Poem in which an extended poem may appropriate elements from sapiential categories such as the instruction or from the major psalmodic genres such as the thanksgiving and the lament, but the structure and content of the poem are developed around a simple proverbial saying.[21]

Psalm 1: "A Didactic Poem Concerning the Righteous and the Wicked"

Introduction. In regard to our methodology for the identification and analysis of the genre of long didactic poems, Psalm 1 may be classified as a didactic poem,[22] and, more specifically as pertains to its structural basis, a Proverb Poem, since, as we shall demonstrate, the structure and the content of the poem are taken from the simple proverb found at the end of this didactic poem in v. 6. As pertains to sapiential forms, the poem contains the following: an *'ashrê*,[23] two parabolic sayings (vv. 3-4),[24] an antithetical proverb[25] which is the central saying around which the psalm is constructed (v. 6), and the form of the didactic poem which embodies the entire piece.[26] Sapiential terminology present in the poem includes the terms עצה ,רשעים ,חטאים ,לצים ,דרך ,חפץ ,ידע, and צדיקים.[27] As regards sapiential themes, this psalm, taking its content from the central proverb in v. 6, contrasts the fate of the righteous (צדיקים) and the wicked (רשעים) which is dealt out in terms of the just retributive system of rewards and punishments by the Lord, the guardian of retribution. One also finds the late developing wisdom theme of meditating on the

"Instruction of Yahweh," the Torah.[28] Finally, as we shall
see, the application of the methodology of New Stylistics reveals a skillfully composed literary structure.

Translation[29] *and Structural Analysis*

Strophe I (E)

'*Ashrê*   A (1) Happy is the man
                    (2)   who neither walks in the community
                           of the wicked,
                    (3)   nor stands in the dominion[30] of sin-
                           ners,
                    (4)   nor sits in the assembly[31] of scof-
                           fers.

Insertion D   (But rather his delight is in the Law of
                           the Lord,)
                        (And in his Law he meditates both day
                           and night.)

Parable   B (5) For he is like a tree planted by channels
                           of water,
                    (6) Which gives forth its fruit in its sea-
                           son,
                    (7) And its foliage does not wither.

Concluding
Observation   C (8) And all which he does shall prosper.

Strophe II (E^1)

Introductory
Observation   C^1 (1) However, the evil ones do not (prosper);

Parable   B^1 (2) Rather they are like the chaff which the
                           wind blows away.

Proverb   A^1 (3) (Therefore) the wicked do not stand in
                           judgment,
                    (4)   Nor sinners in the assembly of the
                           righteous.

Central Proverb

               E   (1) (Because) God knows the way of the righ-
                           teous,
                    (2) But the way of the wicked will perish.

As is apparent from our analysis, the poem consists of two
strophes which exhibit external, antithetical parallelism, and
each strophe consists of three chiastically arranged units (A,
B, C; C^1, B^1, A^1). Thus A is contrasted with A^1 (the righteous man is not a part of the community of the wicked even as
the wicked are not a part of the community of the righteous);

B with B[1] (the parable of the fruitful tree and the parable of
the windswept chaff); and C with C[1] (the prosperity of the
righteous and the misfortune of the wicked).[32] Furthermore,
the first strophe exactly doubles the length of the second, in
that the first possesses 8 hemistichs, whereas the second has
4. The structure of the two strophes of the poem parallels the
key proverb, a chiastic, antithetical saying, which independently stands outside the structure of the two three unit
strophes. And yet in terms of content and structure the proverb is the locus around which the content and the structure of
the highly artistic didactic poem has been built. The first
hemistich of the proverb provides the basis for the first
strophe, whereas the second hemistich that for the second
strophe.[33] The two hemistich unit D, placed in Strophe I, may
be regarded as an insertion, since it contains no parallel in
Strophe II, has an imperfect verb (יהגה) following a series
of perfect verbs and thus is syntactically awkward, and, if
omitted, allows for a smooth transition from A (4) to B (5).
This insertion was made probably by a pious scribe of Torah
similar to the picture we have drawn of Sirach who wishes to
emphasize that the one who is truly righteous will find guidance for his life in the meditation on Torah.[34]

Exegesis.[35] In this didactic poem, the author has ampli-
fied an antithetical proverb which contrasts the divine retribution of the righteous with that of the wicked by means of an
artistically constructed didactic poem consisting of two
strophes, the first of which presents the activities and prosperity of the righteous, and the second of which concerns the
misfortune and punishment of the wicked.

Strophe I pertains to the righteous man who does not, by
means of his behavior, associate himself with the community of
the wicked. In unit A, three terms: הלך, עמד, and ישב, are
used by the sage to describe metaphorically the behavior of the
righteous man who does not associate with the wicked, and com-
prise the basic positions of the human body--"walking," "standing," and "sitting." The sagacious poet also demonstrates his
flair for synonyms by referring to the wicked by three nouns of

comparison: רשעים, חטאים, and לצים, terms found in wisdom
literature to denote those whose behavior is opposed to the
mores and laws of the righteous society based on the just order of the cosmos.[36] Further, three synonyms are used also by
the sage for referring to the religio-ethical category of the
wicked: "community" (עצה), "dominion" (דרך), and "assembly"
(מושב). Thus, the man who maintains his distance from the
group of the wicked is deemed "happy," a term denoting in wisdom literature a congratulatory remark made by an observer as
well as the state of blessing into which the decorum of the
righteous man has led him.

The poet then proceeds in unit B to illustrate the key
proverb which speaks of the divine care for the righteous by
the utilization of a parabolic saying based on the "Parable of
the Fruitful Tree." Such a tree parable is common to the literatures of the ancient Near East, as may be seen in Amen-em-
Opet, IV, Jer. 17:5-8, and Ezek 29:1-5.[37] Several of these
texts demonstrate that this specific type of parable is not
limited to the symbols and motifs of the king, and argues
against the attempt of Engnell to regard the righteous man as
the king, who in Near Eastern myth is the caretaker of the tree
of life, and to classify the psalm as a royal psalm.[38] This
parable is used to illustrate by means of a common sapiential
metaphor the prosperity of the righteous man who is not a part
of the community of the wicked. Finally the concluding observation in unit C points back to the righteous man who is con-
gratulated in unit A, and concludes that he succeeds in everything that he seeks to accomplish and to do.

The second strophe amplifies the second hemistich of the
key proverb (E) by describing the destruction which seeks out
the wicked. The first unit, C^1, forms a chiastic antithesis
with C of Strophe I, and thus introduces us to the wicked by
observing that whatever he seeks to accomplish does not succeed. The second unit, B^1, chiastically parallels B of Strophe
I, and is likewise a parabolic saying paralleled in other wisdom literature (Job 21:18) and used to depict metaphorically
the wicked as the chaff which is blown away by the wind, a
primitive method of separating the grain from the chaff by

pitching the grain into the air and allowing the currents of the wind to blow away the chaff. The third unit, A^1, is a concluding observation, also in chiastic antithesis with its counterpart in the first strophe, and it affirms that the wicked will not escape their destruction by being included among the religio-ethical category of the "righteous." Thus, in an example taken from Israelite jurisprudence, they are presented as those who are declared "guilty" (רשעים) in a law-case, and not as צדיקים, "innocent" of charges levelled against them.

Finally, the key proverb (E) is a common one in wisdom literature, and it observes that Yahweh "knows," "is aware of," those who belong to the category of the righteous who live in accordance with the divinely instituted laws of social and cosmic order, whereas, the wicked, of whom he is also aware, are accorded the destruction of divine wrath.[39]

As pertains to the question of whether or not the poem is a wisdom psalm intended for the cult, we are not convinced the poem contains any cultic terminology or characteristics comparable to cultic genres that would allow us to make a cultic classification. The reference to the assembly could be a cultic assembly, but this is more of a reflection over a group of the righteous, rather than a direct reference to a cultic community that is present and listening to the poem.

Psalm 34: "Concerning the Salvation of the Righteous"

Introduction. Scholarly opinion has been divided with respect to the genre to which the 34th psalm belongs. The poem has been classified in three different categories: an individual psalm of thanksgiving, influenced by wisdom forms and content,[40] a combination of an individual thanksgiving psalm (vv. 1-11) and a wisdom writing (vv. 12-22),[41] and a wisdom psalm which contains certain characteristics of an individual song of thanksgiving.[42]

But is this a didactic poem? Applying to our psalm the form critical test, we find the following sapiential forms: the *'ashrê* saying (v. 9),[43] positive admonitions with or without

the motive clause introduced by $k\hat{\imath}$ (vv. 10, 14, 15), a series
of proverbs (vv. 16-23), a rhetorical question (v. 13),[44] and
the acrostic framework which in this case is alphabetic.[45]
Sapiential vocabulary includes the words רשע, צדיק, לב, למד,
and יראת יהוה, and the typical sapiential introduction to an
instruction (לכו בנים שמעו לי) is present also. Wisdom themes
are the typical ones of retribution, the contrast of the wicked
and the righteous, and the testing of the thesis in the arena
of personal experience (vv. 5-7). Yet the determination of the
form of the poem is complicated by the fact that it contains
characteristics of an individual song of thanksgiving, especially in vv. 1-11: the characteristic introduction whereby the
individual announces his intent to thank and praise the Lord
(in the jussive and cohortative moods--אברכה, ישמחו, ישמעו,
ונרוממה) and invites the assembly to join in his worship (v.
4);[46] the typical reference to his own past distress (vv. 5b-7);
the description of his deliverance by Yahweh who "heard" (שמע,
vv. 5, 16, 18), "answered" (ענה, v. 5), and "delivered" (נצל,
vv. 5, 18, 20; ישע, vv. 7, 19; and פדה, v. 23); the expressions
of confidence and trust in the Lord (vv. 6, 8, 9, 11, 16, 18,
19, 20, 21, 23); the general inferences of salvation for all
those who trust in Yahweh (especially vv. 11-23); and the key
words תהלה ("praise"), הלל ("boast"), גדל ("magnify"), and
נרוממה ("exalt").[47] However, it is our view that the psalm
should be classified as a didactic poem which contains a reflective and educative instruction concerning the psalm of
thanksgiving and its theology (vv. 12-22), presents a model
individual thanksgiving psalm for students to study (vv. 2-11),
and is a development in terms of structure and content of the
key proverb which occurs in v. 23.

Translation and Structural Analysis

Superscription

A Psalm of David, when he feigned madness before Abimelech, with the result that he drove him away, and he departed.[48]

Strophe I The Model Thanksgiving Psalm[49]

Introduction

א   Let me bless the Lord at all times;
     Continually his praise shall be in my mouth.
ב   Let me boast in the Lord;
     Let the afflicted hear and rejoice.
ג   Magnify the Lord with me,
     And let us extoll his name together.

Body

ד   I sought the Lord and he answered me;
     For he delivered me from all my terrors.
ה   Look[50] to him and be radiant,[51]
     And your faces will not be ashamed.[52]
ז   This afflicted one called and the Lord heard,
     And he delivered him from all his troubles.
ח   The angel of the Lord encamps around those who fear him,
     And he delivers them.
ט   Taste and drink deeply[53] for the Lord is sweet;[54]
     Happy is the man who seeks refuge in him.
י   Fear the Lord, his saints,
     For there is no want to those who fear him.
כ   The young lions[55] are poor and hungry,
     But the ones who seek the Lord will not lack any
      good.

Strophe II An Instruction concerning the Thanksgiving

Introduction

ל   Come, O sons, listen to me;
     The fear of the Lord I shall teach you.
מ   Who is the man who desires life,
     Who loves days in order to see good?[56]

Body

נ   Keep your tongue from evil,
     And your lips from speaking deceit.
ס   Turn from evil and do good;
     Seek peace and pursue it.
ע   The eyes of the Lord are upon the righteous,
     And his ears toward their cry for help.[57]
פ   The face of the Lord is against the doers of evil,
     In order to cut off their remembrance from the
      earth.
צ   They cry and the Lord hears;
     And he delivers them from all their distress.
ק   The Lord is near the contrite of heart,
     And he saves the crushed in spirit.
ר   The righteous man has many miseries,
     But the Lord delivers him from all of them.
ש   He keeps intact all his bones,
     Not one of them is broken.
ת   Evil will kill the wicked men,
     And the ones hating the righteous will be held
      guilty.

Central Proverb

The Lord redeems the soul of his servants,
  And all those who trust in him will not be held
  guilty.

Once more we find a didactic poem which is structured
around a proverb, in this case a synonymous, two hemistich saying found in v. 23, which is independent of the alphabetic
acrostic, a fact that indicates that the proverb is the central
saying of the poem.[58] The first strophe takes the form of an
individual thanksgiving, though in vv. 8-11 it begins to make
the transition to sapiential forms. It is our opinion that the
thanksgiving strophe serves as a model for instructing young
scribal novitiates in the ideology and literary form of the
thanksgiving which is affirmed as part of the procedure by
which redemption of the Lord is obtained: the process of the
lament-thanksgiving cycle. The lament is alluded to in the
following: "I sought the Lord and he answered me," and "This
afflicted one called and the Lord heard, and he delivered him
from all his troubles."[59]

The second strophe is a sapiential instruction concerning
the thanksgiving and develops in detail the content of the key
proverb, especially in the proverbial series in vv. 16-22,
while the admonitions in vv. 14-15 admonish the sagacious
students to appropriate the general decorum of the ones who are
God-fearers, thus picking up on the "fear of God" motif which
was introduced in the proverbial ending (vv. 8-11) of Strophe
I. Therefore, those who are "God-fearers" like the psalmist
may depend upon the redemption of the deity in times of distress. The thesis of the proverb which concerns Yahweh's redemption of the pious is restated in the second hemistich of
verses 5 and 7 of Strophe I and vv. 18 and 20 of Strophe II.

Key words in the psalm appear to be the synonyms for redemption: פדה, חלץ, נצל, and ישע, while the following serve as
mots crochets: Yahweh (found in almost every line), טוב (vv.
11, 13, and 15), יראת יהוה (vv. 8, 10, and 12), רע (vv. 14, 15,
17, 20, and 22), and צדיק (vv. 16, 20, and 22).

Exegesis. Strophe I is presented primarily in the form of
an individual song of thanksgiving, though wisdom forms begin

to appear in vv. 8-11. Verse 2 initiates the thank offering
which apparently is the result of a "vow" made by the psalmist
during his period of distress.[60] The psalmist sets forth his
praise in the midst of the cultic assembly, and intends his
praise and his deliverance by Yahweh to serve as an example for
the ענוים[61] who are encouraged to take heart (v. 3). In v. 4
he invites the assembly to participate in his exaltation of
Yahweh (נרוממה, גדלו). Verses 5-7 include the *Bekenntnis*[62]
which is typical in thanksgiving psalms and which relates the
past experience of distress (צרה, מגורה) which had encompassed
the psalmist, and then speaks of his seeking of Yahweh (דרש,
קרא), Yahweh's answer (ענה), and his deliverance (ישע, נצל).
דרש (vv. 5, 11) in cultic contexts refers to the quest for admission to the sanctuary (cf. Amos 5:4f.)[63] whereby the individual in distress hoped for a *Heilsorakel* (ענה)[64] from a cultic official assuring the lamenter of Yahweh's imminent deliverance (ישע, נצל). Upon the basis of his own experience, the
psalmist then invites the assembly, especially other ענוים, to
look to his deliverance as a positive example of Yahweh's salvation, and, thereby, to gain confidence and hope (v. 6).

The psalmist seeks to emphasize the surety of Yahweh's
salvation of the pious by drawing from proverbial literature
a number of sayings, the content of which affirms the saving
power of God. In vv. 8 and 11 we have didactic proverbs.
Verse 8 draws upon the old exodus and conquest traditions involving the מלאך יהוה who aided and guided Israel during her
early experiences.[65] In the present context, the term is used
metaphorically to refer to Yahweh's protection of the pious
(יראים), and, in fact, may be a term for Yahweh himself due to
the pronominal suffix attached to יראים which seems to point
back to the מלאך (cf. Gen 16:13; Jud 13:22). Verse 8 has the
first of four occurrences of the word ירא which refers to the
obedience and trust of the pious in the absolute authority of
Yahweh, the creator who has established the just orders for
pious living. Those who observe this rule of orders and follow
the direction of the admonitions and commands based upon it will
receive the reward of חיים for themselves and their community.[66]

Verses 9 and 10 are admonitions (*Mahnsprüche*) given in the typical imperative form (שמעו, יראו), and v. 9b also inserts an *'ashrê* form. The assembly is addressed, vocatively, as the קדשיו, the only occurrence in the Old Testament in which the term "saints" is used as a noun to refer to the human assembly of worshippers.[67] The strophe closes with the proverbial contrast of the כפירים, probably a metaphor for the rich and powerful who suffer want, and the pious (דרשי) who have every good thing. טוב in wisdom literature, according to von Rad, is to be regarded as a beneficent "power," a life-giving force which creates "well-being" and "life" for the wise-righteous in terms of possessions, fortune, name, children, longevity, etc., for both him and the community in which he lives. Thus, טוב is a "lebens- und gemeinschaftsfördernden Macht."[68]

Strophe II is an instruction by a wise teacher who is instructing his schoolboys both in the theology and the literary form of the thanksgiving. The instruction typically contains the introduction (v. 12), the body which has a rhetorical question (v. 13) and admonitions (vv. 14-15), and the conclusion which consists of proverbs (vv. 16-22). In v. 12, one finds the typical sapiential introduction (cf. Prov 1:8, 2:1, etc.) in which the sage announces he is about to instruct his students in the יראת יהוה which he identifies with the attitude and cultic response of the "God-fearer" in the thanksgiving psalm.

Beginning with the catechetical question, the wise man places in interrogative form the basic concerns of the wise "who desire life (חיים) and to experience the good (טוב)." Bauer-Kayatz has defined "life" in wisdom as "langes, ruhiges, gesichtertes Leben ohne Mangel und Störung."[69] The catechetical answer to the question is given by the sage in vv. 14-15 in terms of two admonitions. One who desires "life" and the experience of "good" must know how to control his tongue (Prov 13:3), one of the primary concerns of the wise who regarded proper speech as the key characteristic of the "silent man."[70] In a more general way, the admonition of v. 15 states the counsel of the entire wisdom ideology: "turn from evil (Prov 3:7, 13:19) and do good" (Ps 37:3, 27; Prov 13:21). The actions and

attitudes of the wise aid in creating the life-producing sphere
(שלום) of order (צדקה), whereas the actions and behavior of the
wicked lead to the destruction of this sphere for himself and
for his community. Thus, the removal of the wicked from the
just society was necessitated for the community to survive
(Prov 2:21-22, 10:30; Ps 37:9, 10, 12, 13, 20, 22).

The remainder of the strophe consists of a series of
proverbs which contrast the righteous and the wicked (cf. Proverbs 10-15), and, as is typical in the instruction genre, serve
as clauses which legitimate the validity of the admonitions.[71]
The righteous man, by practicing צדקה, is one who is able to
integrate himself within the salvific order of righteousness
established by Yahweh, is able to create life for the community in which he lives,[72] and, if in distress, may turn to the
deity for his redemption. By contrast, the wicked are those
whose behavior leads not only to a disregard of the orders of
life but also to the dissolution of order, and consequently they
must be removed from the community by the retributive action of
the deity, destroyed to the point of utter extinction so that
even their "remembrance" will be obliterated, thus denying to
them even this small semblance of immortality: להכרית מארץ
זכרם.[73]

In v. 23, the key proverb around which the entire psalm
has been developed is presented which emphasizes the main thesis of both strophes: Yahweh's redemption of the pious.

Finally, once more we doubt that this didactic poem was
originally intended to be a piece of cultic literature and used
in the cult. Certainly the thanksgiving psalm of strophe I was
originally a cultic psalm, but it has been taken by a wisdom
teacher and used as a model thanksgiving for the instruction of
young schoolboys in the "fear of the Lord." Even so, the poem
still indicates to us that this sage was supportive of the ritual and theology of the cultic lament-thanksgiving cycle and
aligns himself with the opponents of Job.

Psalm 37: "An Instruction Concerning the Righteous and the
Wicked"

Introduction. Psalm 37 is a third example of a Proverb
Poem, for though it is clothed in the sapiential dress of an

instruction, the instruction is built around a repeated proverb found in certain key positions throughout the poem. The categorization of this psalm as a wisdom composition is easily proven.[74] The entire poem is an instruction[75] consisting of admonitions, both positive and negative, often coupled with motive clauses introduced by $k\hat{\imath}$ (vv. 1 and 2, 3 and 4, 5 and 6, 8 and 9, 27 and 28a, 34, 37 and 38), a "better" saying (v. 16), different types of didactic proverbs scattered throughout the poem, and the acrostic arrangement.[76] Wisdom language includes the terms תורת, ישר, תם, עולה, מדמה, לב, ידע, דרך, בין, חכמה, אלהיו, אחרית, צדק, רשע, and לשון. Typical wisdom themes include the central emphasis of the poem upon the principle of retribution justly meted out to the righteous and the wicked, the contrast of the behavior of the righteous man and the wicked man, an evil time, correct speech, and the late wisdom theme of the guidance of the pious wise by the Torah of Yahweh (v. 31). The artistically built structure of the poem is fashioned in the same way that other proverb poems have been built: the development of structure and content around a central proverb (vv. 9, 22, 28b and 29a, 34b, and 38b).

Translation and Structural Analysis.

A. Strophe I: "Be not Envious of the Evil-Doers"

א Do not anger yourselves on account of the wicked,
Nor be envious of the evil-doers,
For they will quickly wither as grass,
And as green herbage they shall droop.

ב Trust in the Lord and do good;
Inhabit the land and enjoy security.
Take delight in the Lord,
And he will give to you the requests of your heart.

ג Turn your way unto the Lord;
Trust in him and he will act.
He will bring forth your innocence as the light,
And your justice as the noontime.

ד Be silent before the Lord,
And wait longingly for him.
Do not anger yourselves on account of the success of
    his way,
On account of the man who commits wicked deeds.

ה Refrain from anger and leave behind wrath;
Do not anger yourselves, for it leads only to evil.

Central Proverb

(For) the wicked will be cut off,
But the ones who wait for the Lord will possess the
    land.

Expanded Observation concerning the Proverb

Yet a little while and the wicked will be no more;
You will look attentively upon his place, but he will
ו   not be there.
But the meek shall inherit the land,
And will be delighted by abundant well-being.

B. Strophe II: Concerning the Righteous and the Wicked

The evil one plots against the righteous,
ז And grinds his teeth against him.
My Lord laughs at him,
For he sees that his day is approaching.

The wicked draw the sword and bend their bow,
In order to bring down the afflicted and needy (to
ח   slay the upright).[77]
Their sword will enter their own heart,
And their bows will be broken.

Better is the little which the righteous man possesses,
ט Than the wealth of many wicked,
For the arms of the wicked will be broken,
But the Lord sustains the righteous.

The Lord knows the days of the innocent,
י And their inheritance will be forever.
They will not be ashamed in an evil time,
And in the days of famine they will be satiated.

Surely the wicked shall perish,
כ For the enemies are like the most precious of pastures.
They vanish in smoke, they vanish.

ל The wicked one borrows but does not repay,
But the righteous man is generous and gives.

Central Proverb

(For) his blessed ones will inherit the land,
But his accursed ones will be cut off.

From the Lord are the steps of a man;
They are established, for he takes delight in his way.
מ Whenever he should fall, he will not be cast down,
For the Lord sustains his hand.

Expanded Observation Concerning the Central Proverb

I have been a lad, and now I am old,
נ But I have never seen the righteous abandoned nor his
    children begging for bread.
All the day he is generous and lending,
And his seed will become a blessing.

C. Strophe III: Concerning the Righteous and the Wicked

Depart from evil and do good,
ס And dwell forever,
For the Lord loves justice,
And will not abandon his pious ones.

ע They are preserved forever.

Central Proverb

(But) the seed of the wicked is cut off,[78]
The righteous will inherit the land.

And they will dwell upon it forever.

The mouth of the righteous expresses wisdom,
פ And his tongue speaks justice.
The torah of his God is in his heart;
His steps will not be moved.

The evil one observes the righteous,
צ And seeks to kill him.
But the Lord will not abandon him into his hand,
And he shall not pronounce him guilty when he is tried.

ק Wait for the Lord and keep his way,

Central Proverb Paraphrased

So that he may exalt you to possess the land,
When the wicked are cut off you will observe it.

Expanded Observation concerning the Proverb

I have seen a ruthless,[79] wicked man,
ר Spreading himself out like a luxurious tree.[80]
And he passed along,[81] and behold he was no more;
I searched for him, but he was not found.

D. Conclusion to the Instruction

Observe the blameless and behold the righteous,
ש For there is a future to the man of peace.
But transgressors shall be destroyed altogether;

Central Proverb

The future of the wicked will be cut off.

The salvation of the righteous is from the Lord;
ת He is their refuge in a time of distress.

He helps them and delivers them.
He delivers them from the evil ones,
And saves them, for they take refuge in him.

While the aesthetic appeal of the poem is somewhat hampered by the strictures of the acrostic arrangement, one still
discovers the structure to be demonstrative of artistic ability
on behalf of the wise poet. As we have indicated, the structure and content of the poem is developed around a central
proverb which is restated in several key places:

v. 9	כי מרעים יכרתון וקוי יהוה המה יירשו־ארץ
v. 22	כי מברכיו יירשו הארץ ומקלליו יכרתו
v. 28b and v. 29a	צדיקים יירשו ארץ וזרע רשעים נכרת
v. 34b	וירוממך לרשת ארץ בהכרת רשעים תראה
v. 38b	אחרית רשעים נכרתה[82]

In addition to the key proverb which occurs in each of the four
major divisions: A, B, C, and D, we also find at the end of
each of the three major strophes (A, B, C) an expanded observation of the proverb which points to personal observation of the
destruction of the wicked:[83]

vv. 10-11 Yet a little while and the wicked will be no more,
You will look attentively (התבוננת) upon his
place, but he will not be there.
But the meek shall inherit the land,
And will be delighted by abundant well-being.

vv. 25-26 I have been a lad, and now I am old,
But I have never seen (ראיתי) the righteous
abandoned nor his children begging for bread.
All the day he is generous and lending,
And his seed will become a blessing.

vv. 35-36 I have seen (ראיתי) a ruthless, wicked man,
Spreading himself out like a luxurious tree.
And he passed along, and behold he was no more;
I searched for him, but he was not found.

Thus, these personal experiences of the blessing of the righteous and destruction of the wicked serve to verify the truth
of the central proverb, and, at the same time, are structurally
conceived as dividers between the major strophes, for each one
occurs at the end of a major strophe.

Key words in addition to those repeated in the central
proverb are רשע and צדיק, again emphasizing the major theme of
the poem: the contrast between the wicked and the righteous.

Strophe I consists of five admonitions followed by the central proverb and the expanded observation. The strophe is primarily concerned with admonishments to the righteous to avoid behaving like the wicked who become angry, lose control of their passions, and consequently perish. The inclusion for this strophe is a synonym for the wicked: מרעים which occurs in v. 1 and v. 9. Words serving as *mots crochets* are אל תחחר (vv. 1, 7, and 8) and החענג (vv. 4, 11).

The second strophe contrasts the behavior and fate of the righteous and wicked in proverbial form, and ends with an auto-biographical observation of the teacher. ראה serves as an inclusion for the strophe, while *mots crochets* are צדיק, רשע, and תשברנה.

Strophe III is likewise a contrast of the behavior and fortune of the wicked with those of the righteous, and consists of admonitions, proverbial sayings, and the first person observation of the teacher. The two admonitions serve as the inclusion for the strophic unit, while רשע, משפט, and צדיק are *mots crochets*.

Finally, vv. 37-40 are a conclusion to the instruction, and serve primarily as a means for the completion of the alphabetic acrostic. The form is an admonition followed by an extended series of motivations and assertions concerning the salvation of the righteous and the destruction of the wicked. *Mots crochets* include אחרית, יהוה, ישב, and רשעים (and its synonyms).

Exegesis. This didactic poem, dressed in the garb of an instruction, serves as a prime example of the principle of retribution, for it repeatedly asserts that the righteous will eventually be rewarded, whereas the wicked will be destroyed. And the overseer of this system of just retribution, of course, is Yahweh. The principle of retribution involved the process of *Tun-Ergehen-Zusammenhang*, that is, the process by which certain behavior led to either well-being or misfortune, and consequently we find our sage equally concerned with the delineation of the characteristics of sagacious behavior as contrasted to the foolish and wicked actions of the evil ones.[84]

The creation of the instruction by the sage seems to be motivated by the perplexion of his students over the problem of

the prosperity of the wicked who succeed even in their persecution of the righteous.[85] This concern has so enraged the righteous audience that their trust in Yahweh as the one who maintains a just order hangs precariously near the chasm of doubt.
In fact, this impatience and anger aroused within the breast of
the righteous is leading them to develop behavior that is characteristic of the wicked, and, as such, is extremely dangerous.
Thus, the sage repeatedly requests his hearers to still their
rage (vv. 1, 7, 8). If they maintain their trust in the justice of Yahweh, so our sage argues, they will continue to reside within the spheres of "life" and "well-being," figurative-
ly expressed in the repeated image of "possessing" or "inherit-
ing the land" (נחלה).[86] And, in addition, they will see the
eventual destruction of the wicked who, along with their descendants, will be "cut off" from success, land, and life.

The sage develops his arguments for the validity of the
principle of retribution and the dogma of theodicy by centering
upon two temporal ideas found within the structure of wisdom
thought: the idea of the "future" and the concept of "time."
One of the key theological terms in the instruction is the word
אחרית, occurring in vv. 37-38, and capable of several nuances.
One idea is that of "posterity," as seen in Ps 109:13, while
another is that of the final result of a course of action
(Prov 14:12). However, the most important nuance is that of
the "future" of a man which includes every element of one's
hopes for his future: longevity, descendants, success, prosperity, well-being, etc. Therefore, the sage seizes upon this
term to affirm his belief that the wicked, in contrast to the
righteous, have no security residing within their אחרית, for
they, their descendants, and their possession of the land "will
be cut off."

In addition, the sage grasps the argument of "time" to
support his faith in the principle of retribution and the justice of God. In the wisdom tradition, there is the idea of an
"evil time" in which those who are foolish and wicked will be
utterly decimated, while the wise-righteous may hope for the
salvation of the deity (cf. Sirach 39:12f.). Thus, our sage
argues that during an "evil time" (עת רעה) the righteous will

not be put to shame, for the Lord serves as their refuge in the
"time of trouble," implying that catastrophic times will sweep
away the wicked in the flooding waters of destruction (cf.
Amen-em-Opet 7). In addition, he argues that the "time" of the
wicked man's success is brief (עוד מעט, v. 10), and that "his
day is coming" (יבא יומו, v. 13), an expression which in wisdom
sources refers to the time when the consummate result of an
evil man's actions will be requited, and he experiences an
"untimely death" (Prov 16:4, Job 20:28, Ecc 7:17).[87]

Thus, our sage places himself squarely in the category of
the pious wise who support, never question, the traditional
dogmas of wisdom literature, even to the extent of blindly arguing that he had "never seen the children of the righteous
begging for bread."

Finally, if we consider whether there is evidence that
this didactic poem was intended to be a psalm composed for cultic liturgy, our conclusion is negative for the same reasons
articulated in the preceding discussions: the absence of cultic
language and the non-similarity to cultic genres of psalms. We
lean towards the view that the poem was originally intended to
instruct a school audience in the problem of theodicy.

Psalm 73: "A Reflection on the Problem of Theodicy"

Introduction. In regard to content, Psalm 73 has generall
been recognized to be a Joban psalm[88] in that the intense questioning of the justice of God and the related dogma of retribution is of critical concern to the theological thrust of the
poem. Like the Joban dialogues, the poem makes use of formal
elements and themes of the lament, but the inner doubts and the
theological questioning of the poet are openly displayed for
accessible scrutiny. Furthermore our poem is more of an intense reflection over and questioning of the theological presuppositions of the lament, thus pointing to the conclusion
that the piece should best be seen as a product of the wisdom
circles, and perhaps is best considered among the category of
Gese's "Paradigm of the Answered Lament."[89] Such a sapiential
classification is derived from the fact that the closest

parallels to the psalm from ancient Near Eastern literature, in addition to Job, are the Sumerian "Man and His God" and the Akkadian "I Will Praise the Lord of Wisdom," both of which are reflective poems dealing with the theological and existential torment of a just sufferer who persistently seeks and eventually discovers his redemption through the battered and worn cultic response of the lament.[90]

With respect to sapiential forms occurring in our poem, we find a maxim (v. 1), the autobiographical style,[91] and the disputative quotation of the wicked in v. 11.[92] Sapiential vocabulary includes the terms דעת, בער, תוכחת, ישר, עצה, בין, חשב, לב, אחרית, רשעים, גאוה, and עמל. Wisdom themes include the above-mentioned questioning of the justice of God, retribution, the contrast of the wicked and the righteous, and the theological answer to the problem of theodicy which is centered in the idea of "nearness to God," or theological existence (cf. Job).

Translation and Structural Analysis

Superscription

A Psalm of Asaph

Introductory Maxim

Surely El is good to the upright,[93]
Elohim to the pure in heart.

Strophe I: The Prosperity of the Arrogant Wicked

But as for me, my feet had almost turned aside,[94]
My steps[95] had almost slipped.
For I was jealous of the proud,
When I perceived the well-being of the wicked.
For they have no pangs,
Their bodies are sound and healthy,
They do not participate in human toil,
Nor are they stricken like other men.
Therefore, pride is their necklace,
And violence clothes them as their garment.
Their eyes swell from fatness,
The conceits of their heart flow forth.
They mock and speak with evil,
They speak oppression as if from on high.
They place their mouths in the heavens,
And their tongue struts upon the earth.

Therefore, bread satiates their hunger,[96]
And plentiful waters are drunk by them.
And they say, "How can God know"?
And, "Is there knowledge in the Most High"?
Behold, these are the wicked;
Forever at ease, they increase their wealth.

Strophe II: The Destruction of the Wicked

Surely it has been in vain that I have kept my heart pure,
And have washed my hands in innocence.
Because I have been stricken all the day,
And my chastisement comes each morning.
If I had said, "I will speak concerning this,"
Then I would have been a deceiver to the generation of
     thy sons.
And I wished to reflect in order to understand this,
Yet it was a wearisome task to my eyes.
Until I went to the sanctuary of God,
Then I perceived their end.
Surely you have placed them in slippery places;
You cause them to fall to their destruction.
How they are destroyed in a moment,
Utterly swept away by terrors,
Like a dream when one awakes, O Lord,
Like a hazy image when one awakes.

Strophe III: "The Nearness of God"

When my heart was bitter,
And my emotions had been spent,
I was stupid, for I did not understand.
I was like a brutish animal with you.
But I am continually with you.
You have taken my right hand.
With your counsel you lead me,
And you have me follow after glory.
Who is mine in the heavens but you?
And I take no delight on earth.
My flesh and my eyes may be weak,
But the rock of my heart and my portion is God forever.

Conclusion

For behold, those who are far from you will perish;
You destroy everyone who is unfaithful to you.
But as for me, my welfare is the nearness of God.
I have made my refuge the Lord God,
In order to recount all of your works.

The sagacious poet has utilized a synonymous maxim from
the wisdom tradition in v. 1 as the basis for the structure and
content of his reflection on the lament. The vocabulary of the

maxim is repeated in strategic places throughout the following strophes, and the affirmation of the justice of God in the saying is the pivotal theological concern of the entire poem.

The content of Strophe I involves the radical questioning of the affirmation of the maxim with respect to the justice of God, a questioning issuing forth from the sage's observation of the prosperity of the arrogant and blasphemous wicked. The strophe is initiated by first person pronouns and verbs (vv. 2-3), and then makes the transition (v. 4) to the third person description of the wicked. The religio-ethical category of the רשעים serves as an inclusion (vv. 3, 12), while the strophe is terminologically linked to the maxim by the repetition of the key words אל and אך in v. 11.

The transition to Strophe II is indicated by the shift from the third person description of the wicked to the first person reflections of the sage who decries the suffering by which he has been tormented even though he had been righteous. He then proceeds to the second person address of the deity, and finally to the third person description once more of the wicked. The language of the introductory maxim is repeated in the terms אך (vv. 13, 18, 19) and לבב (v. 13). Verse 13 disputes momentarily the theology of the maxim, for the sage bemoans his own suffering which has come in spite of his "clean heart." אך also serves as an inclusion for the demarcation of this second strophe.

Once more the transition to the third strophe is noticed in the change to the first person pronouns and verbs, though finally the sage proceeds to the second person in addressing the deity. The repetition of the words לבב (vv. 21, 26) and אלהים (v. 26) links this strophe with the language of the maxim. The *mot crochet* of this strophe is עמד (vv. 22, 23, 25), while לבב serves as an inclusion.

Finally, the conclusion, which reaffirms the theology of the maxim but gives it a new insight, parallels the language of the maxim in regards to the following clauses which, in addition, serve as the inclusion for the demarcation of the entire psalm:

Maxim   טוב לישר אל

Conclusion   אלהים לי טוב

In addition, אני serves as an inclusion for the entire psalm
(vv. 2, 28), and the words אך and לבב are the *mots crochets* of
the complete poem.

    Exegesis. Psalm 73 is a sapiential reflection concerning
the Israelite dogmas of the justice of God and retribution
which are the foundation blocks of sapiential as well as penitential theology. Like the just sufferer in "I Will Praise the
Lord of Wisdom," our poet rigorously questions, anguishedly
doubts, and almost blasphemously denies the justice of God and
the related principle of retribution. His faith was shaken not
only because of his observation that the arrogant wicked pros-
pered and were at ease, but also because of the prodding of the
pain of his own intense suffering, suffering which was supposedly undeserved by the righteous.[97]

    In the first strophe, the sage admits he has doubted the
justice of God when he observed the welfare of the wicked whose
prosperity and well-being seemed to increase in spite of their
oppression, violence, promethean pride, and defiant, mocking
blasphemy of the knowledge and power of God.[98]

    The sage then speaks with bitterness of his own suffering
in spite of his self-proclaimed innocence, an experience which
almost led to the brink of angry blasphemy hurled against
God.[99] Incapable however of uttering his thoughts aloud, the
sage tries intellectually to grasp why he has suffered and the
wicked apparently were at ease, but finally concludes that such
an intellectual task proved to be "wearisome toil."[100] He
finally resorts to the sanctuary of God[101] in his despair, and,
presumably on the basis of a revelatory message,[102] or even a
theophanic experience,[103] he is led to conclude that the "fate"
of the wicked eventually will overtake them, for suddenly,
without warning, they will be decimated by the God they had
accused of being impotent.

    A further theological point is made in the third strophe
concerning the justice of God which supports our suggestion
that a theophanic experience occurred in the sanctuary. In

similar fashion to Job, the sage articulates the theological concept that meaningful existence may come only to the righteous who find true meaning in the "nearness of God."[104] In other words, theological existence is the keystone of the righteous and meaningful life, for the one who has this intimacy of relationship with God finds his security in him, which, in times of distress, provides him with deliverance, whereas the wicked, not sharing this relationship, are destroyed in times of catastrophe.

The conclusion reaffirms the theology of the maxim, though the sage adds a reflective note by defining the "good" of the maxim in terms of the "nearness to God." Thus this sage discovers, at least for his own theological understanding, that an intellectual understanding of evil is impossible, and that it is only in the cultic experience of God that one is able to transcend the intellectual incongruities between wisdom teaching concerning retribution and one's own sapiential experience.

In our assessment of the poem, we tend to regard it as a theologically reflective poem concerning the problem of the good fortune of the wicked and the validity of the lament-thanksgiving response to the problem of suffering. It does not appear to be a thanksgiving psalm intended to be sung in the cult, since its formal structure does not correspond to the typical structure of the thanksgiving. The poem does not possess such characteristic elements as the introduction which usually involves the psalmist announcing his intention to praise the Lord and the invoking of the assembly to join him. Furthermore, the poet does not address the congregation and admonish them to look upon his own salvation as an example that they should follow. Though, in our opinion, the text was not intended to be a cultic psalm, it still remains important for assessing the views of the wise pertaining to cult, for once again we find a text examining the validity of the lament-thanksgiving cycle.

Psalm 112: "Concerning the Righteous and the Wicked"

Introduction. An examination of Psalm 112 reveals a rather striking similarity with respect to content, form, and

structure to Psalm 1,[105] and, like the first psalm, should be
classified as a didactic poem.[106] Sapiential forms present in
this psalm include the 'ashrê saying in v. 1, the two part
proverb in 6b and 10c, and the form of the entire psalm which
is clothed in the apparel of an acrostic, didactic poem.[107]
Themes common to wisdom literature which are found in our psalm
include the description of the behavior of the righteous as
contrasted to that of the wicked, the principle of just retribution, the stress upon the "fear of God," and the piety of the
wise man who "delights in the commandments." Sapiential vocabulary includes the terms יראת יהוה, תאוה, ישרים, צדק, לב, and
רשע. Finally, the application of the method of New Stylistics
discloses an artistically structured didactic poem.

Translation and Structural Analysis

Superscription

Praise the Lord

Introduction: An *'Ashrê* Saying

Happy is the man who fears the Lord,
Who delights exceedingly in his commandments.

Strophe I: Concerning the Blessings of the Righteous Man

His offspring shall be a mighty man in the land.
The generation of the upright will be blessed.
Wealth and riches are in his house.

Refrain (Proverb a)

And his righteousness endures forever.

Strophe II: Concerning the Behavior of the Righteous Man

The sun rises for the righteous man even in darkness;
Gracious and merciful is the righteous man.
It goes well for the one who shows favor and lends.
He conducts his affairs with justice,
For he shall not be moved forever.

Refrain (Proverb a)

The righteous man shall have an eternal remembrance.

Strophe III: Concerning the Faith of the Righteous Man

He shall not fear an evil report.
His heart is secure, trusting in the Lord.
His heart is steady, he shall not be afraid,
Even when he sees his adversaries.
He gives freely to the needy.

Refrain (Proverb a)

His righteousness endures forever.

Strophe IV: "Concerning the Wicked"

His horn[108] shall be exalted in honor.
The wicked man sees it and is angry;
He gnashes his teeth and grows fearful.

Antithesis to the Refrain (Proverb b)

The desire of the wicked will perish.

Even with the rather stringent limitations imposed by the
acrostic device,[109] our poet has been able to construct an artistic poem around an antithetical proverb which he has divided
into its two hemistichs, and has placed them at the conclusion
of each of the four major strophes. The proverb[110] is as follows:

לזכר עולם יהיה צדיק

a The righteous man shall have an eternal remembrance

וצדקתו עמדת לעד

(And his righteousness endures forever)

צדקתו עמדת לעד

(His righteousness endures forever)

(ו) תאות רשעים תאבד

b (But) the desire of the wicked will perish

Thus, once more we find a didactic poem structured around a
simple, sapiential saying which, in addition, provides the
theme for the artistically developed poem. Furthermore, the
single unit lines of the strophes number respectively 3, 5, 5,
3, thus making the arrangement of the strophes in terms of
structure a chiasm. Repetitions include the key words צדק (vv.
3, 4, 6, 9) ישריב (vv. 2, 4), רשע (twice in v. 10), לעד ועולם

(vv. 3, 6, 9), ירא (vv. 1, 7, 8), ראה (vv. 8, 10), and עמד (vv. 3, 10). The psalmist also has a penchant for the number two: two strophes of three lines and two strophes of five lines, the terms for the righteous (יאר, צדיק) and the wicked (רשעים, צרים), and words occurring in pairs: הון and עשר, v. 3; רחום and חנון, v. 4; מלוה and הונן, v. 5; בטח and נכון, v. 7; יירא and סמוך, v. 8; נתן and פזר, v. 9; כעס and יראה, v. 10; and נמס and יחרק, v. 10.

Exegesis. Psalm 112 is an artistically constructed didactic poem contrasting the behavior and lot of the righteous with those of the wicked. The righteous man's behavior is characterized by fear of God, delighting in the commandments, generosity to those in need, just dealings, and lack of fear, whereas, in contrast, the wicked man is consumed by his jealousy and anger aroused by the just behavior and good fortune of the righteous man. While the righteous man receives his due rewards for his sagacious behavior (prosperity, family, honor, and, above all, a measure of immortality in his being remembered for his righteousness), the wicked man's desires in life come to naught, for he is consumed by his own jealous rage. This demonstrates that our sagacious author regards himself to be a devotee of the sapiential dogma of retribution, and thus places himself in the company of the pious wise.

Finally, we are not convinced that there is any evidence that this poem was intended to be a psalm for use in the cult. Rather, we believe the piece is a well constructed didactic poem which contrasts sagacious behavior and the reward of the righteous with foolish behavior and the destruction of the wicked.

Psalm 19B: "In Praise of Torah and A Prayer for Deliverance from Sin"

Introduction. Psalm 19B combines elements of praise of Torah with those of an individual lament and is, therefore, comparable to Psalm 119. We have concluded that this psalm most probably rests within the category of didactic poetry on the basis of the following.[111] Sapiential forms include the

comparative sayings in v. 11 and the rhetorical question embedded in v. 13.[112] Themes prominent in wisdom literature that
are expressed in the poem include the dogma of retribution (v.
12), the exaltation of torah and its identification with wisdom
(vv. 8-10),[113] and the emphasis upon prayer, in this case a
prayer for deliverance from sin. Wisdom vocabulary includes:
יראת יהוה, and מאיר, לב ,ישר ,פתי ,חכם ,רצון ,תם ,בין ,תורה
צדק. Finally, structural analysis further supports a wisdom
classification.

Translation and Structural Analysis

Strophe I: In Praise of Torah

The law (תורה) of the Lord is perfect,
   refreshing the soul.
The testimony (עדות) of the Lord is sure,
   making the simple wise.
The precepts (פקוד) of the Lord are upright,
   making the heart rejoice.
The commandment (מצוה) of the Lord is pure,
   enlightening the eyes.
The fear of the Lord (יראה) is clean,
   enduring forever.
The ordinances (משפט) of the Lord are true,
   and altogether righteous.

Comparative Sayings

(The Ordinances of the Lord)[115] are more desirable than
   and more than much fine gold.   [gold,
They are sweeter than honey,
   even the fine honey of the honey-combs.

Strophe II: A Prayer for Deliverance from Sins

Also, your servant is warned by them,
   in the observing of them is great reward.
Who can discern hidden sins?
   Make me innocent of secret faults.
Keep back your servant from presumptuous sins,
   let them not rule over me.
Then I shall be blameless,
   and I shall be innocent of great transgression.
May the words of my mouth,
   and the meditation of my heart,
   be acceptable unto you,
   O Lord, my rock and my redeemer.[116]

The structure of the psalm involves two strophes which are divided by an intervening couplet consisting of two comparison sayings which metaphorically describe the law as "sweeter than honey" and "more desirable than gold," a description elaborated upon in the two major strophes. The first emits an exultant praise of the superb qualities and beneficent merits of Torah, and the second is a description of the law as a tutor which instructs one in the awareness of sins, and, upon the basis of that important knowledge, allows the informed devotee to ask for divine forgiveness.

Strophe I is uniformly structured, consisting of 6 stichs (12 hemistichs), each of which has the following sentence structure: the subject consisting of a different synonym for law which is placed in construct with Yahweh, a predicate adjective which immediately follows, and a participial noun placed in construct with an absolute noun which serves as the direct object. In demonstrating an artist's flair for vocabulary and a penchant for the number 6, the author has constructed a six line strophe possessing 6 synonyms for law, 6 predicate adjectives descriptive of torah, and 6 different verbs.

The second strophe likewise consists of 6 lines (12 hemistichs) of varying sentence structure, interlinked by the following *mots crochets*: רב (vv. 12, 14), נקה (vv. 13, 14), and עבד (vv. 12, 14). The second strophe is yoked to the comparative sayings by the two-fold repetition of the word רב (v. 11). An inclusion for the entire psalm is the word חם (vv. 8, 14).

Exegesis. Strophe I, which presents us with a laudatory praise of torah, is quite comparable to Psalm 119 and to the description of wisdom in Wis 7:22f. Once more we find a didactic poem which identifies wisdom and torah in comparable fashion to Sirach. The second strophe is also comparable to Psalm 119 in that it consists of a penitential prayer[117] in which the sage, tutored by torah, is able to recognize his sins and to turn to God for divine forgiveness.[118] Yahweh serves not only as the one who forgives sin, but in addition is the one to whom a prayer for guidance in the avoidance of sin is made, and thus is connected with the same function of torah. But most

important for our concerns is the evidence contained in this
psalm that the wise not only participated in prayer, primarily
in terms of the lament-thanksgiving cycle, but apparently wrote
their own, giving us another primary source for the cultic
piety of the Israelite wise.[119]

As such, we tend to regard the psalm as a cultic wisdom
psalm, intended by its wise author for use in the cult. We
draw his conclusion from the close parallels of the psalm to
the lament, for the psalm seems to be a penitential prayer
which combines a praise of Torah, the locus of post-exilic
wisdom, with a beseeching of God to protect the poet from sin.
Furthermore, the dedicatory formula, occurring at the end of
the psalm, demonstrates its dedication to Yahweh and thus would
support Mowinckel's view that at least some of these poems were
possibly votive texts.

Psalm 127: "Concerning Vain Toil and the Blessing of Sons"

Introduction. Psalm 127 appears as though it had been a
leaf taken from a collection of Proverbs, for it contains two
"strophes" of proverbial materials: two conditional proverbs
(v. 1), an admonition (v. 4), a synonymous proverb (v. 3), a
comparative proverb (v. 4), and an *'ashrê* saying (v. 5). The
two sapiential themes respectively are "labor done in vain" and
"the blessing of sons." Because of the dominance of the proverb
form, we have chosen to classify the psalm among the proverb
poems, though it should be stressed that in contradistinction
to the other proverb poems we have examined, there is no central proverb around which the strophes have been structured.[120]

Translation and Structural Analysis

Superscription

A Song of Ascents. By Solomon.

Strophe I: "Concerning Vain Toil"

A If the Lord does not build the house,
    Its builders labor in vain.
B If the Lord does not guard a city,
    Its watchman has watched in vain.

C It is vain for you to rise early in the morning,
   Following a night of rest,
   In order to eat the bread of wearisome toil,
   For such a one gives to his beloved[121] nothing.[122]

Strophe II: "The Blessings of Sons"

D Behold, sons are the heritage given by the Lord,
   A laborer's wage is the fruit of the womb.
E Like arrows in the hand of a warrior,
   So are the sons of one's youth.
F Happy is the man who has filled his quiver full of them.
   Such ones are not ashamed when they speak with their
   enemies in the gate.

The first strophe contains two conditional proverbs (A and B, "If...then...") which are intimately yoked together in terms of form, content (the vanity of labor not supported by the Lord), and terminology ("If the Lord does not...then...is vain").[123] Unit C is an admonition linked to the conditional proverb both in content and by the recurrence of the key word שוא, found twice in C and twice in AB.

The second strophe contains a synonymous proverb (D), a comparative proverb (E), and an 'ashrê saying (F). The repetitions include בנים (vv. 3, 4), and גבר וגבור (vv. 4, 5). The theme of the strophe is the blessing one finds in the birth of sons.

Exegesis. At first glance, the two strophes appear disparate, unrelated units as pertains to content, structure, and language. However, it may well be that they have been linked together by a wise man who used the second strophe to elaborate upon part C. Thus, overwork leads to exhaustion along with little time and energy for the marriage bed, with the obvious consequence of failing to produce male offspring who are not only a source of familial pride and loyalty, but support as well in the father's toils.

Be that as it may, the two themes of vain toil without the support of Yahweh[124] and the blessing of male offspring[125] are common wisdom themes, and thus further support the classification of the poem as wisdom literature. However, it is doubtful that this poem was intended to be a cultic text, since liturgical formulae and parallels to the formal structures of cultic

genres are absent. Furthermore, its content does not contain
any thoughts concerning the cult.

C. *'Ashrê Poems*

A second sub-category of didactic poetry is the *'Ashrê*
Poem in which a "happy" saying provides the basis for the content and structure of the developed poem. There are two such
didactic poems in the Psalter: 32 and 119.

Psalm 32: "Concerning the Forgiveness of Sins"

Introduction. Psalm 32 also belongs to the genre of didactic poems, since it is a poem whose content and structure
are developed around the two introductory "happy" sayings in
vv. 1 and 2 which deal with the forgiveness of sins. The poet
seeks to demonstrate the means by which such a state of "happiness" is obtained, and the answer is the lament-thanksgiving
cycle.[126] The classification of the psalm as a didactic poem
may be determined upon the basis of our previously discussed
and applied methodology of genre identification and analysis.
Sapiential forms found in this poem include an instruction (vv.
8-10) and the two *'ashrê* sayings (vv. 1-2). The individual
thanksgiving that is found in vv. 3-7 is not a genre limited to
the literary creativity of the wise, but such a genre certainly
belonged to the literary repertoire of the sages as we have
seen (cf. Psalm 34). Furthermore, it will be our argument that
vv. 3-7 are presented as a model thanksgiving psalm, the ru-
brics of which are to be mastered by the young scribal novitiates, and its theology affirmed and put into the cultic devotion of the pious sages. Sagacious language includes: בין, דרך,
חרש, חשב, ידע, לב, רמיה, עצה, ירה, שכל, רשע, ישר, and צדיק.
Sapiential motifs include the typical dichotomy drawn between
the wicked (רשע) and the righteous (צדיק, חסיד, ישר), just
retribution dispensed by the divine judge (v. 10), the interpretation of suffering as caused by sin, and the affirmation of
the theology of the lament-thanksgiving cycle.[127] Finally, we
shall demonstrate that the structure of the poem is supportive
of a sapiential classification.

Translation and Structural Analysis

Introduction: The Two *'Ashrê* Sayings

a (1) Happy is he
  (2)   whose transgression is forgiven,
  (3)   whose sin is covered.
b (1) Happy is the man
  (2)   whose sin is not reckoned to him by the Lord,
  (3)   and who has no deceit in his spirit.

Strophe I: The Model Thanksgiving Psalm

A
Narrative

When I was silent, my body wasted away
  In a state of moaning throughout the day.
Both day and night
  Your hand was heavy against me.
My body's life-giving juices[128] were dried up
  As though by the summer's heat.

B
Confession and Forgiveness

I confessed my sin unto you,
  I did not conceal my iniquity.
I said, "I shall confess my transgressions to the Lord."
  And you bore the iniquity of my sin.

C
Admonition to the Assembly

Therefore, let every pious person make entreaty unto you,
  At the time of distress.[129]
During the rushing of many waters,
  They will not reach him.
You are a hiding place to me;
  You keep me from destruction;
  Deliverance encompasses me.[130]

Strophe II: The Instruction Concerning Sin

c[1]
Introduction

I shall instruct and teach you in the way that you should go.
  I shall give counsel[131] concerning my iniquity.[132]

B[1]
Admonition

Do not be like a horse or mule
  Which does not pay heed to bridle and bit.
For when it is approached for curbing,
  It will not come near to you.[133]

A[1]
Gnomic Conclusion

Many are the pains of the wicked,
  But steadfast love envelops the one who trusts in the Lord.

Conclusion: The Thanksgiving

a[1]
b[1]

Delight in the Lord, and exult, O righteous ones,
  And utter a joyous shout all you who are upright.

As is the case with most of the didactic poems, Psalm 32
has as the basis for its structural and thematic development
simple wisdom forms, in this case the two initial *'ashrê* sayings.[134] The major *mots crochets* which recur throughout the
poem are the synonyms for sin: פשע ("transgression"), חטאה
("sin"), and עון ("iniquity"). These are found in the "happy"
sayings and are repeated in the two major strophes (vv. 5, 8,
11). In fact, the sagacious psalmist has a preference for the
number three, a point that provides us with some incisive insight into the literary structure of the entire psalm: the
three synonyms for the "righteous" (ישר, חסיד, צדיק), the three
references to the confession of sin (v. 5; לא כסיתי, אודיעך,
אודה), the three expressions for instruction (v. 8; ירה, שכל,
עצה), and the three imperatives issued to the audience to rejoice with him (רנן, גיל, שמח).[135] In addition, each of the
two introductory sayings consists of three hemistichs which are
paralleled by the three units of the model thanksgiving in vv.
3-7 (A, B, C) and by the three constitutive units of the instruction in vv. 8-10 (C^1, B^1, A^1). The two introductory sayings (a, b) are paralleled by the two major strophes which develop the content of the sayings, as well as a^1 and b^1 of the
thanksgiving conclusion. In terms of external parallelism, the
two introductory sayings which bespeak the state of happiness
experienced by the one who has received forgiveness of sins are
paralleled also by the conclusion of the thanksgiving which
tells those righteous who are assured of "forgiveness of sins"
to "rejoice," "exult," and "shout for joy." Finally, in terms
of external parallelism, the two major strophes are chiastically structured in terms of content: A=A^1, B=B^1, and C=C^1.

Exegesis. This didactic poem seeks to affirm to the pious
wise the proper response to suffering, which is understood as
punishment or chastisement for sin, in order that the suffering
and the sin which precipitated it might be removed, and subsequently the forgiven sinner may experience the state of well-
being, happiness, and the love of the deity. This response is
the same one that had been supported by the traditional wise
opponents of Job as they counseled him to repent from his

blasphemy and to make the proper response: the cultic response of the lament-thanksgiving cycle.

Therefore, the state of happiness and the entrance into the sphere of well-being which envelop the forgiven sinner is ably introduced in the two initial *'ashrê* sayings. Then follow the two major strophes of the psalm. Strophe I, we believe, should be considered as a didactic model for instructing sages in the formulation of the typical thanksgiving psalm, and contains the major characteristics of such a genre: the narrative in which the speaker tells of his past suffering, the confession and acknowledgement of sin followed by the exultant declaration of forgiveness and salvation by the deity, and the didactic admonition to the congregation to do likewise, for the psalmist points to his own experience as validating the fact that God is a haven and redeemer to those in distress. Verse 5 is the key verse in the second strophe for, by referring back to ab, it affirms paradoxically that one's sins are concealed (כסוי) by the sinner's refusal to conceal them from God (לא כסיתי), and that one's sins are borne (נשוי) by allowing them to be borne away by the deity (נשאת עון).[136]

The second strophe consists of a typical instruction of three parts. The first is the introduction in which the sage announces his intent to instruct his students concerning his own iniquity. The second part is the admonition in the form of a prohibition in which a metaphorical comparison is drawn between the wicked, stubborn fool who refuses to swallow his pride and make the proper cultic response and the disobedient, rebellious horse or mule which lacks self-control and rejects the "guidance" of bridle and bit. The comparison is made by the sage in order to convince young students to adhere to his counsel and, more specifically, to emphasize the acceptance of the validity of the cultic response to sin and suffering. The final segment of the instruction is the typical conclusion which consists of an antithetical proverb pertaining to retribution: only the wicked suffer greatly, presumably because of their sins, but the ones who trust in the deity enjoy the special gift of his steadfast love. Therefore, those who participate in the proper cultic response to sin and suffering receive forgiveness and enter once more into the state of happiness, well-being, and the steadfast love of God.[137]

Finally, a thanksgiving conclusion ends our psalm in which the צדיקים, those who have been forgiven of their sins, are told to express their happiness and joy in praise to the righteous deity.

We are not convinced the poem was written for use in the cultic service. Rather, we tend to regard the poem as intended for the instruction of young schoolboys in the literary features and theology of the lament. Nevertheless, the poem is still fertile ground for assessing the views of the wise which pertain to cult, especially in the area of the lament-thanksgiving cycle.

Psalm 119: "The Study of Torah and A Sapiential Lament"

Introduction. With the identification of wisdom and Torah in the circles of the scribes of Torah in the Post-Exile, it is not surprising to find poems which exude this spirit of sagacious piety.[138] The most extensive and well-structured among such poems is the massive 119th Psalm. The classification of this poem as a didactic poem, and more specifically, as an *'ashrê* poem, is supported by the occurrences of wisdom forms (*'ashrê* sayings, vv. 1-2; the catechetical question and answer, v. 9; and two better sayings, vv. 72, 127); wisdom themes (the identification of wisdom and torah,[139] the study and love of torah in late wisdom piety,[140] the fear of God, praying for wisdom, the efficaciousness of the prayer of a righteous, wise man, God as creator and overseer of world order, God as the source, giver, and instructor of true wisdom, retribution, the dichotomy drawn between the righteous and the wicked, and suffering as chastisement); and sapiential vocabulary[141] (למד, שיה, ירא, עצה, בין, זקנים ("ancestral wise"), חכם, ישר, צדק, עות, עולה, נתיבה, לב, חוש, דרך, רשעים, פתי, שכל, דעת, ידע, חשב, ריב, and תם.

Translation and Structural Analysis

א Strophe I

The *'Ashrê* Sayings

Happy are those whose way is blameless,
　　Those who walk in the Torah (תורה) of the Lord.
Happy are those who keep his testimonies (עדות),
　　Who seek him with all their heart,
　　Who commit no evil,
　　But rather walk in his ways.
You have commanded that your precepts (פקוד) be closely kept.
O that my ways may be sure
　　By keeping your statutes (חק).
　　I shall not be ashamed,
　　For I have observed all your commandments (מצוה).
I will praise you with an upright heart,
　　When I learn your righteous ordinances (משפט).
I will keep your statutes (חק),
　　Do not completely abandon me.

ב Strophe II

How can a youth make his path pure?
　　By keeping your word (דבר).
With all my heart I have sought you,
　　Do not allow me to stray from your commandments (מצוה).
I have stored your word (אמרה) in my heart
　　In order that I might not sin against you.
Blessed are you, O Lord,
　　You have taught me your statutes (חק).
With my lips I recount
　　All the ordinances (משפט) of your mouth.
I exult in the way of your testimonies (עדות),
　　As I would exult over all prosperity.
I will meditate on your precepts (פקוד),
　　And I will observe your paths.
In your statutes (חק) I will take delight,
　　And I will not forget your word (דבר).

ג Strophe III

Act for your servant, that I may live,
　　And that I may keep your word (דבר).
Open my eyes that I may observe
　　Miracles from your law (תורה).
I am a sojourner in the land,
　　Do not hide your commandments (מצוה) from me.
My soul is consumed with longing
　　For your ordinances (משפט) at all times.
You rebuke the accursed proud,
　　Those who stray from your commandments (מצוה).

Take from me scorn and contempt,
    For I have kept your testimonies (עדות).
Though princes have taken their seats to plot against me,
    Your servant will meditate on your statutes (חק).
Your testimonies (עדות) are my delight,
    As well as my counsellors.

ד Strophe IV

My life cleaves to the dust,
    Give me life according to your word (דבר).
I have recounted my ways, and you did answer me.
    Teach me your statutes (חק).
The way of your testimonies (פקוד) make me understand,
    So that I may meditate on all your wonders.
My soul melts for grief,
    Raise me up according to your word (דבר).
Make me turn away from the path of falsehood,
    And show mercy according to your law (תורה).
I have chosen the way of truth,
    I have set forth your ordinances (משפט).
I cleave to your testimony (עדות), O Lord;
    Do not make me ashamed.
I shall run the course of your commandments (מצוה),
    Because you have enlarged my understanding.

ה Strophe V

Teach me, O Lord, the way of your statutes (חק),
    And I shall keep it to the end.
Give me understanding so that I may keep your law (תורה),
    And I shall keep it with all my heart.
Direct me in the path of your commandments (מצוה),
    Because I take delight in it.
Incline my heart toward your testimonies (עדות),
    And not toward profit.
Make my eyes to turn from beholding vanity,
    Make me live according to your word (דבר).[142]
Establish your word (אמרה) for your servant,
    Which is for fear of you.
Turn away my reproach which I dread,
    Because your ordinances (משפט) are good.
Behold, I long for your precepts (פקוד),
    Give me life in your righteousness.

ו Strophe VI

Let your steadfast love come to me, O Lord,
    Your salvation according to your word (אמרה),
So that I may answer those who reproach me,
    For I have trusted in your word (דבר).
Do not take completely from my mouth the word of truth,
    For I have waited for your ordinances (משפט).
Let me keep your law (תורה) continually,
    Forever and ever.

Let me walk in a broad expanse,
    For I have sought your precepts (פקוד).
Let me speak of your testimonies (עדות) before kings,
    And let me not be ashamed.
Let me delight in your commandments (מצוה),
    Which I love.
And I will lift up my hands to your commandments (מצוה)
which I love,
    And I shall meditate on your statutes (חק).

ז Strophe VII

Recall thy word (דבר) concerning your servant,
    By which you have made me hope.
I have been comforted by this in my affliction,
    Because your word (אמרה) gives me life.
The proud have mocked me exceedingly,
    Yet I have not turned from your law (תורה).
I have remembered your statutes (משפט) from of old,
    O Lord, and I am comforted.
Indignation grips me because of the wicked,
    Those who abandon your law (תורה).
Your statutes (חק) have been my songs,
    In the house of my sojourning.
I remember your name at night, O Lord,
    And I have kept your law (תורה).
This has been mine,
    Because I keep your precepts (פקוד).

ח Strophe VIII

I said, "The Lord is my portion,"
    In order to keep your words (דבר).
I entreat your face with all my heart,
    Have mercy upon me according to your word (אמרה).
I have considered my ways,
    And I have turned my feet toward your testimonies (עדות).
I make haste, and I do not tarry,
    To keep your commandments (מצוה).
Though the cords of the wicked have surrounded me,
    Yet I have not forgotten your law (תורה).
During the middle of the night I arise to praise you,
    For your righteous ordinances (משפט).
I am a companion to all who fear you,
    To those who keep your precepts (פקוד).
Your steadfast love, O Lord, has filled the earth;
    Teach me your statutes (חק).

ט Strophe IX

You have acted beneficently with your servant,
    O Lord, according to your word (דבר).
Before I was afflicted[143] I went astray,
    But now I keep your word (אמרה).

You are good, and you do good;
    Teach me your statutes (חק).
The proud have smeared me with falsehood,
    Yet I continue to keep your precepts (פקוד) with all
    my heart.
Their heart is gross like fat,
    I rejoice in your law (תורה).
It is good for me that I was afflicted,
    In order that I might learn your statutes (חק).
The law (תורה) of your mouth is better to me,
    Than thousands of pieces of gold and silver.

י Strophe X

Your hands made me and fashioned me,
    Enlighten me so that I may learn your commandments
    (מצוה).
Those who fear you will see me and rejoice,
    Because I hope in your word (דבר).
I know, O Lord, that your ordinances (משפט) are just,
    And in faithfulness you have afflicted me.
Let your steadfast love be my comfort,
    According to your word (אמרה) to your servant.
Allow your mercies to come to me so that I may live,
    Because your law (תורה) is my joy.
Let the proud be ashamed because they have subverted me
with falsehood.
    I will meditate on your precepts (פקוד).
Let those return to me who fear you,
    So that they may know your testimonies (עדות).
Let my heart be blameless by your statutes (חק),
    So that I may not be ashamed.

כ Strophe XI

My soul wastes away for your salvation,
    I await your word (דבר).
My eyes have grown dim for your word (אמרה),
    I say, "When will you comfort me"?
For I have become like a wineskin in the smoke.
    I have not forgotten your statutes (חק).
How long will your servant suffer?
    When will you mete justice out to my persecutors?
The proud have dug pitfalls for me,
    Those who are not in accordance with your law (תורה).
All your commandments (מצוה) are faithful,
    They persecute me falsely, Help me!
They have almost consumed me on earth,
    But I have not abandoned your precepts (פקוה).
According to your steadfast love give me life,
    And let me keep the testimony (עדות) of your mouth.

ל Strophe XII

Forever, O Lord,
   Your word (דבר) is established in the heavens.
Generation by generation is your faithfulness,
   You have established the earth to endure.
According to your ordinances (משפט) they stand unto this day,
   For all your servants.
If your law (תורה) had not been my joy,
   Then I would have perished in my affliction.
I shall never forget your precepts (פקוד),
   Because you have given me life by them.
I am yours, save me,
   Because I seek your precepts (פקוד).
The evil ones lie in the way to destroy me,
   But I consider your testimonies (עדות).
I have seen an end of every perfect thing,
   But your commandments (מצוה) are limitless.

מ Strophe XIII

O how I love your law (תורה),
   It is my meditation all the day.
By your commandments (מצוה) you have made me wiser than all my enemies,
   For they are mine forever,
I have been wiser than all my teachers,
   Because your testimonies (עדות) are my meditation.
I have been more intelligent than the ancestors,
   Because your precepts (פקוד) I have kept.
I have withdrawn my feet from every path,
   In order that I might keep your word (דבר).
I have not turned aside from your ordinances (משפט),
   Because you have instructed me.
How your word (אמרה) is smooth to my palate,
   More than honey to my mouth.
I have been enlightened by your precepts (פקוד),
   Therefore I have despised every deceitful path.

נ Strophe XIV

Your word (דבר) is a lamp unto my feet,
   And a light for my path.
I have sworn, and I have established my oath,
   To keep your righteous ordinances (משפט).
I have been afflicted severely,
   O Lord, revive me according to your word (דבר).
The offerings of my mouth, accept, O Lord,
   And teach me your ordinances (משפט).
My life is in my hands always,
   And I have not forgotten your law (תורה).
The wicked have devised a snare for me,
   But I have not wandered from your precepts (פקוד).

My heritage forever is your testimonies (עדות),
    Because they are the exultation of my heart.
I have inclined my heart to practice your statutes (חק),
    Forever without end.

ס Strophe XV

I despise half-hearted men,
    But I love your law (תורה).
You are my hiding place and my shield,
    I hope in your word (דבר).
Depart from me practitioners of evil,
    That I may keep the commandments (מצוה) of my God.
Support me according to your word (אמרה), and I shall live,
    And do not let me be put to shame in my hope.
Hold me up that I may be safe,
    And I will behold your statutes (חק) continually.
You abandon those who stray from your statutes (חק),
    Because their deceit is falsehood.
You have considered as dross all the wicked of the earth,
    Therefore I have loved your testimonies (עדות).
My body trembles because I fear you,
    And I am afraid of your ordinances (משפט).

ע Strophe XVI

I have acted justly (משפט) and righteously,
    Do not leave me to my oppressors.
Act as a surety for your servant to his benefit,
    Let not the proud oppress me.
My eyes grow dim for your salvation,
    And for your righteous word (אמרה).
Deal with your servant according to your steadfast love,
    And teach me your statutes (חק).
I am your servant, give me understanding,
    So that I may know your testimonies (עדות).
It is time for the Lord to act,
    They have broken your law (תורה).
Therefore, I love your commandments (מצוה)
    Better than gold and fine gold.
Therefore, I esteem as right all your precepts (פקוד);[144]
    Every path of falsehood I have hated.

פ Strophe XVII

Your testimonies (עדות) are wondrous,
    Therefore my soul has kept them.
The doorway of your word (דבר) emits light,
    Making wise the simple.
I pant with my mouth open,
    Because I desire your commandments (מצוה).
Turn to me and be gracious unto me,
    According to the ordinance (משפט) to those who live by
    your name.

Establish my steps by means of your word (אמרה),
  And do not allow every evil to rule over me.
Redeem me from human oppression,
  So that I may keep your statutes (פקוד).
Make your face to shine upon your servant,
  And teach me your statutes (חק).
Channels of water have streamed down from my eyes,
  Because they have not kept your law (תורה).

צ Strophe XVIII

You are righteous, O Lord,
  And your ordinances (משפט) are upright.
You have commanded righteously your testimonies (עדות),
  And exceedingly faithfully.
My zeal has consumed me,
  Because my adversaries have forgotten your words (דבר).
Your word (אמרה) is well tested,
  And your servant loves it.
I am small and despised,
  Yet your precepts (פקוד) I have not forgotten.
Your just righteousness endures forever,
  And your faithful law (תורה).
Adversity and anguish have found me,
  But your commandments (מצוה) are my joy.
Your testimonies (עדות) are righteous forever,
  Make me understand so that I may live.

ק Strophe XIX

I called with all my heart,
  Answer me, O Lord! I will keep your statutes (חק).
I cry unto you, save me,
  So that I may keep your testimonies (עדות).
I rise up before the break of day, and I cry out,
  For I await thy word (דבר).
My eyes arise as the watches of the night,
  To meditate on your word (אמרה).
Hear my voice according to your steadfast love,
  O Lord, revive me according to your ordinances (משפט).[145]
Evil persecutors draw near,
  They are far from your law (תורה).
You are near, O Lord,
  And all your commandments (מצוה) are true.
I long have known from your testimonies (עדות)
  That you have established them forever.

ר Strophe XX

Look upon my affliction and rescue me,
  Because I have not forgotten your law (תורה).
Plead my case and redeem me,
  Give me life according to your word (אמרה).
Save me far from the wicked,
  For they have not sought out your statutes (הק).

Your mercies are many, O Lord,
   Give me life according to your ordinances (משפט).
Many are my persecutors and my adversaries,
   I have not turned away from your precepts (עדות).
I have looked upon the treacherous ones and have loathed them,
   Those who have not kept your word (אמרה).
See how I love your precepts! (פקוד).
   O Lord, revive me according to your steadfast love.
The sum of your word (דבר) is true,
   And each of your righteous ordinances is forever.

ש Strophe XXI

Princes persecute me without reason,
   But my heart fears your word (דבר).
I exult over your word (אמרה),
   Like one who finds great spoil.
I hate and regard as abominable falsehood,
   But I love your law (תורה).
I praise you seven times each day,
   On account of your righteous ordinances (משפט).
Abundant peace is to those who love your law (תורה),
   And there is no stumbling-block to them.
I hope for your salvation, O Lord,
   For I have acted according to your commandments (מצוה).
My soul has guarded your precepts (עדות),
   And I love them exceedingly.
I have kept your precepts (פקוד) and your testimonies (עדות),
   For all my ways are before you.

ח Strophe XXII

Let my cry come before you, O Lord,
   Give me understanding according to your word (דבר).
Let my supplication come before you,
   Deliver me according to your word (אמרה).
Let my lips pour forth praise,
   Because you will teach me your statutes (חק).
My tongue will answer according to your word (אמרה),
   Because all your commandments (מצוה) are righteous.
Let your hand help me,
   Because I have chosen your precepts (פקוד).
I desire your salvation, O Lord,
   For your law (תורה) is my joy.
Give my soul life, and I will praise you,
   And allow your ordinances (משפט) to help me.
I have wandered like a lost sheep,
   Seek out your servant, for I have not forgotten your commandments (מצוה).

The structure of this psalm is that of an alphabetic acrostic, consisting of 22 strophes of 8 lines and 16 hemistichs.

The number 8 results from the sage's penchant for the 8 major synonyms for "law": משפט, תורה, עדות, חק, מצוה, דבר, אמרה, and פקוד. Each strophe contains from 6 to 9 of these synonyms. In fact, only 3 lines do not contain one of these words for law: 3, 90, and 122.

In addition, the content, if not the structure, of the psalm is contained in the two introductory *'ashrê* sayings, affirming once again that the central element of a didactic poem is one or two simple sayings which provide the basis for the development of the entire poem. Repetitions are numerous in such a lengthy poem, but in addition to the 8 major synonyms for law, the following are frequently found: צדק, לב, שמר/נצר, שכה, טוב, רשע, ירא, בין, זדים, and חיה.

Exegesis. This didactic poem borrows heavily from the form of lament in which a sage asks for God to deliver him from his suffering and his persecutors, a plea based upon his extensively repeated avowal that he has been a devoted student, follower, and lover of torah, whereas his wicked persecutors have flaunted the precepts of the law. In addition, he asks for a bestowal of additional wisdom by God so that he might more closely and rigorously follow the divine commandments, and, thereby, avoid the mistakes that have precipitated his present state of suffering. His identification of torah and wisdom, that is, his regarding of torah as the locus of true wisdom, is a hallmark of the late post-exilic sage, the most prominent example being Sirach.

It is an important point to stress that the penitential character of the contents of the psalm further illustrates a conclusion we have reached in our investigation: the wise not only exalted prayer as the single most important cultic act,[146] but considered themselves to be able creators and gifted speakers of prayers, based on their ability to write artistic poetry and to speak cogently, and upon their conviction that the prayer of a wise and righteous person possessed an extremely efficacious character. As such, we regard the poem to be intended for the cult, and thus is a wisdom psalm.

D. *Riddle Poems*

A third category of didactic poetry is that of Riddle
Poems, a classification based upon the presence of one or two
riddles which provide the structure and content of the developed poem. We shall include two psalms within this category:
49 and 19A.

Psalm 49: "Mythology, Wisdom, and Divine Salvation"

Introduction. In addition to the construction of didactic
poems around the proverb and the *'ashrê* saying, we also find
the wise doing the same with riddles. A case in point is Psalm
49, a poem which we have investigated extensively in another
context.[147] The identification of this psalm as a didactic
poem,[148] and more specifically as a riddle poem, is based upon
the occurrence of wisdom forms (the two riddles, a sapiential
instruction introduction, an instruction consisting of an admonition and several result and circumstantial clauses in vv.
17-18, and a rhetorical question, v. 6), sapiential language
(חידה, בין, דרך, משל, חכם, הגות, כסל, ישר, לב, בינה, תבונה,
and בער), and sapiential themes (the foolish and wicked rich
and retribution involving punishment for the wicked rich in
terms of death and the reward of salvation for the wise poet).
Finally, the poem is artistically structured around two riddles
and their solutions which we shall demonstrate as follows.

Translation and Structural Analysis

Superscription

Concerning Death.[149] To the Choir Director.

A Psalm of the Sons of Korah

Introduction

Hear all you peoples,
   Give ear all inhabitants of the world.[150]
Both sons of affluence and sons of poverty,
   Rich and poor[151] together.
My mouth shall speak wisdom,[152]
   And the meditation of my heart, understanding.
I shall incline my ear to a proverb,
   I shall solve my riddle[153] to the tune of my lyre.[154]

Strophe I

Why should I fear evil days,[155]
    And the iniquity of my oppressors[156] which surrounds me?
The ones who trust in their wealth,[157]
    And praise themselves in their abundant wealth?

Riddle B, part 1

Surely,[158] a (rich) man cannot redeem himself,[159]
    For he is unable to give to God his ransom.
The ransom of his life[160] is costly,
    So that he must come to an end forever.

Strophe II

For shall a (rich) man live forever?
    Shall he not see the Pit?[161]
Surely he sees that even the wise man will die,
    Along with the fool and the brute who perish.
Their tomb[162] is their home forever,
    Their tents for generation after generation.
Though they have called lands by their own names,[163]
    They will leave to others their wealth.

Solution A[1]

A wealthy man cannot abide,[164]
    He is like fattened cattle who are butchered.

Strophe III

This is their way, the "confidence"[165] which is to them,
    This is the way[166] of those who have self-confidence.
Like sheep they have been appointed[167] to Sheol,
    Mot will pasture and rule over them![168]
Their form[169] will waste away,[170]
    Sheol will be their prince![171]

Riddle B, part 2

Surely God will redeem me,
    For he will take me from the hand of Sheol.

Strophe IV

Do not fear when a man becomes rich,
    When the glory of his house may increase.
For when he dies, he will take nothing with him,
    His glory shall not follow after him.
While he is alive, his life may be blessed,
    And he may even praise you[172] saying there is benefit
    to you also.

But he shall pass away[173] unto the generations of his
fathers;
    The wealthy man shall never again see[174] the light of
day.

Riddle A

A rich man is like cattle, for he has no understanding,
    He is like the fattened cattle who are dumb.[175]

In this poem we have an artistically contrived didactic
poem, consisting of an introduction and four strophes structured around two riddles (A, B) and one solution (A^1). The
poet, having assembled his audience, announces that he is about
to "unlock" or solve (אפתח) a riddle.[176] And though he does
not specifically state what that riddle is, it is our opinion
that the solved riddle is contained in v. 21 and its solution
in v. 13. Now a number of scholars have considered vv. 13 and
21 to be a refrain,[177] and have changed one of the two verses
to conform exactly to the other, but if we listen closely to
the text, such changes destroy the binary structure of the artistic riddle and its solution.

Riddle A (1st hemistich)	אדם בקר ולא יבין
Solution A^1 (1st hemistich)	ואדם ביקר בל-יליין
Riddle A (2nd hemistich)	נמשל כבהמות נדמו
Solution A^1 (2nd hemistich)	נמשל כבהמות נדמו

That the verses (13, 21) consist of a riddle and its solution may be argued from the following. First of all, as concerns texture, these verses exhibit poetic features characteristic of the riddle genre: the meter of the riddle and its solution is 3 + 3, the typical binary construction of a riddle and
its solution is present, both the riddle and the solution consists of one stich with two hemistichs, and in terms of syllabification each of the 4 hemistichs appears to have 8 syllables.
As concerns rhyme, assonance, and alliteration, note the following:

	Z	Y	X
Riddle A--	וְלֹא יָבִין	בָּקָר	אָדָם
Solution A^1	בַּל יָלִין	בִּיקָר	וְאָדָם
Riddle A--	נָדַמּוּ	כְּבְהֵמוֹת	נִמְשַׁל
Solution A^1	נִדְמָה	כַּבְּהֵמוֹת	נִמְשַׁל

Synonymous parallelism is most noticeable between the hemistichs in the riddle and the two in the solution. Finally,
metaphor and simile are recognized, for man is said to be an
"ox" and "like fattened cattle."

Secondly, as concerns the formal definition of the riddle,
a riddler takes one characteristic feature of his subject and
attempts to state it obscurely enough to mislead his audience
into seeking the answer in the common language, while the real
answer, disguised in certain keys given in the riddle itself,
is to be derived from the *Sondersprache* of the riddler or his
group. If we place the riddle in the form of a question, we
have: "How is an unperceiving man like a dumb animal"? In
terms of common language, one would expect the answer to be:
"They are both stupid." However, such a response has no meaning in the context of the poem, so that in turning to the solution in v. 13, as well as the superscription, the real answer
is "They both die." Yet the wit of the poet is not as yet
fully completed, for our wise poet in the course of his psalm
has considered the word איש to be a key word for a wealthy man;
thus he is referring to a particular group of men, that is the
wealthy, and he makes the point that the wealthy, like their
fattened beasts which they fatten for sumptuous dining, grow
fat; but also like their domesticated animals they are dumb as
well, for they fail to understand that they, like their fattened cattle, are being fattened for the crushing jaws of
"Prince Death" (cf. Koh. 3:18). Thus it is being fattened for
death, the cattle for their aristocratic owners and the rich
for the banquet of prince Mot, that is the one factor which
makes the two subjects, the rich and their cattle, an essential
unity. The riddler, therefore, exploits an unexpected ironic
relation between the wealthy and their cattle. So a wise man
has taken a riddle from sapiential lore, and, in the course of
his writing, has developed an artistically constructed poem
which makes an explicit reference to the wealthy.

It is our opinion that the structural analysis of this
poem supports our conclusion concerning vv. 13 and 21. Leaving
aside the introductory strophe, the body of the psalm consists
of 4 strophes, each of which has four stichs and eight

hemistichs with each stich having 3 + 3 meter. The riddle of
v. 21 and the solution (v. 13) are not placed in any one of the
four strophes, but rather we find them placed at the end of the
second and fourth strophes, serving as strophic demarcations.
Thus, it appears that a skilled poet has taken a one stich, two
hemistich riddle and an identically formed solution with 3 + 3
meter and equal syllabification (8 + 8 = 8 + 8) and has built
a poem of four strophes, each of which has four stichs and
eight hemistichs.

But we have also concluded that in the course of his didactic poem, the wise riddler has proposed a second riddle
which he leaves to his puzzled audience to unravel. We propose
that this second riddle is found in vss. 8 and 16[178] which fit
together quite smoothly on the basis of texture, thought, and
structural position, since each stich concludes a major strophe:

Riddle B

אך לא-פדה יפדה איש לא יתן לא לחם כפרו

v. 8   Surely a man cannot redeem himself, he cannot
       give his ransom to God.

אך אלהים יפדה נפשי מיד שאול כי יקחני

v. 16 Surely God will redeem my soul; certainly he
       will take me from the hand of Sheol.

The poet has constructed a paradoxical enigma: death is the one
state from which neither rich nor poor, foolish nor wise can be
ransomed (vv. 7-10),[179] and yet our sage affirms that he is an
exception, that is, he will not suffer death. Now the key to
the riddle is embedded in the language he has used to speak of
his ransoming from death: מיד שאול כי יקחני. In the "translation" stories of Enoch and Elijah, the same verb, לקח, is used
to speak of God's taking these rather strange and enigmatic
people from this life into the heavenly realm, thus allowing
them to escape death (Gen 5:24, I Kgs 2:1).[180] Thus the poet
seems to be speaking of the same redemption by God that these
two figures experienced. Now the question which confronts us
is "Why"? Suggestions of piety and faith are possible, but are
never explicitly stated. To understand the intention of the
wise man, it is important to refer to Jolles' masterful analysis

of the "life and death" situation in which riddles are found, a situation so strongly depicted in this psalm.

Within the context of many ancient Near Eastern myths and legends, one finds a number of legendary wise and primordial heroes whose success or failure in their efforts to gain eternal life or divine status depended upon their obtaining the secretive wisdom of the gods: Adam, Enoch, Adapa, Etana, Noah, Utnapishtim, and Gilgamesh. Perhaps the best parallel to our poem is the myth of Utnapishtim who is saved from the flood and eventually given a place as a deity in the heavenly world by learning the secretive wisdom of the gods concerning the imminent deluge, a decision revealed to him by the god of wisdom, Ea. When Utnapishtim asks what he should tell the city of Shuruppak concerning his activities in building a ship to escape the flood, Ea responds with an enigmatic oracle which, on the surface, seems to mean Utnapishtim will be forced from the city to dwell with Ea while Shuruppak will be blessed with prosperity. However, due to the wordplays involving *kukku* and *kibāti*, which mean both "food" and "misfortune," the real implication of the oracle, recognized only by Utnapishtim because of his instruction in the secret by Ea, is coming destruction. Lacking Utnapishtim's knowledge and insight, the people of the city fail to discern the oracle's true meaning and are consequently destroyed in the deluge. Of course, Utnapishtim is saved from the flood's destruction and is eventually deified.[181]

Now it may well be that our sage is referring to a similar situation in that, because of his secretive wisdom which he alone possesses, he is sure of his ransom from death, whereas his foolish audience, including even the powerful rich, are doomed to languish forever within the grip of Mot and Sheol.

While the poet refers to his lyre and addresses an audience, there is no indication that the situation is specifically a cultic one. Rather, we consider the poem to be a didactic poem written either within the context of a school or even within the milieu of the court, especially since the wealthy and "men of the world" (diplomats?) are among the audience. Furthermore, there is nothing present in the psalm that speaks directly to matters of cultic theology and ritual, except that

the references to Mot and to the poet's escape from death may
possibly demonstrate the wise man's debt to Canaanite mythology.

Psalm 19A: "Riddles Concerning the Cosmos and the Sun God"

Introduction. Though almost every major scholar of the
Psalms has typed this psalm as a hymn,[182] we shall also argue
that Psalm 19A (19:1-7) should be classified as a didactic
poem, and in terms of structural analysis, as a riddle poem,
since the structure of the poem is formed around two cosmological riddles (Riddle A, vv. 4-5 ab; Riddle B, vv. 6-7 ab) and
their respective answers.[183]   Our classification once more is
supported by the presence of sapiential forms (the occurrence
of two riddles) and wisdom themes (God as creator, the knowledge of the God of creation by means of his created order, and
the metaphorical depiction of the sun god as the retributive
judge and overseer of world order).[184]

Translation and Structural Analysis

Superscription

To the Choirmaster. A Psalm of David

Strophe I

Solution A[1] (1) The heavens recount the glory of El,
           (2) And the firmament proclaims the work of his
                hand.
           (3) Day pours forth speech unto day,
           (4) And night declares knowledge unto night.

Riddle A   (1) There is no speech, and there are no words;
           (2) Their voice is not heard.
           (3) Yet throughout all the earth their speech
                goes forth,[185]
           (4) And their words unto the end of the world.

Strophe II

Solution B[1] (1) Concerning the sun (Shamash) who pitches his
                tent in the sea,[186]
           (2) And nothing is hidden from his heat.[187]

Riddle B   (1) He is like a bridegroom who goes forth from
                his bridal chamber.
           (2) He is like a strong man who exults when
                running his course.
           (3) His gate is found at the end of the heavens.
           (4) And his circuit extends to their end.

The classification of A as a poetic riddle may be concluded from the application of our methodology for genre analysis of riddles. In terms of the definition of a riddle, A is
an obvious enigmatic paradox: apparently, people are able to
speak, be heard, and be understood, and yet without the formulation of words or the utterance of audible sounds. Thus the
task of the riddler's audience is to determine an answer that
may possibly remove the paradox. They must ask themselves:
"What speaks and is understood, and yet without language or the
utterance of sounds"? With regard to content, the riddle and,
as we shall see, its answer should be considered as a cosmological riddle, paralleled by the "impossible questions" in Job
38-39. The texture of the riddle and its solution (A^1) exhib-
its the typical binary construction. The riddle itself is a
chiasm, (1) = (4) and (2) = (3),[188] which consists of four
hemistichs paralleled by the four hemistichs in the solution.
Other elements pertaining to texture include the repetition of
certain key words and synonyms (לילה, יום ;שמים, רקיע ;אין;
ארץ, and קום, קולם ;מספרים, מגיד ;מליחם, דברים ;אמר, חוה; יביע
חבל), assonance in the third (qâmeṣ) and fourth (ṣerê) hemistichs of the riddle, and 4 + 3 meter.

The solution given is the idea of creation and the orderly
cycle of time which, though they utter no audible sounds nor
proclaim human speech, still speak a "language" which is understood by all as praise to the creator of the structured order
of creation, a typical wisdom motif. The poet has given this
riddle a hymnic character to praise the creator deity, El, for
the order of his creation.

Strophe II also consists entirely of a riddle (B) and its
solution (B^1). B is a mythic, cosmological riddle. The circuit of the sun god in his journey through the expanse of the
heavens is metaphorically described as a virile bridegroom
leaving his bridal chamber to run his path through the heavens.
The texture of the riddle and its solution involves the typical
binary construction, 4 + 4 meter, and the repetition of three
different synonyms for "tent": אהל, חפה, and המת.[189] The riddle itself contains two stichs, or 4 hemistichs, which exhibit
synonymous parallelism, while the solution possesses one line,
or two hemistichs.

After the audience places the riddle in an interrogative form, they must determine who or what possesses the characteristics of a virile bridegroom who runs unexhaustingly a course which extends from one horizon to the other. The special language of the riddle is to be found in A.N.E. mythological texts which speak of the sun-god as a "hero, mighty man"[190] who travels by chariot, boat, horse, or wings his circuit across the expanse of the skies and dwells at night in his abode in the sea.[191] Thus "tent" ("Bridal-chamber," חפה),[192] "heavens" (שמים), and "mighty man, hero" (גבור) are the key words which should "unlock" the riddle and provide the answer: "the sun (Shamash) who pitches his tent in the sea, and nothing is hidden from his heat." The poetic stich which explains the answer, "Concerning the sun (Shamash)," states that the sun god dwells in the sea in his tent (חמה), and that nothing is hidden from his all-seeing rays (חמה).

Exegesis. As suggested above, the two strophes are fashioned from two cosmological riddles and their respective solutions which borrow heavily from ancient Near Eastern mythological texts.[193] Strophe I speaks of the "heavens," the "firmament," "day," and "night" as a divine choir made up of members of the royal astral entourage of the council of El, and is comparable to other mythologically influenced Hebrew texts (Pss 89:5-6, 97:6, 148:1f., and Job 38:7), the P account of creation, and the Akkadian Creation myth (especially Tablets IV-VI) which speaks of the divine praise of Marduk following his destruction of Tiamat, the creation, and the ordering of the cosmos.[194] The strophe is also similar to several Ugaritic texts, especially "The Birth of the Gods," in which Dawn and Dusk, given birth by the wives of El, take their place in the heavens, and receive Shapsh and the stars.[195] Thus, it may well be that "day" and "night" parallel these two Canaanite astral deities who give praise to El, their progenitor. Furthermore, the idea of "night" and "day" pouring forth speech (יביע)[196] and declaring knowledge intimates not only the sapiential theme that they instruct their successors in the proper cosmological cycle of time through the calendrical year, but also that they reveal to the sapiential observer the creator who ordered their existence.

Another mythological text which parallels our riddle is
the second half of a speech of Baal made to Anat through Baal's
divine messengers:

> I've a word I fain would tell thee,
>   A speech I would utter to thee:
> Speech of tree and whisper of stone,
>   Converse of heaven with earth,
>   E'en of the deeps with the stars;
> Yea a *thunderbolt* unknown to heaven,
>   A word not known to men,
>   Nor sensed by the masses on earth.
> Come, pray, and I will reveal it
>   In the midst of my mount godly Zaphon:
> In the sanctuary, mount of my portion,
>   In the pleasance, the hill I possess.[197]

As is the case in our riddle, this text also speaks of a "language" of nature which speaks a riddle known in this case only
to Baal.

The second riddle (B) also borrows heavily from the imagery and language of ancient Near Eastern mythology, in this
case, the mythology of the sun-god who in ancient cosmology
"disappeared" each day when he descended into his nightly abode
in the sea in the West there to illuminate the underworld, only
to appear the following day on the eastern horizon to repeat
his heavenly journey across the expanse of the heavens. For
example, the references in Akkadian literature to Shamash as a
"mighty man," the judge of the universe "from whom no deeds are
hid," the one who enters the "gate of Heaven" to "traverse the
Heavens," to his route which covers the earth, to his descent
into the deep, and to his bridal chamber parallel the language
and thought of our riddle,[198] thus leading us to suggest that
such a riddle concerns the sun god Shamash, even as the first
riddle is based on the Canaanite deity El.[199]

Since our text is a didactic poem with hymnic characteristics, it is difficult to determine if the poem may also be a
cultic psalm, certainly not intended for a Yahwistic cult, but
rather for a polytheistic, Canaanite one. Our own view is that
the text consists of two originally independent riddles and
their solutions which originated in a Canaanite wisdom school.
The riddles were then made into a didactic poem by a skilled

poet, possibly intended to be used as a hymn praising the deities El and Shamash. Finally, the poem made its way into Israelite cultic circles, was evidently demythologized somewhat, and used to praise Israel's God and his creation.

E. *Conclusion*

Our examination of a number of psalms in the Psalter according to our three-pronged methodology has suggested that these psalms appear to be long didactic poems written by the wise. These poems include: 1, 19A, 19B, 32, 34, 37, 49, 73, 112, 119, and 127. In our analyses, it is our conclusion that not only are these poems characterized by wisdom language (forms and terms) and themes, but also by a didactic structure that at times focuses upon a brief wisdom form: a proverb, a riddle, or an *'ashrê* saying. Consequently, in speaking of subcategories of didactic poetry, we have chosen to classify poems in terms of which simple wisdom form seems to play this central role. Thus, we have included among the subcategory "Proverb Poems" Psalms 1, 19B, 34, 37, 73, 112, and 127, while Psalms 32 and 119 we have placed in the subcategory "*'Ashrê* Poems" and Psalms 19A and 49 in the subcategory "Riddle Poems". As we have repeatedly noted, these poems are comparable in terms of content and structure to a number of poems embedded in the wisdom literatures of Israel and the ancient Near East: Job 28, Sir. 39:12-35, "The Harper's Song," etc.

Another complicated matter has involved us in the assessment of the milieu and purpose of the poems. We have tended to regard the poems as originating in a wisdom context, possibly a school, and used for instructional purposes, though it is possible that several were intended to serve as the contributions of certain sages to cultic literature, and thus may be rightly classified as psalms: 19A, 19B, and 119. The last two combine the praise of torah and prayers: 19B (the "Prayer for Righteousness") and 119 (the lament). These two psalms were probably written by pious, post-exilic sages who considered torah (the Hebrew scriptures, including law, prophets, and some of the writings) to be the focal point of true, divine wisdom. In addition, they demonstrate the affirmation of the importance of prayer by the wise and their participation in the writing of didactic prayers. Psalm 19A is also possibly a piece of cultic literature, more specifically a hymn, at least in its final form. Two mythological riddles from the wisdom traditions of Canaan have been taken by a poet and shaped into a hymn in praise of the gods El and Shamash and creation.

In addition, we have concluded that several didactic poems, while they were not written for use as psalms in the cult, were, nevertheless, reflective poems which dealt with the theology and ritual of the lament-thanksgiving cycle as the proper, sagacious response to suffering. Psalms 32 and 34 contain model thanksgiving psalms, followed by positive instructions concerning the thanksgiving. We have argued that these two poems are intended to instruct wisdom adherents in the writing and theology of the thanksgiving. This corresponds to the statements by the sages that wise people possessed the ability to write psalms (Sir. 15:9-10 and Wis. 10:20-21), to the extollment of prayer as a virtuous cultic activity of the wise (Prov 15:8, 29, and 28:9, Sir. 39:1f., and Wis. 16:28-29), and to the presence of thanksgivings and laments in wisdom literature (e.g., Sir. 33:1-3 and 36:16-22 and 51:1-12). Psalm 73 is comparable to the Sumerian "Man and his God," "I Will Praise the Lord of Wisdom," and Job, in that the poet anguishes over the authenticity of the faith and practice of the lament-thanksgiving cycle. We tend to agree with Gese that the genre of this type of poem is not a cultic one, but rather is the didactic "paradigm of the answered lament."

Finally, a number of these didactic poems in terms of tenor and purpose do not appear to belong to either of the above categories, i.e., they are neither cultic literature nor reflections and instructions which broach the cultic realm: Psalms 1, 37, 49, 112, and 127. Their inclusion in the Psalter, we would suggest, is probably due to the editorial work of post-exilic scribes who included these didactic poems along with the cultic psalms.

[1]We prefer to use the general classification, "Didactic Poems," to refer to sapiential poems in general, while we shall reserve the category, "Wisdom Psalms," for those poems which seem to have been intended by their wise authors to be utilized in the cultic services.

[2]Ivan Engnell, "The Book of Psalms," *A Rigid Scrutiny* (Nashville: Vanderbilt University Press), p. 99. Engnell's rejection of this genre rests upon his rather rigid cultic interpretation of the Psalter and his questionable belief that the wise had nothing to do with the cult. For Murphy's brief, but important, investigation, see "A Consideration of the Classification 'Wisdom Psalms,'" VTSup 9 (Leiden: E. J. Brill, 1963), pp. 156-67.

[3]Hermann Gunkel and Joachim Begrich, *Einleitung in die Psalmen* (Göttingen: Vandenhoeck und Ruprecht, 1933), pp. 386-97. Fichtner also briefly examined the wisdom psalms in his introduction: "Die Weisheitspsalmen sind nach einem an der übrigen bibl. Chokmaliteratur gebildeten inhaltlichen und formalen Massstab aus dem Psalter auszusondern. An Hand dieses Massstabes kann man einige Psalmen bzw. Psalmenteile als Proverbien-Psalmen (34:12-23, 37, 112, 128, ähnlich 127 und 133), einige als 'Hiob-Psalmen' (49, 73) bezeichnen. Dazu treten das Wshtslied, das den Psalter einleitet (Ps 1), einige Psalmen, die von Wshtsmotiven durchsetze sind (32:8-11, 94:8ff., 111, bes. 10) und zwei, die sich mit der Wsht, wie sie das Gesetz bietet, beschäftigen (119, bes. 97-103, wohl auch 19b, bes. 8). Wir halten Ps 1, 19b, 94, 111, 112, und 119 für jünger als die übrigen und meinen, sie um 300 ansetzen zu dürfen" (*Die altorientalische Weisheit*, p. 9).

[4]Sigmund Mowinckel, "Psalms and Wisdom," VTSup 3 (1955), pp. 205-24. Also see his article, "Traditionalism and Personality in the Psalms," *HUCA* 23 (1950/51), pp. 2f.

[5]Herman Ludin Jansen, *Die spätjüdische Psalmendichtung. Ihr Entstehungskreis und ihr 'Sitz im Leben.'* (Oslo: I Kommisjon Hos Jacob Dybwab, 1937).

[6]*Weisheit in Israel*, pp. 70f.

[7]Murphy, *op. cit.* He ends his essay by concluding: "We may conclude that it is feasible to speak of 'wisdom psalms' as a literary form parallel to other psalm types. They merit separate classification....Other types of psalms incorporate wisdom elements but remain formally hymns, or thanksgivings, etc." (p. 167).

[8]James L. Crenshaw, "Wisdom," pp. 247-53.

[9]"The Canonical Wisdom Psalms of Ancient Israel--Their
Rhetorical, Thematic, and Formal Elements," *Rhetorical Criticism: Essays in Honor of James Muilenburg* (Pittsburgh Theological Monograph Series 1; Pittsburgh: Pickwick Press, 1974), pp.
186-222.

[10]*The Way of Wisdom*, p. 121.

[11]See "Examination Text A" from the Old Babylonian II
Period, translated and analyzed by Benno Landsberger, "Scribal
Concepts of Education," *City Invincible*, A Symposium on Urbanization and Cultural Development in the Ancient Near East (Chicago: The University of Chicago Press, 1958), pp. 94-123. He
comments: "We learn that the well-trained scribe had to be acquainted with the art of the *nar*, the musician, and with all
the different genres of this highly developed Sumerian special-
ty" (p. 99). The lines which are germane to our point are
translated:
> no. 10. To understand the occult language of all classes of
> priests and members of other professions.
> 12. All categories of songs and how to conduct a choir.
> 14. Other complicated and intentionally distorted lan-
> guages of professional groups like the shepherds and
> scribes.
> 15. The use and technique of various musical instruments.
(*Ibid.*, p. 100). In the legendary narratives concerning Solomon, the wise king is credited with writing among other wisdom
forms 1,005 "songs" (שירים), a point supporting the argument
that the wise composed didactic songs.

[12]The methodology used to identify wisdom psalms does contain certain hazards and limitations. First of all, in a cultural milieu shared by prophet, priest, and sage, it is not
surprising to discover possible examples of borrowing of formal
elements of language. Furthermore, many vocabulary words were
obviously shared by these different groups. A case in point is
the polarity of the "wicked" and the "righteous," religio-
ethical categories of people found in cultic, prophetic, and
sapiential texts. Finally, certain themes are common to the
three groups; especially is this true of the theme of retribution. Thus, while these criteria are useful in the identification of wisdom psalms, they cannot bring to bear a much needed
precision. We shall argue that these criteria coupled with
structural analysis will provide us with such precision.

[13]"The Riddles of Psalm 49," *JBL* 93 (1974), pp. 533-42.
For introductions to "New Stylistics," see David Greenwood,
"Rhetorical Criticism and *Formgeschichte*," *JBL* 89 (1970), pp.
418-26; James Muilenburg, "Form Criticism and Beyond," *JBL* 88
(1969), pp. 1-18; Luis Alonso Schökel, *Estudios de Poética
Hebrea* (Barcelona: Juan Flors, 1963), and Meir Weiss, *The Bible
and Modern Literary Theory* (Mod. Heb.) (Jerusalem: The Bialik
Institute, 1967). For an application of the method to wisdom
literature, see Addison Wright, "The Riddle of the Sphinx," pp.

313-34. For studies of the psalms which utilize the method, see N. H. Ridderbos, *Die Psalmen*, BZAW 117 (Berlin: Walter de Gruyter, 1972); and Meir Weiss, "Wege der neuen Dichtungswissenschaft in ihrer Anwendung auf die Psalmenforschung," *Bib* 42 (1961), pp. 255-302.

[14]*Einführung in die alttestamentliche Weisheit*, pp. 9f. Also see Crenshaw, "Wisdom," pp. 227f. For the tribe or family, see Erhard Gerstenberger, *Wesen und Herkunft des 'Apodiktischen Rechts'*, WMANT 20 (Neukirchener Verlag, 1965), pp. 110f.; for the court, see W. Richter, *Recht und Ethos* (München: Kösel, 1966); and for the wisdom school, see H.-J. Hermisson, *Studien zur israelitischen Spruchweisheit*, pp. 96f.

[15]Hermisson surmises that a wisdom school in Israel may have existed from the period of the *Grossreich* of David and Solomon, being patterned upon an Egyptian model, though most probably mediated through Canaanite schools under significant Egyptian influence from especially the Amarna period. It is here that the major wisdom materials of the pre-exilic period (Proverbs) were composed, collected, and transmitted. During the same period, cultic materials were collected in a separate temple school by the priests. After the end of the kingdom period, according to Hermisson, the two schools merged, and, of course, cult became the dominant institution in the post-exilic times. Among the literature written during this period were the wisdom psalms in the context of the temple school (*op. cit.*). While such a thesis is suggestive, the lack of explicit evidence relegates Hermisson's ideas to the realm of tentative theory.

[16]Mowinckel suggests that such psalms were included in the Psalter due to their possible production as votive stelae written by the sages and then offered by them in the temple ("Psalms and Wisdom," pp. 204f.).

[17]We would argue that on the basis of language and themes at least the following show every tendency of being pre-exilic: 19A, 34, 49, and 73.

[18]For example, Scott, *The Way of Wisdom*, pp. 190f.

[19]Of course, our lack of detailed knowledge of the Hebrew cultic services keeps us from making any more than a tentative suggestion, but it is possible that during the liturgy a place was given to the recitation of didactic poetry, intended to instruct the cultic assembly. If this were the case, then the didactic poems could have had a cultic function as well.

[20]See our discussion of Sirach's wisdom hymn (39:12-35).

[21]The identification of a saying within a larger poetic unit is no simple task. In our efforts to identify and isolate an individual proverb which may provide the locus for the structure and thesis of the proverb poem, we shall utilize the following criteria:

1. First, the presumed saying should contain the major
   characteristics of a Hebrew proverb: one stich consisting of two hemistichs which demonstrate parallelism and
   other elements of proverbial poetry.
2. Second, the presumed saying should be a third person
   observation of reality which "registers a conclusion
   based on experience" (Crenshaw, "Old Testament Form
   Criticism," p. 231).
3. Third, one should be able to isolate the saying from
   the larger, didactic unit into which it has been placed.
   For example, this can easily be done, if the presumed
   saying initiates, concludes, or exists apart from the
   major strophes of the poem.
4. Fourth, the saying should be paralleled in the proverbs
   of other wisdom literature of the ancient Near East,
   especially those in Proverbs, Koheleth, and Sirach.

[22]Most scholars have classified the poem as a wisdom psalm
(B. Duhm, *Die Psalmen*, KHAT 14 [Tübingen: J. C. B. Mohr (Paul
Siebeck) 1899], p. 1; Mitchell Dahood, *Psalms* 1, AB 16 (Garden
City: Doubleday, 1966), p. 1; Hermann Gunkel, *Die Psalmen*, HKAT
16 (Göttingen: Vandenhoeck und Ruprecht, 1926), p. 1; H.-J.
Kraus, *Psalmen* 1, 2nd ed. (Neukirchener Verlag, 1961), p. 2;
and Jansen, *Die spätjüdische Psalmendichtung*, p. 136). Engnell
attempts to regard the psalms as originally a royal, cultic
psalm, due to the motif of the "tree of life" ("Planted by
Streams of Water," *Studies Orientalia Ioanni Pedersen* [Einar
Munksgaard, 1953], pp. 85-96). Lipiński regards the psalm as a
"psalm of congratulations" extended to pilgrims who, having
been healed from illness, are granted access to the temple area
to worship God ("Macarismes et psaumes de congratulation," *RB*
75 [1968], p. 338).

[23]The *'ashrê* form has been extensively investigated by
Waldemar Janzen ("*'Asrê* in the Old Testament," *HTR* 58 [1965],
pp. 215-26) and Lipiński, *op. cit.*, pp. 321f. Janzen draws the
questionable conclusion that אשרי should be translated "to be
envied," for it is an expression issuing forth from one who
makes the exclamation concerning another person who is in a
more enviable position than he. One wonders if this is what
the early Christian redactionists had in mind when they placed
a series of these sayings in the mouth of Jesus! Lipiński's
study deserves close attention, though his argument that the
form originated in the language of the cult, and not that of
wisdom, is based on the questionable antithesis he draws between wisdom and cult, and upon the presupposition that the
psalms are entirely cultic and contain no wisdom forms or even
wisdom psalms. He does demonstrate in an important discussion
that a parallel expression which may well have influenced the
Hebrew one is found in Egyptian psalms from the Theban necropolis in the epoque of the Ramesside Kings of the 13th century, an
expression which is used concerning pilgrims who are coming
to worship in the temple. However, our own investigation of
the form reveals that of the 45 times that the form occurs in
Hebrew literature, 26 are in sapiential contexts, while the
majority of the remaining 19 are in contexts either influenced

by wisdom language or redacted by wisdom scribes. The only passage supporting Lipiński's thesis of a cultic origin is Ps 65:4. But the overwhelming evidence that the form is a sapiential one cannot be negated by one psalm where the term is used in a cultic context. We agree, therefore, with Gerstenberger who comments: "The woe as well as the bliss-formula had its origin in the wise men's reflection about the conditions of this world" ("The Woe-Oracles of the Prophets," *JBL* 81 [1962], p. 261). In addition, Dupont's observation that the Egyptian expression *rš wj* also occurs in sapiential as well as cultic contexts (see the last line of the "Prayer to Thoth," *ANET*, p. 379; Amen-em-Opet XXIV, 19-20; and Ptah-hotep, l. 557) demonstrates not only a possible borrowing of the term from Egypt by the Israelite sages, but also supports the wisdom origin of the expression (Jacques Dupont, "'Béatitudes' égyptiennes," *Bib* 47 [1966], pp. 185-22).

[24]Parabolic sayings and parables are common in ancient Near Eastern wisdom literature, and are most often used to illustrate gnomic sayings (see Ecc 9:13-16, Ecclus 13:2, James 1:7-11, Matt 13:1-52, etc.).

[25]Similar proverbs are found in Prov 3:33, 10:27, Ps 37:18, 28, etc.

[26]Unfortunately the didactic poem has not received the close attention of scholars up to this time (cf. von Rad, *Wisdom in Israel*, pp. 38f.). A comparable wisdom poem to Psalm 1 is that found in Sirach 14:20f. In addition, the "Poem on the Ideal Housewife" in Prov 31:10f. is another well known didactic poem.

[27]For a tabulation of wisdom vocabulary, see Scott, *The Way of Wisdom*, p. 121. In the main, we are following Scott's list, though we have added several words to his list.

[28]This is common in Sirach and the Torah Psalms (19b, 119).

[29]There exist no major textual problems in this poem.

[30]See Ugaritic *drkt* (Dahood, *Psalms* 1, p. 2).

[31]The translation of עצה as "assembly, community" is argued by Roland Bergmeier who also believes that the term should be translated "assembly" in certain Qumran texts (IQS 5:7, 6:3, 14, 16, and 8:2, 24, 11:8) ("Zum Ausdruck עצת רשעים in Ps. 1:1, Hi. 10:3, and 22:18," *ZAW* 79 [1967], pp. 229f.).

[32]This poem was first recognized as a chiastic psalm by Nils Lund, "Chiasmus in the Psalms," *AJSL* 49 (1932-33), pp. 294-95, though he failed to regard the proverb in v. 6 as independent of the two strophes.

[33]Paul Auvray also concludes that the poem is written to amplify the maxim of V. 6 ("Psaume I," *RB* 53 [1946], p. 370).

[34]Unit D is closely paralleled by Jos. 1:8 which is part of the sapientially influenced redaction of the Deuteronomistic History. Thus, both may have been the result of the sapiential redaction by Torah sages.

[35]For a detailed analysis of the poem, see J. Alberto Soggin, "Zum ersten Psalm," *ThZ* 23 (1967), pp. 81-96.

[36]In addition to the frequently occurring חטאים, רשעים is also found in wisdom literature: Prov 1:3, 13:21, 23:17, and so is לצים: Prov 1:22, 9:7, 8, 15:12, 13:1, 14:6, 24:9, etc.

[37]Amen-em-Opet metaphorically describes the "silent man" in a parabolic saying as a fruitful tree which prospers, whereas the "heated man" is presented as a desiccated tree which is eventually cut down. The close parallel in Jer 17:5-8 has produced the suggestion that Psalm 1 may have borrowed the parabolic saying from Jeremiah. However, we follow Hyatt's conclusion that the passage in Jeremiah "is more likely...to have been comprised by a part of the wisdom school...," especially since the parabolic saying is found in a larger, sapiential context in Jeremiah (see vv. 9f.; "Jeremiah," *IB* 5 [1956], p. 952).

[38]Engnell, *op. cit.* This is not to deny the fact that the imagery and symbols of the king's role in overseeing the "tree of life" are frequently found in A.N.E. literature and art (see Geo Widengren, *The King and the Tree of Life in Ancient Near Eastern Religion*, Uppsala Universitets Årsskrift 4 [Uppsala: Lundequistska Bokhandeln], 1951). However, there is no convincing evidence that the "righteous man" in this poem is a Near Eastern king, nor that this metaphor is limited to the royal association with the tree of life.

[39]Psalm 1 has been placed in its position most probably to serve as an introduction to the Psalter by a scribal redactor (cf. Prov 1:1-7). Such a proverbial thesis is often used to attack the wicked who charge Yahweh with both the inability to know of and the impotency to punish their wicked ways (see, e.g., Psalm 73 and Wisdom 2).

[40]Mitchell Dahood, *Psalms* 1, p. 205; and Gunkel and Begrich, *Einleitung in die Psalmen*, pp. 276-80. Gunkel refers to this Psalm as a *Danklied*, though he believes that there was a development toward a more sapiential character in this genre during the Post-Exile. H.-J. Kraus essentially agrees: "Ps 34 gehört zur Gattung der individuellen Danklieder...tendiert jedoch stark zur Form des Lehrgedichtes..." (*Psalmen* 1, p. 267).

[41]Schmidt states concerning both Psalms 25 and 34: "Auch darin gleichen die beiden Psalmen dass ihr Verfasser in die Form des Weisheitsspruches, die ihm offenbar geläufig ist, hinübergleitet. Hier geschieht das in 12 so ausdrücklich und betont, dass man sich nicht wundern würde, den zweiten Teil des Psalms im Buch der Proverbien oder in den Sprüchen des Jesus ben Sirach zu lesen" (*Die Psalmen*, HAT 15 [Tübingen: J. C. B. Mohr (Paul Siebeck), 1934], p. 64).

[42]Murphy, "A Consideration of the Classification 'Wisdom Psalms,'" pp. 166f.

[43]Murphy, *Introduction to the Wisdom Literature of the Old Testament* (Collegeville, Minnesota: The Liturgical Press, 1965), p. 41.

[44]See Walter Baumgartner, "The Wisdom Literature," *The Old Testament and Modern Study* (London: Oxford University Press, 1951), p. 211.

[45]See H. Wiesmann, "Ps. 34 (Vulg. 33)," *Bib* 16 (1935), p. 416. Examples of the acrostic in Hebrew literature include: Psalms 9, 10, 25, 34, 37, 111, 112, 119, and 145; Lamentations 1-4; and Ecclus 51:13f. From Mesopotamia we have "The Babylonian Theodicy."

[46]Gunkel and Begrich refer to the introduction as hymnic in form (*op. cit.*, p. 394), but Kraus has correctly argued that such a hymnic introduction is most common in the *Danklied* (*Psalmen* 1, p. xlvii).

[47]For a succinct analysis of the thanksgiving genre, see Kraus, *Psalmen* 1, p. xlvii.

[48]The prose superscription is a rather odd one, for it connects the psalm with "David's feigning madness" in I Sam 21: 14. Why such a note would be added is difficult to ascertain, but the redactional לדוד and the word טעם in v. 9 provided a connection with I Sam 21:13, at least to one editor who wrote the superscription.

[49]The strophe has lost the *waw* line in the transmission of the psalm. If one were to allow for the missing line, then each strophe would consist of 11 lines.

[50]Read הַבִּיטוּ for הִבִּיטוּ with the LXX, Syriac, Vulgate (LXX and Heb.), and a number of Heb. MSS. Cf. BH³, and Schmidt, *op. cit.*, p. 1.

[51]Read וּגְהָרוּ for וְנָהָרוּ with the LXX, Syriac, Vulgate (LXX and Heb.), and ᴵA. Cf. BH3.

[52]Read וּפְנֵיכֶם for וּפְנֵיהֶם once more with the LXX, Syriac, and Vulgate (LXX and Heb.). Cf. BH³.

[53]Dahood derives ראו from ירא ("to be fat, sated, drink deeply") which is cognate with רוה ("to be saturated, drink one's fill") (*op. cit.*, p. 206). Cf. Prov 11:25, Ps 91:16, Isa 53:11, and Job 10:15. Also see G. R. Driver, "Problems in the Hebrew text of Proverbs," *Bib* 32 (1951), pp. 173f. Though we accept Dahood's suggestion, the versions do not agree, for they support the meaning "to see."

[54]The translation of טוב as "sweet" is also suggested by Dahood (*op. cit.*) on the bases of Ugaritic *yn ṭb* ("sweet wine," UT, 1084:1), the Song of Solomon 1:2, and the Vulgate (*quonian suavis est Dominus*).

[55]BH[3] makes note that some scholars have proposed כֹּפְרִים
("rebels," "liars"), while others have suggested כבירים
("mighty ones") for כפירים. The LXX has translated the word
πλούσιοι while the Vulgate (LXX) has *divites*. The Targum has
בני אריון along with the Vulgate (Heb.) which reads *leonis*.
We follow the MT and regard כפירים as a metaphor for the rich
and powerful as it is used elsewhere: Pss 35:17, 58:7, and Jer
2:15.

[56]The syntax of 13b is rather difficult. In what appears
as an effort to smooth out the syntax, the LXX reads τίς ἐστιν
ἄνθρωπος ὁ θέλων ζωήν ἀγαπῶν ἡμέρας ἰδεῖν ἀγαθάς. Thus, ἀγαθάς
is made to modify ἡμέρας. Both versions of the Vulgate follow
the LXX. Couroyer has solved the problem by arguing that the
plural ימים means longevity, and he translates the hemistich:
"Qui est celui qui désire la vie, qui aimerait une existence où
l'on voie le bonheur" ("Idéal sapiential en Égypte et en
Israël," *RB* 57 [1950], p. 175).

[57]According to Schmidt, *op. cit.*, and BH[3], vv. 16 and 17
should be transposed, since צעקו in v. 18 should refer to the
righteous of v. 16, not the "doers of evil" in v. 17. This is
an acceptable change, since in a number of acrostics פ precedes
ע (Lamentations 2, 3, 4).

[58]Cf. Prov 28:18, 25, 29:25, 30:10; Sir. 33:1, 34:13f. We
use the term "poem" rather loosely here, since the two strophes
are rather disparate units: a thanksgiving psalm and an instruction.

[59]We have repeatedly asserted that the main cultic action
for the wise was prayer, especially as seen within the framework of the lament-thanksgiving cycle. Thus we do not find it
unusual to suggest that vv. 2-11 appear as a model thanksgiving
psalm. Sirach wrote at least one thanksgiving psalm in 51:1-12.
Also see our discussion of Job in Chapter IV.

[60]Kraus, *op. cit.*, p. 268. Cf. "The Babylonian Theodicy,"
ANET, pp. 601f.

[61]A number of studies have been made concerning the ענוים
(עני) in laments and songs of thanksgiving along with their
opponents, the פעלי און. Mowinckel has argued that the פעלי
און were magicians who inflicted upon the ענוים demonic forces
(*Psalmenstudien* 1 [reprint; Amsterdam: Schippers, 1961]). H.
Schmidt has regarded the laments as the prayers of the oppressed who have been accused by their enemies of breaking the
law and must have their cases decided by Yahweh in the sanctuary (*Das Gebet der Angeklagten im Alten Testament*, BZAW 49
[Giessen: A. Töpelmann, 1928]). Birkeland had accepted Mowinckel's ideas in his *'ani und 'anaw in den Psalmen* (Videns-
kapsselkapets Skrifter 2. Hist.-Filos. Klasse 1932, no. 4,
1933), though in his later work appearing the same year, he
discarded Mowinckel's thesis for one which interpreted the
"enemies" as "foreigners" and the "I" of psalms as a king, army
commander, high priest, or Jewish governor (*Der Feinde des*

Individuums in der israelitischen Psalmenliteratur [Oslo: I Kommisjon hos J. Dybwad, 1933]). Finally, J. van der Ploeg has considered the *'āni* as the economically poor, a term which came to be used along with the term *'ānāw* to refer to the humble in a religious sense, since they were not as likely to be guilty of pride as were the rich ("Les pauvres d'Israel et leur pieté," *OTS* 7 [1950], pp. 236-70). We follow van der Ploeg in regarding the term as primarily a religious one for the humble, for only they will debase themselves to achieve the proper spirit for forgiveness.

[62]Gunkel, *Die Psalmen*, p. 142.

[63]For a complete discussion, see Westermann, "Die Begriffe für Fragen und Suchen im Alten Testament," pp. 2-30. Also cf. Ps 73:17 and *Ludlul bel Nēmeqi*.

[64]See Joachim Begrich, "Das priesterliche Heilsorakel," *ZAW* 52 (1934), pp. 81-92. For examples of the *Heilsorakel*, see Lam 3:5bf. and especially II Isaiah.

[65]Cf. Ex 14:19, Jos 5:14. The term מלאך יהוה came to be used metaphorically not only to refer to the protection of the pious (Ps 91:11), but also to the destruction of the wicked (Ps 35:5f.). For a complete discussion, see W. Baumgartner, "Zum Problem des Jahwe-Engels," *Zum Alten Testament und seiner Umwelt* (Leiden: E. J. Brill, 1959), pp. 240-47.

[66]Bauer-Kayatz, *Einführung in die alttestamentliche Weisheit*, pp. 31f. S. Plath remarks concerning יראת יהוה: Es handelt sich um die Benennung einer noch näher zu bestimmenden geschlossenen Menschengruppe als 'Jahwefürchtige' in der Bedeutung der Jahvetreuen und Gerechten im Unterschied zu den Gottlosen und Bösewichten." He indicates that in wisdom the term also implies *Lebensglück*, the result of following wisdom (Prov 10:27, 14:27, etc.) (*Furcht Gottes* [Stuttgart: Calwer Verlag, 1962], pp. 54f.).

[67]See M. Noth, "The Holy Ones of the Most High," *The Laws in the Pentateuch* (Philadelphia: Fortress Press, 1966), pp. 215f. Noth indicates that with the exception of Psalm 34, the O.T. usages refer to divine beings. Also see Coppens, "Les saints dans le Psautier," *ETL* 39 (1963), pp. 485-500.

[68]*Weisheit in Israel*, p. 106. Cf. Prov 13:21, Ecc 2:3.

[69]Bauer-Kayatz, *op. cit.*, p. 33. Cf. Prov 10:27, 14:26. A similar concern is expressed in Amen-em-Opet 4:1f. "Thou wilt find my words a storehouse of life and thy body will prosper upon the earth." Couroyer has pointed to an Egyptian tomb inscription which parallels 13a: "O tout (homme) aimat la vie, desirant une existence heureuse." According to him, the statement exactly parallels 13a except for the מי (*op. cit.*, p. 178).

[70]Cf., e.g., Amen-em-Opet, chap. III.

[71]See Schmid, *Wesen und Geschichte der Weisheit*, p. 161, and Noth, "The Laws in the Pentateuch," *The Laws in the Pentateuch*, p. 102, note 238.

[72]Bauer-Kayatz, *op. cit.*, pp. 18f. She refers to such acts as *Gemeinschaftstreu* and *Rechtverhalten*.

[73]Such an expression is similar to Psalm 37 (throughout), Prov 15:23, 25:11, and Sir. 14:20.

[74]The classification of this psalm as a wisdom psalm has been almost unanimously accepted by the major wisdom and psalmodic scholars (see our introduction to this chapter).

[75]We prefer to refer to this psalm as a poem and not merely as an instruction, since strophes, consistently uniform couplets consisting of two lines and four hemistichs, and a repeated proverb are discernible.

[76]Holm-Nielsen remarks concerning the psalm's acrostic arrangement: "The alphabetic structure in this psalm consists of periods of two lines, each of two hemistichs, which, again, are introduced by a new letter, so that the whole psalm gets twice as many lines as the number of letters in the alphabet. Even though this is not carried through with full consistency, it seems that the poet has endeavored to make each letter period constitute an independent whole also as determined from the contents just as he obviously aims at a sentence connexion between the two lines in each period" ("The Importance of Late Jewish Psalmody for the Understanding of Old Testament Psalmodic Tradition," *ST* 14 [1960], p. 42).

[77]BH³ suggests deleting the words in parentheses.

[78]BH³ suggests נשמדו ("are destroyed"). Cf. LXX.

[79]LXX reads ὑπερυψούμενον ("exalting himself"). BH³ notes that עליץ ("exultant") and עליז ("proud") have been suggested by some scholars.

[80]The LXX reads καὶ ἐπαιρόμενον ("rise up") ὡς τὰς κέδρους τοῦ Λιβάνου. Thus one might read מתעלה כארז (ארזי) הלבנון), or מתעדן ("luxuriant"), or מתעבה ("thick").

[81]One should read ואעבר (cf. LXX, Jerome, S): "and I passed by."

[82]This repeated proverb seems to have been a common one in Israelite sapiential sources, since it is found almost word for word in Prov 2:21a, 22a. Parts of the proverb also occur in vv. 3, 11, and 27 of this poem.

[83]Crenshaw points to Meri-ka-Re, Amen-em-het, and Koheleth as prime examples of the autobiographical style of the wisdom teacher (*op. cit.*, p. 206).

[84]Such a principle was derivative of wisdom thought which saw as its primary purpose "der Gedanke an die Beglückung und Befriedigung des Menschen" (Fichtner, *Die altorientalische Weisheit*, p. 60).

[85]Stamm states concerning this wrestling with the problem of evil: "Das Problem, über welches der Psalmist Belehrung gibt, ist die Beobachtung, dass so vielen Gottlosen alles wohl gerät (7), und dass sie ohne Hemmungen ihre Macht gegenüber den Frommen ausüben können" (*Das Leiden des Unschuldigen in Babylon und Israel* [Zürich: Zwingliverlag, 1946], p. 44). For a discussion of the questioning of the dogma of theodicy, see J. L. Crenshaw, "Popular Questioning of the Justice of God," pp. 381-95. G. von Rad's discussion of the various approaches to the problem is cogently and succinctly presented (*Weisheit in Israel*, pp. 251f.).

[86]The possession of the land is a concept thoroughly rooted in Israelite tradition (Ps 25:13, Isa 57:13, 60:21, 65:39). But, of course, the idea of the conquest tradition and the *heilsgeschichtliche* נחלה is not included within the wisdom tradition until Sirach and especially the Wisdom of Solomon. Unless we give an extremely late date to this psalm, such a concept does not seem to be a part of the sage's thinking, but rather he uses the idea of נחלה as the "inheritance" of the familial land by the family's sons throughout the generations. Thus the righteous are guaranteed the ability to keep their land within the family forever, whereas the wicked will eventually loose their land. נחלה to our sage is then a sociological term of familial land ownership. P. A. Munch has seen the expression as an indication of a class struggle between the rich landowners (רשעים) and the oppressed small landowners (ענוים). Thus he states: "Die armen Kleinbauern sollen wieder das Ackerland zu eigen haben" ("Das Problem des Reichtums in den Psalmen 37, 49, 73," *ZAW* 55 [1937], pp. 36f.).

[87]Thus Fichtner indicates that the "evil day" (Prov 16:4) and the "day of wrath" (Prov 11:4, Job 21:30) do not refer to an apocalyptic day of judgment, "sondern um von Jahve immer wieder einmal gesandte innerzeitliche und innerweltliche Unglückstage, die dem Frevler zum Verderben werden, aber dem Gerechten nichts anhaben können" (*op. cit.*, p. 65).

[88]The Psalm has been classified as a thanksgiving (Schmidt, *op. cit.*, p. 140), a didactic psalm (Gunkel, *Die Psalmen*, p. 312), and a mixture of both genres (Kraus, *Psalmen*, p. 504).

[89]*Lehre und Wirklichkeit*.

[90]See our discussion in Chapter III.

[91]The repetition of the pronoun אני for emphasis and as a parenthetic "as for me" is paralleled by Koheleth.

[92]Crenshaw, "The Problem of Theodicy in Sirach," pp. 48f.

[93]Reading ליֹשר אל for MT לישראל, a suggested example of the improper joining of two separate words. For similar sayings, see Prov 2:7-8, 3:13, 34, 10:3, 29.

[94]Following the Qere נטיו.

[95]אשרי is figurative for "mode of life," and is a frequent metaphor in wisdom language (Job 23:11, 31:7; Prov 14:15; Ps 37:31).

[96]Reading ישבעמו לחם for MT ישב עמו הלם.

[97]Such an observation of the prosperity of the wicked and the misfortune of the righteous led Koheleth to abandon the twin concepts of theodicy and retribution. While Koheleth never mentions that he suffered, personal suffering, of course, is what precipitated the crisis of Job.

[98]The fact of the sage's acquaintance with mythological texts is derived from his description of the wicked in v. 9 which parallels UT 52, 60f., and 67, II, 2-3 (cf. H. Ringgren, "Einige Bemerkungen zum 73. Psalm," *VT* 3 [1953], pp. 265-72).

[99]The ritual of "washing one's hands in innocence" occurred in juridical proceedings by which one proved his innocence, as well as in the cultic sphere when one wished to demonstrate symbolically his innocence to the deity (cf., e.g., Dt 21:6, and our discussion of the Dialogues of Job).

[100]עמל. This also is paralleled in Koheleth (cf. 2:20, 4:4, 6, 8; 6:7, etc.).

[101]מקדשי אל may be seen as a plural of majesty (cf. Jer 51:51, Ezek 21:7, Ps 68:36). See Ernst Würthwein, "Erwägungen zu Psalm 73," *Festschrift Alfred Bertholet* (Tübingen: J. C. B. Mohr [Paul Siebeck], 1950), p. 547; and A. A. Anderson, *The Book of Psalms*, New Century Bible (London: Oliphants), p. 533. Birkeland has attempted to see in the "sanctuaries of El" a reference to illegitimate sanctuaries which were destroyed, thus placing the poem within the struggle between the righteous Israelites and the wicked Canaanites or apostate Israelites. He adds that זונה in v. 27 supports the idea of pagan fertility rites and idolatry ("The Chief Problem of Ps. 73:17f.," *ZAW* 55 [1967], pp. 99-103). This is suggestive, but totally unprovable, since the description of the wicked involves their blasphemous mockery of God, not apostasy.

[102]Würthwein suggests a prophetic oracle has been received by the psalmist in the cult (*op. cit.*, p. 548).

[103]Anderson, *op. cit.*, p. 534. This may be the idea suggested by the term כבוד in v. 24, since כבוד is often used for the theophany of God.

[104]P. A. Munch, "Das Problem des Reichtums in den Ps. 37, 49, 73," p. 40.

[105]Both poems have in common the following: the introductory *'ashrê* saying, a structure built around an antithetical proverb, the form of the didactic poem, and the contrasting of the righteous and wicked.

[106]Most scholars of the psalms have classified this psalm as wisdom literature (e.g., see Kraus, *Psalmen*, p. 771).

[107]Such a didactic poem describing the righteous is found in other wisdom texts as well: Psalm 1, Prov 31:10-31 ("The Ideal Housewife"), Sir. 14:20-27, and 39:1-11.

[108]"Horn" is a metaphor for an increase in dignity and strength (cf. I Sam 2:1, 10; Pss 75:11, 89:18, 25).

[109]The acrostic arrangement is frequently found in wisdom literature: Psalms 34, 37, Sir. 51:13-30, and "The Babylonian Theodicy."

[110]Cf. Prov 10:7, 24, 11:23.

[111]Cf. Dahood, *Psalms* 1, p. 121.

[112]Gunkel points to the rhetorical question in "I Will Praise the Lord of Wisdom" (Tablet II, 11. 36-38) as a parallel (*Die Psalmen*, p. 79).

[113]Kraus comments: "Vorstellungen der חכמה-Theologie verbunden sich auch in Ps. 1 und 119 mit dem nachexilischen תורה-Verständnis, aus der Weisung Gottes störmt Leben und Weisheit. Die Thora ist Anweisung zum Leben" (*Psalmen*, p. 159).

[114]See Prov 29:13 and Ecc 8:1.

[115]The words in parentheses are not found in the text, but are understood from the lines which have preceeded. Similar proverbs are found in Prov 3:14-15, 16:16; Sir. 40:25-27.

[116]Verse 15 is a "dedicatory formula." Gunkel believes this was also presented at the times of sacrifice: "Und wie der Opfernde, wenn das Opfer angerichtet ist, die Weiheformel spricht, in der er seine Gabe der Gottheit darbietet, so legt er jetzt sein Gedicht vor Gott nieder" (*Die Psalmen*, p. 79). However, we feel such dedicatory formulae were typical in the scribal circles, for scribes dedicated their artistic creations to the gods and goddesses of wisdom and order (e.g., see the dedicatory formula at the end of Kramer's "Schooldays: A Sumerian Composition Relating to the Education of the Scribe," 11. 74f.).

[117]Kraus, *op. cit.*, p. 153, and Gunkel, *op. cit.*, p. 204.

[118]The sins which apparently most concern our sage are those done inadvertently or in ignorance (שגיאה), presumptuous sins (זד, v. 14), and rebellion (פשע, v. 14).

[119]This prayer is quite similar to Sirach's "Prayer for Self-Control" (22:27-23:4).

[120]Most scholars have regarded the poem as a wisdom psalm (Gunkel, *Die Psalmen*, pp. 553f.; Kraus, *Psalmen*, p. 858), though Lipiński ("Macarismes et psaumes de congratulation," p. 351) regards it as a song of congratulations sung at the birth of a son. With the exception of *'ašrê*, no wisdom vocabulary is present.

[121]ידידו, the masculine form of the adjective, may be explained as an example of the usage of masculine forms instead of the appropriate feminine forms, a grammatical phenomenon quite common in Hebrew. In fact, this occurs with regard to ידיד in Jer 11:15.

[122]MT reads שנא (an Aramaism for שנה, "Sleep"). If followed, the point would be a rejection of the practice of overwork which leads one to give only "sleep" to his beloved, and not sexual intimacy. However, we have emended the reading to שוא, due to the facts that the two words are most similar in spelling and that שוא is the key word of the strophe and initiates unit C, thus providing a nice inclusion for the unit.

[123]E.g., cf. Koh. 10:10, 11.

[124]Cf. Prov 21:31, James 4:13f., and especially Koheleth.

[125]Cf. Ani, III, 2-3, and the Joban Narrative.

[126]Because the poem includes the major components of an individual psalm of thanksgiving, a number of scholars have typed the psalm accordingly (e.g., Kraus, *Psalmen*, p. 254; and Ridderbos, *Die Psalmen*, p. 231).

[127]Cf. our discussions of Job and Sirach in Chapter IV.

[128]לשדי, literally "to Shaddai," should probably be read as לשד, "bodily juices" (Num 11:8).

[129]מצא רק in the MT, "the discovery of only" is without grammatical and logical sense, and thus should probably be regarded as מצר ("distress") or מצא רע ("the discovery of evil").

[130]The MT contains a dittography, חצ(רני) רני, which should be excised.

[131]Reading אעצה for איעצא.

[132]We are omitting the ך in עליך, and are reading עוני for עיני.

[133]We have followed the translation of Castellino who seeks to solve the major problems of this quite difficult verse ("Psalm XXXII 9," *VT* 2 [1952], pp. 37-42). He suggests that עדיו should be regarded as an example of the textual critical

error of transposition of letters, in this case the *yôdh* and the *hôlem*, and therefore derives עדרי from עדה, "to approach" (Job 28:8).

[134]Another didactic poem structured around an *'ashre* saying is Prov 3:13-18.

[135]Ridderbos, *Die Psalmen*, p. 234.

[136]נשא חטאה is a frequent expression for forgiveness of sins.

[137]Such parallels our arguments regarding Prov 16:6 as concerns the proper way that sins are "forgiven." See Chapter IV.

[138]Most scholars have argued for including the psalm among the wisdom psalms (Anderson, *op. cit.*, p. 806; and Alfons Deissler, *Psalm 119 (118) und seine Theologie*, MthSt 11 [München: Karl Zink Verlag, 1955], pp. 269f.). Also see A. Robert, "Le Psaume CXIX et les sapientiaux," *RB* 48 (1939), pp. 5-20.

[139]See Sirach. Yet it is apparent from the anthological nature of the psalm the "law" is not simply the Pentateuch, but includes the prophetic and sapiential traditions as well (Anderson, *op. cit.*, pp. 806f.).

[140]See H.-J. Kraus, "Freude an Gottes Gesetz," *EvT* 10 (1951), pp. 337-51.

[141]Deissler, *op. cit.*, pp. 272-73.

[142]Read דבר with two Heb. MSS. instead of דרך.

[143]Read the niphal of ענה, "afflicted," with the LXX instead of MT ענה, "answer."

[144]Read פקודיך for MT פקודי כל.

[145]Read the plural, following a number of Heb. MSS., instead of the singular.

[146]His penitential prayer is even metaphorically described as נדבות ("free-will offerings") in v. 108.

[147]For an analysis of this poem and a description of the methodology for riddle analysis, see my article, "The Riddles of Psalm 49," *JBL* 93 (1974), pp. 533-42. For a precise discussion of the three major facets of the analysis of the riddle genre, see C. Scott, "Persian and Arabic Riddles," *International Journal of American Linguistics* 31 (1965), pp. 1-135. Among the more important studies concerning riddles in general, one should consult A. Aarne, *Vergleichende Rätselforschungen*, FF Communications, 26-28 (Helsinki: Suomalaisen Tiedeakatemian Kustantama, 1918-20); H. Bausinger, *Formen der 'Volkspoesie'*,

Grundlagen der Germanistik 6 (Berlin: Erich Schmidt, 1968), pp. 119-30; M. Hain, *Rätsel*, Realienbücher für Germanisten 53 (Stuttgart: Metzler, 1966); A. Jolles, *Einfache Formen*, 2nd ed. (Halle: Niemeyer, 1956), pp. 104-23; and R. Petsch, *Kenntnis des Volksrätsels*, Palaestra 4 (Berlin: Mayer and Müller, 1899). For literature concerning O.T. riddles, see S. H. Blank, "Riddle," *IDB* 4 (1962), pp. 78-79; J. L. Crenshaw, "Wisdom," pp. 239f.; "The Riddle and Related Forms in the Old Testament" (Unpublished Manuscript, 1974); H.-P. Müller, "Der Begriff 'Rätsel' im Alten Testament," *VT* 20 (1970), pp. 465-89; and H. Torczyner, "The Riddle in the Bible," *HUCA* 1 (1924), pp. 125-49.

[148]Psalm 49 has been typed by several scholars as a wisdom psalm (J. Fichtner, *Die altorientalische Weisheit*, p. 9; and R. E. Murphy, "A Consideration of the Classification 'Wisdom Psalms,'" pp. 156f.).

[149]Several scholars have correctly regarded על מות as the original superscription of Psalm 49, and not as the conclusion to Psalm 48 (e.g., Gunkel, *Einleitung in die Psalmen*, p. 48).

[150]A rather interesting textual variant in one Heb. MS. is חדל for חלד, thus paralleling Isa 38:11--"inhabitants of Sheol." This variant would have our poet addressing even those who have been taken captive by Mot in the realm of the dead.

[151]Podechard remarks in a cogent observation: "L'opposition entre eux des termes du premier vers et le fait que les termes parallèles des collectifs occupent une place inverse dans le second ne laissant aucun doute sur le sens de בני אדם 'gens du commun' et de בני איש 'homes de condition'" ("Psaume LXIX," *RB* 31 [1922], p. 8).

[152]The form of חכמות has been explained by Dahood and Albright as the Phoenician form of the Hebrew חכמה (*Psalms* 1, pp. 296f., and "Some Canaanite-Phoenician Sources of Hebrew Wisdom," p. 8).

[153]Kraus believes that this is an example of the inspiration of the wisdom teacher in the composition of a משל (*Psalmen* 1, p. 364).

[154]For a discussion of the lyre as an ancient musical instrument, see Kurt Galling, "Musik," *Biblische Reallexikon* 1, HAT (Tübingen: J. C. B. Mohr [Paul Siebeck], 1937), pp. 389-94. From ancient Near Eastern sources it is evident that the wise were at times trained in the use of various musical instruments.

[155]That such has been regarded as a rhetorical question by the Syriac translation is seen in the translation: "I shall not fear."

[156]Read עקבי ("oppressors") for MT עקבי ("feet, heels") on the basis of Origen's hexapla and the Syriac translation.

[157]For the relative usage of the article, see Gesenius, no. 126, p. 404.

[158]Read with 8 Heb. MSS. אַך for אַח.

[159]Read the niphal יִפָּדֶה for qal יִפְדֶּה (cf. Kraus, *op. cit.*).

[160]Read with the LXX נפשו ("his soul") for MT נפשם.

[161]שחת is an epithet for Sheol (cf. Job 33:25 and Ps 16:10).

[162]Read קברם for קרבם with the LXX, Syriac, and Targum.

[163]Omit the ב with the LXX and Syriac. Kraus observes: "Ein alter Rechtsbrauch bestand darin, dass im Akte der Übereignung der Name des neuen Eigentümers über einem Objekt ausgerufen wurde. M ist durch die Phrase קרא בשם irregeführt worden" (*op. cit.*).

[164]We accept the MT ילין ("abide"). Cf. Job 17:2, 19:4. The LXX and Syriac try to make v. 13 and v. 21 a refrain. Such an attempt demonstrates that they are removing difficulties in translation, a frequent textual error.

[165]כסל ("confidence"--Job 31:24) also has the meaning of "stupidity" (Ecc 7:25).

[166]Read ארחות for אחרים due to the parallelism with דרכם in the preceding hemistich, or possibly אחריתם ("their end") with the Targum and Syriac.

[167]BDB locates שתו as a qal of שתח and translates: "They have been appointed like sheep for Sheol."

[168]ישרים לבקר should be taken as an apocalyptic addition.

[169]Read the *Qere* for the *Kethibh* (צורם for צירם).

[170]ל + היה plus the infinitive (or understood) implies "to become something, i.e., to meet with a particular fate" (Gesenius no. 114k, p. 349).

[171]We have taken מזבל to be a participle of זבל, "prince."

[172]Read with the Syriac, V, and { יודך for MT יורךָ.

[173]Read יבוא for MT תבוא.

[174]Read יראה for יראו with LXX and Syriac.

[175]We suggest reading בָקָר for בִיקָר and keeping יבין. For our pointing of the riddle and its solution, consult "The Riddles of Psalm 49," pp. 538, notes 27-29.

[176]Against Müller ("Der Begriff 'Rätsel,'" pp. 481-42, note 5) who argues *ḥidāti* should be *yiḥîdatî* ("my innermost self").

[177]B. Duhm, *Die Psalmen*, p. 202; Gunkel, *Die Psalmen*, p. 209; and H.-J. Kraus, *Psalmen* 1, pp. 362-63.

[178]Several scholars erroneously have suggested vs. 16 may be a gloss (Gunkel, *Die Psalmen*, p. 310; and W. O. E. Oesterley, *The Psalms* 1 [London: SPCK, 1939], p. 16). For an analysis of this riddle in terms of texture and definition, as well as our repointing, see "The Riddles of Psalm 49," pp. 540-41.

[179]Cf. Prov 13:8.

[180]Dahood, *Psalms* 1, p. 301. For examples of sapiential interest in Enoch, see Sir. 49:14 and Wis. 4:10f. Sirach also refers to Elijah's journey into heaven (48:9).

[181]See *ANET*, p. 93, note 190. The oracle Utnapishtim is to deliver reads:
I have learned that Enlil is hostile to me,
So that I cannot reside in your city,
Nor set my f(oo)t in Enlil's territory.
To the Deep I will therefore go down,
To dwell with my lord Ea.
(But upon) you he will shower down abundance,
(The *choicest*) birds, the rarest fishes,
(*The land shall have its fill*) of harvest riches.
(He who at dusk orders) the husk-greens.
Will shower down upon you a rain of wheat.

[182]Dahood, *Psalms* 1, p. 31, Gunkel, *Die Psalmen*, p. 74, and Kraus, *Psalmen*, p. 152.

[183]Torczyner was the first to argue that the poem contained two riddles, and while his analysis of the first riddle and solution parallels ours, his analysis of the second differs slightly in that he has considered v. 7 to be the riddle and 5c-6 to be the solution ("The Riddle in the Bible," *HUCA* 1 [1924], pp. 141f.).

[184]Wisdom vocabulary is limited to חוה, ארח, and דעת.

[185]BH[3] suggests reading קולם for קום. However, Kraus may be correct in arguing the MT should be maintained, since קו means "sound" or "speech" in Isa 28:10, 13 (*op. cit.*, p. 155).

[186]We are following BH[3] which suggests reading בים ("in the sea") for בהם ("in them").

[187]We propose that 7a should follow 5c as the second half of the solution (B[1]) to riddle B.

[188]See Ridderbos, *Die Psalmen*, p. 58.

[189]חמת is probably a word play since the term may mean "heat" as well as "tent" (cf. Ugaritic *hmt*).

[190]VAT 8249 (Otto Schroeder, "Zu Psalm 19," *ZAW* 34 [1914], pp. 69-70).

[191] For a discussion of Shamash, see Ringgren, *Religions of the Ancient Near East*, pp. 57f.

[192] For the reference to the bridal-chamber of Shamash, see "The Hymn to Shamash," 1. 200, BWL, p. 138.

[193] For a discussion of the mythological character of the psalm, see J. Morgenstern, "Psalms 8 and 19A," *HUCA* 19 (1945/46), pp. 491-523.

[194] *ANET*, pp. 66f.

[195] UT 52.

[196] נבע is found to mean "to burst forth in ecstatic praise" (cf. Pss 119:171, 145:7), as well as "to speak riddles" (Ps 78:2).

[197] UT, 'NT, III, 18f. For a discussion, see A. Jirku, "Die Sprache des Gottheit in der Natur," *TLZ* 76 (1951), p. 631.

[198] Kraus concurs that the text has been influenced by the Shamash tradition (*op. cit.*, p. 156). See our discussion of the "Shamash Hymn" in Chapter III.

[199] The relationship between myth and wisdom has not yet been rigorously examined, and certainly the numerous instances of mythological ideas and symbols point to the knowledge and use of myth by the wise. Hopefully, such a study will soon be undertaken. For initial efforts, see H.-P. Müller, *Hiob und Seine Freunde*, ThSt 105 (Zürich: EVZ-Verlag, 1970), pp. 27-54.

CHAPTER VI

CONCLUSIONS

A. *Introduction*

It has been our primary task to demonstrate in our analyses of the views of cult in the wisdom literatures of the ancient Near East the questionable position of earlier scholarly generalizations picturing the wise as a body of international, cosmopolitan humanists and secularists who functioned with empirical and rational epistemologies, were indifferent to the sphere of cult and its demands for confrontation and participation, were often disdainful of cultic observances and participants, and negatively criticized matters of cult. We believe these are tenuous generalizations, lacking any real foundation in the primary texts themselves. Now it is true that not every sage tended to view cultic matters in the same way, for we have found differences in viewpoints with respect to cult, its values, validity, theological bases, practices, and observances. However, even with some exceptions, much of the sapiential literature in the ancient Near East deals with cultic matters in substantive, not merely incidental, ways.

Furthermore, only one piece of ancient Near Eastern wisdom literature, the Mesopotamian "Dialogue of Pessimism," rejects the values and validity of the cultic sphere. However, this is not surprising, since the section on cult in this wisdom text is embedded in a series of exchanges between a master and his slave which deny the possibility of discovering meaning and security in human existence. Thus, even here cultic religion is not singled out as the solitary whipping boy by this Mesopotamian sage, since every human activity deemed important by the traditional sages is satirically attacked.

Thus, from the massive documentation to which we have referred in the preceeding chapters, we must conclude, first of all, that the sages did not extricate themselves from the sphere of cultic religion, but rather seriously reflected over its theology and often counseled participation in its practices.

B. *The Approaches of the Wise to Cultic Religion*

Cult as a Compartment of Order

In returning to our introductions to the thought of the
wise in the ancient Near East, we have indicated that wisdom is
the quest for self-understanding, an understanding derived from
the sapiential exploration of the wise man's relationships with
the various compartments of an ordered reality--creation (the
phenomena of the natural world), society (persons, social
groups, institutions), and deity (god or gods of creation, order, and retribution). As the wise man reflected on the seg-
ments of reality, he posited the idea of an all embracing order, most often defined in terms of justice and truth, which
permeated reality and served as the cohesive structure of a
well integrated whole of the elements of reality. Each element
of reality was believed to have its own laws and regulations
for existence and its orderly functioning within the gamut of
world order. By observing the elements of order, the task of
the wise man was, first of all, that of setting forth in
sapiential language those rules and laws which he believed
governed each component of order; secondly, to observe and follow the dictates of order with the purpose of integrating himself harmoniously within the composite structure of reality;
and, thirdly, to experience the beneficence which he attributed
to the areas of order. Thus, wisdom was the key which enabled
the wise man to find his own place, function, and time within
the beneficent spheres of world order. This quest for self-
understanding was motivated by the desire of the wise to master
life, that is, to know how and when to act with respect to
every conceivable situation, so that a semblance of security in
his personal existence might be obtained in what was very often
an insecure world. If his quest were successful, the wise man
knew who he was and what his tasks in life were, and he could
expect to experience the security and joys of what is often
referred to as the state of well-being, or, more simply, the
"good."

Now it has been suggested by many scholars that the efforts of the wise to understand every conceivable element of
reality were comprehensive in their scope, so that every segment

of reality came within the aegis of the sage's analysis. And,
as we have demonstrated, the realm of the cult was no exception, for this segment of reality also came under the investigative efforts of the sage, not simply in flippant or disdainful, but rather in substantive ways. However, the sages do not
always simply borrow the priestly teachings and understandings
concerning the matters of cult, but rather the various components of cult are given at times reflective sapiential analyses, and, consequently, sometimes bear what is often a demonstrative sapiential character. Thus when the wise reflect over
and submit conclusions about an element of the cultic compartment of world order, these very often bear a sapiential stamp.[1]

Elements of Cult in Ancient Near Eastern Wisdom Literature

In examining the references to the various elements of the
cultic sphere, it is apparent that almost every major element
of cult is mentioned by the wise. The following should serve
not only as a useful index to the references to the elements of
cult in wisdom texts, but also should underline in a conclusive
way the importance of the matters of cult in sapiential literature:

I. References to Elements of Cult in Egyptian and Mesopotamian
    Wisdom Literature

Sacred Rituals:

> General References: Sumerian Proverbs 2.1; Babylonian
>   Theodicy, 135, 219; I Will Praise the Lord of Wisdom,
>   I, 104, II, 17, 29, IV (?), 101; Dialogue of Pessimism,
>   61; The Tamarisk and the Palm, b, Reverse, 3; Assyrian
>   Proverbs, BM 38596=80-11-12, 480, I. 2-9.

> Sacrifices and Offerings: Ipu-wer, viii, 12f.; xi, 2f.;
>   Meri-ka-Re, 65f., 128f; Dialogue of a Man with his
>   Soul, 146; Ani, iii, 5f., iv, 1f., vii, 12; Amen-em-
>   Opet, ii, 1f.; 'Onchsheshonqy, Col. 14, 1.10; Papyrus
>   Insinger, 16:1; Advice to a Prince, 44; Counsels of
>   Wisdom, 136f.; Counsels of a Pessimist, 12; Shamash
>   Hymn, 14, 151, 172f., 196, 197; Babylonian Theodicy, V,
>   51-55; I Will Praise the Lord of Wisdom, II, 20, 24,
>   IV (?), 93, 94, 100; Dialogue of Pessimism, 55f.; The
>   Ox and the Horse, C, 7; Fable of the Fox, Z, Reverse,
>   10; Nisaba and Wheat, Reverse IV, 10; Babylonian Prov-
>   erbs, R. Borger, *Asarhaddon*, 105. 29-30.

Libations: Ipu-wer, xi, 1; Meri-ka-Re, 129f.; 'Onchsheshonqy, Col. 14, 1. 10; Papyrus Insinger 16:1; Sumerian
Proverbs; Shamash Hymn, 157f.; I Will Praise the Lord
of Wisdom, II, 12, IV (?), 95, 97; The Tamarisk and the
Palm, A, Reverse, 9, b, Reverse, 2.

Incense: Ipu-wer, xi, 1; Ani, iii, 5f., vii, 16, 17; I Will
Praise the Lord of Wisdom, IV (?), 92; The Tamarisk and
the Palm, b, Reverse, 7.

Ablutions and other Rites of Purification and Desacralization: Ipu-wer, xi, 3f.; I Will Praise the Lord of Wisdom, III, 24f.; IV (?), 26, 88; Dialogue of Pessimism,
54; The Tamarisk and the Palm, A, Reverse, 6, b, Reverse, 7, c, 6; Babylonian Proverbs, R. Borger, *Asar-
haddon*, 105. 29-30.

Egyptian Mortuary Rituals: Hor-dedef; Ptah-hotep, 298f.;
The Dialogue between a Man and his Soul; A Harper's
Song; Ipu-wer, iii, 5f., vii, 3f., xiii, 10; Meri-ka-
Re, 69f., 77f., 127f.; Amen-em-het, iii, 1f.; Sehetep-
ib-Re, 18f.; In Praise of Learned Scribes; Ani, iv,
14f.; Amen-em-Opet, ii, 9f., x, 21-xi, 1, 5, xxiv, 17;
'Onchsheshonqy, Col. 12, 1. 5; Papyrus Insinger, 2:9-
11, 16:2.

Pharaonic Cult: Ptah-hotep, 38, 199, 593f.; Ipu-wer, vii,
3f.; Amen-em-het, 1f.; Instruction of a man for his
Son; Instruction of Sehetep-ib-Re.

Divination, Exorcism, and Incantation: Ipu-wer, vi, 7f.;
Meri-ka-Re, 136f.; Sumerian Proverbs, 1. 70, 2. 4;
Shamash Hymn, 53-54, 129, 151, 155; Babylonian Theodi-
cy, V, 49; I Will Praise the Lord of Wisdom, I, 49-54,
II, 108-111, III, 1f., Si 55 (q), Reverse, 4f., IV (?),
84f.

Sacred Psalms (Hymns):

Ipu-wer, vii, 13f.; Meri-ka-Re, 131f.; The Instruction
of Sehetep-ib-Re; Sumerian Proverbs, 1. 70; I Will
Praise the Lord of Wisdom, I, 1f.; Nisaba and Wheat,
Reverse, IV.

Sacred Prayers:

General References: Ani, iii, 5f., iv, 1f.; Amen-em-Opet,
x, 11f.; 'Onchsheshonqy, Col. 28, 1. 10, Col. 24, 1.
11; Papyrus Insinger, 29:1; Counsels of Wisdom, 136f.;
Counsels of a Pessimist, 11f.; Shamash Hymn, 130f.,
163f.; Babylonian Theodicy, IV, 39, VII, 71, 73; I Will
Praise the Lord of Wisdom, II, 3-15, 23-24, 27, III,
52, IV (?), 76-77, 91; Nisaba and Wheat, Reverse, IV,
21; Fable of the Fox, Z, Reverse, 11, 14; Akkadian
Popular Sayings, VAT 8807, Reverse, IV, 4, 13; BM 53309
and BM 53555, 5.

Lament-Thanksgiving Cycle: The Dialogue of a Man with his
Soul, 20f., 86-149; Amen-em-Opet, vii, 7-10; Papyrus
Insinger 29:2; A Man and his God; Babylonian Theodicy,
XXVII, 295f.; I Will Praise the Lord of Wisdom.

Sacred Seasons:

Ipu-wer, xi, 4; Ani, iii, 3f.; Shamash Hymn, 156f.;
I Will Praise the Lord of Wisdom, II, 16, 24; The
Tamarisk and the Palm, A, Reverse, 13, b, Reverse, 8;
Akkadian Popular Sayings, BM 53309 and BM 53555, 6-7.

Sacred Drama:

Processions: Meri-ka-Re, 125; Ani, vii, 12; I Will Praise
the Lord of Wisdom, II, 25.

Dancing: Ani, iii, 5f.

Sacred Places (Temples):

The Dialogue of a Man with his Soul, 143f.; Ipu-wer,
xi, 3, xiii, 10; Meri-ka-Re, 63, 110, 135; Ani, iv.
1f.; Amen-em-Opet, vi, 1, vii, 7-10, x, 21; 'Onchsheshonqy 8, 1. 18; Advice to a Prince, 55f.; I Will
Praise the Lord of Wisdom, Commentary, o-p, IV (?),
77f.; The Tamarisk and the Palm, A, Reverse, 6; Sumerian Proverbs 1. 142, 2. 61a, 2. 69; Fable of the Willow,
K 13771, 12; Nisaba and Wheat, Obverse, I, 13-15; Fable
of the Fox, Z, Reverse, 8; Akkadian Popular Sayings,
VAT 8807, Reverse, III, 15.

Sacred Paraphernalia (images, altars, etc.):

Ipu-wer, xi, 3f.; Meri-ka-Re, 63, 125; Ani, vii, 12f.

Sacred Personnel:

Ipu-wer, xi, 4, 5; Meri-ka-Re, 63; Amen-em-Opet, ii,
15f.; 'Onchsheshonqy, 8, 1.18, 24, 1. 11; A Man and
his God, 67; Sumerian Proverbs, 1. 63, 2. 54, 2. 69,
2. 97 - 2. 106; Advice to a Prince, 55-56; Shamash
Hymn, 53-54, 155, 195; Babylonian Theodicy, the acrostic; I Will Praise the Lord of Wisdom, II, 6-9, 108-
111, III, 1f.; The Tamarisk and the Palm, A, Reverse,
6, b, Obverse, 26, Reverse, 7, c, 36; The Ox and the
Horse, A, Reverse, 6; Fable of the Fox, E, Obverse, I,
12, 18; Akkadian Popular Sayings, VAT 8807, Reverse
IV, 3-5; Proverbs, Assyrian Collection, ii, 27-28.

Sacred Texts:

Ipu-wer, vi, 6f., xi, 4; Meri-ka-Re, 51, 63, 87, 130;
Ani, iii, 5f.; Counsels of Wisdom, 73f.; I Will Praise
the Lord of Wisdom, III, 41f.

II. References to Elements of Cult in Israelite Wisdom
Literature

Sacred Rituals:

General: Koh. 8:10.

Sacrifices and Offerings: Prov 3:9-10, 7:14-15, 9:2f.,
15:8, 17:1, 21:3, 27; Job 1:5, 33:24, 42:8; Koh. 4:17,
9:2; Sir. 7:31, 14:11, 30:19, 34:18, 19, 20, 35:1-9,
12, 38:11, 45:14, 16, 20-21, 46:16, 47:2, 50:12, 14;
Wis. 18:8.

Libations: Prov 9:2f.; Sir. 50:14-15.

Incense: Sir. 24:15, 45:16; Wis. 18:21.

Cultic Meals: Prov 7:14f., 9:2f., 17:1; possibly Job 1:4f.

Vows: Prov 7:14, 20:25, 31:2; Job 22:27; Koh. 5:3-4; Sir.
18:22f.

Fasting: Sir. 34:26.

Ablutions and other Rites of Purification and Desacralization: Job 1:4-5, 9:30-31, 22:30; Koh. 9:2; Sir. 34:24-
25, 45:15.

Divination: Prov 16:10, 33; Koh. 5:2, 6; Sir. 34:1-8.

Sacred Psalms (Hymns):

General References: Job 36:24; Sir. 15:9-10, 32:13, 36:14,
43:28f., 47:8, 10.

Hymns: Prov 3:19-20, 8, 9; Job 5:9f., 9:4f., 12:13f., 26:
5f., 36:24f.; Sir. 1:1f., 4:11-19, 24:1-29, 16:24-17:
14, 39:12-35, 42:15-43:3; Psalm 19A.

Sacred Prayer:[2]

General References: Prov 15:8, 29, 28:9; Job 31:26-28,
33:24f., 42:8-10; Koh. 5:1-2; Sir. 3:5, 4:6, 7:10,
14, 17:25, 28:2, 34:24, 26, 36:17, 37:15, 38:14, 34,
39:5-6, 46:4f., 16f., 47:5f., 50:19; Wis. 7:7-8, 8:21,
11:3-4, 18:21.

The Lament-Thanksgiving Cycle: Joban Dialogues, Sir. 17:
25-29, 21:5, 35:13-20, 38:9f., 47:8, 48:20f., 51:9, 11;
Wis. 16:27-29; 19:22; Psalms 19B, 32, 34, 73, 119.

Prayers for Guidance or Wisdom: Sir. 22:27-23:6, 39:5-6,
51:13; Wis. 9:1-18.

Sacred Seasons: Prov 7:20; Sir. 33:7-9, 47:10, 50:5f.;
Wis. 18:6f.

Sacred Places (Temple): Prov 9:1f., 14, 17:1; Job 33:26;
Koh. 4:17, 8:10; Sir. 24:10f., 36:13f., 45:9, 24,
47:10, 13, 49:6, 12, 50:1-2, 7, 11, 51:14; Wis. 9:8-9.

Sacred Paraphernalia (Lots, Lampstand, Altar, Temple Cur-
tain): Prov 16:33; Sir. 26:17, 33:3, 45:10, 47:9,
49:8, 50:5, 11-16; Wis. 9:9.

Sacred Personnel: Job 12:19, 33:23; Koh. 5:5; Sir. 7:29-31,
44:5, 45:6-26, 47:9, 49:12, 50:1-24; Wis. 18:20-25.

Sacred Texts (Torah, Commandments): Prov 28:9; Koh. 5:5;
Sir. 1:26, 3:22, 6:37, 9:15, 10:19, 15:1, 15, 17:11,
19:17, 20, 24, 21:3, 11, 23:23, 27, 24:23, 28:6-7,
29:1, 32:15, 23-24, 33:2-3, 34:8, 35:1, 37:12, 39:1, 8,
41:8, 42:2, 44:20, 45:5f., 17, 46:14, 49:4; Wis. 9:9,
16:6, 18:9.

Illicit Cults and Cultic Practices: Proverbs 7, 9; Job 31:
26-28; Sir. 30:18-19, 34:1-8; Wis. 11:15-26, 12:23-27,
13:1-16:1, 18:13.

Affirmations of Cultic Dogmas

It is indeed the case that we find the traditional wise
voicing their assent to the validity of ideas and dogmas which
regulated the sphere of the cult. And this is apparent in
their statements which pertain to cultic phenomena associated
with the concept of the "sacred and profane" (sacred space,
objects, times, and personnel). The cults of the ancient Near
East were centered around certain sacred places, especially
temples, believed to be associated in some manner with divine
presence and regulated by means of rituals and festivals designed to preserve the sanctity of the gods. The acceptance
of the phenomenon of the holy at times appears when the sages
counsel their adherents in the proper sagacious behavior in the
cultic realm or when they speak to the matter of a righteous
order which permeates reality and must be followed by mankind.
Thus the "Advice to a Prince" is primarily concerned to warn
the Babylonian ruler to observe the rules of justice, especially as pertains to the privileges of certain esteemed Babylonian
cities, though one of the motivations which were to bolster the
royal observance of these privileges was the cultic affirmation
that each of the major deities in the pantheon, having his own
sacred city and dwelling in his own shrine, would leave his

city and shrine if the integrity of these privileges was subverted. In similar fashion, Sirach entertains the cultic idea
of holy space, especially in his prayer for Jerusalem, when he
appeals to Yahweh for divine action on the basis of Jerusalem's
position as the holy city which contains the temple in which
Yahweh dwells and which presumably had been profaned by foreign
enemies. Likewise, Ani has in mind the concept of the holy
when he warns that boisterous activity by the foolish cultist
profanes the silence of the holy (a common religious idea concerning the dwelling of a deity) and leads to destruction. In
addition he warns his 'son' to maintain a discreet distance
from the veiled idol when it passes in procession, since the
eager, zealous desire to press too close may result in profan-
ing the idol and bring destruction. Even Koheleth encourages
reserved behavior in the realm of the holy, apparently accepting the cultic idea that profanation of the holy by foolish
behavior may lead to the destruction of the fool.

The ritual of sanctification of the worshipper before his
participation in the cultic realm is alluded to in wisdom literature, including the rites of consecration by Job for his
three sons (the prologue), the ritual of purification by the
nobleman before his intended sacrifice ("Dialogue of Pessimism"), and the purification of the redeemed lord before his
participation in the rites of thanksgiving in the Esagil ("I
Will Praise the Lord of Wisdom").

The sanctity and mystery of cultic ritual and magical
texts which were to be only in the possession of cultic personnel in order that they might be effective is affirmed by
Ipu-wer who laments the impotency of these texts and their prescribed rituals due to their being read and practiced by profane laymen. Likewise, the need for sanctified priests to
serve in the sacred sphere may very well rest in the background
of Sirach's personal involvement in the religious and political
struggles involving the offices of priest and high priest in
the Jerusalem cult.

Finally, we find the pious sages affirming the cultic idea
of sacred time in their counsels, including Ani's indication
that the revelation of the god occurs especially during the

festive times and his remarks that the wise man participates in
the festival of his god in order to achieve divine blessing.
Likewise, the "Shamash Hymn" refers to the monthly festival of
Shamash and notes that during this time the sun god is re-
vitalized by cultic service and in gratitude grants the requests of his faithful worshippers. Sirach speaks of the importance of David's actions in establishing the festive times,
especially the pilgrimage festivals, and enters into a dialogue
concerning the rationale behind sacred seasons as differentiated from secular time.

Besides the concept of the holy, the major *raison d'être*
of the cult, the claim that the cult was the channel to the
world of the divine through which would flow the life-giving
forces of the gods, is accepted by the traditional sages who
place the dogma within the aegis of their concept of retribution. Thus, the offering of first fruits is counseled by a
sage in Proverbs 3 and cultic worship to one's personal god and
goddess is admonished in Babylonian wisdom literature, since
cultic service was believed to result in the beneficence of the
gods for the faithful cultist. In the same vein, we find the
wise affirming the idea that atonement for sins and a return to
the good graces of and beneficent relationship with the gods is
effectuated by the appropriate cultic rituals. This is especially the case in their reflections pertaining to the lament-
thanksgiving cycle ("Man and his God," "Counsels of Wisdom,"
"I Will Praise the Lord of Wisdom," the Joban Narrative, the
poetic Job, Sirach, and Psalm 73).

The belief that the cult was a means for communication
with the gods is also a dogma to which the pious sages acqui-
esce, especially in their counsels concerning prayer and divination. Prayer, especially the thanksgiving and the lament, was
considered to be an important cultic activity of the sages,
some of whom even participated in the writing of their own
prayers as the statements of Sirach and the author of Wisdom
and the presence of prayers in sapiential literature attest.
Divination, though controversial, was considered by the traditional sages to be a proper means of ascertaining the divine

will in Mesopotamia, and the casting of lots and the interpretation of dreams were affirmed as proper means of obtaining
divine revelations in Israel (Sirach).

Finally, the cultic prohibition of apostasy in Israel
seems to have permeated the ideology of the wise in Israel, as
may be seen in the close relationship of the language of the
self-imprecation in Job 31:26-28 to that of Deuteronomic legis-
lation´ prohibiting apostasy (Dt 13:6f.) and in the agreement of
Job and cultic legislation that death was the proper punishment
for this cultic crime.

Motivations for Cultic Participation

In the reflections and instructions of the wise with respect to matters of cult, we often find a number of motivations
which prompt the adherents of wisdom to participate in cultic
observances. As we have stated, the primary motivation which
is repeatedly given is the one based on the overwhelming desire
to enjoy the beneficence which comes to those who have observed
the laws and rules regulating the various elements of cult, a
beneficence administered through the conduit of the principle
of retribution. Those who faithfully and correctly observed
cultic legislation and rituals were believed to enjoy the
blessings derived from orderly existence. Thus we find the
traditional wise affirming the ability of cult to produce beneficence for the cultically observant. The wise not only affirmed the beneficence-working sphere of the cult, but in addition believed that cultic devotion gave to the wise man the
basis for divine aid in deliverance from the powers of evil.[3]

A second oft found motivation for cultic observance is the
desire to avoid the destructive wrath of the gods which is incurred against those who are cultically negligent, demonstrating again the sapiential affirmation of a cultic dogma for a
component of the *raison d'être* of cult.[4]

Thirdly, the wise were motivated to participate in cult by
their sagacious teachers not only in terms of gaining the
blessings which flow forth to the cultic observer and of
avoiding the destructive anger of the gods consuming those who

neglect the cultic sphere, but also by an appeal to their social conscience, for the priests as well as the poor received
their sustenance from the sacrifices and offerings given to the
cult.[5]

A fourth motivation for sapiential participation within
the realm of the cult is based upon the affirmation that such
has been commanded by the deity. Therefore, the wise-righteous
who fulfill their cultic observations are deemed "pleasing" to
the deity, whereas those who are cultically negligent or who
attempt to participate in cult while being wicked and foolish
are categorized as "displeasing" and their service as an "abomination."[6]

Finally, we discover a fifth motivation for sapiential
observance of cultic regulations to be that based on the desire
to praise and to give thanks to the gods of creation, order,
and retribution, praise and thanksgiving often found in the
forms of thanksgiving psalms, hymns, and prayers.[7]

The Decorum of the Wise within the Realm of the Cult

One of the most important concerns of the wise in speaking
to the matters of cultic religion and the sapiential participation within its realm was to instruct their adherents in the
proper, sagacious decorum within the cultic sphere, and, as we
have demonstrated, the standards for wise behavior within the
cult are exactly those which have been established for wise behavior in the various compartments of world order, including
the court, social institutions, professions, etc.[8]

Thus we find the wise arguing that the proper and acceptable worship to the gods is that offered by the wise-righteous
who have shaped their thoughts and actions in the mould of the
ideal wise man. This intimates that cultic and non-cultic
arenas were considered to be integrally entwined within the
structure of world order. In addition, one who was not sagacious in his decorum inside and outside the realm of cult received the punishment and even total destruction which was his
due according to the principle of retribution. The sages especially ridicule and lambast the wicked fool who does not live

in accordance with the laws of world order and yet foolishly
believes that cultic participation will still garner for him
divine blessing. Thus the sage who worships in the realm of
the holy should incorporate the behavior of the wise in general, including the characteristics of silence, solemnity, and
reverence, and should avoid the passionate outbursts of the
fool whose ecstatic and garrulous behavior leads to his punishment and even destruction by the gods.[9]

C. *The Wise as Critics of the Cult*

Though we have demonstrated from numerous wisdom texts
that the wise considered cult to be an important compartment of
world order and, therefore, sought to instruct their followers
in the proper participation within the cultic realm, it is by
no means to be argued that they simply bowed the knee to cultic
demands without intensely reflecting over and even severely
criticizing various elements of the cultic realm.

The satirical proverbs aimed at the pomposity of the *Kalû*
priest in Sumer demonstrate that the Sumerian wise had no reticence whatsoever in attacking foolish behavior and conceit even
when it characterized the behavior of supposedly "sacral"
groups. The warning issued to the chief priest by the Papyrus
Insinger that failure to intercede on behalf of the people who
were cultically observant would result in the verdict of death
and Sirach's gentle but firm prodding of the priests of his
period to fulfill carefully their cultic responsibilities
demonstrate that the wise believed it to be their duty to instruct priestly officials, not in the precision of proper cultic rituals, but rather in terms of the importance of their
cultic responsibilities as sacred functionaries.

In addition to this criticism of sacred functionaries, we
also find the wise attacking the popular misunderstanding of
cultic practices, primarily in terms of lambasting a magical
view of cultic rituals. A case in point is the casting of lots
in Israelite divination, a process which could easily be seen
by popular understanding to be a magical means of determining
the future. Thus the sages emphasize that such a process is

not automatically tied to some causal nexus, but rather is
entirely dependent upon the will of the deity who gives the
proper answer through the means of Urim and Thummim.[10] A similar criticism of the magical understanding of sacrifice seems
to be at work in the affirmation that sacrifice has the potential to remove the destructive powers of sin only because the
ritual is based upon the faithfulness and steadfast love of the
deity who has promised his followers to remove sins through the
means of sacrificial offerings.[11]

Idolatry was a cultic practice which received the critical
assessments of the sages. The Egyptian wise (Meri-ka-Re and
Ani) wrestled with the incongruity between the cultic idea of a
transcendent overseer and the belief in the deity who was
present in an idol. While the sages conclude by emphasizing
the idea of the transcendent watchman, they, nevertheless,
argue that the god is revealed in many ways, including the
process of idolatry, especially during holy seasons. Idolatry
was rejected by the Hebrew sages, not on the basis of sacral
law, but because the practice was considered contrary to reason.

Certain types of cultic behavior which were considered to
be out of harmony with sagacious decorum also fell beneath the
bludgeoning of sapiential attacks, including, for example,
Ani's lambasting of the garrulous behavior of the passionate
man within the sphere of the holy, and Koheleth's comparable
attack of the worship of fools who, in their ecstatic devotion
to the deity, often become entrapped in the destructive side of
the holy and are consumed by divine rage. In addition, these
two sages reject the understanding of cultic activity as *opus
operatum*. More specifically, the interpretation of dreams as
omens and signs sent by the gods to warn the pious of impending
doom is singled out by some of the ancient Near Eastern sages
for special criticism ("Counsels of a Pessimist" and Koheleth),
since the frenzied cultic activity of the recipients of dreams
is based upon the false assumption that dreams are omens of the
gods, whereas in truth they are the result of overwork and the
subsequent mental duress which accompanies overwork. Fertility
rites are another example of a cultic practice which receives
the barbed criticisms of the wise, for the wise person is not

one who loses his self-control even in cultic participation,
nor does he participate in cultic practices which breach the
code of ethical behavior as drawn up by the wise.[12] The vow is
a cultic activity that receives sapiential concern, and we find
the sages, like their priestly contemporaries, warning against
hasty and foolish vows which may not be fulfilled by the worshipper and thus could bring him divine punishment. This process is usually considered as one ingredient of potentially
foolish behavior, though we never find the sages counseling
their followers to refrain from making vows. Finally, in terms
of the ethical code of the sages, it is apparent that the wise
totally reject as "abominable" cultic participation by the unrighteous who engage in improper activities outside the cultic
sphere. It is imperative, according to sapiential teaching,
that the person who participates within the realm of the cult
be one who is righteous and upright in all of his activities.

Now it is most apparent that certain of the sages engaged
in poignant reflections and even severe doubts about the validity and value of cultic religion, while others affirm without
question its importance to the followers of wisdom. This polarity in thought may best be explained in terms of the polarity existing in wisdom circles which encompass both traditional
and critical wisdom. Thus, during periods of historical and/or
personal crises and despair, we often find the sages reflec-
tively criticizing and even doubting the validity and values of
cultic religion. In Egypt both mortuary religion and the cult
of the pharaohs were lambasted by the critical wise of the
First Intermediate Period,[13] while in Mesopotamia personal crises coupled with societal disruptions gave vent to the agonizing despair of the authors of "The Babylonian Theodicy" and "I
Will Praise the Lord of Wisdom" whose doubts concerning the
validity of cultic claims led them to the brink of abandoning
cultic religion, though the conclusions still point to the
avowal of the validity of cult.

In Israel, the Joban poet takes to task the theology and
practice of the lament-thanksgiving cycle, and though the theological basis of the ritual becomes altered from the expectation of reward for piety to disinterested piety, the Joban poet

still places cultic piety in terms of the lament in the mouth
of Job. However, the belief that the cult could both influence
a righteous deity and bring about the refurbishing of the vital
forces of nature is totally rejected. The new basis for cultic
piety offered by the poet is the feeling of awe in response to
divine, majestic mystery. Koheleth, who was unable to perceive
any just order permeating the universe and who viewed God as an
inscrutable, incalculable, transcendent despot, questions the
efficacy of prayers, especially enthusiastic and passionate
outpourings of speech to a transcendent deity made with the
expectation of the divine blessing, the cultic dogma of divine
immanence, and the idea of beneficence achieved through the
channel of cult in general. To Koheleth, the destructive power
of the holy was the only divine power which one confronted as
he entered the cultic realm. Further, he reminds his students
that death comes to all men, regardless of their response to
cultic commands.

And yet in the intense struggles and doubts of the critical wise, we find only one text which completely denies the
validity and value of cultic observance: "The Dialogue of
Pessimism." In this text a *du-ut-des* understanding of cultic
religion is especially subjected to ridicule. Otherwise, the
questionings of the wise during times of crisis often were the
arrows aimed at, but always eventually diverted from, the heart
of cultic religion, allowing once again the eventual reconcili-
ation of wisdom and cult in sapiential circles.

D. *The Question of Sapiential Avoidance of Cultic Provincialism*

It has become commonplace to suggest that the wise, especially the wise in the older periods of their respective traditions in the ancient Near East, were cosmopolitan internationalists who, being possessors of a worldly *savoir-faire*, disdained and, therefore, remained apart from the provincialism
of local and national cults. However, when Egypt ruled the
East during the Amarna Age, and Amon-Re sat enthroned over the
state pantheon, Ani apparently speaks of the wondrous rule of
this Egyptian sun god. Furthermore, the Egyptian sages, with

duly noted exceptions, are intimately involved in mortuary
religion and service to the divine pharaohs, cults which are
uniquely Egyptian. Divination, exorcism, and service to one's
personal god and goddess are characteristically Mesopotamian,
while the attacks levelled against other religions and illicit
cultic practices belong to the Israelite circles of wise men,
including the writers of Proverbs 1-9, the Joban poet, Sirach,
and the author of Wisdom.

Thus, it is highly questionable whether the sages, even
the earliest wise, were quite the internationalists we have
often depicted them to be. At least this would seem the case
with respect to the question of cults.

E. *The Wise as Creators of Cultic Literature*

It may well have been the case that certain wise participated in the realm of the holy by contributing wisdom psalms
meant to be used in the cultic services. At least this is a
tenable hypothesis, since we do find a number of wisdom psalms
in the Psalter such as 19A, 19B, and 119 which could have
served such a function. We also find other examples of psalms
embedded in the writings of the wise, some of which possess the
character of sapiential poetry, and, we believe, are not simply
borrowed by the formulators of sapiential tradition who insert
them into wisdom texts. Thus Meri-ka-Re, "The Dialogue of a
Man Tired of Life with his own Soul," and Sirach contain hymns,
laments, and thanksgivings, while "The Instructions of Sehetep-
ib-Re" and the "Shamash Hymn" are didactic poems possibly used
in cultic service. Thus, we find the sages emulating the
writers of cultic psalms.

In addition, some didactic poems reflect over and teach
about cultic theology and ritual, especially pertaining to the
theology and ritual of the lament-thanksgiving cycle.[14] Though
some texts intensely question the validity of the process, only
Job emaciates its theological foundations.

F. *The Question of Sapiential Usage of Cultic Language*

We have only briefly touched on the issue of the sapiential
usage of cultic language, and thus are able to offer only a few

tentative suggestions in this regard. The wise often use the term "abomination" and the opposite term "pleasing" to speak of cultic behavior by the wicked-foolish as contrasted to that of the righteous-wise. If such pronouncements were originally cultic, and it is by no means certain that this is the case due to the presence of comparable designations in ancient Near Eastern wisdom texts,[15] this may be an example of the appropriation of cultic language by the wise to express the sapiential emphasis on wise and righteous behavior as contrasted to that of wicked and foolish behavior. Thus, it is ethical behavior and not the concept of sacral taboos and ideas of clean and unclean that primarily concern the wise. However, it would be incorrect to suggest that the priests did not use the designations of "abomination" and "pleasing" as ethical categories.

We are on more certain ground when examining the usage by the wise of cultic language with respect to the descriptions of Dame Wisdom and the Strange Woman, since in several instances it is obvious that religious language, in this case mythological language depicting fertility goddesses, is appropriated to contrast the love for wisdom which leads to life with the lust for illicit sexual intrigue which leads to death.

Finally, the sapiential usage of the term 'ashrê, a designation which possibly may have derived from the cultic practice of cursings and blessings ($b^e r \hat{a} \underline{k} \hat{a} h$), may have been taken from the sphere of the holy to speak of those who are characterized by wise and righteous behavior in every sphere of world order, including cult, and who have come to experience well-being.

G. *Sapiential Forms and References to Cult*

An interesting point that we have made from our analysis of the views of cult in the wisdom literature of the ancient Near East is that only a very small number of references to cult are found in proverbial literature, thus leading us to conclude that when the wise spoke of cult they clothed their remarks in the garb of the instruction (e.g., "Counsels of Wisdom," Psalms 32 and 34), the *Streitgespräch* (e.g., Job), and the "Reflection on the Lament-Thanksgiving Cycle" (e.g., Psalm 73). Thus, the conclusion made by some scholars that the pre-exilic wise in Israel were disinterested in or even disdainful of cult is tenuous, since this conclusion rests primarily upon Proverbs 10-31, most of which consists of the various types of simple sayings of sapiential language.

H. *Conclusion*

We set as our task the two-fold purpose of critically examining the references to cult in the wisdom literature of the ancient Near East and of analyzing the didactic poems written by the wise. We have sought to question the general argument of many scholars that the cult was of little or no concern to the wise, and that when the subject of cult was broached, it was done so with a critical bias. It is our conclusion, supported by extensive documentation from the primary sources, that the traditional wise regarded the realm of cult to be an important compartment within the orders of reality, and, therefore, merited sapiential scrutiny and demanded sagacious participation. Secondly, our structural analyses of the didactic poems composed by the sages should point the way to a means of identifying didactic poems in the Psalter and distinguishing them from psalms influenced by wisdom forms and language. It is conceivable that the composing of some of these poems by the wise was done with an eye to their being used in the sacred liturgies (Psalms 19A, 19B, and 119).

We have not entered into the complicated efforts to draw up extensive comparisons and contrasts between the ideologies of the priests and the sages of the ancient Near East, say, for example, in their views of order, their relationships to myth, their understandings of deity, and their ideas of time. We shall leave these to future investigation. And it is here that we shall end our task.

[1]One prominent example of this, already discussed earlier, is the basis upon which idolatry is condemned by the Hebrew sages. Idolatry is not condemned as a breaking of cultic apodictic law, as an act considered to be cultically "abominable," nor as a cultic practice upon which is placed the destructive power of the curse. But rather idolatry is condemned by the wise primarily on the basis that such a cultic practice was considered to be foolish and contrary to reason.

[2]It appears that the cultic action deemed most important by the wise was prayer, which we have argued is not based primarily on "spiritualizing" or "individualizing" tendencies of the wise with respect to cult, but rather is connected to the fact that the sages most often speak of cultic concepts and practices which are closely akin to their own abilities and perspectives. Thus, a sage, trained in proper speech, able to compose, because of his training, cultic prayers, and indoctrinated in the dogma concerning the efficaciousness of the prayers of the righteous, would find in prayer the most important and most conducive cultic action for pious devotions and sagacious worship. This major interest of the wise in cultic practices and ideas which most readily corresponded with their own thinking and behavior may also be seen in the references to the communion sacrifices, the vows, and the genre of the hymn, especially those hymns which concern creation and retribution.

[3]See Meri-ka-Re, 63f.; The Instruction of a Man for his Son, 8-9, 18-19; Sehetep-ib-Re; Ani, iii, 3-9; Amen-em-Opet, x, 13f.; 'Onchsheshonqy, Col. 6, 1.1, Col. 18, 1.17; Papyrus Insinger, 10:1, 29:1-2; The Counsels of Wisdom, 135-147; The Counsels of a Pessimist, 131; The Shamash Hymn, 100; The Babylonian Theodicy, II, 21-22; I Will Praise the Lord of Wisdom, IV (?); Prov 3:9-10; the Joban Narrative; the Joban Dialogues; Sir. 35:10-11.

[4]See Meri-ka-Re, 110; The Instruction of Sehetep-ib-Re; 'Onchsheshonqy, Col. 19, 1.14, 24, 1.11; I Will Praise the Lord of Wisdom, II, 12-22; Job 1:5, 42:7f.; Koh. 5:3f.; Sir. 45:23f.; Wis. 18:7f., 20f.

[5]See the Papyrus Insinger, 16:1-3; and Sir. 7:29-31, 45: 20-22. This motivation is also found in cultic legislation (Num 18:8f.; Dt 26:12f., etc.).

[6]See Meri-ka-Re, 63f., 129f.; Papyrus Insinger 2:9; Man and his God, 117f.; the Shamash Hymn, 100, 106, 119; I Will Praise the Lord of Wisdom, II, 33-35; Prov 15:8, 21:27, 28:9; Job 31:26-38, 42:7f.; Koh. 5:3f.; Sir. 34:18-35:20; Wis. 14:11.

[7]Meri-ka-Re, 131f.; Amen-em-Opet, vii, 7-10; the Shamash Hymn; Sir. 39:12-35, 51:1-12; Wis. 9, 10:20-21, 16:28-29, 18:9; Psalms 19A, 19B, 32, 34, 73, 119.

[8]See Ani, iv, 1-4, vii, 12-17; Amen-em-Opet 4; and Koh. 4:17-5:6.

[9]Koh. 4:17-5:6.

[10]Prov 16:33.

[11]Prov 16:6.

[12]Proverbs 7; Wis. 12:2f., 14:22f.

[13]See The Dialogue of a Man Tired of Life with his own Soul, Ipu-wer, and A Harper's Song.

[14]"Man and his God," "I Will Praise the Lord of Wisdom," Job, and Psalms 32, 34, and 73.

[15]Amen-em-Opet, xiii, 15, xv, 20, etc.; Shamash Hymn 100, 106, and 119; and the Counsels of Wisdom 64.

BIBLIOGRAPHY

Major Reference Works

Erman, Adolf. *The Ancient Egyptians*. New York: Harper and Row, 1966; Harper Torchbook.

Gordon, E. I. *Sumerian Proverbs*. Philadelphia: The University of Pennsylvania, 1959.

Kittel, Rudolf, ed. *Biblia Hebraica*. 3rd ed. Stuttgart: Württembergische Bibelanstalt, 1937.

Lambert, W. G. *Babylonian Wisdom Literature*. Oxford: At the Clarendon Press, 1960.

Pritchard, J. B. *Ancient Near Eastern Texts*. 3rd ed. Princeton: Princeton University Press, 1969.

Rahlfs, Alfred, ed. *Septuaginta*, 2 vols. Stuttgart: Württembergische Bibelanstalt, 1935.

Books

Aarne, A. *Vergleichende Rätselforschungen*. FF Communications, 26-28. Helsinki: Suomalaisen Tiedeakatemian Kustantama, 1918-20.

Abel, F.-M. *Histoire de la Palestine* 1. Études Bibliques. Paris: Gabalda et Cie, 1952.

Anthes, Rudolf. *Lebensregeln und Lebensweisheit der alten Ägypter*. Der Alte Orient, 32. Leipzig: J. C. Hinrichs, 1933.

Barton, George A. *The Book of Ecclesiastes*. International Critical Commentary. New York: Charles Scribner's Sons, 1908.

Barucq, André. *Le livre des Proverbes*. Paris: J. Gabalda et Cie, 1964.

Bauer-Kayatz, Christa. *Einführung in die alttestamentliche Weisheit*. Biblische Studien, 55. Neukirchen-Vluyn: Neukirchener Verlag, 1969.

_____. *Studien zu Proverbien 1-9*. Wissenschaftliche Monographien zum Alten und Neuen Testament, 22. Neukirchen-Vluyn: Neukirchener Verlag, 1966.

Baumgartner, Walther. *Israelitische und altorientalische Weisheit*. Tübingen: J. C. B. Mohr (Paul Siebeck), 1933.

Bausinger, H. *Formen der 'Volkspoesie'*. Grundlagen der Germanistik, 6. Berlin: Erich Schmidt, 1968.

Bell, H. I. *Cults and Creeds in Graeco-Roman Egypt*. Liverpool: At the University Press, 1953.

Bleeker, C. J. *The Religion of Ancient Egypt*. Historia Religionum, Vol. 1. Leiden: E. J. Brill, 1969.

Boeser, P. A. A. *Transkription und Übersetzung des Papyrus Insinger*. Oudheidkundige Mededeelingen, 3. Uit 'Srijksmuseum van Oudheden Te Leiden, 1922.

Boström, Gustav. *Proverbiastudien*. Lunds Universitets Årsskrift, N. F. Aud. 1. Bd. 30, Nr. 3. Lund: C. W. K. Gleerup, 1935.

Brunner, Hellmut. *Altägyptische Erziehung*. Wiesbaden: Otto Harrassowtiz, 1957.

_____. *Die Lehre des Cheti*. Ägyptologische Forschungen, 13. Glückstadt: J. J. Augustin, 1944.

Castellino, G. R. *Sapienza Babilonese*. Rome: Società Editrice Internazionale, 1962.

Cerfaux, L. and J. Tondriau. *Le cult des souverains*. Tournai: Desclée and Cie, 1956.

Cody, Aelred. *A History of Old Testament Priesthood*. Analecta Biblica, 35. Rome: The Pontifical Biblical Institute, 1969.

Crenshaw, James L. *Prophetic Conflict*. Beiheft zur Zeitschrift für die alttestamentliche Wissenschaft, 124. Berlin: Walter de Gruyter, 1971.

Cumont, Franz. *The Oriental Religions in Roman Paganism*. New York: Dover Publications, 1956.

Dahood, Mitchell. *Proverbs and Northwest Semitic*. Scripta Pontificii Instituti Biblici, 113. Rome: Pontifical Biblical Institute, 1963.

_____. *Psalms*. Anchor Bible, 16. Garden City: Doubleday, 1966.

Dalbert, Peter. *Die Theologie der hellenistisch-jüdischen Missionsliteratur unter Ausschluss von Philo und Josephus*. Hamburg-Volksdorf: Herbert Reich, 1954.

De Boer, P. A. H. *De Vorbeede in het Oud Testament*. Oudtestamentische Studiën, 3. Leiden: E. J. Brill, 1943.

Deissler, Alfons. *Psalm 119 (118) und seine Theologie*. Münchener theologische Studien, 11. München: Karl Zink Verlag, 1955.

De Vaux, Roland. *Ancient Israel* 2. New York: McGraw-Hill, 1965.

_____. *Studies in Old Testament Sacrifice*. Cardiff: University of Wales Press, 1964.

Dhorme, E. *A Commentary on the Book of Job*. Translated by Harold Knight. London: Nelson, 1967.

Di Lella, Alexander A. *The Hebrew Text of Sirach*. London: Mouton and Co., 1966.

Dürr, D. Dr. Lorenz. *Das Erziehungswesen im Alten Testament und im alten Orient*. Mitteilungen der vorderasiatisch-ägyptischen Gesellschaft, 36. Leipzig: J. C. Hinrichs, 1932.

Duesberg, Hilaire, and Paul Auvray. *L'Ecclésiastique*. La Sainte Bible. Paris: Les Éditions du Cerf, 1958.

Duhm, B. *Die Psalmen*. Kurzer Hand-Commentar über das AT, 14. Tübingen: J. C. B. Mohr (Paul Siebeck), 1899.

Ebeling, Erich. *Ein babylonischer Kohelet*. Berliner Beiträge zur Keilschriftforschung, 1. Berlin, 1922.

Ehrlich, Ernst L. *Der Traum im Alten Testament*. Beihefte zur Zeitschrift für die alttestamentliche Wissenschaft, 73. Berlin: Alfred Töpelmann, 1953.

Eichrodt, Walther. *Ezekiel*. Old Testament Library. Philadelphia: Westminster Press, 1970.

Eissfeldt, Otto. *The Old Testament. An Introduction*. New York: Harper and Row, 1965.

Engnell, Ivan. *Studies in Divine Kingship in the Ancient Near East*. Oxford: Basil Blackwell, 1967.

Fecht, Gerhard. *Der Habgierige und die Maat in der Lehre des Ptahhotep*. Mitteilungen des deutschen archäologischen Instituts, 1. Glückstadt: J. J. Augustin, 1958.

Fichtner, Johannes. *Die altorientalische Weisheit in ihrer israelitisch-jüdischen Ausprägung*. Beihefte zur Zeitschrift für die alttestamentliche Wissenschaft, 62. Giessen: Alfred Töpelmann, 1933.

_____. *Weisheit Salomos*. Handbuch zum AT, 6. Tübingen: J. C. B. Mohr (Paul Siebeck), 1938.

Fohrer, Georg. *Das Buch Hiob*. Kommentar zum AT, 16. Gütersloh: Gerd Mohn, 1963.

_____. *Introduction to the Old Testament*. Nashville: Abingdon Press, 1968.

Fohrer, Georg. *Studien zum Buche Hiob*. Gütersloh: Gerd Mohn, 1963.

Frankfort, Henri. *Ancient Egyptian Religion*. Harper Torchbook. New York: Harper and Brothers, 1948.

Galling, Kurt. *Die Fünf Megilloth*. 2nd ed. Handbuch zum AT, 18. Tübingen: J. C. B. Mohr (Paul Siebeck), 1969.

_____. *Prediger Salomo*. Handbuch zum AT, 18. Tübingen: J. C. B. Mohr (Paul Siebeck), 1940.

Gardiner, A. H. *Egypt of the Pharaohs*. New York: Oxford University Press, 1966.

_____. *The Admonitions of an Egyptian Sage*. Leipzig: J. C. Hinrichs, 1909.

Gemser, Berend. *Sprüche Salomos*. 2nd ed. Handbuch zum AT, 10. Tübingen: J. C. B. Mohr (Paul Siebeck), 1963.

Gerstenberger, Erhard. *Wesen und Herkunft des 'apodiktischen Rechts'*. Wissenschaftliche Monographien zum Alten und Neuen Testament, 20. Neukirchen-Vluyn: Neukirchener Verlag, 1965.

Gese, Hartmut. *Lehre und Wirklichkeit in der alten Orient*. Tübingen: J. C. B. Mohr (Paul Siebeck), 1958.

Gilbert, Maurice. *La critique des dieux dans le livre de la Sagesse*. Analecta Biblica, 53. Rome: Pontifical Biblical Institute, 1973.

Ginsberg, H. Louis. *Studies in Koheleth*. New York: The Jewish Theological Seminary of America, 1950.

Glanville, S. R. K. *The Instructions of 'Onchsheshonqy*. Catalogue of Demotic Papyri in the British Museum, 1955.

Glasser, Étienne. *Le procès du bonheur par Qohelet*. Lectio Divina, 16. Paris: Les Éditions du Cerf, 1970.

Goedicke, Hans. *The Report about the Dispute of a Man with his Ba*. Baltimore: The Johns Hopkins Press, 1970.

Goodrich, A. *The Book of Wisdom*. New York: The MacMillan Co., 1913.

Gordis, Robert. *Koheleth the Man and His World*. 3rd ed. New York: Schocken Books, 1968.

Gray, G. B. *The Book of Job*. International Critical Commentary, 14. Edinburgh: T. and T. Clark, 1921.

Gray, John. *The Legacy of Canaan*. Supplement Vetus Testamentum, 5. Leiden: E. J. Brill, 1965.

Grumach, Irene. *Untersuchungen zur Lebenslehre des Amenemope*. Münchener ägyptologische Studien, 23. München: Deutscher Kunstverlag, 1972.

Gunkel, Hermann. *Die Psalmen*. Handkommentar zum AT, 16. Göttingen: Vandenhoeck und Ruprecht, 1926.

_____, and Joachim Begrich. *Einleitung in die Psalmen*. Göttingen: Vandenhoeck und Ruprecht, 1933.

Gunneweg, A. H. J. *Leviten und Priester*. Forschungen zur Religion und Literatur des Alten und Neuen Testaments, 89. Göttingen: Vandenhoeck und Ruprecht, 1965.

Guthrie, W. K. C. *The Greeks and their Gods*. Boston: Beacon Press, 1950.

Hain, M. *Rätsel*. Realienbücher für Germanisten, 53. Stuttgart: Metzler, 1966.

Hallo, William W., and William Kelly Simpson. *The Ancient Near East*. New York: Harcourt, Brace, Jovanovich, Inc., 1971.

Harrelson, Walter. *From Fertility Cult to Worship*. Garden City: Doubleday, 1970.

Haspecker, Josef. *Gottesfurcht bei Jesus Sirach*. Analecta Biblica, 30. Rome: Pontifical Biblical Institute, 1967.

Helck, Wolfgang. *Der Text der Lehre Amenemhets I. für seinen Sohn*. Kleine ägyptische Texte, 1. Wiesbaden: Harrassowitz, 1969.

Hengel, Martin. *Judentum und Hellenismus*. Wissenschaftliche Untersuchungen zum Neuen Testament, 10. Tübingen: J. C. B. Mohr (Paul Siebeck), 1969.

Hermission, Hans-Jürgen. *Studien zur israelitischen Spruchweisheit*. Wissenschaftliche Monographien zum Alten und Neuen Testament, 28. Neukirchen-Vluyn: Neukirchener Verlag, 1968.

Herrmann, Siegfried. *Untersuchungen zur Überlieferungsgestalt mittelägyptischer Literaturwerke*. Deutsche Akademie der Wissenschaften zu Berlin Institute für Orientforschung, 33. Berlin: Akademieverlag, 1957.

Hertzberg, H. W. *Der Prediger*. Kommentar zum AT, 17. Gütersloh: Gerd Mohn, 1963.

Humbert, Paul. *Recherches sur les sources égyptiennes de la littérature sapientiale d'Israël*. Neuchâtel: Paul Attinger, 1929.

Jansen, Herman L. *Die spätjüdische Psalmendichtung: Ihr Entstehungskreis und ihr 'Sitz im Leben'*. Oslo: I Kommisjon Hos Jacob Dybwad, 1937.

Janssen, Enno. *Das Gottesvolk und seine Geschichte.*
Neukirchen-Vluyn: Neukirchener Verlag, 1971.

Jaubert, Annie. *La notion d'alliance dans le Judaïsme.*
Patristica Sorbonensia, 6. Paris: Éditions du Seuil,
1963.

Jepsen, Alfred. *Das Buch Hiob und seine Deutung.* Arbeiten
zur Theologie, 14. Stuttgart: Calwer Verlag, 1963.

Johnson, N. B. *Prayer in the Apocrypha and Pseudepigrapha.*
Society of Biblical Literature Monograph Series, 3.
Philadelphia: Society of Biblical Literature, 1948.

Jolles, André. *Einfache Formen.* 2nd ed. Halle: Niemeyer,
1956.

Kaufmann, Yehezkel. *The Religion of Israel.* Translated and
Abridged by Moshe Greenberg. Chicago: University of
Chicago Press, 1960.

Kluger, Rivkah S. *Satan in the Old Testament.* Evanston: The
Northwestern University Press, 1967.

Kramer, Samuel Noah. *Sumerian Mythology.* rev. ed. New York:
Harper and Brothers, 1961.

_____. *The Sumerians.* Chicago: The University of Chicago
Press, 1963.

Kraus, H.-J. *Die Psalmen.* 2nd ed. Neukirchen-Vluyn:
Neukirchener Verlag, 1961.

_____. *Worship in Israel.* Richmond: John Knox, 1966.

Kroeber, Rudi. *Der Prediger.* Berlin: Akademie Verlag, 1963.

Kuhn, Gottfried. *Beiträge zur Erklärung des salomonischen
Spruchbuches.* Beiträge zur Wissenschaft vom Alten und
Neuen Testament, 16. Stuttgart: W. Kohlhammer, 1931.

_____. *Erklärung des Buches Koheleth.* Beihefte zur Zeit-
schrift für die alttestamentliche Wissenschaft, 43.
Giessen: Alfred Töpelmann, 1926.

Lamparter, Hellmut. *Die Apokryphen* 1. Stuttgart: Calwer Verlag, 1972.

Lang, Bernhard. *Die weisheitliche Lehrrede.* Stuttgarter
Bibelstudien, 54. Stuttgart: KBW Verlag, 1972.

Lange, H. O. *Das Weisheitsbuch des Amenemope aus dem Papyrus
10,474 des British Museum.* Det Kgl. Danske Videnska-
bernes Selskab. Historisk-filologiske Meddelelser, 11, 2.
Kopenhagen: Bianco Lunos, 1925.

Langdon, S. *Babylonian Wisdom*. London: Luzac and Co., 1923.

Larcher, C. *Études sur le livre de la Sagesse*. Études Bibliques. Paris: J. Gabalda et Cie, 1969.

Lévêque, Jean. *Job et son dieu*. Vol. I. Paris: Librairie Lecoffre, 1970.

Lindblom, Johannes. *La composition du livre de Job*. Bulletin de la société royale des lettres de Lund, 3. Lund: C. W. K. Gleerups Förlag, 1945.

Loretz, Oswald. *Qohelet und der Alte Orient*. Freiburg: Herder, 1964.

McKane, William. *Proverbs*. Old Testament Library. London: SCM Press, 1970.

McKay, John. *Religion in Judah under the Assyrians*. Studies in Biblical Theology, 26. London: SCM Press, 1973.

Marböck, Johann. *Weisheit im Wandel*. Bonner biblische Beiträge, 37. Bonn: Peter Hanstein Verlag, 1971.

Marcus, Ralph. *Law in the Apocrypha*. Columbia University Oriental Studies, 26. New York: Ams Press, 1960.

Marzal, Angel. *La Enseñanza de Amenemope*. Madrid: Instituto Español de Estudios Eclesiasticos Y Ediciones Marova, 1965.

Meissner, Bruno. *Babylonien und Assyrien* 2. Kulturgeschichtliche Bibliothek. Edited by W. Foy. Heidelberg: Carl Winters Universitätsbuchhandlung, 1925.

Mercer, S. A. B. *The Religion of Ancient Egypt*. London: Luzac and Co., 1949.

Morenz, Siegfried. *Ägyptische Religion*. Stuttgart: W. Kohlhammer, 1960.

Mowinckel, Sigmund. *He That Cometh*. Oxford: Basil Blackwell, 1956.

_____. *Psalmenstudien* 1. Oslo. Reprint; Amsterdam: P. Schippers, 1961.

Müller, H.-P. *Hiob und seine Freunde*. Theologische Studiën, 105. Zürich: EVZ-Verlag, 1970.

Nilsson, Martin P. *Geschichte der griechischen Religion* 2. Handbuch der Altertumswissenschaft, 5. München: C. H. Beck, 1950.

Nougayrol, J., E. Laroche, C. Virolleaud, and C. F. A. Schaeffer. *Ugaritica* 5. Mission de Ras Shamra, 16. Paris: Imprimerie Nationale, 1968.

372

Oppenheim, A. Leo. *Ancient Mesopotamia*. Chicago: The University of Chicago Press, 1964.

_____. *The Interpretation of Dreams in the Ancient Near East*. Philadelphia: The American Philosophical Society, 1956.

Otto, Eberhard. *Der Vorwurf an Gott*. Hildesheim: Gerstenberg, 1951.

Petsch, R. *Kenntnis des Volksrätsels*, Palaestra 4. Berlin: Mayer und Müller, 1899.

Pfeiffer, R. H. *A History of New Testament Times with an Introduction to the Apocrypha*. New York: Harper and Row, 1949.

Pope, Marvin H. *Job*. Anchor Bible, 15. Garden City: Doubleday and Co., 1965.

Posener, G. *Littérature et politique dans l'Égypte de la XIIe Dynastie*. Bibliothèque de l'École des Hautes Études, 307. Paris: Librairie Ancienne Honoré Champion, 1956.

Preuss, Horst Dietrich. *Verspottung fremder Religionen im Alten Testament*. Beiträge zur Wissenschaft vom Alten (und Neuen) Testament, 92. Stuttgart: W. Kohlhammer, 1971.

Reese, James M. *Hellenistic Influence on the Book of Wisdom and Its Consequences*. Analecta Biblica, 41. Rome: Pontifical Biblical Institute, 1970.

Reider, Joseph. *The Book of Wisdom*. New York: Harper and Brothers, 1957.

Ridderbos, N. H. *Die Psalmen*. Beiheft zur Zeitschrift für die alttestamentliche Wissenschaft, 117. Berlin: Walter de Gruyter, 1972.

Ringgren, Helmer. *Israelite Religion*. Philadelphia: Fortress Press, 1966.

_____. *Religions of the Ancient Near East*. Philadelphia: The Westminster Press, 1973.

_____. *Word and Wisdom*. Lund: Hakan Ohlssons Boktryckeri, 1947.

Römer, W. H. Ph. *The Religion of Ancient Mesopotamia*. Historia Religionum, 1. Leiden: E. J. Brill, 1969.

Rowley, H. H. *Job*. The Century Bible. Don Mills, Ontario: Thomas Nelson and Sons, 1970.

_____. *Worship in Ancient Israel*. Philadelphia: Fortress Press, 1967.

Rüger, H. P. *Text und Textform im hebräischen Sirach*. Beihefte zur Zeitschrift für die alttestamentliche Wissenschaft, 109. Berlin: Walter de Gruyter, 1970.

Rylaarsdam, J. Coert. *Revelation in Jewish Wisdom Literature*.
Chicago: University of Chicago Press, 1946.

Sanders, J. A. *The Psalms Scrolls of Qumran Cave II*. Dis-
coveries in The Judean Desert of Jordan, 4. Oxford: At
the Clarendon Press, 1965.

Schaeder, Hans Heinrich. *Esra der Schreiber*. Beiträge zur
historischen Theologie, 5. Tübingen: J. C. B. Mohr (Paul
Siebeck), 1930.

Schilling, Othmar. *Das Buch Jesus Sirach*. Herders Bibelkom-
mentar, 3. Freiburg: Herder, 1956.

Schmid, II. H. *Wesen und Geschichte der Weisheit*. Beihefte zur
Zeitschrift für die alttestamentliche Wissenschaft, 101.
Berlin: Alfred Töpelmann, 1966.

Schmidt, Hans. *Die Psalmen*. Handbuch zum AT, 15. Tübingen:
J. C. B. Mohr (Paul Siebeck), 1934.

Schmökel, Hartmut. *Das Land Sumer*. 3rd ed. Stuttgart: W.
Kohlhammer, 1962.

Schökel, Luis Alonso. *Estudios de Poética Hebrea*. Barcelona:
Juan Flors, 1963.

Scott, R. B. Y. *Proverbs. Ecclesiastes*. Anchor Bible. Garden
City: Doubleday and Co., 1965.

_____. *The Way of Wisdom*. New York: The MacMillan Co.,
1971.

Skladny, Udo. *Die ältesten Spruchsammlungen in Israel*.
Göttingen: Vandenhoeck und Ruprecht, 1962.

Snaith, John G. *Ecclesiasticus*. Cambridge: Cambridge University Press, 1974.

Snaith, Norman. *The Book of Job*. Studies in Biblical Theology, 11. Naperville, Ill.: Alec R. Allensen, Inc., 1968.

Spiegel, Joachim. *Das Werden der altägyptischen Hochkultur*.
Heidelberg: F. H. Kerle Verlag, 1953.

Stärk, W. *Lyrik*. Die Schriften des AT, 3. Göttingen: Vandenhoeck und Ruprecht, 1911.

Stamm, J. J. *Das Leiden des Unschuldigen in Babylon und Israel*.
Zürich: Zwingliverlag, 1946.

Suys, Émile. *La sagesse d'Ani*. Analecta Biblica, 11. Rome:
Pontifical Biblical Institute, 1935.

374

Tcherikover, Victor. *Hellenistic Civilization and the Jews*. New York: Atheneum, 1959.

Terrien, Samuel. "The Book of Job," pp. 877-1198. *The Interpreter's Bible* 3. Edited by G. A. Buttrick. Nashville: Abingdon Press, 1955.

Tur-Sinai, N. H. *The Book of Job*. Jerusalem: Kiryath Sepher, 1967.

Van der Weiden, W. A. *Le livre des Proverbes*. Biblica et Orientalia, 23. Rome: Biblical Institute Press, 1970.

Van Dijk, J. J. A. *La sagesse suméro-accadienne*. Commentationes Orientales, 1. Leiden: E. J. Brill, 1953.

Volten, Aksel. *Das demotische Weisheitsbuch*. Kopenhagen: Einar Munksgaard, 1941.

_____. *Studien zum Weisheitsbuch des Anii*. Det. Kgl. Danske Videnskaberneg Selskab. Historisk-Filologiske Meddelelser, 23. Copenhagen: Levin and Munksgaard, 1937.

_____. *Zwei altägyptische politische Schriften*. Analecta Aegyptiaca, 4. Kopenhagen: Einar Munksgaard, 1945.

Volz, Paul. *Weisheit*. Die Schriften des AT, 2. Göttingen: Vandenhoeck und Ruprecht, 1911.

Von Rad, Gerhard. *Theology of the Old Testament* 1. Translated by D. M. G. Stalker. New York: Harper and Row, 1962.

_____. *Wisdom in Israel*. Nashville: Abingdon Press, 1972.

Vriezen, Th. C. *The Religion of Ancient Israel*. Philadelphia: The Westminster Press, 1967.

Weinfeld, Moshe. *Deuteronomy and the Deuteronomic School*. Oxford: At the Clarendon Press, 1972.

Weiss, Meir. *The Bible and Modern Literary Theory* (Modern Hebrew). Jerusalem: The Bialik Institute, 1967.

Westermann, Claus. *Der Aufbau des Buches Hiob*. Beiträge zur historischen Theologie, 23. Tübingen: J. C. B. Mohr (Paul Siebeck), 1956.

Whybray, R. N. *The Book of Proverbs*. Cambridge: At the University Press, 1972.

_____. *Wisdom in Proverbs*. Studies in Biblical Theology, 45. London: SCM Press, 1965.

Williams, Ronald J. *Hebrew Syntax*. Toronto: University of Toronto Press, 1967.

Wilson, John A. *The Burden of Egypt*. Chicago: University of Chicago Press, 1951.

Wolff, H. W. *Amos' geistige Heimat*. Wissenschaftliche Monographien zum Alten und Neuen Testament, 18. Neukirchen-Vluyn: Neukirchener Verlag, 1964.

Ziener, Georg. *Die theologische Begriffssprache im Buch der Weisheit*. Bonn: Peter Hanstein, 1956.

Zimmerli, Walther. *Sprüche. Prediger*. Das Alte Testament Deutsch, 16. Göttingen: Vandenhoeck und Ruprecht, 1962.

Articles

Albright, W. F. "Some Canaanite-Phoenician Sources of Hebrew Wisdom." *Supplement Vetus Testamentum* 3 (1955), 1-15.

_____. "The Goddess of Life and Wisdom." *American Journal of Semitic Languages and Literatures*, 36 (1919/20), 258-94.

Alt, Albrecht. "Zur literarischen Analyse der Weisheit des Amenemope." *Supplement Vetus Testamentum* 3 (1955), 16-25.

_____. "Zur Vorgeschichte des Buches Hiob." *Zeitschrift für die alttestamentliche Wissenschaft* 14 (1937), 265-68.

Anthes, Rudolf. "Die Funktion des vierten Kapitels in der Lehre des Amenemope." *Archäologie und Altes Testament*. Tübingen: J. C. B. Mohr (Paul Siebeck), 1970, pp. 9-18.

_____. "The Legal Aspects of the Instruction of Amenemhet." *Journal of Near Eastern Studies* 16 (1957), 176-91.

Bauckmann, Ernst G. "Die Proverbien und die Sprüche des Jesus Sirach." *Zeitschrift für die alttestamentliche Wissenschaft* 72 (1960), 33-63.

Baumgartner, Walter. "Die literarischen Gattungen in der Weisheit des Jesus Sirach." *Zeitschrift für die alttestamentliche Wissenschaft* 34 (1914), 161-98.

_____. "The Wisdom Literature." In *The Old Testament in Modern Study*, pp. 210-37. Edited by H. H. Rowley. Oxford: At the Clarendon Press, 1951.

Begrich, Joachim. "Das priesterliche Heilsorakel." *Zeitschrift für die alttestamentliche Wissenschaft* 52 (1934), 81-92.

Bell, Harold. "Graeco-Egyptian Religion." *Museum Helveticum* 10 (1953), 227-37.

Bickermann, Elias J. "The Civic Prayer for Jerusalem." *Harvard Theological Review* 55 (1962), 163-85.

Blackman, A. M. and T. E. Peet. "Papyrus Lansing: A Translation with Notes." *Journal of Egyptian Archaeology* 11
(1925), 284-98.

Blank, Sheldon H. "Men against God." *Journal of Biblical
Literature* 77 (1953), 1-14.

_____. "The Curse, Blasphemy, the Spell, and the Oath."
Hebrew Union College Annual 23 (1950/51), 73-95.

Bleeker, C.-J. "L'idée de l'ordre cosmique dans l'ancienne
Égypte." *Revue d'histoire et de philosophie religieuses*
42 (1962), 193-200.

Böhl, F. M. Th. "De Zonnegod als de Beschermer der Nooddruftigen." *Jaarbericht 'Ex Oriente Lux'* 8 (1942), 665-80.

Bottéro, Jean. "Le 'Dialogue Pessimiste' et la transcendance."
Revue de théologie et de philosophie 16 (1966), 7-24.

Botti, Giuseppe, and Aksel Volten. "Florentines-Fragmente zum
Texte des Pap. Insinger." *Acta Orientalia* 25 (1960), 29-
42.

Brunner, Hellmut. "Das hörende Herz." *Theologische Literaturzeitung* 79 (1954), 697-700.

_____. "Die 'Weisen', ihre 'Lehren' und 'Prophezeiungen,'
in altägyptischer Sicht." *Zeitschrift für ägyptische
Sprache und Altertumskunde* 93 (1966), 29-35.

_____. "Die Weisheitsliteratur." In *Ägyptologie*, pp. 90-
110. Handbuch der Orientalistik, Vol. 1. Leiden: E. J.
Brill, 1952.

_____. "Eine neue Entlehung aus der Lehre des Djedefhor."
Mitteilungen des deutschen archäologischen Instituts 14
(1956), 17-19.

_____. "Ein weiteres Djedefhor-Zitat." *Mitteilungen des
deutschen archäologischen Instituts* 19 (1963), 53.

_____. "Gerechtigkeit als Fundament des Thrones." *Vetus
Testamentum* 8 (1958), 426-28.

Brunner-Traut, Emma. "Die Weisheitslehre des Djedef-Hor."
Zeitschrift für ägyptische Sprache und Altertumskunde 76
(1940), 3-9.

_____. "Der Lebensmüde und sein Ba." *Zeitschrift für
ägyptische Sprache und Altertumskunde* 76 (1940), 6-15.

Bryce, Glendon. "Omen-Wisdom in Ancient Israel." *Journal of
Biblical Literature* 94 (1975), 19-37.

Buccellati, G. "Tre saggi sulla sapienza Mesopotamica - II. IL Dialogo del Pessimismo: La scienza delgi oppositi come ideale sapienziale." *Oriens Antiqvvs* 11 (1972), 81-100.

Budge, E. A. W. "The Precepts of Life by Amen-em-apt, the Son of Ka-nekht." In *Recueil d'études égyptologiques*, pp. 431-46. Paris: Édouard Champion, 1922.

Büchler, A. "Ben Sira's Conception of Sin and Atonement." *Jewish Quarterly Revue* 13 (1922/23), 303-35.

Burrows, Millar. "The Voice from the Whirlwind." *Journal of Biblical Literature* 47 (1928), 117-32.

Buzy, Denis. "La notion du bonheur dans l'Ecclésiaste." *Revue Biblique* 43 (1943), 494-516.

Caquot, André. "Ben Sira et le messianisme." *Semitioa* 16 (1966), 43-68.

Castellino, George. "Qohelet and his Wisdom." *Catholic Biblical Quarterly* 30 (1960), 15-28.

Cazelles, Henri. "Bible, sagesse, science." *Recherches de science religieuse* 48 (1960), 40-58.

_____. "Des débuts de la sagesse en Israël." In *Les sagesse du Proche-Orient*, pp. 27-39. Paris: Universitaires de France, 1963.

Conrad, Joachim. "Die innere Gliederung der Proverbien." *Zeitschrift für die alttestamentliche Wissenschaft* 79 (1967), 67-76.

Couroyer, B. "Le chemin de vie en Égypte et en Israel." *Revue Biblique* 56 (1947), 412-32.

_____. "Mettre sa main sur sa bouche." *Revue Biblique* 67 (1960), 197-209.

Crenshaw, James L. "Popular Questioning of the Justice of God in Ancient Israel." *Zeitschrift für die alttestamentliche Wissenschaft* 82 (1970), 380-95.

_____. "The Eternal Gospel." In *Essays in Old Testament Ethics*, pp. 23-56. Edited by James L. Crenshaw and John Willis. New York: Ktav, 1974.

_____. "The Influence of the Wise upon Amos." *Zeitschrift für die alttestamentliche Wissenschaft* 79 (1967), 42-52.

_____. "The Problem of Theodicy in Sirach: On Human Bondage." *Journal of Biblical Literature* 94 (1975), 47-64.

_____. "Wisdom." In *Old Testament Form Criticism*, pp. 225-64. Edited by John H. Hayes. San Antonio: Trinity University Press, 1974.

Dahood, Mitchell J. "Canaanite-Phoenician Influence in Qoheleth." *Biblica* 33 (1952), 30-52.

_____. "Qoheleth and Northwest Semitic Philology." *Biblica* 43 (1962), 349-65.

Daumas, F. "La naissance de l'humanisme dans la littérature de l'Égypte ancienne." *Oriens Antiqvvs* 1 (1962), 155-84.

De Boer, P. A. H. "בבריתם עמד זרעם" Sirach xliv 12a." *Supplement Vetus Testamentum* 16 (1967), 25-29.

De Buck, A. "Het Religieus Karacter der oudste egyptische Wijsheid." *Nieuw theologisch Tijdschrift* 21 (1932), 322-49.

_____. "La composition littéraire des enseignements d'Amenemhet." *Muséon* 59 (1946), 183-200.

De Buck, H. "The Instruction of Amenemmes." In *Mélanges Maspero*, pp. 847-52. Orient Ancien, 1. Cairo: Imprimerie de l'institute français d'archéologie orientale, 1935-38.

Dennefeld, Louis. "Les discours d'Élihou." *Revue Biblique* 48 (1939), 163-80.

Dhorme, P. "Ecclésiastes ou Job." *Revue Biblique* 32 (1923), 1-27.

Di Lella, Alexander. "Conservative and Progressive Theology: Sirach and Wisdom." *Catholic Biblical Quarterly* 28 (1966), 139-54.

Dobrovits, A. "Sur la structure stylistique de l'enseignement de Ptaḥḥotep." *Acta Antiqua* 16 (1968), 21-37.

Drioton, Étienne. "Le livre des Proverbes et la sagesse d'Aménémopé." In *Sacra Pagina* 1, pp. 228-41. Gembloux: Éditions J. Ducolot, 1959.

_____. "Sur la sagesse d'Aménémopé." In *Mélanges Bibliques André Robert*, pp. 254-80. Paris: Bloud and Gay, 1955.

Drubbel, Adrian. "Le conflit entre la sagesse profane et la sagesse religieuse." *Biblica* 17 (1936), 45-70.

Dunand, M. "La maison de la sagesse." *Bulletin du Musée de Beyrouth* 4 (1940), 69-84.

Ebeling, Erich. "Aus den Keilschrifttexten aus Assur." *Mitteilungen der deutschen Orient-Gesellschaft* 58 (1917), 22-50.

_____. "Quellen zur Kenntnis der babylonischen Religion." *Mitteilungen der vorderasiatisch (-ägyptisch)en Gesellschaft* 23 (1919), 50-70.

Edel, Elmar. "Inschriften des Alten Reichs. II. Die Bio-
    graphie K3j-gmjnj (Kagemni)." *Mitteilungen des Instituts
    für Orientforschung* 1 (1953), 210-26.

Eising, H. "Der Weisheitslehrer und die Götterbilder."
    Biblica 40 (1959), 393-408.

_____. "Die theologische Geschichtsbetrachtung im Weis-
    heitsbuche." In *Vom Wort des Lebens*, pp. 28-40. Neu-
    testamentliche Abhandlungen, 1. Münster: Aschendorff,
    1951.

Engnell, Ivan. "The Book of Psalms." In *A Rigid Scrutiny*, pp.
    68-122. Translated and Edited by John Willis. Nashville:
    Vanderbilt University Press.

Erman, Adolf. "Das Weisheitsbuch des Amen-em-ope." *Oriental-
    istische Literaturzeitung* 27 (1924), 240-52.

Falkenstein, Adam. "Die babylonische Schule." *Saeculum* 4
    (1953), 125-37.

Faulkner, R. O. "Notes on 'The Admonitions of an Egyptian
    Sage.'" *Journal of Egyptian Archaeology* 50 (1964), 24-36.

_____. "The Admonitions of an Egyptian Sage." *Journal of
    Egyptian Archaeology* 51 (1965), 53-62.

_____. "The Installation of the Vizier." *Journal of
    Egyptian Archaeology* 41 (1955), 18-29.

_____. "The Man who was Tired of Life." *Journal of
    Egyptian Archaeology* 42 (1956), 21-40.

Federn, Walter. "Notes on the Instruction to Kagemni and his
    Brethren." *Journal of Egyptian Archaeology* 36 (1950),
    48-50.

Festugière, A. J. "À propos des Arétalogies d'Isis." *Harvard
    Theological Review* 42 (1949), 209-34.

Fichtner, Johannes. "Die Stellung der Sapientia Salomonis in
    der Literatur- und Geistesgeschichte ihre Zeit." *Zeit-
    schrift für die neutestamentliche Wissenschaft* 36 (1937),
    113-32.

_____. "Zur Probleme Glaube und Geschichte in der
    israelitischen-jüdischen Weisheitsliteratur." *Theo-
    logische Literaturzeitung* 76 (1951), 146-50.

Fohrer, Georg. "Kritik an Temple, Kultus und Kultusausübung
    in nachexilischer Zeit." In *Archäologie und Altes Testa-
    ment*, pp. 101-16. Tübingen: J. C. B. Mohr (Paul Siebeck),
    1970.

Fohrer, Georg. "The Righteous Man in Job 31." In *Essays in Old Testament Ethics*, pp. 1-22. Edited by James L. Crenshaw and John Willis. New York: Ktav, 1974.

Fox, Michael. "Aspects of the Religion of the Book of Proverbs." *Hebrew Union College Annual* 39 (1968), 55-69.

Galling, Kurt. "Das Rätsel der Zeit im Urteil Kohelets." *Zeitschrift für Theologie und Kirche* 58 (1961), 1-15.

Gardiner, Alan H. "A Didactic Passage Re-examined." *Journal of Egyptian Archaeology* 45 (1959), 12-15.

_____. "Kagemni Once Again." *Journal of Egyptian Archaeology* 37 (1951), 109-10.

_____. "New Literary Works from Ancient Egypt." *Journal of Egyptian Archaeology* 1 (1914), 20-36.

_____. "The Earliest Manuscripts of the Instruction of Amenemmes I." In *Mélanges Maspero*, pp. 479-96. Orient Ancien, 1. Cairo: Imprimerie de l'institut français d'archaéologie orientale, 1935-38.

_____. "The Instruction Addressed to Kagemni and his Brethren." *Journal of Egyptian Archaeology* 32 (1946), 71-74.

Garnot, Jean Saint Fare. "La vie et mort d'après un texte égyptien de la haute époque." *Revue de l'histoire des religions* 127 (1944), 18-29.

Gemser, B. "The Instructions of 'Onchsheshonqy and Biblical Wisdom Literature." *Supplement Vetus Testamentum* 7 (1960), 102-45.

Germann, Heinrich. "Jesus ben Siras Dankgebet und die Hodajoth." *Theologische Literaturzeitung* 19 (1963), 81-87.

Gese, Hartmut. "Die Krisis der Weisheit bei Koheleth." In *Les sagesses du Proche-Orient ancien*, pp. 139-51. Paris: Universitaires de France, 1963.

Gilbert, Maurice. "La structure de la prière de Salomon." *Biblica* 51 (1970), 301-31.

Gilbert, Pierre. "Les chants du harpiste." *Chronique d'Égypte* 15 (1940), 38-44.

Gill, David. "The Greek Sources of Wisdom XII 3-7." *Vetus Testamentum* 15 (1965), 383-86.

Ginsberg, H. L. "Job the Patient and Job the Impatient." *Conservative Judaism* 21 (1967), 12-28.

_____. "The Structure and Contents of the Book of Koheleth." *Supplement Vetus Testamentum* 3 (1955), 138-49.

Goedicke, Hans. "Die Lehre eines Mannes für seinen Sohn." *Zeitschrift für ägyptische Sprache und Altertumskunde* 94 (1967), 62-71.

_____. "Ein Verehrer des Weisen *DDFHR* aus dem späten alten Reich." *Annales du service des antiquités de l'Égypte* 45 (1958), 35-55.

Gordis, Robert. "Qoheleth and Qumran - A Study of Style." *Biblica* 41 (1960), 395-410.

_____. "The Social Background of Wisdom Literature." *Hebrew Union College Annual* 18 (1944), 77-118.

_____. "The Temptation of Job - Tradition versus Experience in Religion." *Judaism* 4 (1955), 195-208.

_____. "Wisdom and Job." In *Old Testament Issues*, pp. 216-38. Edited by Samuel Sandmel. New York: Harper and Row, 1968.

Grapow, Hermann. "Die Einleitung der Lehre des Königs Amenemhet." *Zeitschrift für ägyptische Sprache und Altertumskunde* 79 (1954), 97-99.

Gray, G. B. "Job, Ecclesiastes, and a New Babylonian Literary Fragment." *Expository Times* 31 (1920), 440-43.

Greenwood, David. "Rhetorical Criticism and *Formgeschichte*." *Journal of Biblical Literature* 89 (1970), 418-26.

Grelot, Pierre. "Sagesse 10, 21 et la targum de l'Exode." *Biblica* 42 (1961), 49-60.

Gressmann, Hugo. "Die neugefundene Lehre des Amen-em-ope und die vorexilische Spruchdichtung Israels." *Zeitschrift für die alttestamentliche Wissenschaft* 42 (1924), 272-96.

Griffith, F. L. "The Teaching of Amenophis the Son of Kanakht." *Journal of Egyptian Literature* 12 (1926), 191-231.

Gunn, Battiscombe. "Notes on Ammenemhes I." *Journal of Egyptian Archaeology* 27 (1941), 2-6.

Hermann, Alfred. "Das Gespräch eines Lebensmüden mit seiner Seele." *Orientalistische Literaturzeitung* 34 (1939), 345-51.

_____. "Review of *Untersuchungen zur Überlieferungsgestalt mittelägyptischer Literaturwerke* by S. Herrmann." *Orientalistische Literaturzeitung* 54 (1959), pp. 251-63.

Herrmann, S. "Die Königsnovelle in Ägypten und Israel." *Wissenschaftliche Zeitschrift Universitäts Leipzig* 3 (1953/54), 51-62.

Humbert, Paul. "Le modernisme de Job." *Supplement Vetus Testamentum* 3 (1955), 150-61.

Irwin, William A. "An Examination of the Progress of Thought in the Dialogue of Job." *Journal of Religion* 13 (1933), 150-64.

_____. "Job's Redeemer." *Journal of Biblical Literature* 81 (1962), 217-29.

_____. "The Elihu Speeches in the Criticism of Job." *Journal of Religion* 17 (1937), 37-47.

Jacobsen, Thorkild. "Mesopotamia." In *The Intellectual Adventure of Ancient Man*, pp. 125-222. Chicago: The University of Chicago Press, 1946.

Janzen, Waldemar. "*'Ashrê* in the Old Testament." *Harvard Theological Review* 58 (1965), 215-26.

Kaiser, Otto. "Die Begründung der Sittlichkeit im Buche Jesus Sirach." *Zeitschrift für Theologie und Kirche* 55 (1958), 51-63.

Kitchen, K. A. "Studies in Egyptian Wisdom Literature." *Oriens Antiqvvs* 5 (1967), 62-71.

_____. "Studies in Egyptian Wisdom Literature." *Oriens Antiqvvs* 7 (1969), 189-208.

_____. "Studies in Egyptian Wisdom Literature - II." *Oriens Antiqvvs* 8 (1970), 203-9.

Koch, Klaus. "Gibt es ein Vergeltungsdogma im Alten Testament?" *Zeitschrift für Theologie und Kirche* 52 (1955), 1-42.

Köhler, Ludwig. "Justice in the Gate." *Hebrew Man*. London: SCM Press, 1956.

Koole, J. L. "Die Bibel des Ben-Sira." *Oudtestamentische Studiën* 14 (1965), 374-96.

Kovacs, Brian. "Is there a Class-Ethic in Proverbs?" In *Essays in Old Testament Ethics*, pp. 171-90. Edited by James Crenshaw and John Willis. New York: Ktav, 1974.

Kramer, Samuel Noah. "'Man and his God.'" *Supplement Vetus Testamentum* 3 (1955), 170-82.

_____. "Schooldays: A Sumerian Composition Relating to the Education of a Scribe." *Journal of the American Oriental Society* 69 (1949), 199-215.

_____. "Sumerian Theology and Ethics." *Harvard Theological Review* 49 (1956), 45-62.

Kramer, Samuel Noah. "The Sumerian Wisdom Literature." *Bulletin of the American Schools of Oriental Research* 122 (1951), 28-31.

Kraus, H.-J. "Freude an Gottes Gesetz." *Evangelische Theologie* 10 (1951), 337-51.

Kuhl, Kurt. "Neuere Literaturkritik des Buches Hiob." *Theologische Rundschau* 21 (1953), 257-317.

Kuhn, Gottfried. "Beiträge zur Erklärung des Jesus Sira I." *Zeitschrift für die alttestamentliche Wissenschaft* 47 (1929), 289-96.

_____. "Beiträge zur Erklärung des Jesus Sira II." *Zeitschrift für die alttestamentliche Wissenschaft* 48 (1930), 100-21.

Kuntz, J. Kenneth. "The Canonical Wisdom Psalms of Ancient Israel." In *Rhetorical Criticism: Essays in Honor of James Muilenburg*, pp. 186-222. Pittsburgh Theological Monograph Series, 1. Pittsburgh: Pickwick Press, 1974.

Lambert, W. G. "Ancestors, Authors, and Canonicity." *Journal of Cuneiform Studies* 11 (1957), 1-14, 112.

_____. "Morals in Ancient Mesopotamia." *Jaarbericht 'Ex Oriente Lux'*, 15 (1957/58), 184-96.

_____. "The Literary Structure, Background and Ideas of the Babylonian 'Poem of the Righteous Sufferer.'" *Akten des vierundzwangzigsten internationalen orientalisten Kongresses München.* Wiesbaden: Franz Steiner Verlag, 1959.

_____, and O. R. Gurney. "The Sultantepe Tablets III. 'The Poem of the Righteous Sufferer.'" *Anatolian Studies* 4 (1954), 65-99.

Landsberger, Benno. "Babylonian Scribal Craft and its Terminology." In *Abstract in the Proceedings of the 23rd Congress of Orientalists*, pp. 123-26. Cambridge, 1954.

_____. "Die babylonische Theodizee." *Zeitschrift für Assyriologie* 43 (1936), 32-76.

_____. "Scribal Concepts of Education." In *City Invincible*, pp. 94-123. A Symposium on Urbanization and Cultural Development in the Ancient Near East. Chicago: The University of Chicago Press, 1958.

Langdon, Stephen. "Babylonian Proverbs." *American Journal of Semitic Languages and Literatures* 28 (1912), 217-43.

Lanczkowski, Günter. "Der 'Lebensmüde' als antiosirianische Schrift." *Zeitschrift für Religions- und Geistesgeschichte* 6 (1954), 1-18.

Lauha, A. "Die Krise des Religiösen Glaubens bei Koheleth." *Supplement Vetus Testamentum* 3 (1955), 183-91.

Leclant, Jean. "Documents nouveux et points de vue récents sur les sagesses de l'Égypte ancienne." In *Les sagesses du Proche-Orient ancien*, pp. 5-26. Paris: Universitaires de France, 1963.

Lehmann, Manfred R. "Ben Sira and the Qumran Literature." *Revue de Qumrân* 3 (1961), 103-16.

Lexa, Frantiŝck. "L'analyse littéraire de l'enseignement d'Amenemopet." *Archiv Orientálni* 1 (1929), 14-49.

Lichtheim, Miriam. "The Songs of the Harpers." *Journal of Near Eastern Studies* 4 (1945), 178-212.

Lipiński, E. "Macarismes et psaumes de congratulation." *Revue Biblique* 75 (1968), 321-67.

Loretz, Oswald. "Zur Darbietungsform der 'Ich - Erzählung' im Buche Qohelet." *Catholic Biblical Quarterly* 25 (1963), 46-59.

Mack, Burton L. "Wisdom Myth and Mytho-logy." *Interpretation* 24 (1970), 46-60.

MacKenzie, R. A. F. "The Purpose of the Yahweh Speeches in the Book of Job." *Biblica* 40 (1959), 435-45.

Martin, M. Françoise. "Le juste souffrant babylonien." *Journal Asiatique* 16 (1910), 75-143.

Mazar, B. "The Tobiads." *Israel Exploration Journal* 7 (1957), 137-45, 229-38.

Milgrom, Jacob. "The Cultic Šegāgā and its influence in Psalms and Job." *Jewish Quarterly Review* 58 (1967), 115-25.

Montet, Pierre. "Les fruits défendus et la confession des péchés." In *Les sagesses du Proche-Orient ancien*, pp. 53-62. Paris: Universitaires de France, 1963.

Müller, Hans-Peter. "Der Begriff 'Rätsel' im Alten Testament." *Vetus Testamentum* 20 (1970), 465-89.

_____. "Wie sprach Qohälät von Gott?" *Vetus Testamentum* 18 (1968), 507-21.

Muilenburg, James. "Form Criticism and Beyond." *Journal of Biblical Literature* 88 (1969), 1-18.

Murphy, Roland. "A Consideration of the Classification 'Wisdom Psalms.'" *Supplement Vetus Testamentum* 9 (1963), 156-67.

_____. "Assumptions and Problems in Old Testament Wisdom Research." *Catholic Biblical Quarterly* 23 (1967), 101-12.

Murphy, Roland. "The Kerygma of the Book of Proverbs." *Interpretation* 20 (1966), 3-14.

Nock, A. D. "Notes on Ruler Cult." *Journal of Hellenic Studies* 48 (1928), 1-43.

Nötscher, Friedrich. "Biblische und babylonische Weisheit." *Biblische Zeitschrift* 6 (1962), 120-26.

Nougayrol, Jean. "Les sagesses babyloniennes: études récentes et textes inédits." In *Les sagesses du Proche-Orient ancien*, pp. 41-52. Paris: Universitaires de France, 1963.

_____. "Une version ancienne du 'Juste Souffrant.'" *Revue Biblique* 59 (1952), 237-50.

Oesterley, W. O. E. "The 'Teaching of Amen-em-ope.'" *Zeitschrift für die alttestamentliche Wissenschaft* 45 (1927), 9-24.

Oppenheim, A. Leo. "A Note on the Scribes in Mesopotamia." In *Assyriological Studies* 16, pp. 253-56. Chicago: The Oriental Institute, 1965.

Otto, Eberhard. "Bildung und Ausbildung im alten Ägypten." *Zeitschrift für ägyptische Sprache und Altertumskunde* 81 (1956), 41-48.

_____. "Die beiden vogelgestaltigen Seelenvorstellungen der Ägypter." *Zeitschrift für ägyptische Sprache und Altertumskunde* 77 (1941), 71-84.

_____. "Monotheistische Tendenzen in der ägyptischen Religion." *Die Welt des Orients* 2. Göttingen: Vandenhoeck und Ruprecht, 1955.

_____. "Weltanschauliche und politische Tendenzschriften." In *Ägyptologie*, pp. 111-19. Handbuch der Orientalistik, 1. Leiden: E. J. Brill, 1952.

Pedersen, J. "Scepticisme israélite." *Revue d'histoire et de philosophie religieuses* 10 (1939/40), 317-70.

Perdue, Leo G. "The Riddles of Psalm 49." *Journal of Biblical Literature* 93 (1974), 533-42.

Peterson, E. "Die geschichtliche Bedeutung der jüdischen Gebetsrichtung." *Theologische Zeitschrift* 3 (1947), 1-15.

Pfeiffer, Egon. "Die Gottesfurcht im Buche Kohelet." In *Gottes Wort und Gottes Land*, pp. 133-58. FS H.-W. Hertzberg. Göttingen: Vandenhoeck und Ruprecht.

Pfeiffer, Robert H. "The Peculiar Skepticism of Ecclesiastes." *Journal of Biblical Literature* 53 (1934), 100-109.

Posener, Georges. "Le chapitre IV d'Aménémopé." *Zeitschrift für ägyptische Sprache und Altertumskunde* 99 (1973), 129-35.

_____. "Le début de l'enseignement de Hardjedef." *Revue d'égyptologie* 9 (1952), 155-57.

_____. "Les richesses inconnues de la littérature égyptienne." *Revue d'égyptologie* 6 (1951), 27-48.

_____. "L'exorde de l'instruction éducative d'Amennakhte." *Revue d'égyptologie* 10 (1955), 27-48.

_____, and Jean Sainte Fare Garnot. "Sur une sagesse égyptienne de basse époque." In *Les sagesses du Proche-Orient ancien*, pp. 153-58. Paris: Universitaires de France, 1963.

Preuss, Horst Dietrich. "Das Gottesbild der älteren Weisheit Israels." In *Studies in the Religion of Israel*, pp. 117-46. Supplement Vetus Testamentum, 23. Leiden: E. J. Brill, 1972.

Reese, James. "Plan and Structure in the Book of Wisdom." *Catholic Biblical Quarterly* 27 (1965), 391-99.

Richter, Hans. "Die Naturweisheit des Alten Testament im Buche Hiob." *Zeitschrift für die alttestamentliche Wissenschaft* 70 (1958), 1-19.

Ricken, Friedo. "Gab es eine hellenistische Vorlage für Weish 13-15?" *Biblica* 49 (1968), 54-86.

Robert, A. "Les attaches littéraires bibliques de Prov. I-IX." *Revue Biblique* 43 (1934), 42-68.

Rosengarten, Yvonne. "Le nom et function de 'sagesse' dans les pratiques religieuses de Sumer et d'Akkad." *Revue de l'histoire des religions* 162 (1962), 133-46.

Sarna, Nahum. "Epic Substratum in the Prose of Job." *Journal of Biblical Literature* 76 (1957), 13-25.

Scharbert, J. "'Fluchen' und 'Segen' im Alten Testament." *Biblica* 39 (1958), 1-26.

Scharff, Alexander. "Die Lehre für Kagemni." *Zeitschrift für die alttestamentliche Wissenschaft* 77 (1941), 13-21.

Schechter, Solomon. "A Glimpse of the Social Life of the Jews in the Age of Jesus the Son of Sirach." In *Studies in Judaism*, pp. 55-101. Philadelphia: The Jewish Publication Society of America, 1908.

Schmidt, Johannes. "Koh. 4:17." *Zeitschrift für die alttestamentliche Wissenschaft* 58 (1940/41), 279-80.

Scott, Charles. "Persian and Arabic Riddles." *International Journal of American Linguistics* 31 (1965), 1-135.

Scott, R. B. Y. "Wisdom in Creation: The *'Amon* of Proverbs VIII 30." *Vetus Testamentum* 10 (1960), 213-23.

Sekine, Masao. "Schöpfung und Erlösung im Buche Hiob." In *Von Ugarit nach Qumran*, pp. 213-23. Beihefte zur Zeitschrift für die alttestamentliche Wissenschaft, 77. Edited by J. Hempel and L. Ross. Berlin: Alfred Töpelmann, 1958.

Sewall, Richard B. "The Book of Job." In *The Book of Job*, pp. 21-35. Englewood Cliffs: Prentice-Hall, Inc., 1968.

Siebeneck, Robert T. "May their Bones return to Life! Sirach's Praise of the Fathers." *Catholic Biblical Quarterly* 21 (1959), 411-28.

_____. "The Midrash of Wisdom 10-19." *Catholic Biblical Quarterly* 22 (1960), 176-82.

Simpson, D. C. "The Hebrew Book of Proverbs and the Teaching of Amenophis." *Journal of Egyptian Archaeology* 12 (1926), 232-39.

Skehan, Patrick W. "Job's Final Plea (Job 29-31) and the Lord's Reply (Job 38-41)." *Biblica* 45 (1964), 51-62.

_____. "The Seven Columns of Wisdom's House in Proverbs 1-9." In *Studies in Israelite Wisdom*, pp. 9-14. CBQ Monograph Series, 1. Washington: The Catholic Biblical Association of America, 1971.

_____. "The Text and Structure of the Book of Wisdom." *Traditio* 3 (1945), 1-12.

Smith, H. S. "A Cairo Text of Part of the Instructions of 'Onchsheshonqy." *Journal of Egyptian Archaeology* 44 (1958), 121-22.

Snijders, L. A. "The Meaning of זר in the Old Testament." *Oudtestamentische Studiën* 10 (1954), 1-154.

Speiser, E. A. "The Case of the Obliging Servant." *Journal of Cuneiform Studies* 8 (1954), 98-105.

Stamm, J. J. "Die Theodizee in Babylon und Israel." *Jaarbericht 'Ex Oriente Lux'* 9 (1952), 99-107.

Staples, W. E. "'Profit' in Ecclesiastes." *Journal of Near Eastern Studies* 4 (1945), 87-96.

_____. "Vanity of Vanities." *Canadian Journal of Theology* 1 (1955), 141-56.

Stricker, B. H.   "De Wijsheid van Anchsjesjong."   *Jaarbericht 'Ex Oriente Lux'* 15 (1933), 11-33.

Suys, Émile.   "Le dialogue du désespéré avec son âme."   *Orientalia* 1 (1932), 57-74.

Terrien, Samuel.   "Amos and Wisdom."   In *Israel's Prophetic Heritage*, pp. 108-15.   Edited by B. W. Anderson and Walter Harrelson.   New York: Harper and Row, 1962.

Thausing, Gertrud.   "Betrachtungen zum 'Lebensmüden.'"   *Mitteilungen des deutschen archäologischen Instituts* 15 (1957), 262-67.

Torczyner, Harry.   "The Riddle in the Bible."   *Hebrew Union College Annual* 1 (1924), 125-49.

Tsevat, Matitiahu.   "The Meaning of the Book of Job."   *Hebrew Union College Annual* 37 (1966), 73-106.

Ugnad, Arthur.   "Zur babylonischen Lebensphilosophie."   *Archiv für Orientforschung* 15 (1945/51), 74-75.

Van de Walle, Baudoin.   "Problemes relatifs aux methodes d'enseignement dans l'Égypte ancienne."   In *Les sagesses du Proche-Orient ancien*, pp. 191-207.   Paris: Universitaires de France, 1963.

Van Seters, John.   "A Date for the 'Admonitions' in the Second Intermediate Period."   *Journal of Egyptian Archaeology* 50 (1964), 13-23.

Vergote, Joseph.   "La notion de Dieu dans les livres de sagesse égyptiens."   In *Les sagesses du Proche-Orient ancien*, pp. 159-90.   Paris: Universitaires de France, 1963.

Volten, Aksel.   "Der Begriff der Maat in den ägyptischen Weisheitstexten."   In *Les sagesses du Proche-Orient ancien*, pp. 73-101.

Von Rad, Gerhard.   "Hiob 38 und die altägyptische Weisheit."   *Gesammelte Studien*.   München: Chr. Kaiser Verlag, 1958, pp. 262-71.

_____.   "The Joseph Narrative and Ancient Wisdom."   In *The Problem of the Hexateuch and Other Essays*, pp. 292-300.   New York: McGraw-Hill, 1966.

Von Soden, Wolfram.   "Das Fragen nach der Gerechtigkeit Gottes im Alten Orient."   *Mitteilungen der deutschen Orientgesellschaft* 96 (1965), 41-59.

_____.   "Der grosse Hymnus an Nabû."   *Zeitschrift für Assyriologie* 61 (1971), 44-71.

Von Soden, Wolfram. "Religion und Sittlichkeit nach den Anschauungen der Babylonier." *Zeitschrift der deutschen morgenländischen Gesellschaft* 89 (1935), 143-69.

_____. "Zur ersten Tafel von *Ludlul bel nēmeqi*." *Bibliotheca Orientalis* 10 (1953), 8-12.

Walcot, P. "Hesiod and the Instructions of 'Onchsheshonqy." *Journal of Near Eastern Studies* 21 (1962), 215-19.

Weill, Raymond. "Le Livre du Désespéré." *Bulletin de l'institut français d'archaéologie orientale* 45 (1947), 89-154.

Weiser, Artur. "Das Problem der sittlichen Weltordnung im Buche Hiob." *Theologisches Literaturblatt* 2 (1923), 158-64.

Weiss, Meir. "Wege der neuen Dichtungswissenschaft in ihrer Anwendung auf die Psalmenforschung." *Biblica* 42 (1961), 255-302.

Wente, Edward. "Egyptian 'Make Merry' Songs Reconsidered." *Journal of Near Eastern Studies* 21 (1962), 118-28.

Westermann, Claus. "Die Begriffe für Fragen und Suchen im Alten Testament." *Kerygma und Dogma* 6 (1960), 2-30.

_____. "Struktur und Geschichte der Klage im Alten Testament." *Zeitschrift für die alttestamentliche Wissenschaft* 66 (1954), 44-80.

Williams, Roland J. "Reflections on *Lebensmüde*." *Journal of Egyptian Archaeology* 48 (1962), 49-56.

_____. "The Alleged Semitic Original of the Wisdom of Amenemope." *Journal of Egyptian Archaeology* 47 (1961), 100-106.

_____. "Theodicy in the Ancient Near East." *Canadian Journal of Theology* 2 (1956), 14-26.

Winter, Paul. "Ben Sira and the Teaching of 'Two Ways.'" *Vetus Testamentum* 5 (1955), 315-18.

Wright, Addison. "The Riddle of the Sphinx: The Structure of the Book of Qoheleth." *Catholic Biblical Quarterly* 30 (1968), 313-34.

_____. "The Structure of the Book of Wisdom." *Biblica* 48 (1967), 165-84.

Würthwein, Ernst. "Die Weisheit Ägyptens und das Alte Testament." In *Wort und Existenz*, pp. 197-216. Göttingen: Vandenhoeck und Ruprecht, 1970.

Žabkar, Louis V. "Ba." *Lexikon der Ägyptologie* 1 (1973), 587-98.

Zeiner, Georg. "Altorientalische Weisheit als Lebenskunde." In *Wort und Botschaft*, pp. 258-71. Edited by Josef Schreiner. Würzburg: Echter-Verlag, 1967.

Zimmerli, Walther. "Das Buch Koheleth - Traktat oder Sentenzensammlung?" *Vetus Testamentum* 24 (1974), 221-30.

_____. "Zur Struktur der alttestamentlichen Weisheit." *Zeitschrift für die alttestamentliche Wissenschaft* 51 (1933), 177-204.

Zink, J. K. "Uncleanness and Sin in Job 14:4 and Ps. 51:7." *Vetus Testamentum* 17 (1967), 354-61.